MONTENEGRO

in your hands

First Edition

Author and Editor:
Vladimir Dulović

Publisher:
KOMSHE d.o.o. Beograd

Managing Director:
Branko Andrić

For Publisher:
Marko Borojević
Branko Andrić

Front cover photo:
MontenegroPHOTO.com

Photos:
Dragan Bosnić
Amer Kapetanović
National Museum of Montenegro
National Tourism Organisation of Montenegro
Lazar Pejović
Theo van der Heijdt
Expeditio
Daniela Aroyo

Maps:
Aleksandar Stanojlović

Proof-reading:
Ivan Kovanović

Design & Pre Press:
Ivan Grujić

For information and distribution contact:
marketing@komshe.com

Special thanks:

National Tourism Organisation of Montenegro

National Museum of Montenegro

BASIC FACTS

MONTENEGRO AT A GLANCE
TOP SIGHTS
HISTORY OF MONTENEGRO
LANDSCAPE & WILDLIFE
ACTIVE & EXTREME
SAILING IN MONTENEGRO
MANIFESTATIONS

Škrčko Lake below Bobotov kuk, the highest pe of Mt Durmitor

MONTENEGRO BY REGIONS   5

BOKA KOTORSKA
DESTINATIONS
ACCOMMODATION

THE LITTORAL
DESTINATIONS
BEACHES OF THE LITTORAL
ACCOMMODATION

ENTRAL MONTENEGRO   152
ESTINATIONS   156
CCOMMODATION   196

ORTHERN MONTENEGRO   200
ESTINATIONS   204
CCOMMODATION   226

Cypresses overlooking Kotor's Old Town, a UNESCO Heritage site

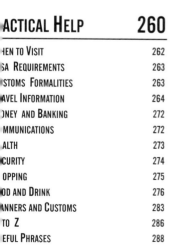

EASTERN MONTENEGRO   230
DESTINATIONS   234
ACCOMMODATION   256

ACTICAL HELP   260
HEN TO VISIT   262
SA REQUIREMENTS   263
STOMS FORMALITIES   263
AVEL INFORMATION   264
NEY AND BANKING   272
MMUNICATIONS   272
ALTH   273
CURITY   274
OPPING   275
OD AND DRINK   276
ANNERS AND CUSTOMS   283
TO Z   286
EFUL PHRASES   288
DEX OF PLACES   290

Majorettes at Herceg Novi's Mimosa Festival

HOW TO USE THE GUIDE

The "Montenegro in Your Hands" tourist guide allows you to quickly access information that will empower you to explore Montenegro simply and with pleasure.

The first of its three parts presents basic facts about Montenegro: first contact with the country, its position and geography, an overview of its history, nature and wildlife, etc. This is fol-lowed by a list of all major manifesta-tions and their short descriptions, listed in chronological order.

The second, largest part covers more than 100 destinations – bigger and smaller cities, monasteries and church-es, mountains and National Parks. All of them are grouped in five sections bearing the names of the regions in which they are to be found.

Panoramic maps of most interesting loca-tions worth exploring

Detailed information on every sight with their history and practical information

Info box for each sight gives data on the number of inhabitants, address and phone number of local bus and railway stations, as well as of the tourist information centre and the distance from the major cities

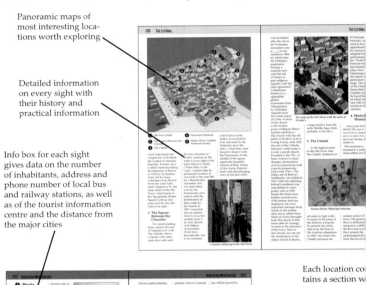

Each location co tains a section w recommended p to eat

Chapters on larger towns include a map with the main sights and other impor-tant institutions (post office, museums, churches, bus and railroad stations...)

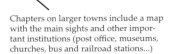

Each section begins with an introductory text and a map presenting you with a general overview of the region's features, thus, allowing you to quickly find your desired location. Denoted by numbers, the destinations follow one another from north to south or from a major centre to the outlaying areas. At the end of each section you will find lists with information on the available accommodation in the region.

The final section provides practical data which you will find useful prior to and during your trip to Montenegro, such as customs policy, money, travel info, health and security risks and so on. At the very end of the guide you will find a basic dictionary and an index.

On the inner side of the cover a detailed road map and a regional overview of Montenegro is made available for your use.

The map of the region with tourist sights

Regional location map in which you can see where the region lies

Each of the eight sections is marked by a different colour

Full list of hotels displaying data on facilities, price category etc.

Practical information boxes offering essential contact data

A list of annual manifestations with dates and short descriptions

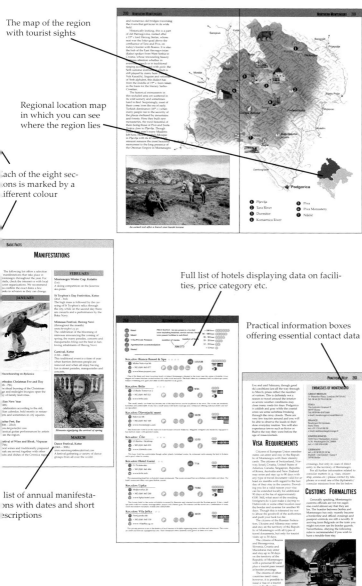

BASIC FACTS

Montenegro at a Glance
Top Sights
History of Montenegro
Landscape & Wildlife
Active & Extreme
Sailing in Montenegro
Manifestations

MONTENEGRO AT A GLANCE

The Gulf of Kotor, enclosed by its high mountains

In May 2006, after 88 years as part of Yugoslavia, Montenegro reappeared on the map of Europe, in the club of independent nations which it joined for the first time in 1878. Although national and tourist promotion portrays it as a Mediterranean land, the landscape resembles much more the etymology of its name: Crna Gora (in Italian *Montenegro*) translates in English as the "Black Mountain" and indeed it is high mountains that occupy more than three quarters of its territory. Until a few years ago the country's beautiful Adriatic coast was the hidden gem of the Mediterranean but its sandy coves and pretty fishing villages are becoming once again the playground for tourists from all around the world. The rugged scenery of the interior, the craggy peaks of the Dinaric Alps and the deep canyons and broad plateaus between them are a delight for adventurers ready to explore some of the least known, yet most beautiful corners of Europe.

Although counted amongst one of the smallest countries in Europe, Montenegro displays a remarkable geographical diversity. Beguiling seascapes with tall mountains looming over the gentle beaches characterize most of the coastland, but it is Boka Kotorska – the Gulf of Kotor – with its fjord-like appearance and medieval townships that represents its most distinguishing feature. In the central region mountains for a moment yield to the flat and fertile plain in which lies the nation's capital Podgorica and the nearby Skadarsko Lake, a marshy bird sanctuary with villages of stone houses scattered along its coast. The north and east seem lost in the endless lines of mountains, carved with deep canyons, amongst them that of the River Tara, the second deepest in the world.

Montenegro is changing rapidly and the contrasts of old and new will at times bewilder the visitor. In the backwater rural communities far from major roads, people stick to the traditional sheep and cattle breading as well as the notions of stoic bravery forged by the centuries-long resistance to the Turks. On the other hand, fashionable coastal resorts such as Svet Stefan, the raving Budva or the posh restaurants of Podgorica embody the other face of this fast-changing nation.

Society

To a foreign observer the population of Montenegro might seem homogenous: the harsh struggle for survival in their high mountains and in fight against the Turks and other conquerors gave birth to a race of very

Craggy landscape of Mt Durmitor

ll, strong people, many of whom have a somewhat scary physique boosted by the piercing looks of their eyes. The same homogeneity is seen in the language, with 95% of the people speaking Serbo-Croatian, a branch of South-Slavic languages which is also spoken in Serbia, Bosnia-Herzegovina and in Croatia. Considering this one will be surprised taking a look at the ethnic composition according to the census of 2003 with Montenegrins, Serbs, Muslims, Bosniaks, Albanians and Croats, all additionally claiming to speak their own language. This dazzling diversity stems from the bloody national conflicts that raged across the area of ex-Yugoslavia during the 1990s and which Montenegro managed to escape, but only narrowly. In the same period the traditional Orthodox Christian majority split into two – ethnic Montenegrins and ethnic Serbs. There is absolutely no way for an outsider to distinguish between the two as the break was so radical that it even divided members of the same family. The whole dispute between the two groups can be reduced to the dilemma of whether the Orthodox populace of Montenegro are Serbs by origin and tradition (which is the established view) or whether they represent a separate ethnicity built up during Montenegro's independent existence as a state. A similar kind of split, though much milder, is seen amongst the Slavic speaking Muslims where

Strolling through the streets of Herceg Novi

older people in remote villages still cling to the old pattern of "Muslims from Montenegro", while the younger and urban communities prefer being called Bosniak, underlining their unity with the Muslim population of the neighbouring Bosnia-Herzegovina. The Croats speak the same language as the previous groups but are Roman Catholics and are concentrated in the maritime region which was long under the rule of Venice and Austria. Ethnic Albanians living in Montenegro have a different language than the rest of the populace but adhere to two religions – the majority is Muslim while some are Catholic. Though this ethnic mish-mash which is still bubbling in its creation causes many disputes, like the one regarding the name of the official language (changed from Serb to Montenegrin in 2007), all of the ethnic and religious groups enjoy broad rights while the situation in which no group has a majority may be the Montenegrin way towards a civic society.

One more confusing element in Montenegrin society are the two official scripts – Cyrillic and Latin, which are equally used. Except in the littoral, Latin letters were virtually unknown in the rest of the country until the Yugoslav unification (1918). Gradually, Latin script penetrated deeper and is nowadays used more often than the traditional Cyrillic letters. Since

MONTENEGRO IN A NUTSHELL

Full name: Republic of Montenegro (*Republika Crna Gora*)
Population: 620,145 (2003)
Area: 13,218 km2
Capital: Podgorica 136,473 (2003)
Ethnic groups: Montenegrins (43%), Serbs (32%), Bosniaks (8%), Albanians (5%), others
Language: Montenegrin
Alphabets: Cyrillic and Latin
Religion: Orthodox Christian, Muslim, Roman Catholic
President: Filip Vujanović
Prime Minister: Milo Đukanović
GDP: $3,4 billion
GDP per capita: $3,800
Unemployment rate: 14,3% (2007)
Annual inflation: 1,8%

there are no regulations on their use you might have some problems in distinguishing which of these you are looking at. For instance "MACHO" might be macho but could also be *masno* – "greasy".

Modern-day Politics

Montenegro is a constitutional and parliamentary democracy with parliament and the president of the state elected for a four year term. Though this practice is observed strictly, the system is still burdened by the legacy of the communist era as the major political party, the Democratic Party of Socialists (DPS) - which

A guard of honour in front of the Presidential palace in Cetinje, the old capital

started in 1990 as the heir to the old communists - has been a crucial actor in all the governments since. Synonymous with DPS is the name of its long time leader, Milo Djukanović, who has been either a prime minister or a president of the Republic from 1991 to 2006 and who continues as the president of DPS and the grey eminence of all its actions. Together with its minor coalition partner, the Social-democrats,

Montenegrin parliament in Podgorica

DPS has won 41 out of 81 seats in the last parliamentary elections held in September 2006. The opposition includes a group of Serb-orientated parties which oppose almost all the doings of the present government, the SNP (Socialist People's Party) which has regrouped from pro-Yugoslav to more socialist and European ways after very bad results in the last elections, and the Movement for Changes (PzP) which maintains a balance between its opposition to DPS and loyalty to the new state. The key to achieving majority in the parliament is often held by one of no less than four Albanian parties as well as the Bosniak one.

Economy & Tourism

During the communist era (1944-90) the country's economy was radically shifted from agriculture to heavy industry. However, the international economic sanctions imposed on Montenegro in the 1990s suffocated most of the state held enterprises which were later either bought by rich businessmen or are still barely functioning and expecting reorganization. The country's single largest employer is the aluminum plant, which accounts for more than

New constructions in Podgorica's business area

Petrovac's town beach in full swing

000 jobs in Podgorica. The plant is
w privately owned but due to its
portance in keeping social peace
still receives state help to continue
perating, although with financial
sses. Other important industries
clude the steel plant in Nikšić, coal
ines of Pljevlja and power generation
om hydro and coal plants. These
e joined by export of raw wood and
ood processing which continue to
rink the surface of
nd under forests,
hich still amount
roughly half of
e total land area.
griculture, with
imal husbandry in
e interior and olive
owing and fishing
ong the coast, has
een reduced to, at
st, production for
e local markets.
ne only substantial
xporter in the
eld is "Plantaže",
company whose
3 million bottles
excellent wine
er year are produced
om the huge vine
antations south of Podgorica.

*Lemon tree ripe for picking on
the Adriatic coast*

Fully aware of the situation as well
s of Montenegro's huge potential,
e government has wisely listed
urism as one of its priorities. A
ever marketing campaign (which
cluded the setting of the latest James
ond movie in Montenegro!), foreign
investments and improvement of
the country's infrastructure have
managed to double the number of
tourists to more than a million in
2007, with the number still growing.
Nowadays, by far the largest share
of county's national revenue comes
from tourism which generates
almost 500 million Euros a year. Still,
there is a lot of work to be done,
one of the problems being that the
Montenegrin Adriatic
coast, where the large
majority of tourists go,
in high summer often
sees water shortages
and traffic jams along
its roads. On the other
hand, the rural north
and east of the country,
with their magnificent
mountains are still
visited by only a small
portion of guests.

The other boom is
recorded in the real
estate business. The
first wave of trading
hit the coast in 2005
with smaller plots,
old and new houses as
well as whole swathes
of land being bought mostly by
the Russians, British and Irish.
According to experts, the prices
have not yet peaked although they
have risen over 60% in the last two
years and are now far from reach of
ordinary Montenegrins. With almost
all of the land and properties bought

Stone house in Boka Kotorska refurbished for modern use

Way of Life

In the span of only a century, Mon tenegro underwent a huge transforma tion from a land of peasants always ready to reach for their swords and make war against the Turks to a land services and touris with almost 70% of people living in towns. Though the stereotypical Mon tenegrin is still portrayed in cartoon strips and caricatures as a splendidly mustached chap with a shallow Mon tenegrin cap on his head, you will be lucky to meet men like this only in the most remote areas, as the national

as far as up the mountains as one can see from the shoreline, the real estate agents are moving inwards with locations near present and future ski-centers becoming increasingly interesting. The huge influx of hard currency (some 750 million Euros in 2006 alone) is also changing the appearance of the capital, Podgorica, the only substantial city in the country. Here the demand and prices of flats have gone sky high, ranking the town amongst the most expensive in Europe when it comes to property.

Tourism and the rise of real estate values significantly increased the country's GDP per capita reaching $5,984 in 2006 with 7% growth. Though Montenegro on the whole can be quite satisfied with its development in the last few years, and especially so after its independence, it is still largely a question whether this growth can be sustained at such a rate. A further problem lies in the fact that only a smaller percentage of the population profited in the last few years and that social differences between the extremely rich and very poor have risen drastically.

Montenegrin cap and moustache caricatured in a cartoon strip

costume is out of use for decades and is now only seen in folklore manifesta tions, special occasions and souvenir shops. While the decades of fast deve opment under communism have wipe out many other forms of traditional behavior, the economic depression of the 1990s and the recent rather uncon trolled progress have introduced the bad aspects of capitalism and consum erism into everyday life Today middle-aged Mo tenegrins from the towr are to be seen drinking espresso in street cafés noon, boisterously wav ing around with their new mobile phones and car keys. These are still not viewed as a means of communication or transport but more as status symbols. There are almost twice as mar cellular phones in the

Summer sunbathers

untry to the total
umber of inhabit-
ts and while
ese gadgets
em necessary to
sinessmen and
ople living in
mote areas with
phone lines,
many it has
come a matter
prestige and the
ligatory sign
the would-be
trepreneurs.
ssessing a fast,
w car far beyond

Main square in Bijelo Polje, a town in Montenegro's north-east

e limits of one's financial capabilities
also a must for many and a fair pro-
rtion of luxury cars stolen in Europe
til recently ended up in Montenegro.
wning such a car also means reckless,
gh-speed driving along the curvy
ads with little respect for anything
t one's own haste, a typical sight on
Montenegrin roads. Many of the
ung don't have anything against this
pe of image but there is also a rising
pulation of fully-European minded
d mannered youths living a life
milar to those of people their age in
e West. Symptomatically, in socialist
goslavia, Montenegro was the only
public that did not produce a single
gnificant rock group, but nowadays
e semi-underground hip-hop culture
luences many of the young, though
st of them stick to the mainstream
p ballads promoted in song contests
ch as those in Budva or Herceg Novi.
contrast to the habits of the middle-
ed and young, the older generations
ll hold to such pastimes as creating

huge family-trees (deriving from the
old oral tradition of remembering fore-
fathers up to 20 or more generations
back), collecting data on their family,
brotherhood or clan, reciting verses of
the national-poet Njegoš, or even (if
asked by friends) playing the *gusle*, a
one stringed instrument - all quite traditional activities, however even they
are now clad in more modern form.

One thing that is certain about
Montenegro is that it is a very small
society in which it is next to impossible
not to know almost all of the people
your age in your town and most of
them with interests similar to your's in
the whole country. Adding that family
ties are often overbearing, this often
leads to migration towards the larger
towns or abroad. Many, however,
leave the country for purely financial
reasons and these factors combined
caused Montenegrins to scatter all over
Europe, North America and Australia.

*hildren spending their summer in **katun**, a traditional shepherd's mountain settlement*

TOP SIGHTS IN MONTENEGRO

Piva Monastery (page 219)
The fact that the monastery church was dissembled and then reassembled stone by stone in the 1970s add to the fantastic feel of its superb 16th c. frescoes and its rich treasury

Perast (page 71)
Face to face with the narrowest part of the Gulf of Kotor, this small baroque town is frozen in time when its fleet defended the glory of Venice against the Ottoman Empire

Kotor (page 78)
One of the most unusual cities in the Mediterranean, Kotor lies at the end of a gulf named after it, with its rear against the cold rocks and with a maze of streets hiding historic churches and palaces

Cetinje (page 174)
Set in the heart of the impassable scenery of Old Montenegro, country's historic capital is a proud city whose edifices tell unusual stories and guard important art collections

Budva (page 120)
The undisputed tourist centre of Montenegro coast is an ancient town with an enwalled town core, long beaches and evening entertainment for everyone

Durmitor (page 210)
his colossal mountain with twenty peaks over
000 meters and many glacial lakes is heaven for
ikers, alpinists and skiers as well as those just
admiring its rough beauty

Location of Montenegro in Europe

River Tara (page 207)
Its immaculately clear waters have carved out the
deepest canyon in Europe whose sides of 1,300
meters height are covered in lush pine forests
and scarred with waterfalls

Prokletije Mountains (page 252)
The green alpine valleys traversed by hurried
streams contrast with the cruel backdrop of
craggy peaks in one of the least known parts of
Europe

Skadarsko Lake (page 165)
largest lake in the Balkans is equally valu-
for its many historic villages, monasteries
forts as for the fantastically varied nature
and richness in its fish and birds

Morača Monastery (page 236)
This medieval monastery in a magnificent setting of Morača River canyon served for centuries
as both a school and a stronghold against
Turkish attacks

HISTORY OF MONTENEGRO

The earliest inhabitants of Montenegro known by name were the **Illyrians**, an Indo-European people living predominantly in the area of the Dinaric Alps. The Illyrians were crude and warlike highlanders, shepherds known for their excellent cheese and who buried their dead in large mounds on hilltops. Nevertheless, the ones who lived by the sea gradually became skilful corsairs. They were organized in large tribes under their "kings" who, periodically, managed to form wider coalitions and attack their neighbours. The most powerful amongst the tribes were the Ardieians, notorious for their pirating and settled in the coastal area between the River Neretva (in Bosnia-Herzegovina) and the Gulf of Kotor. The Enheleans also lived by the sea, inhabiting the area from Rhizon (today Risan), one of the most important Illyrian towns, to Buthua (Budva). The Labeates inhabited the area around Lake Skadarsko, which is mentioned in Latin texts as the "Labeatian Lake", with important towns here being Scodra (Shkoder) and Meteon (Medun). The Docleates were centered around the town of Doclea close to present day Podgorica. The north of Montenegro was inhabited by the Autariates whose memory remains preserved in the name of the River Tara, and by the Pirustes who were known as skilful miners and therefore probably lived around Pljevlja, the area rich in ore.

Fully justifying their reputation, the first historical event in Illyrian history was a war. In 231 BC King Agron and his Queen Teuta, at the head of a coalition centered around the Ardieians, led a fleet of light ships in the sacking of Adriatic and Ionian islands and along the Greek coast all the way to Peloponnesus. The threatened Greeks called in the **Romans** who swiftly defeated the Illyrians, spreading their influence to the east coast of the Adriatic for the first time. Rome's crisis in war with Hannibal created an opportunity for King Gentius of Labeates to join forces with the Macedonians and act against the Romans, but he was defeated in **168 BC** and taken to Rome to be displayed in triumph. Thus perished organized Illyrian resistance, though the Roman influence remained effective only along the coast while the interior wasn't subdued until Christ's birth.

After fully subjugating the Balkan Peninsula the Roman Empire started to build on its influence by means of roads, trade and colonization of Roman citizens. During the following centuries most of the natives gradually became romanized, embracing the Latin language and Roman gods together with the benefits of civilized living in a great empire. The territory of Montenegro, as part of the province of Dalmatia, lived its life almost undisturbed until the turbulent 4th century AD. At the beginning of this century, in 305 AD, the southernmost part of Dalmatia was separated into a new province – **Prevalitana**, which included most of the present day Montenegro, and which later – in contrast to Dalmatia – became part of the East Roman Empire. By this time Christianity had spread across the province and firmly established itself the littoral. The final blow to the Roman way of life was inflicted by the barbarian invasion. Though only briefly passing through the territory of present-day Montenegro, Visigoths and Ostrogoths plundered as they went bringing insecurity and announcing the arrival of the dark ages.

By far the greatest change in the history of the region came with

Queen Teuta and the Roman envoy, a 19th c. engraving

A Roman tombstone in Duklja near Podgorica

e Slavic invasion at the beginning of e 6th c. These numerous newcomers om the north, together with the siatic Avars broke the borders of the mpire and spilled across the Balkans. ontrary to the other barbarians who oted and then continued further, e **Slavs** were intended on settling e territories. By 602 AD their raids ached the Adriatic coast, and in the ext decade all but the strongest of e towns were taken and destroyed. mong the Slavic tribes of the west alkans the most powerful were the erbs, who took the upper hand over e other Slavs and formed six states, ree of which lay on the territory of esent day Montenegro. The most nportant of these three was **Duklja**, amed after the ruined town of Doclea. uklja lay around Lake Skadarsko, corporating the plain of the River eta and stretching along the coast om Kotor to Shkoder in present-day lbania. The northern tip of the coast as a part of **Travunija** that reached to ubrovnik and had its seat in Trebinje. he whole of the mountainous part of Montenegro became known simply as erbia (later also called Raška) with the alley of Lim as its centre.

In the second part of the 9th c. these ates adopted Christianity on the basis f a Slavic liturgy created by the Greek rothers Cyril and Methodus, often ubbed the "Apostles of the Slavs". evertheless, the proximity of these rincipalities both to Rome and to Constantinople left them open to both influences which were absorbed in equal measure in spite of the increasing differences between them in the following centuries. Hence it was that Papal influence was prevalent in the maritime states while the interior clung to Eastern Orthodoxy.

The 9th and 10th c. saw these states struggling for survival against their mightier neighbours, the Byzantine Empire and the Bulgarians. At the end of this period lived the ruler of Duklja, Prince **Jovan Vladimir**, who died in 1018 as a martyr at the hands of the Bulgarian Emperor (*see p. 172*). The year of his death saw the Byzantines regaining control over the whole of the Balkans including Duklja. Vladimir left no heir but under the **Vojislavljević dynasty** in the 11th c. Duklja emerged as a leader among the Serb states. Its founder was Stefan Vojislav (c. 1034 – c. 1055) who escaped from Byzantine captivity to his homeland, forced out the imperial troops and managed to defeat two armies sent against him. His son Mihailo (c. 1055 – c. 1081)

King Mihailo of Duklja, a 11th c. frescoe (National Museum of Montenegro)

ruled in relative peace and was even crowned king. Although to the outside world Duklja seemed as one state under a Slavic king it actually had two distinctive characters. On the one side were the Latins, descendants of the Romans who escaped to the fortified towns where they organized their own communities and who were usually artisans, traders and priests; on the other were the predominant Slavs, inhabiting the countryside and engaged in agriculture and war. The last important ruler of the Vojislavljević lineage was King Bodin (c.1081 – c. 1097) who for a brief period united all Serb states under his rule but then succumbed to consecutive Byzantine attacks. His successors were weak figures unable to restore any of the former glory of Duklja. During the 12th c. the name "Duklja" faded and gave way to the name Zeta, after the river of the same name.

Prince Stefan of the Nemanjić dynasty depicted on a frescoe Morača monastery (13th c.)

The supremacy among the Serb states now passed on to Raška which contested Byzantium in installing rulers to the Dukljan throne. This trend ended with **Stefan Nemanja** (1168-1199), who in the 1180s united all Serb states (except Bosnia) under his rule. The territory of Montenegro constituted the core of his state and it was in the Serbia of the Nemanjić dynasty that it remained for the next two centuries, during which period the character of the land was changed for good.

Nemanja gave the rule over Duklja to his eldest son Vukan while he left the throne to his other son, Stefan. After his death the two clashed over the throne but were pacified by their youngest brother, the monk Sava, later known as St Sava. Nemanja's legacy was strengthened when in 1217 Stefan got the crown from the Pope, an act that earned him international recognition. Two years later (1219) Sava secured the independence of the Serb Orthodox Church from Byzantium and spread the network of churches, monasteries and Orthodox bishoprics. Even though **Nemanjić** rulers were highly tolerant of Catholicism, their strong support for the Orthodox church meant that in the next two centuries Catholicism lost ground and was present only inside the city walls of the Latin maritime communes, which retained their old autonomies. Of these towns it was Kotor that profited the most, expanding its estates while its merchants roamed across the country controlling much of its trade. Peace, stable central power and a codified legal system meant growth in all fields: new churches

and monasteries were founded and in them schools were opened and books transcribed, the population rose and n villages grew beside the old ones. The first mine to be opened after almost a thousand years was Brskovo by presen day Mojkovac, managed by Saxon min and populated with traders from Koto and Dubrovnik, who profited from its silver. In the 14th century Zeta enjoyed the status of a large fiefdom ruled by the queen-mother or by the heir to the throne. The territory of Montenegro gradually lost its importance as the borders of Serbia were expanded to the east and the south.

The height of this expansion was reached under Stefan Dušan (1331-55) who assumed the title of Emperor. However, Dušan's son Uroš V (called "The Weak", 1355-1371), as it turned o the last of the Nemanjićs, lost control over the mighty barons who disregard his authority and usurped royal privileges. These unruly attitudes cam at the worst time, just as the Ottoman Turks pushed deeper into the Balkans. The north and the west of present day Montenegro were for a period of time ruled by the house of Altomanović, whose power was crushed in 1373 whe their land was annexed by Bosnia. In the Littoral, virtually out of the blue, appeared the three **Balšić** brothers wh started as petty landowners but within only a decade managed to become rule of the area stretching from the Adriatic to Prizren in Kosovo and from Trebinj in Herzegovina to Durres in Albania. The next generation of Balšićs wasn't s successful, loosing a good deal of the territories and ended up clinging to th coastal towns only by pledging allianc with the Turks or Venetians. Not least

f their problems was dealing with
e new rivals, the **Crnojevićs**, who
pied their model of grabbing power.
he last in the lineage, Balša III (1403-
) decided not to play a puppet in
enetian hands and spent most of his
ule in warfare against the Republic
f St Mark. On his deathbed, Balša
ft his lands to his uncle, the Serbian
espotes Stefan, who from 1410 already
uled over the eastern half of present
ay Montenegro. Learning of Balša's
ecision, the Venetians quickly seized
l of his maritime towns, an act that
d to a long and inconclusive
ar with Serbia. The most
rofit from the war was
ained by Stefan Crnojević
ho became a champion of
enetian rule in the towns
hile securing for himself
semi-independent area
ound Lake Skadarsko. In the
eantime the central power
Bosnia also waned and the
orthwest of Montenegro,
om Risan to Pljevlja,
as now held by the
ouse of Kosača. After its
ost powerful member
jepan Hranić proclaimed
mself Herzog of St Sava
s lands became known as
erzegovina, the name
which this region of
ontenegro was known
til the late 19th c.

*Coat-of-arms of
the Balšić family*

The Turkish conquests were as a
le preceded by constant raids and
otings. Running for their lives or just
caping the rule of Islam caused mass
ovements of the population. Most
them were running to the coastal
rip ruled by Venice and Dubrovnik,
hers moved to the north and west
hile some just hid higher in the
ountains. This process, along with the
sappearance of central or any other
fective and lasting power, opened the
ay for the formation of Montenegrin
ans. The
ghland
epherds who
ere allowed to
rry weapons for
eir protection
came
ominant over
e agricultural
opulation in the
wlands which
st the protection
ovided by

the nobles. The highlanders took
power over whole regions, absorbing
gradually the lowland population into
their ranks. The Turks decided to use
this clan organization and their war
skills and gave them autonomy in
return for their services as auxiliary
forces. The clans kept to themselves as
much as they could: they had their own
unwritten laws or used the codes of
medieval Serbia since they didn't like
the Turks arbitrating their disputes. A
clan decided all matters in the assembly
of armed men and had communal
pastures and woods used by all
members.

After all of Serbia fell to the
Turks in 1459, Stefan Crnojević
found himself ruling over the last
parchment of the former Serbian
state - Upper Zeta, which was by
now equally well known by the
name of Crna Gora. This name is
first found in a document from
1296 but was officialy used as
a name for the region only
from the early 15th c. Stefan
appropriated court titles,
scribes and the two-headed
eagle of the Nemanjićs.

His Crna Gora lived both as
the last of the Serb lands of the
Middle Ages, by keeping to the
traditions of Serbia, as well
as the first Montenegrin
state, by the independent
existence of the region under this
name. Stefan's son Ivan (1465-90), had
to rely on Venetian help to fight off
the Turks who had by now conquered
all of the Balkans with the exception
of a few regions on the Adriatic. His
dependency was more than evident
after the Turkish campaign of 1479
forced him to flee across the sea. Ivan
returned to Montenegro in 1482 but
his domain was shrinking year by year
and he had to move his seat deeper
into the mountains – from Žabljak to
Rijeka and then in 1484 to the field of

Seal of Ivan Crnojević (National Museum of Montenegro)

A page from Oktoih, a book printed in Cetinje in 1494 (National Museum of Montenegro)

Cetinje where he transferred the seat of the orthodox bishopric and built his court. This small, besieged Montenegro had its last hour of glory in 1494 when Djuradj, the last of the Crnojevićs, brought a printing press which produced several fine volumes, the first Serb printed books and indeed the first of all the South Slavs. Two years later, Djuradj fled to Venice in fear of the Turks and in **1496** Montenegro became part of the Ottoman Empire.

In the beginning the Turks did the same in Montenegro as in other lands they conquered introducing taxation, feudal estates and mandatory labor. The population which ran to the barren hills to escape this met these measures with revolts and defiance. Soon the Turks discovered that this craggy and infertile region with a population more willing to take up arms than pay taxes would be of more use if it safeguarded the Empire's border towards Venetian possessions in the Adriatic. In **1523** the feudal estates were abolished and taxes cut down on the condition that the Montenegrins should wage war against the Sultan's enemies in their territory. The taxes were gathered by local chieftains and disputes were settled in county courts without the intrusion of the Turks. There even existed the "general Montenegrin assembly" that regulated the problems between the clans. Such advantageous privileges lured the men from surrounding areas, and Montenegro quickly doubled

its population. We find the semi-autonomous land now more or less in its classic shape from Virpazar on Skadarsko Lake to Ostrog Monastery in the north and from Kotor to River Zeta. The loyalty of the Montenegrins was won to such an extent that when in 1537 Papal and Spanish forces conquered Herceg Novi there was no reaction at all inland and the Turks won it back the next year. After 1557 the Turks allowed the renewal of the Serb Patriarchy and a renaissance of the Orthodox Church followed. Having consolidated, the Church turned to rebuilding its churches and monasteries, while also founding new ones such as Piva or Sveta Trojica in Pljevlja.

By the mid 16th c. the Ottoman Empire entered a period of crisis: the system of this enormous state became inefficient causing repeated rises of the levies, which led to resistance and further to the brutality of the tax-collectors, while the lands given for services to the Sultan were turned into hereditary possessions which were unlawfully expanded. As only non-Muslims paid taxes this also led to more conversions to Islam. When in 1593 war broke out between the Ottoman and Habsburg Empires, Vienna sought to profit from the growing dissatisfaction of the Balkan Christians and called on them to revolt against the Turks. The Serbs rose up in **1597** simultaneously in Banat (NE of Belgrade) and in Herzegovina; this large scale rebellion was soon bloodily suppressed but the attacks on caravans and Turkish towns continued. In 1605 the Montenegrins routed a Turkish unit sent to forcibly collect taxes, the first of many such conflicts to follow. In 1608 the Serb patriarch and clan

The Gulf of Kotor on a 17th c. engraving

aders from Herzegovina, Montenegro nd the Highlands (*Brda*) convened in Morača monastery calling for unity in the fight against the Turks and even ecting the king f Savoy to the mptied post of the rbian king. All opes of liberation nd help from the West vanished in 606 when the two mpires concluded eace; this, however, ould not stop the cursions against he Turks (or anyone se who was rich) at became a means f survival for most Montenegrins. The ext chance to rebel gainst the Turks ame in **1645** when he Ottomans made ar against the enetian Republic. t the moment his happened the Montenegrins were

Patriarch Arsenije III Crnojević

ready fighting the Turks, asking for eir autonomous rights to be more rictly observed and refusing to pay xes. In a few years almost all of erzegovina, Montenegro and the ighlands rose up in arms. In 1648 the eneral Montenegrin assembly, led by e orthodox metropolitan of Cetinje, y now the only and undisputed ader of the Montenegrins, decided acknowledge the rule of Venice n condition that their privileges be oadened. The Turks responded y vicious attacks on the clans and unding of fortified military garrisons Nikšić, Kolašin and Plav, a measure at tried to prevent attacks on loyal pulations and Muslims in the wlands. The war ended in 1669 with change for the Montenegrins, who mained nominally under Turkish thority but continued resistance gainst the paying of any taxes and tacking the neighboring districts, well as one another in many clan sputes.

After the disastrous defeat of the urks at the gates of Vienna in 1683 e Habsburg-Venetian coalition met uccess beyond their wildest dreams enetrating deep into Ottoman rritory. The Christians of the Balkans et them with joy and so did the

Serb Patriarch Arsenije III who for this reason had to flee from his seat in Peć to his native Cetinje. Here he met with Venetian representatives but in the end decided to join the much mightier Habsburgs. The Montenegrins and Highlanders were, needles to say, already at war with the Turks, managing to drive back several large expeditions sent against them. However, their disunity and clan obstinacy brought them devastating defeats culminating in **1692** with the destruction of the Cetinje Monastery, the religious and political hub of Montenegro.

Nevertheless, by now it was clear to all that the Ottomans had lost the upper hand and that their further defeats were just a matter of time. Nowhere was this feeling so prevalent as in Montenegro that waged a continuous war against the Turks for more than a century now. More organized Montenegrin resistance was, however, paralyzed by the clan clashes over fertile land and by blood feuds. The only authority outside the clan pattern was the Cetinje metropolitan (*vladika*), but even this figure was elected by the clan assembly and then only ratified by the Serb patriarch. The first step towards the organisation of a permanent state was the reign of vladika **Danilo** (1697-1735) from the Petrović family of the Njeguši clan. He coordinated the actions of the clans against the Turks into a more consistent policy, promoted the decisions of the clan assembly as obligatory to all, banned blood feuds and even organized a short-lived court that would peacefully resolve disputes. Most importantly, with his huge authority he managed to make the title of *vladika* hereditary in the house of Petrović-Njegoš. His rule is remembered by two bloody events. The first one was the elimination of the Muslims from Montenegro on Christmas Eve of **1707** when all those who did not convert to Christianity were cut down – a bitter and unpleasant event, which constitutes the historical background of Njegoš's epic "The Mountain Wreath", but a necessary action by which Montenegro severed its last tie with the Turks and attained religious unity. Danilo was dissatisfied with Venice which supported the Montenegrin fight only when it was at war with the Ottomans and suppressed it whenever it made peace. Therefore he decided to establish connections with Orthodox Russia, which emerged as a great power during the last war and was furthermore too far away to have pretensions on Montenegrin independence. When in 1710 the Tsar made war with the Sultan, Russian colonel Miloradović, a Serb from Herzegovina, arrived in Montenegro bringing with him financial help and moral support from Russia. In return he asked the Montenegrins to intensify their actions against the Turks and coordinate them with those of the Herzegovinians and Highlanders. The new liaison with Russia was deemed very dangerous by the Turks and in **1712** they gathered a large army with the plan to finally uproot all resistance. Venice, angered at the fact that it had lost a client state, had no objections to this plan and sealed off its border so that the Montenegrins could not purchase guns and gunpowder. The fierce resistance and the tactics of "scorched earth" were futile against the far mightier adversary and the Turkish army reached Cetinje where it burnt down the monastery and than waited until some of the clans paid their taxes and gave hostages to secure against further rebellions. However, this brutal campaign further impoverished the Montenegrins which led to new raids of the lowlands. A new Turkish campaign launched in **1714** was more a punitive expedition than a military one: the resistance was easily crushed but then the Turks stayed in Montenegro for a whole month burning, pillaging and killing anyone they could lay their hands on. After this campaign, Montenegro was a desolate and blood drenched land. Danilo saw his mistakes: first he brought the sad news to Saint Petersburg where he got a yearly allowance for his land

Venetian winged lion of St Mark

and then, pressed by the demands of many chieftains, he straightened out relations with Venice. These chieftains went to Venice and made a suggestion that Montenegro should become its protectorate. This was accepted and the Republic started subsidizing Montenegrin chieftains and instigated a new position in the country - *guvernadur* ("governor"), a secular head of the land who ruled in the name of Venice and whose main task was to block the decisions of the Russian-minded metropolitans. Nevertheless, the last hope of serious Venetian help faded away in 1718 when it concluded peace with Turkey leaving Montenegro in its hands while seizing from it four maritime clans – Grbalj, Brajići, Pobori and Maine. The position of guvernadur survived and their clashes with vladikas lay a further burden on Montenegro for a whole century.

As all the Orthodox metropolitans are monks, Danilo could not produce an heir to the throne of the

Sabre, a typical weapon of Montenegrin highlanders

metropolitan but left it over to his cousin **Sava**. Unfortunately, Sava was a meek man who turned towards ecclesiastical matters and who was not able to suppress clan hostility and was indulgent to the demands of Venice and Turkey.

A feeble personality like Sava could not rule over a land like Montenegro and in 1750 he yielded his powers to his cousin **Vasilije**, an energetic man with a firm vision of salvation coming

m Russia. He traveled there three
nes offering to add Montenegro to
e list of the Tsar's lands. To arouse
eir interest he even wrote a "History
 Montenegro" (1754), the first of its
nd, which glorified the Montenegrin
ght against the Turks and the merits
 the Petrović-Njegoši. The Russian
urt decided to stick to financial
pport but Vasilije's agitation against
e Sultan's taxes instigated another
ody expedition that reached Cetinje.
hen in 1766 Vasilije died during his
st trip to Russia there was no one
lling to listen to
va who had lost
 credibility and
e land once again
pped back to clan
archy.

In the spring of
67 a mysterious
aracter appeared
 Podmaine
onastery on
e border with
ontenegro. This
aler who called
mself **Šćepan
ali** ("Šćepan the
ttle") claimed that
 was the Russian
ar Peter III for who was said to
ve survived poisoning. His arrival
 Montenegro aroused great interest
d soon the whole country believed
s prophetic speeches, promises of
tter days and liberation under his
idance. The people of Montenegro
ere willing to believe and his stories
ere supported by some chieftains
d monks who were fed up with
wlessness. When vladika Sava
ticed that his position was in danger
was already too late and he was put
der custody of Šćepan Mali. Later
 he was freed, but left only as the
ligious head of the land. The new
ler had no respect for the bad side of
ontenegrin traditions and with his
disputed authority banned blood
uds, robbery and clashes between the
ans. Those who did not obey were
nished by beating or fines in sheep.
e organized a court which dealt with
ese offences and his guards put its
cisions into life. Šćepan's emergence
oduced widespread interest amongst
e Orthodox in the neighbouring lands
d even caused a rebellion amongst
e clans in the littoral. Although he
blicly stated that he wanted peace
ith his neighbors, Venice sealed off

its border and Turkey sent an army
against him in 1768. At the first sight
of defeat, Šćepan Mali fled and could
not be found for days. This seriously
shook his reputation amongst the
Montenegrins but he was saved, most
unexpectedly, by a Russian mission
sent to dispose of him. The Russian
envoy made it clear that he was a
crook and imprisoned him but soon
learned that with Šćepan Mali gone
there was no one to govern the land
appropriately. As Russia entered a new
war with Turkey, Šćepan was reinstated

"Resolving a blood feud" by Vialla de Sommiers
(National Museum of Montenegro)

and left as a useful Russian ally. His
curious life was ended in 1773 when
he was killed by his Greek servant
bribed by the pasha of Shkoder. This
brief episode in Montenegrin history
was very important as it showed that
much needed peace and order could be
achieved by authority.

With Šćepan's death things
returned to where they were before.
Metropolitan Sava had no authority
and the leading role was taken by the
ambitious **guvernadur Jovan Radonjić**
who secured his title as hereditary for
his family, thus establishing a second
"dynasty" in Montenegro. However,
Sava soon died (1781) opening the way
to Petar Petrović-Njegoš (later known
as **Petar I**, and after his death as St
Petar of Cetinje), a strong character and
a good organizer who soon equaled
the authority of the guvernadur. As an
orthodox metropolitan, Petar urged
alliance with Russia and tried to forge
Montenegrin unity from within, while
Radonjić, also predisposed by his title,
sought help from Venice and Austria.

For the moment Montenegro had
a new urgent problem to deal with
- the hostile pasha of Shkoder, Kara
Mahmud Bushati, a renegade from the
Turkish Sultan who demanded taxes

for himself. He successfully bribed and blackmailed the Highland clans and stimulated Montenegrin disunity so that when he attacked in 1785 his troops met merely sporadic resistance on their way to Cetinje where they burned down the monastery. Back from Russia, Petar I started organizing Montenegrins, persistently pleading them not to fight among themselves, cursing the killers in blood feuds and asking for unity against the Turks. His tireless efforts were crowned in **1796** when he called an assembly of the clans and pledged them to a common decision (called **"Stega"** – "The Discipline") on mutual peace and common defense against any attacker. The decision was soon put to the test when a few months later Mahmud-pasha attacked again. This time the Montenegrins faced him united and defeated his army at **Martinići**. Pasha regrouped, gathered an army several times larger than the Montenegrin and attacked from two sides. The Highlanders joined their

The original historic document "Stega" fr 1796 (National Museum of Montenegro)

Metropolitan Petar I by Vialla de Sommiers (National Museum of Montenegro)

brothers in need and beat off one army, while the Montenegrins stood firm at **Kruse** in their hour of glory and routed the pasha's army who met his death on the battleground. These decisive victories removed the little influence the Turks had over Montenegro, which was from this point *de facto* an independent country. They also showed Montenegrins what

they could achieve if they worked together. Furthermore the Highland clans of Bjelopavlići and Piperi decide to join the Montenegrins, and now all the Orthodox Christians from the surrounding lands looked to Petar for advice, guidance and help. Vladika Petar used this historic opportunity to capitalize on these victories and in the **1798** clan assembly he passed the **"Common Law Book of Montenegro and the Highlands"**, a set of basic law leaning strongly on tradition, with the main article prohibiting any kind of murder. Another novelty was the introduction of the State Court-of-Law a group of clan leaders headed by Pet himself, whose almost sole task was to settle problems between the clans in a peaceful manner. Although the new laws met with a lot of resistance from some quarters and the article on taxation could never be enforced, thes laws set the basis for organizing the government in Montenegro.

In the meantime the Venetian Republic was put to an end by Napoleon and **Boka Kotorska** came into the hands of Austria. After Napoleon's victories over Austria in 1805 Boka should have been handed to the French but this was challenged by the Russians (still at war with Napoleon) when their fleet sailed into the Adriatic calling on the Montenegrins to join them. Together they governed Boka until the peace treaty of 1807 when it was handed to the French. The new authorities set on reorganizing the province introducing

freedom of religion and promoting
e use of the Serbian language in
ministration but also stripped
etropolitan Petar of his religious
thority over Boka. When French rule
lapsed in **1813** Petar returned to
ka victoriously, this time with plans
unification: a commission made up
representatives of Montenegro and
ka voted for this and proclaimed
tar I as a common ruler. The great
wers, of course, disregarded this
d returned Boka Kotorska to
ustria. The instigation of Habsburg
le to the province did not proceed
thout fighting but in the end the
ontenegrins had to give it up.

When in 1804 in Serbia, on the other
le of the Montenegrin horizon, broke
t a quickly spreading insurrection, its
der Djordje Petrović – Karadjordje
ho although by ancestry from
e Highlands wasn't related to the
trovićs of Montenegro) established
otherly contacts with metropolitan
tar and agreed on moving together
ainst the Turks. Karadjordje made
to the present day border between
rbia and Montenegro where he
is joined by many Highlanders, but
tar was stuck besieging Nikšić. As
aradjordje had to redeploy to the
er front the whole plan failed.

The closing years of Petar's rule
re marked by another success.
hen in **1820** the Highland clans of
oračani and Rovca defeated the
rkish forces sent against them they
cided to embrace the rule of Cetinje.
now Montenegro became a point to
iich the surrounding orthodox Serbs
clined, led by the will to fight the
mmon enemy, the Turks.

The work of Petar I was continued
his young nephew **Petar II**, better
own just as Njegoš, who came to
e seat of the metropolitan in 1830.
ough one side of his personality
mained focused on poetry and
ilosophy (*see also p. 192*), Njegoš was
le to impose his authority on the
ontenegrins, not least because of the
ntinuity of his rule with that of his
e uncle whom he swiftly canonized.
s first step was to deal with the dual
wer in the state: when letters from
vernadur Vuko Radonjić to the
ustrians were intercepted, he was at
st charged with treason and stripped
his title and then in 1832, due to his
ots against the metropolitan, expelled
om Montenegro. Continuing in the
ps of his uncle, Njegoš established

the Senate which passed judgments
on capital crimes and settled quarrels
between the clans. The next institution
was the *gvardija*, units of armed men
led by a *kapetan*, which represented
local authorities, enforced the decisions
of the Senate and brought offenders
to justice. He also organized his own
bodyguard, called the *perjanici*, made
up of strong young men from all the
clans. The real novelty was that all of
these positions were paid. In order

*Petar II Petrović Njegoš by Johan Bess
(National Museum of Montenegro)*

to secure this Njegoš introduced the
paying of taxes, a very unpopular
measure at the time. Even so, there
wasn't enough money for the state
to function and in 1833 Njegoš set
out on his first journey to Russia.
There he obtained money for state
administration, an annual subsidy,
books for schools and even a printing
press, the first one in Montenegro
since the one of Djuradj Crnojević
in the 15th c. On his second trip four
years later he managed to persuade
the Emperor to raise the subsidy from
1000 to 9000 gold rubles a year, an
amount with which Montenegro could
finally start functioning as a state. The
Russians counted on Montenegrin
help in case of war but at Njegoš's
objections about the Turkish threat
he was advised to stay calm and
friendly. This was not an easy matter:
Montenegro of Njegoš was involved in
constant skirmishes with the Turks. In
1836 Montenegrins were defeated by
Herzegovinian Turks at Grahovo but
this resulted in negotiations in which
the Turks *de facto* treated Montenegro
as a separate entity. This was also the

Njegoš with his entourage by A. Orou (National Museum of Montenegro)

case with Austria, to which Njegoš, under great pressure, had to sell the parts of Montenegro nearest to the sea; in this way the two states finally regulated their mutual borderline. In 1840 the Turks were defeated in the regions inhabited by Moračani and Uskoci clans who now felt free enough to join Montenegro. A serious blow was inflicted to Montenegro in 1843 when the Turks from Shkoder captured Vranjina and Lesendro, two islands on Lake Skadarsko whose control meant that Montenegrin trade and fishing were to be under constant threat. During Njegoš's rule the first schools were opened in Montenegro and efforts were made to help the poorest, but the land was still frequently hungry and masses of people migrated to Serbia to find arable land they could live on.

Njegoš died in 1851, aged only 38. According to the wish expressed in his testament, his successor was to be his nephew **Danilo** who hurriedly came back to Montenegro from his schooling in Russia. In the meantime, all power was seized by Pero, Njegoš's brother and the president of the Senate and Danilo managed to ascend to the throne only after fierce disputes and with the Russian help. When he came to be the ruler of the country Danilo

Prince Danilo (National Museum of Montenegro)

was only 22; without the heroic stature of his uncle he had to win his respect only by his deeds, his wit and his strong will to rule. In order to strengthen his power Danilo broke with tradition and instead of becoming a monk and a metropolitan he proclaimed himself to be the hereditary prince of Montenegro and Highlands – a crucial step in the modernization and perception of Montenegro as a state. This, of course, provoked the response of the Ottoman Empire and in **1852** an army three times larger than the total number of Montenegrins under arms attacked. After fierce fighting in which the Montenegrins melted even the letters of their printing house to make more bullets, the Turks were within reach of Cetinje and only the intervention of Russia and other European powers prevented the fall of the capital. The war made it obvious to Danilo that Montenegrins should reorganize from groups of armed men into a real army and he took upon forming the first units led by commanding officers. To strengthen his grip on power he installed his close relatives and fiercest supporters to all the important positions in the country, increasing the number of senators and *kapetani* and raising their incomes. In 1855 he proclaimed a revised law book and ordered its strict obeyance. With those who refused to abide Danilo dealt mercilessly and his attacks on the clans of Bjelopavlići and Piperi who failed to do so are still remembered for their bloodiness. When his efforts to gain international recognition for his country at the Paris peace conference in 1856 failed, prince Danilo decided to provoke new clashes with the Turks and force Europe to consider the Montenegrin question. He decided on helping the insurrection in Herzegovina which started a few years earlier; in **1858** the Turkish army sent to punish Montenegro was encircled at **Grahovo**, attacked and heavily defeated. The news of

"Funeral procession of Prince Danilo" by Anton Karinger (National Museum of Montenegro)

this victory rang out across Europe, boosting the reputation of Montenegro. European diplomacy urged a peaceful conclusion and forced Turkey to regulate the border with Montenegro (1859-60), an act of silent acceptance of its independence. The rule of prince Danilo ended in 1860 when he was assassinated by a man from the Bjelopavlići clan as an act of revenge.

Danilo was succeeded by his nephew **Nikola** (19), another in the line of very young rulers. The stability created by Danilo's efforts is best seen from the fact that Nikola's coming to the throne wasn't disputed by anyone. Nevertheless, in 1861 Montenegro was still a land with no roads or towns exceeding the population of 1,000, in which all but a few inhabitants were shepherds in high mountains living on the brink of hunger, where all men were armed and prepared for war with their eyes on the fertile plains still controlled by the Turks. Nikola's reign started with the Turkish ultimatum to stop helping the rebels in Herzegovina.

When Nikola rejected it, Montenegro was attacked in **1862** by a far more numerous enemy and only Russian intervention saved the land from total defeat. Knowing well that a new war with the Turks was only a matter of time, Nikola joined an alliance with Serbia, from where he was sent guns, cannons as well as officers to train his troops. Further attempts were made to organize the state: ministries were founded, the prince's and state treasuries divided (1868), the first high school was opened (1869) and the first newspapers printed (1871).

After some years of silent discontent, in **1875** a large uprising broke out in Herzegovina, quickly spreading to Bosnia and further beyond. Prince Nikola could not ignore it and soon managed to impose his protégés as the leaders of the insurrection, coordinating their actions with those of the Montenegrins. In 1876 he declared war on Turkey simultaneously with his ally, Serbia; in this war the Montenegrins did excellently, defeating Ottoman troops in the Fundina and Vučji Do battles and winning great acclaim and respect with all Serbs. The Turks brought in reinforcements and were ready for another attack towards Cetinje when Russia joined the war. The majority of the Turkish army was sent against the new foe and so the Montenegrins were left with an easy task, taking Nikšić, Podgorica, Bar and Ulcinj before the ceasefire. The war was concluded with the **Berlin Congress (1878)** by whose decrees Montenegro got international recognition as a sovereign state and was enlarged to double its prewar size, including the first real cities as well as a portion of the Adriatic coast. The fertile land in the lowlands, previously owned by Turkish landlords, was divided into smaller lots and awarded to many Montenegrins who had no land at all. However, large tracts of land also fell into the hands of Prince Nikola himself, his cousins and his closest associates who now resembled a kind of a new landed aristocracy.

Sovereign Montenegro was now changing rapidly from its centuries

"Going to the market" by Theodore Valerio (National Museum of Montenegro)

old ways: the towns, populated still mostly by Muslims, became centres of economic development and administration. To connect them, the first roads in Montenegro were built by compulsory labor paid for in wheat. The first industrial enterprises were based on exploitation of forests and other natural goods and were owned mostly by Italian and Austrian capital. In spite all of its efforts, Montenegro never managed to become self-sufficient and the deficit of its budget was filled regularly by Russia, which regarded the small princedom as its most loyal ally. The administration was also undergoing changes: the Senate was abolished and its functions were taken over by the six ministries, the State Council (comprising of ministers) and the High Court, but all of the dignitaries were appointed by the prince, whose will was the highest law in the land. This situation met with opposition first amongst some of the free-spirited chieftains who thought that the distribution of power would result in less willfulness of the Prince (and Nikola was a man with whom one could never be sure) and abuses by his cronies. Since these efforts were the work of just a few men, Nikola dealt with them easily. His real problems started when the same ideas, amplified by demands for democratization, were propagated by a growing body of young men educated abroad, mostly in Serbia. Their voices were eagerly heard,

though perhaps not fully understood, by the majority of Montenegrins who were still living hand to mouth. New problems for the Prince appeared in 1903 as Serbia got rid of its autocratic king and started developing a fully democratic system whose example the Montenegrin youth were eager to follow. Belgrade again took on the cause of Serb and Yugoslav unification (which also included Montenegro), renounced Austrian tutorship and gained the support of Russia who now saw Serbia as its most important Balkan ally.

Upon the news that the Russian Emperor had granted a constitution, Nikola took the same steps in **1905** and Montenegro became a constitutional monarchy. Parliament was also chosen by a public ballot amongst all male tax payers but had no prerogatives, since ministers and governments were appointed and dismissed by the Prince. At first the parliament was devoted to Nikola but in 1907 divergent voices began to be heard and the first parties were formed: the opposition People's Party (*Narodna stranka*) and, in response to it, the governmental True People's Party (*Prava narodna stranka*). Nikola accused the opposition of being tools in the hands of Belgrade and suppressed their activity. In 1907 a group of Montenegrin students educated in Belgrade were caught as they tried to smuggle bombs in from Serbia. Very few members of the People's Party had knowledge about this, but Nikola decided to use the occasion to eliminate his adversaries and organized staged trials sentencing the opposition leaders to jail terms and death. The accusations between Cetinje and Belgrade were for a moment halted by the Austro-Hungarian annexation of Bosnia-Herzegovina (1908) to which both Montenegro and Serbia strongly

Portrait of Prince Nikola on a 100 perpe coin (National Museum of Montenegro)

King Nikola with his numerous family

joined the military alliance of Serbia, Bulgaria and Greece whose aim was to push the Ottomans from the Balkans. Montenegro had the honour of starting operations in the **First Balkan War (1912)**: the battles in the narrow belt of land which divided it from Serbia were completed without much trouble but then the Montenegrin army found itself stuck with the siege of the well fortified Shkoder (now in Albania), suffering severe casualties in charging its cannons and machine guns. When in the end, with the help of the Serbian army, Shkoder surrendered, Austria-Hungary threatened war if the town was not ceded to the newly founded Albanian state. In spite of this futile campaign, Montenegro was enlarged with the regions surrounding the towns of Pljevlja, Bijelo Polje, Berane, Plav as well as the fertile lowlands around Peć and Djakovica in present-day Kosovo. Now that Montenegro and Serbia got the long desired mutual border new thoughts on unification arose and many were not clear why a border between the two Serb states should even exist but Nikola ignored these ideas as he rightly saw that the smaller Montenegro would be devoured by Serbia.

rotested, coming close to the brink of ar against their mutual enemy. The ling of opposition leaders forced e discontent underground and in 09 a secret organization plotting ainst the "tyranny" of Prince Nikola as discovered; mass arrests and a w diplomatic quarrel with Serbia llowed. The situation between the o countries was further entangled hen in **1910**, on the 50th anniversary his rule, Nikola decided to adopt e title of **king**; by doing so Nikola gnaled that he didn't feel inferior to e king in Serbia and set his sights leading the liberation of Serbs in e Ottoman Empire, the idea that spired every last part of society in oth Montenegro and Serbia. Setting differences with Serbia aside to lfill this assignment, Montenegro

When in July of **1914** Austria-Hungary declared war on Serbia, King Nikola did not lose a moment in joining his brothers in this challenge. Officers were exchanged between the two high commands to coordinate the operations, and troops of both armies established a common front towards Bosnia. In 1914 Montenegrins fearlessly defended Mt Lovćen from attacks coming from the coast while on the Bosnian front they even joined an offensive that almost reached Sarajevo. In late **1915** the Serbian front succumbed to the joint attack by Austrians, Germans and Bulgarians and the Serbian army started retreating in the only possible direction – the mountains of Montenegro – in the hope of reaching the

King Nikola accepting the Turkish surrender of Shkoder

Adriatic and receiving help from its allies. This retreat was sheltered by the Montenegrin army which had its hour of glory in the **battle of Mojkovac** (January 1916) where it held the Austrians long enough to let Serbians escape to Albania. However, on the maritime front Lovćen fell into Austrian hands leaving a clear path towards Cetinje. The Montenegrin army was still undefeated, and the

officers and clerks. King Nikola, who spent his long rule guided by the same idea and which he steadfastly spread amongst his subjects, was now in dire straits since it was obvious that one state could not have two kings and that his reputation was dissolving rapidly. Though nominally open to the idea, Nikola did nothing to support it and the initiative was taken fully by the Serbians. In **September 1918** the Serbian army breached the front in Macedonia pushing relentlessly northwards and soon Montenegro was liberated by the units of volunteers from Boka, Herzegovina and America under Serbian command and aided by the guerillas. The situation in Montenegro

Postcard from World War I, Montenegro on the far right

Allies suggested that the Montenegrins should join the Serbians and leave their homeland to continue the fight. However, King Nikola left the country for France and the few ministers he left behind ordered the men to lay down their arms, an act that was viewed by the majority as humiliating and equal to treason. All of the officers and the government clerks the Austro-Hungarians could lay their hands on were arrested and sent to camps across the Empire. After the initial confusion, the occupation was met with guerilla attacks that kept the fight alive and forced the enemy to station large forces in Montenegro.

Both the Montenegrin and Serbian governments were now in exile, but while the Serbian one went with an almost complete state structure and even more importantly with a 200,000 strong army, the Montenegrin one had nothing to bargain with except for its allied status. In its plans for the end of the war the Serbian government stated the concept of Yugoslav unification whose first step would be the unification of Serbia with Montenegro. The idea enjoyed broad (though not unanimous) support amongst the Montenegrins, including most of the members of the exiled government and most of the encamped

was now controlled by the Serbian government who had no intention of letting Nikola back into the country. Deputies from all Montenegro were hastily elected and met on 13th November in the so-called **Podgorica Assembly** (*Podgorička skupština*) where they voted for the unification with Serbia, accepting the Serbian dynasty, the ruling regent Aleksandar Karadjordjević (grandson of King Nikola) and accusing Nikola of treason and forbidding him to return to the country. The body of unionists was made up not only of the pro-Serbian minded and the old opposition to King Nikola but also embraced most of the young and educated including the communists who saw the unification as a progressive move. This almost revolutionary overthrow was seen as dangerous by the older generation of chieftains who ruled by power granted to them by the king, the ministers of the state, many high ranking officers and clerks who had much to lose for their undisputed support of Nikola. Thus two parties emerged, known for the colours of their lists of candidates for the Podgorica Assembly – white for the unionists (*bjelaši*) and green for the supporters of King Nikola (*zelenaši*). In order to return to power, Nikola sought support from Italy who

d plans to annex most
 the east Adriatic and
ho was opposed to the
eation of a unified and
rong Yugoslav state.
ith the help of Italian
oops who had already
iled into Boka Kotorska,
inisters loyal to Nikola
ganized groups opposed
 the overthrow of their
ng and prepared the
unterattack. They struck
 Orthodox Christmas
anuary 1919, thus the event
 known as the Christmas Rebellion -
žićna pobuna) blocking several towns;
e unionists organized to fight back. In
ost of places bloodshed was avoided
t the strongest of the loyalist groups
tacked Cetinje and was beaten off
ily after a day of bloody fighting. The
yalist plan failed and they dispersed,
me to Italy, others to the woods
d mountains. Nikola died in Nice
rance) in 1922 but the attacks on the
w authorities by his loyalists lasted
 the way to 1926. Police and army
sts were attacked and unionists
led to which the police responded in
utal actions that included the burning
 the guerillas' homes and reprisals on
eir families.

 In the new, large state Montenegro
came just one region far from any
roic importance it held in the minds
 its inhabitants and other South Slavs.
eographically isolated, it had barely
y roads or rail, while its inhabitants
ere living in poor conditions,
ditionally suffering from the
nsequences of war and occupation.
ough efforts were made to improve
ucation, health services and the
ltural level of the people, the local
onomy lagged behind. Similar to the
tuation in the rest of the state, the rich
d developed regions prospered while
e poor ones were not interesting
r investment. The benefits of the
odern age such as electricity, radios
 cars were limited to the littoral
d the few cities while the villages
emed almost frozen in time. In terms
 administration the land itself was
named to Zeta Region (Zetska oblast).
was limited to the 1878 borders but
as instead widened by Boka Kotorska
d the Littoral. In 1929 Montenegro
came the core of Zetska banovina,
arge region including also East
erzegovina, Dubrovnik, south-west
rbia and Metohija. Cetinje remained

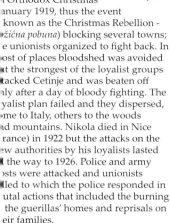

Cetinje in the 1930s

the administrative centre. Political life
was turbulent: in the first elections 4
out of 10 seats allocated to Montenegro
were won by the communists,
reflecting the dissatisfaction and the
will for change but also the traditional
admiration for all things Russian. The
Communist Party, whether legally
or acting underground during its
prohibition, remained successful in
the interwar period, receiving much
acclaim amongst the free-spirited
Montenegrins. The mainstream was
dominated by other parties active
across Yugoslavia (Democratic, Radical,
Peasant etc.). The only party specific to
Montenegro was the Federalist Party,
the offspring of the *zelenaši* faction of
1918, which stood for the federalization
of the state, with Montenegro as one
of its units. The high expectations of
unification failed to materialize in
terms of both the economic and the
political progress achieved.

 In April of 1941 Yugoslavia
crumbled under the attack of Hitler's
Germany and its allies. Montenegro
was occupied by the Italians who
annexed the coastal region while
the rest the country was intended
to become a puppet-state. However,
the proclamation of "independent"
Montenegro by the occupiers through
the parliament made out of the right-
wing Federalists was met with great
discontent among the people and a
day later, on **July 13th**, the uprising
began. The Italians were attacked and
in a few days of fighting their rule was
limited to a few cities encircled by the
rebel forces. The additional troops
brought in by the Italians and Germans
managed to beat of the insurrectionists
who regrouped in the mountains.
The communists who organized units
under the name of *partizani* held the
largest sway over the guerilla forces.
The other group were the *četnici*, Serb-
orientated royalists; the two groups

Partizan leader Tito (middle) with his closest associates

coordinated their actions against the occupiers in the beginning but by 1942 became bitter rivals engaged in a brutal conflict that would split the land in two. The Muslims and Albanians largely supported the occupation and, as a reaction to the slaughters committed by the četnici, joined SS divisions formed by the Nazis. Over-confident, the communists managed in 1942 to ruin their dominant position by reprisals against all who disagreed with their uncompromising ideology. However, the partizani proved to be the best organized and motivated and by 1943 they returned to the position of strength taking control over the mountains in the north of the country. By late **1944** the whole of Montenegro was liberated and firmly controlled by the communists; their wartime and ideological enemies as well as the bourgeoisie were decimated.

The huge contribution to the partizan victory by Montenegrins is seen clearly from the fact that 8 out 32 members of the Supreme Command as well as 36% of all partizan generals were Montenegrins, though they constituted only 2% of the Yugoslav population! In the new, socialist Yugoslavia, Montenegro became one of the six constituent federal republics, equal in all matters with the other five. In 1945 the present day frontiers of the country were established and a year later the capital was transferred to devastated Podgorica which was renamed Titograd in celebration of the country's leader Josip Broz "Tito". The war torn country started its transformation along the lines of the Soviet model. However, in **1948** Tito clashed with Stalin and in order to maintain his power cleansed the

lines of his communists of all who dared to believe that Soviet dogma was better than the "Yugoslav way to communism". This purge hit the traditionally Russian-inclined Montenegrins hardest of all the Yugoslav nations: during the dispute more than 5,000 people – 1% of the population - were arrested, sent to "correction" camps (most notorious of them being Goli Otok island) where they were tortured physically and mentally, a great number of them never to return.

In the post WWII period Montenegro's traditional social and economic structures were utterly transformed. Montenegrins from the poor areas hardest hit by the devastation of the war made up a fair proportion of the colonists to Vojvodina, northern Serbian province. Belgrade and other major centers in Serbia (joined later by Sarajevo and Zagreb) during the period presented the focus points of migration from the republic, so that in 1991 31% of Montenegrins lived outside of their native land. The agricultural population was brought to the towns decreasing from 78% in 1948 to just 7% in 1991. New industrial facilities were established, such as the aluminum plant in Titograd, the ironworks in Nikšić and the ore mine in Pljevlja. New roads were built and in 1974 the Belgrade-Bar railway, currently still one of the main arteries of the country economy, was opened. These decades were marked with a long period of stability and economic growth, Yugoslav "consumer-socialism", state secured jobs, health care and pensions, credits from the Western Block and als

Emblem of Montenegro during the socialist era

rise of tourism. Education, social and
...tural life were controlled solely by the
...mmunist party but satisfaction was
...h so that there were few dissidents.
...Montenegro, as well as all the other
...ublics of Yugoslavia, also got a
...te TV channel (1976), the university
...Podgorica (1974), the Academy of
...s and Sciences (1976) and other
...rogatives of a nation-state into
...ich the Yugoslav republics were
...nsforming with the weakening of
...o's control. The national question
...s deemed solved
...h an administrative
...e of thumb stating
...t all the Orthodox
...Montenegro were
...nic Montenegrins. To
...y this would be to
...llenge the system.
...When in the late 1980s
...goslavia started to
...ntegrate along the
...ional lines, the old,
...gnant communist
...rarchy in Montenegro
...ck to the model of
...ntenegrin nationality
...ile the opposing
...ces introduced the
...b nationalist rhetoric.

*Milo Djukanović, a longstand-
ing leader of Montenegro*

...action of the Party, led
...younger members Momir Bulatović,
...o Djukanović and Svetozar Marović,
...ed forces with the leader of the
...bian communists, Slobodan Milošević
...rn of a Montenegrin father) and
...rthrew the old establishment (1989).
...e parliamentary elections followed in
...0 and the first multi-party parliament
...s formed with Bulatović becoming
... president while Djukanović was
...ed as the youngest prime-minister
...Europe. The reformed communist
...ty changed their name to the
...nocratic Party of Socialists (DPS),
...ping all power in their hands. The
...p from Serbia was repaid by loyalty
...he last days of Yugoslavia and as
...nic tensions rose DPS tolerated Serb
...ionalism. In 1991 fighting broke
... in Slovenia and Croatia as they
...eded; the Yugoslav army units from
...ntenegro, combined with the local
...ervists, were sent against Croatian
...es in Dubrovnik. This mini-war
...led quickly with no gains for
...ntenegro but a hundred dead and
...ined reputation in what seemed
...e an unprovoked attack. In the
...rendum on the status of Montenegro
...April **1992** 64% of the population

voted to form, together with Serbia,
the **Federal Republic of Yugoslavia**,
which now had only two members.
For its help to Serbs from Croatia and
Bosnia (whose leader, Radovan Karadžić
was also from Montenegro) in the
summer of the same year the new state
had international economic sanctions
imposed upon it; this ruined the
country's economy and drove inflation
sky-high. The government turned a
blind eye to the smuggling of petrol and
cigarettes and to the black-market, the
two activities which gave
rise to numerous criminal
groups who now became
the country's *noveau riche*.
During these dark years the
government gave support
to all decisions reached
in Belgrade by Slobodan
Milošević. Change came
in late 1996 as Milošević's
power was paralyzed by
massive demonstrations
all over Serbia; Djukanović
decided that it was time
to leave the sinking ship
while Bulatović continued
his support for the Serbian
leader. Soon the two were
in bitter dispute, their party
split and in the presidential
elections of **1997** they both became
presidential candidates. Djukanović's
victory by a narrow margin was
followed by a political stand-off on
the edge of civil war since his oponent
had support of the army and he that of
the police. In the end Djukanović took
control completely and Bulatović was
forced to form a new, opposition party.
Milo Djukanović adopted a policy of
distancing himself from Serbia and the
long threatening hand of Milošević,
gradually setting the course towards
an independent Montenegro. During
the NATO bombing campaign against
Yugoslavia Montenegro was targeted
only slightly and its hardest test were
the refugees escaping war struck
Kosovo. By the time of Milošević's
downfall, Montenegro was independent
in all but name and this course was
continued in the following years
though the international community,
fearful of new crisis, promoted the new
loose confederacy named simply State
Union of Serbia and Montenegro. After
much internal tension, in May of 2006
Montenegro voted (with 55.5%) in favor
of a separate state.

LANDSCAPE AND WILDLIFE

The landscape of Montenegro is extraordinarily varied primarily for the reason that from sea level to the top of the coastal mountains there is no more than a few kilometers by air and from the sea to the main chain of the High

A winter morning in the village of Stoliv, Gulf of Kotor

Dinaric Alps, with peaks up to 2,500m, no more than 50km. The same contrast is to be observed in the climate, with conditions changing from one region to the other forming specific associations of flora and fauna.

Coastland

The coastline of Montenegro is 293km long. It has two distinct parts: in the north is Boka Kotorska (The Gulf of Kotor), a series of four basins connected by straits and ringed with hills. At its north and east edge these hills climb almost horizontally from the sea to the peaks of Mt Orjen (1895m) and Lovćen (1749m). Warm air that comes from the sea rises along the cliffs cooling rapidly and generating rain in such quantities that it keeps the whole of the Gulf pleasantly green even in the warmest of summers and makes the highlands of the Krivošije clan the region with

most precipitation in the whole of Europe! The rest of the coastland is open towards the sea, with a small number of coves and just a few tiny islands. The feature it shares with Boka is the mountainous hinterland, which here also limits the extent of the Mediterranean climate to the narrow coastal belt. Prevalent in this region is Mediterranean vegetation of thick evergreen bushes (maquis) with many aromatic plants. Oak woods, tall cypress trees, maritime pine and olive groves are also found in abundance. The summers are long and hot and the winters mild and rainy.

Sub-Mediterranean Montenegro

Between the coast and the mountain giants that rise to the east of Podgorica and Nikšić lays the region affected to an extent by the Mediterranean climate. In its north the extremely rugged terrain of "fierce karst" (*ljuti krš*) prevails an 800m high plateau dotted with holes and scarred with small rocky vales. The inhospitable looking scenery is dominated by sparse shrubbery while the hillsides rising from this tableland are almost bare. The scattered houses of relatively numerous villages cling to the little arable land available. There

Clear waters near Sveti Stefan

Barren peaks of Mt Lovćen in sub-Mediterranean Montenegro

...re just two fields with some more land ...itable for agriculture and these are ...ominated by the towns of Grahovo ...d Cetinje. Though the region sees a ...t of rain during the colder part of the ...ar there are no rivers or streams here ... all the water ...uickly disap-...ears through the ...orous limestone ...cks. To protect ...emselves from ...e draught the ...habitants gather ...in water in ...rotected basins ... man-made ...nks. Somewhat ...fferent from this ...rsh region is the ...ld of Nikšić, the ...rgest karst field ... Montenegro ...6km²). It abounds ... hydrological phenomena getting its ...ater from the 330 springs and losing ...through 886 sinks, with 30 more ...tavelles (*see p. 225*) and one intermit-...nt spring. The river Zeta also emerges ...re only to sink at the edge of the field ...d reappear again some kilometers ... the south. The valley of Zeta is a

narrow thread of green, arable land stretching between the cliffs of the adjoining mountains from the NW to the SE. The river ends in the plain of Zeta (*Zetska ravnica*) in which lies Podgorica, the country's capital and largest city. Watered by the Zeta, Cijevna and Morača rivers this flat piece of land makes up most of the 13% of territory suitable for agriculture in Montenegro. To the south, the plain ends with Lake Skadarsko (also called Lake Scutari), the largest lake in the Balkans. As the lake considerably varies in size due to the uneven flow of water it abounds in wetland areas rich in birds, amphibians, plants and fish.

Misty morning on Mount Durmitor

Mountains

Most of Montenegro is mountainous and in the area to the east of the Zeta River there are only a few flat places, nearly all of them high plateaus between the main mountain ridges. The highest strip of the Dinaric Alps with mountains such as Durmitor (2523m), Stožac (2226m), Bjelasica (2139m), Komovi (2487m) or Prokletije (2693m) cuts through the middle of the land. The Durmitor massif is especially beautiful for its diverse relief, contrasting between the wide Jezera plateau

Parceled farmland in the plain of Zeta

snow that remain all through the summer are a valuable source of water for shepherds. The predominant occupation in the mountains is livestock farming, mostly sheep and goat but nowadays also cattle, while there are also good conditions for growing potato, cabbage and corn.

Pastures on Mt Durmitor

and the craggy tops towering above its numerous glacial lakes. Most of the mountains are well forested while some even retain primeval woods (Biogradska gora on Bjelasica and Perućica on Mt Maglić) but there are also those like Sinjajevina where deforestation for firewood and pastureland have turned them into grasslands, with a thin layer of earth spiked with stones and rocks. Between these mountains flow the rivers Tara, Piva and Morača which have cut astoundingly deep canyons, impassable obstacles formed over eons. In the eastern part there are a few wider river basins, occupied by the towns Pljevlja, Bijelo Polje and Berane.

The karst landscape also features many caves which are to be found all over the country including such rarities as the Djalovića pećina in the hills east of Bijelo Polje which has more than 15km of tunnels or the Cetinjska Cave which lies in the middle of the city! Sadly, none of the caves in Montenegro are open for tourist visits.

The mountains of Montenegro enjoy a cold and wet climate, especially those in the far east of the country. Snow is usual already in October and can continue to fall until May. In higher altitudes the patches of

Rivers & Canyons

The range of High Dinaric Alps forms a watershed between the two drainage systems of Montenegro that cut the land in half. To the west and south flow rivers ending in the Adriatic Sea, while those flowing to the north and east carry their waters to the Danube and eventually to the Black Sea. The coastal area is characterized with short streams which rapidly descend to the sea. One exception is the river Bojana at the very south of the country: this 44km long river which takes the waters from Lake Skadarsko to the sea is even navigable for smaller ships. The two most important rivers of the Adriatic system are the Morača and its tributary Zeta. Formed from numerous springs in central Montenegro the Morača pushes SW cutting the astounding Platije canyon with sides up to 1000m high and then enters the Zeta plain, passing through Podgorica and flowing into Lake Skadarsko. Tara is the longest river in the country (150km) and its second part forms a canyon regarded as the second deepest in the world (1300m deep). Equally impressive are the canyons of Komarnica and Piva, one following the other. The river Lim in the east of the country has a more tame appearance but also several smaller gorges which interchange with

Pines on the clifs of the River Piva canyon

Deep luscious forest by the Biogradsko Lake

wider parts that are occupied by ... lages.

...ora

Montenegro's fabulous richness in ...ant species stems from the diversity ... geographic and climactic conditions. ...epending on the distance from the ...a and on the latitude (both having a ...ominent effect of the precipitation ...d temperature in different seasons), ...ontenegro displays a surprising vari-...y of vegetation types often occurring ... close proximity. Here one can find ...ound 3000 species (roughly twice ... many as in Great Britain!), some 22 ...ing endemic only to Montenegro.

Some places are real botanical gardens in the wild, as for example the Biogradska Gora National Park where a trained eye can spot 86 different trees. The diversity of microclimatic conditions is equally important: on the north sides of the highest mountains grow plants characteristic to the Arctic, on peat bogs around the lakes those found in Siberian taiga, while on the steep sides of the inaccessible canyons of Tara or Piva there are species which survive here from the time of the last Ice Age.

The coastland sees flowers blossoming already from January, starting with the mimosa in whose honor the festival in Herceg Novi takes place. By the beginning of May nature is in full bloom. Given that the costal areas have been under human influence for several millennia it is not possible to deduce with certainty which species where introduced and which are native to the region. Most likely the natives were various kinds of evergreen and semi-deciduous oak and coniferous forests of several species of juniper, pine and possibly cypress, as well as maquis in more exposed areas. Today, figs and olives introduced by man dominate the area.

As one moves further from the sea

centuries old olive tree

to the sub-Mediterranean zone more exposed to the continental influences, the evergreen forests are replaced by deciduous forests of oak (mostly downy oak), manna ash and Oriental hornbeam. Further inland areas in low and mid-altitudes are dominated by temperate continental deciduous forests, mostly of beech. Cold and wet high mountains are covered by thick coniferous forest of spruce, fir and pine. Several rare tree species make Montenegro their home; among which are whitebark and Macedonian pines, Macedonian oak and Turkish hazel.

A bountiful haul of carp

Wildlife

Due to the high demographic pressure even in the most remote areas of the country, the wildlife of Montenegro has been seriously imperiled by hunting and exploitation. In times of peace warriors could easily transform to skilful hunters, and carnivores had to compete with humans for pray and territory. Most threatened were the larger mammals and fish while many smaller species adapted to living close to people. Fish and birds, on the other hand, enjoyed the unpolluted environment and the variety of living habitats.

Skadarsko Lake is a major fishing ground, both commercial and recreational. The major target of anglers is the famous exceptionally elongated and vividly colored wild form of common carp, called *krap* by the locals. Due to its very tasty meat the wild carp has become very rare in most of Europe, but populations here survive in spite of the impact of heavy fishing, both legal and illegal. Eels and mullets frequently wonder into Bojana and Skadarsko Lake from the sea. Brown and occasionally rainbow trout are common in cold mountain rivers, many small mountain lakes and reservoirs. Grayling can be found in most medium and large mountain rivers, while huchen is common only in the River Tara.

The waters of the Adriatic are rich in Mediterranean fish species the most common being dentex, mullet, mackerel, hornback ray, sea bream and tuna fish, the last one being the most important kind for the fishing industry. Shrimps, lobsters and octopuses are also to be found here. Amongst the most interesting kinds are the flying fish (such as gurnard), the large conger and moray eels and sea horses. Dolphins are relatively frequently seen in the waters of the Adriatic during the summer. Very rarely a blue shark loses its way and approaches the coast spreading unjustified terror amongst swimmers before it becomes

Heron in the marshland near Lake Skadarsko

...phy of local fishermen; ...attacks on people have ...en recorded.

The marshland of ...adarsko Lake, the area ...ound Ada Bojana and ...sko Lake are attrac-...ve stopping points for ...merous bird species ...uring their north-south ...igrations as well as for ...ntering of many others. ...ese conditions have ...ade them into areas with ...e largest variety of birds ... Europe attracting waders, ...rmorants, pelicans, herons, ibises, ...terns, ducks and warblers. The ...ountains and woods of the interior ...n't lag too far behind this variety and ...re one can spot eagles, owls, wood-

Two young boars

rare but weasels and badgers have survived and are commonly seen close to villages and towns. The pollution of major rivers has made otter one of the species under threat of extinction.

Beware of the nose horned viper (locally called *poskok*), recognized for the zigzag lines on its short body, one of the most poisonous snakes of Europe which inhabits the rocky areas of south and coastal Montenegro. The other poisonous snake here is the European adder (*šarka*) found in the continental mountains. Grass snakes

Eagles abound in far-flung areas of the country

...ckers, buntings, thrushes, larks, ...ghtingales, tits, partridges etc.

The wild boar lives in deciduous ...oods all around Montenegro and is ...e most common target for hunters. ...e once numerous chamois has been ...duced by hunting to rare sightings ...the high mountains such as Durmi-...r, Komovi or Prokletije. Mouflons ...ve been reintroduced in the areas ...ound Lake Skadarsko while the ...newed population of red deer in the ...tional parks of Durmitor and Bjela-...a is growing steadily. From the car-...vores the most numerous are foxes ...d wolves, whose presence close to ...man dwellings has left a clear mark ...local folktales as well as plenty ...names deriving from *vuk* (wolf). ...e coastal mountains are inhabited ...jackals. Wild cats are rarely seen ...nile the population of brown bear ...under protection and is limited to ...e north and east of the country. Pine ...d beech martens have become very

are very common in Skadarsko Lake but should not be feared as they are not poisonous.

Wolf, rarely seen nowdays

ACTIVE AND EXTREME

One thing no one can ignore in Montenegro is its stunning natural environment which simply entices you to immerse yourself, to get out and get active, to explore it and to get the most out of it. Due to the many faces of its wilderness every kind of activity here has a touch of adventure and provides a new and unforgettable experience.

The rugged landscape of Montenegro carries on underwater with a number of interesting caves being a unique attraction for **diving**; moreover the layers of history from Illyrian and Roman times have left many archeological remains, while the wars in the last two centuries have produced several shipwrecks which lie along the coast.

Diving Club "Nikšić";
069/015-655; *www.rknk.cg.yu*
"Hobotnica", Bar; 069/020-660;
www.divemontenegro.com
"Marina", Herceg Novi;
069/637-915; *www.dcmarina.com*

With plenty of good locations for take off, incredible vistas (be it mountains or the seaside) and suitable places to land, Montenegro is perfect for **paragliding**. For those looking for a more serene atmosphere the capital Podgorica has a ballooning club satisfying the tourists' needs.

"Eco Tours", Kolašin;
020/860-700; *www.eco-tours.cg.yu*

Ballooning Club "Budućnost", Podgorica; 067/254-669;
www.balloon.cg.yu

One of the nicest ways to explore the wilderness is on a **mountain bike**.

Kite surfer having fun

The coast of Montenegro facing the open sea has plenty of wind to get you kite or wind surfing, while places such as Velika plaža south of Ulcinj and Ada Bojana are well known as prime locations amongst the lovers of these sports. **Windsurfing** is now made easy with new wide boards which allow also the beginners to feel the excitement of this sport. It is possible as well to windsurf on the warmer waters of Lake Skadarsko with its mild winds which are good for beginners. For **kite surfing** you need no more than a board, ropes and a favourable wind for your kite.

"Dragon", Ulcinj;
069/62-44-29;
www.dragonproject.net
"Pelikan", Vranjina;
020/403-835;
www.pelikansurf.cg.yu

Exploring the depths of the Adriatic

Preparing for take-off

You can choose a route depending on your physical condition and the level of risk you want to take, from riding on unpaved foot paths to descending down mountain slopes.

"Drum i putokazi", Žabljak;
www.drumiputokazi.com

beginning of every July brings together the best European off-road drivers and their crews.

"Montenegro Trophy", Nikšić, 040/212-509;
www.monttrophy.cg.yu

"Eco Tours", Kolašin;
020/860-700;
www.eco-tours.cg.yu

If we bear in mind that Montenegro abounds with caves and caverns of all depths it is not surprising that it has many **speleology** clubs and enthusiasts. The most fascinating sight amongst the country's caves is certainly Djalovića pećina (also known as Pećina nad Vražjim firovima) of which 16km have been explored but it is believed to be a lot deeper. The sides of Mt Orjen above Herceg Novi abound with all types of karst relief.

"Nikšić"; 069/013-583

"Subra"; 069/360-803;
www.subra.users.cg.yu

Off-road adventures

An activity not to be missed in Montenegro is **rafting** along one of its whitewaters while surrounded by the magnificence of some of Europe's most breathtaking canyons, including the one of the beautiful River Tara, second deepest in the whole world. You can choose the means of your descent - wooden rafts, rubber boats and kayaks are all very popular.

"Tara Tour", Plužine; 040/27-13-59;
www.tara-tour.com

„Grab", Nikšić; 040/200-598;
www.tara-grab.com

„Fram"; 069/028-715;
www.rafting-fram.com

„Soko", Podgorica; 069/402-213;
www.raft-soko.cg.yu

Though horsemanship has never been a tradition in Montenegro one can find several agencies organizing **horse riding** tours.

"Vila Jelka", Kolašin;
069/031-392;
www.vilajelka.cg.yu

A more popular way to roam around Montenegro and its wild nature is **jeeping** with skilled drivers taking you along the roads and paths you never thought possible. The jeep-rally Montenegro Trophy which takes place at the

Whitewater rafting on River Tara

Montenegro is a genuine heaven for **hiking and mountaineering**: from Trnovačk Lake just below the peak of Maglić at the border of Bosnia-Herzegovina to the Hajla near Rožaje, and all the classic trekkin routes on Durmitor and Bjelasica The network of mountain huts is not substantial but those carryin a tent are about to set foot on so of the most interesting terrains in Europe.

"Komovi", Podgorica; 069/676-2
www.komovi.cg.yu

„Javorak", Nikšić; 040/214-110;
www.psdj.cg.yu

„Gorica", Podgorica; 069/606-14
www.planinarskogorica.cg.yu

There are two marked routes for **free climbing**, one in Kotor and one in Podgorica as well as several unmarked ones such as the one in Djurdjevića Tara but t real pleasure here are the many uncounted rocks which wait to b discovered.
Contact – the mountaineering societies

Free-climbing a cliff near Kotor

The two best known mountains for **winter sports** are Durmitor and Bjelasica, which have the finest facilities but there are also several ski-lifts in Lokve near Berane, Turjak by Rožaje and Vučjak not far from Nikšić. The snow that remains on the tracks until late March is the best guarantee skiers and snowboarders can ask for.

"Drum i putokazi", Žabljak;
www.drumiputokazi.com

In Montenegro one can see 57% of a European bird species, an astonishing rate due to the variety of living and nesting conditions. The most interestin areas for **bird watching** are Lake Skadarsko, Lake Šasko, saltpans of Ulcinj and Tivat, etc.
www.birdwatchingmn.org

The Adriatic Sea, many smaller and larger rivers as well as lakes provide a variety of conditions for **fishing**. A fishing permit on all rivers and lakes outside national parks can be obtained for €15 with the Fishing Association of Montenegro.

Fishing federation (*Sportski ribolovni savez*); 020/621-007

"Eco Tours", Kolašin; 020/860-700;
www.eco-tours.cg.yu

Fishing and relaxing

SAILING IN MONTENEGRO

For anyone who has ever cruised a boat even for a day or two it needless to point out what an amazing experience it is. Freedom to wander, independence from those on the mainland, new perspectives, the vastness of water and the sky above you are just some of the amazing array experiences and new feelings it rouses, definitely making sailing a thing one should enjoy at least once in his life. Whether you own a boat of your own or you're looking for a

Preparing to dock in Perast

"charter" (renting of a ship for a few days) here's some advice on what to expect and plan your trip more successfully.

Montenegrin coast is not long but nevertheless it offers many breathtaking sights. Its northernmost part is Boka Kotorska ("Gulf of Kotor") an extraordinarily long gulf dotted with historic churches and old villages. The conditions for sailing here are superb due to favourable winds and mountains sheltering it from the strong south winds. Almost all of the coastal villages here provide basic conditions for mooring of ships so one can leap from one to another exploring them both from the sea and from land. The rest of the coastline (referred to in the guide as the Littoral) faces the open sea and therefore has much better beaches and cleaner water but lacks sheltered coves and adequately equipped marinas.

The entry to the territorial waters of Montenegro should be announced to the harbour master's office in Kotor (north) or Bar (south) on VHF channel

16. Sailing in from abroad, you should **register** with the customs at the ports of entry in Zelenika, Risan, Kotor, Budva, Bar and Ulcinj. If sailing in from the north (Croatia) the most convenient port is Zelenika, east of Herceg Novi, which serves mostly cargo ships and is quite polluted. Arriving from the south your choice should be Bar, the chief port of Montenegro; as the customs office is hard to locate you are advised to dock in the marina and inquire locally. The customs formalities are generally dealt with quickly and without hassle. You should visit customs for clearance when you decide to leave. For sailing in Montenegro you will need a **permit** from the harbour master's office which costs between €150 and €200 (depending on the type of your ship) and lasts for one whole year.

On the whole, Montenegro has favourable cruising conditions. The **winds** here are the same as in the rest of the east Adriatic: in summers, during the day there is a permanent breeze from the NW - mistral (called locally *maestral*), or the NNE bora (*bura*) of moderate strength. Nights are generally still or have a slight bora. Most of the forceful storms come from the west. Sirocco (*jugo*) grows gradually from the SW but once at full strength it blows strongly for several days (mostly not more than three) bringing rain and creating high waves.

Boka Kotorska enjoys natural protection from the winds

Town harbour of Herceg Novi

One of the main advantages of Montenegro over the other Mediterranean countries is its relative anonymity and thus also a lack of sailing crowds. On the other side, this also means that marinas are still under equipped and that only a few of the restaurants have considered offering a place to berth. There aren't many locals sailing around since most of them enjoy motor boats and yachts. The larger amongst these can be quite dangerous as they pay little respect to others, especially so in narrow Boka Kotorska where their high speeds create high waves which can damage the berthed boats at the unsheltered quays (pay special attention to this in Perast).

Here are some hints on marinas and other places to harbor your ship along the Montenegrin coast, arranged from north to south. Prices are given for a 14m long boat including water and electricity recharging.

Town harbour of **Herceg Novi** (*tel. 031/32-30-15; €45*) is used mostly by fishing and tourist boats but there are a few places to moor along its massive quay under the breakwater with plug-ins for water and electricity. The harbor is not very clean and the closest toilets are those in local cafés. However, the main problem here poses the fact that during the season the whole place is noisy all day and night long, and enjoys almost no privacy.

In the village of **Rose** across the gulf there is a small quay as well as anchorage buoys in front of the restaurants. The same goes for the beach of **Žanjice**. At the entrance to Boka Kotorska there is the **Dobreč** cove where one can berth his ship to a buoy in front of the restaurant visited mostly by the sailing crowds.

In **Tivat** there is a small marina Kaliman but this one is unsuitable for sailing ships. On the other hand you can dock by the main promenade in calm weather.

In **Risan** there is a small quay with the sea depth of 4.5m and with space for four boats.

In **Perast** it is possible to dock in the tiny town quay by the beacon. If this one is full you can try asking to moor your boat at one of the jetties in front of the houses. South of Perast by the spring of Ljuta is a scenic restaurant "Stari mlini" with a quay providing space for several boats. Close by is the fish and crab hatchery where one can dock and pick his lunch or dinner.

Marina „Kordić" in **Prčanj** (*032/33-61-62; €30*) is a friendly, privately owned place enjoying unspoiled peace whose only disadvantage is that it can harbor only up to 8 middle-sized yachts. A

Competitors in the local regatta

good alternative to the neighbouring Kotor.

Quay in **Kotor** (*telefon 082/325-208; €35*) is well kept and with place for some 50 yachts. Plug-ins for water and electricity but no toilets. The quay is located across the street from the main gate of the Old Town and enjoys little to no privacy as it lies by the city's walkway and highway. A new marina is being planned.

Bigova cove with the tiny village of the same name is the best natural harbour outside Boka Kotorska. There

a small quay by the lighthouse, just
tside "Grispolis", one of the best
afood restaurants in the country.

The coves of **Jaz** and **Trsteno** near
dva with their beautiful sandy
aches have bottom favourable for
choring. As they are fully open
wards the south this is possible only
calm weather.

The yachting marina of **Budva**
33/541-227; €60) lies just beneath
e walls of the Old Town. Modern
d with plug-ins for electricity and
ater but still without the toilets and
orishly expensive. Those looking
a more serene place can berth their
ats by the quay on the Isle of Sveti
kola in front of the town.

South of Budva there is a number
nice beaches suitable for anchoring
r instance Čanj) but again none of
ese is protected from the southern
nds. One is not allowed to anchor
s yacht in front of the exclusive
aljičina plaža beach next to Sveti
efan. In **Petrovac** there is a small
ay where a few boats can be
rthed, weather permitting.

The large port of **Bar** includes four
arinas. The largest amongst them is
veti Nikola" (030/31-39-11; €30) with
0 commercial yacht berths including
ose for ships larger than 54ft. This
by far the most serious place for
y larger repairs. In addition, it
s incredibly low prices for yearly
rboring (€100-150 per meter). Other
arinas in Bar are "Marina"
30/31-77-86), "Jug" (030/314-262)
d "Nautilus" (030/303-276). The bad
de to the port of Bar is that it still is
t oriented towards tourism with

many cargo and ferry ships around
and with long distances from the
nearest shop, restaurant and similar.

Smaller motor boats can go
up the northern branch of river
Bojana to the group of excellent fish
restaurants on the water.

In near future it is expected that
modern marinas will be built in
Kotor, Tivat's arsenal, Budva's Sveti
Nikola Isle and in Perazića do (next
to Petrovac) in front of hotel "As".

USEFUL PHONES

Marine safety direction (*Uprava
pomorske sigurnosti*) 030/313-241

Harbor master's office in Bar (*Lučka
kapetanija Bar*) 030/312-733

Harbor master's office in Kotor
(*Lučka kapetanija Kotor*) 032/325-578

WEATHER FORCAST

"Bar radio" radio station VHF ch.24
or
www.meteo.cg.yu

CHARTER COMPANIES

Yachtingadria
Based in Bar and offering a dozen
sailing ships from 30 to 50ft long
and a few motor yachts, with or
without skippers.
web: *www.yachtingadria.com*

Montenegro Charter Company
Based in Kotor. Offering several
brand new sailing vessels 30 to 54ft
long, a catamaran and several motor
yachts, with or without skippers.
web: *www.montenegrocharter.com*

Favourable winds and nice vistas in the Gulf of Kotor

MANIFESTATIONS

The following list offers a selection of manifestations that take place in Montenegro throughout the year. For details, check the internet or with local tourist organizations. We recommend you confirm the exact dates a few weeks in advance as they can change.

JANUARY

Snowboarding on Bjelasica

Orthodox Christmas Eve and Day
(6th - 7th)
The ritual burning of the Christmas logs and midnight liturgies open the day of family festivities.

Julian New Year
(14th)
A celebration according to the old, Julian calendar, held mostly in restaurants and sometimes in city squares.

Guitar Fest, Bar
(16th – 23rd)
www.barguitarfest.com
Classical guitar performances by artists from the region.

Festival of Wine and Bleak, Virpazar
(27th)
Local wines and traditionally prepared bleak are served together with other fruits and dishes of the Crmnica region.

FEBRUARY

Montenegro Winter Cup, Kolašin
(1st)
A skiing competition on the Jezerine ski-pistes.

St Tryphon's Day Festivities, Kotor
(2nd – 3rd)
The high mass is followed by the carrying of St Tryphon's relics through the city, while on the second day there are concerts and a performance by the Boka Navy.

Mimosas Festival, Herceg Novi
(throughout the month)
www.hercegfest.cg.yu
The celebration of the blooming of mimosas announcing the coming of spring; the many parades, concerts and masquerades bring out the best in fun-loving inhabitants of Herceg Novi.

Carnival, Kotor
(13th – 24th)
This traditional event is a time of year when barriers between people are removed and when all enjoy having fun in street parades, masquerades and concerts.

Mimosis signifying the arrival of spring

MARCH

Dance Festival, Kotor
(24th – 30th)
www.montenegrodancefestival.com
A festival gathering a variety of dance groups from all over the world.

...ays of Camellia, Stoliv (28th-30th)
...ought by seafarers from the Far East,
...is exuberant flower is the pride of Sto-
...'s gardeners and the basic material for
...eating splendid flower arrangements.

...olden Eagle of Durmitor, Žabljak
...skiing competition in slalom and giant
...lom.

APRIL

...rnival, Budva
...8th – 5th of May)
...e carnival consists of many open-air
...ncerts, parades, majorettes' competi-
...ns, parades and masquerades.

...A happy face at the Budva Carnival

MAY

...uvenir Fair, Budva
...·d)
...w.suveniri.cg.yu
...display of the most imaginative sou-
...nirs from all over Montenegro.

...ooting of the Rooster, Perast
...5th)
...aditional manifestation in celebration
...· the 1654 victory over the Turks; the
...·d rooster on a small raft is a target
... the marksmen. The shooting is fol-
...·wed by traditional dances.

**...ver Lim Regatta, Plav-Berane-Bijelo
...lje**
...5th – 28th)
...descent down the river from the Plav
...ke to Prijepolje in Serbia, passing
...rough changing scenery and over
...any exciting rapids.

The rapids of Lim River

Vladimir's Cross, Bar-Mt Rumija
(late May or early June)
In this traditional event which has taken
place for centuries Orthodox, Muslims
and Catholics join the procession in
which the Cross of St Jovan Vladimir is
carried to the top of Mt Rumija.

JUNE

Folklore Festival, Budva
(7th – 8th)
Folklore ensembles from Europe perform their songs and dances.

The Boka Navy Day, Kotor
(26th)
The feast day of this historic organization is marked by a march through
Kotor's streets, the receiving of the
town keys from the town mayor and
the dancing of the ceremonial *kolo*.

JULY

Sunčane skale, Herceg Novi
(7th – 9th)
A festival of pop music in which
perform singers and groups from the
region.

Ars et Musica Antiqua, Kotor-Perast
(8th – August 19th)
In this festival old music blends with
unique ambient of old churches and
palaces in which it is performed.

Days of Music, Herceg Novi
(10th – 20th)
The festival gathers European artists
which perform classical music.

Grand Summer Concert, Budva
(13th)
A pop-rock concert that ends with
fireworks.

Parading in traditional costume during the **Fašinada**

Guitar Art Summer Festival, Nikšić
(17th – 25th)
www.niksicguitarfestival.com
Guitar performances of various kinds.

City-Theatre, Budva
(July and August)
www.gradteatar.cg.yu
The newest theatrical performances from the region are staged in a number of interesting settings, with many other happenings in the streets.

Fašinada, Perast
(22nd)
The line of boats sets out from Perast accompanied by song and music and goes to the Lady of the Rock Island where each of the participants delivers a stone, growing the island slightly.

The Days of Mrkojevići, Pečurice near Bar
(last week of July)
A display of local traditions, dances and music accompanied by sport and cultural events.

Boćarska olimpijada, Tivat
A miniature "Olympics" in *boćanje*, a Mediterranean version of bowls, a beloved pastime of the local populace.

Summer Carnival, Kotor
(28th – August 2nd)
A larger and better attended twin of the February carnival in the same city.

Folklore Festival, Cetinje
(end of month)
Performance of dances and songs by folk ensembles from the region.

AUGUST

Film Festival, Herceg Novi
(1st – 6th)
www.hercegfest.cg.yu
The most important film festival in Montenegro, a review of the new relea from the country and the region.

Tamburitza Festival, Bijelo Polje
(beginning of the month)
The tamburitza string orchestras of the Balkans gather and perform for severa days their traditional and newly composed songs.

Refresh Music Festival, Kotor
(7th – 10th)
Organized in several clubs in the town the festival brings well-known interna tional DJ's to Kotor's audience.

Klapa Festival, Perast
(8th – 10th)
The festival of traditional choral music of the Adriatic with *klape* (groups) from Boka Kotorska and Dalmatia.

Don Branko's Days of Music, Kotor
(9th – 12th)
Classical and jazz music in various op spaces and indoor venues.

Guitar Summer Festival, Herceg Nov
(14th – 21st)
Festival of classic and other guitar per formances.

Jamming at Petrovac's Jazz Festival

Bowling competition

Boka Night, Kotor
(16th)
Boats from all over Boka bring merry crowds to the party on the streets of the Kotor's Old Town which last till late in the night.

Petrovačka noć, Petrovac
(30th)
Brass bands, folk and pop performances, lots of food and drink and, not to forget, socializing and fun.

Njeguška trpeza, Njeguši village
A culinary fest centered on the famous cheese and ham from this historic village.

Njeguš smoked ham

Jazz Festival, Petrovac
(1st – 2nd September)
http://petrovacjazzfestival.tripod.com
Currently the only manifestation of jazz found in Montenegro gathers the artists from the country and the region.

Down the River Zeta, Danilovgrad
(30th – 31st)
A merry group of boats and rafts goes down the river, fish soups are prepared on the banks while the bravest jump from the old stone bridges.

SEPTEMBER

Festival of International Alternative Theatre (FIAT), Podgorica
(th – 28th)
Experimental performances take place in theatres and on the streets providing a rare opportunity to go alternative in Podgorica.

Montenegro Open, Budva
(mid September)
The main tennis tournament in the country.

OCTOBER

Dan Širuna, Budva
(4th)
Everybody gets to savour tastefully grilled bastard mackerel and then enjoy and take part in the festive program.

Kostanjada, Stoliv
(25th)
This manifestation includes tasting of chestnuts and traditional products made from them and walking through the chestnut woods around Stoliv.

NOVEMBER

Riječki Pazar, Rijeka Crnojevića
Folk performances and local products brought to sale recreate the times of the old market days in Rijeka.

DECEMBER

Maslinijada, Stari Bar
(13th)
Olives of all kinds and in a range of dishes garnish the tables of local producers.

New Year's Eve, Kotor
(31st)
The best known and best visited amongst the many New Year's Eves that take place in town squares and streets.

A variety of olives and olive products in Maslinijada

MONTENEGRO BY REGIONS

Boka Kotorska
The Littoral
Central Montenegro
Northern Montenegro
Eastern Montenegro

BOKA KOTORSKA

Boka Kotorska (in Italian *bocche* meaning "mouth") is a region surrounding one of the grandest natural features of east Adriatic - the Gulf of Kotor, a series of four bays penetrating 25km inland. Sailing in from the open sea, one first comes across the Herceg Novi bay with Mt Orjen (1895m) above it, than through the Kumbor straits to the lofty Tivat Bay. Through Verige, the narrowest point of the Gulf, one sees the bay of Risan to the north and the long bay of Kotor to the south, both surrounded with lofty mountains and ending with the historic town of Kotor, nested directly below the steep sides of Mt Lovćen (1749m). The gulf is often mistakenly considered to be a fjord but is in fact a river bed which sank

olive or lemon trees and a variety of other Mediterranean flora along the coast stand in stark contrast to the forbiddingly bare sides of the mountains to the rear, rich in caves and various karst formations.

To the surprise of many, the Gulf of Kotor is one of the rainiest regions in Europe, with the village of Crkvice above Risan holding the record with annual average of 5317mm of rainfall per square meter. This is due to the fact that the warm sea air cools off abruptly as it climbs the vertical sides of the mountains surrounding Boka. The same mountains shelter most of the Gulf from the sun and create a climate and vegetation in many aspects different to the rest of the coastline. On a sunny winter's day one can enjoy

Mist covering the waters in Perast

When the sea level rose in the distant geological past. The magnificent and unique natural beauty of Boka Kotorska doesn't allow one to stay indifferent and the exclamation of poet Ljuba Nenadović "and I wonder if the sun, how it can set, when a beauty such as this nowhere will be met" reflects precisely the kind of sentiment one takes with him. Small towns with baroque mansions erected by sea captains and villages with stone houses dot the sides of the bay. The lush greenery of cypresses,

the mild climate of the coast and then make an excursion to the snow covered mountains surrounding the Gulf.

The whole of Boka is one huge harbour sheltered from the strong winds with ideal conditions for sailing. It is therefore no wonder that its inhabitants (the *Bokelji*, as they are called) have always been noted for their nautical skills and that in the era of sailing ships they roamed the Mediterranean, trading in times of peace and fighting against the Muslims in times of war. Until recently the only

winding coastline of the Gulf of Kotor

thing connecting the villages of the Gulf was the sea, and also it was their only connection to the outer world. Today a road circulates around the Gulf but to fully enjoy its wonders one should embark on a boat trip.

Boka had a turbulent history. In ancient times it was called *Sinus Rhisonicus* – the Bay of Risan, after its largest town, formerly the seat of Illyrian kings and their fleet. In times of the first Slavic princedoms of the Middle Ages which were not of a seafaring nature its waters presented the border between Travunija in the north and Duklja in the south. The first to regain nautical glory were the mariners of Kotor during the times of Nemanjić Serbia as they amassed great wealth through trade and adorned their town with palaces and churches. Facing the Turkish threat the townships of the Gulf embraced Venetian rule and after several wars between these two world powers Boka was divided into half, exactly as it was in the early Middle Ages. In 1689 the Turks were driven away and Boka lived its hay day with many of its townships gaining prosperity through their skilful sailors – Perast, Prčanj, Dobrota, Topla, Orahovac, Herceg Novi, Morinj - all of these places had substantial fleets and gave many famous captains such as Matija Zmajević, the admiral of the Russian Baltic fleet, or Ivo Visin, the first captain of Austria-Hungary to sail around the world. From their journeys these men brought exotic plant species, oriental treasures and the air of the world travellers to their Gulf but never lost the love for their native region, their language and customs. These feelings came to life after the fall of the Venetian Republic when Boka changed hands several times between the Austrians, French, Russians and the English but the Bokelji tried to unite with their brethren from Montenegro on two different occasions. Boka was awarded to Austria who quickly started developing its potential as a natural harbor and turned it into the main base for its war fleet. Since 1918 Boka is united with Montenegro with whom it shares many similarities but is also very different in many aspects. Although fierce warriors on their unbeatable ships, the Bokelji also grew to be refined and gentle in comparison with the roughness of the highlanders and to be more inclined towards the Mediterranean and Italy, canzone and pastas. A mix of Orthodox and Catholics who have lived here peacefully for centuries adds to the variety of customs and traditions of the region celebrated through the carnivals of Kotor, religious ceremonies of Perast or the Mimosa festival of Herceg Novi.

Playing with the rich history of Boka Kotorska

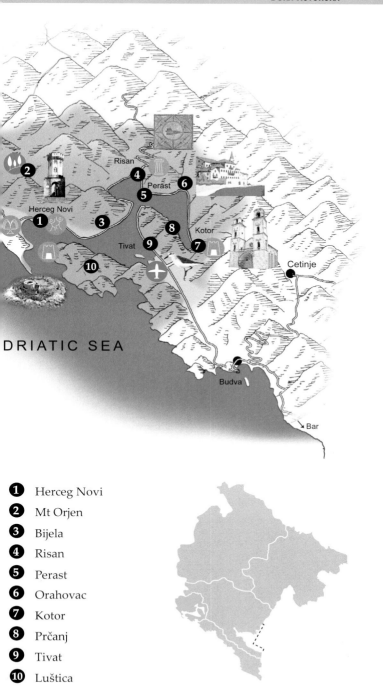

1. Herceg Novi
2. Mt Orjen
3. Bijela
4. Risan
5. Perast
6. Orahovac
7. Kotor
8. Prčanj
9. Tivat
10. Luština

❶ Herceg Novi

- 👥 16,500
- ℹ️ Jova Dabovića 12, 031/350-820
- 🚌 Dr Jova Bijelića 1, 031/321-225
- 🎭 Mimosa festival, beginning of February

Herceg Novi sits in a most beautiful position at the entrance of the Gulf of Kotor with which it shares its breathtaking views but not the climate: the town faces south and the open sea and enjoys a favourable climate with many sunny days. These qualities have made it one of the most visited holiday resorts in Montenegro, popular both in summer and during its mild winters. The town, the largest in Boka, spreads along the coast and has merged with Igalo and Topla, once separate villages, to the west. Another of Herceg Novi's outstanding characteristics is Mount Orjen (1895m) emerging behind it, where, just a few kilometers away from the mild coastal climate, it is possible to enjoy in the pleasures of snow (*see next chapter*).

If not a prime target in terms of monuments and heritage, the town compensates with its liveliness, high spirits and humor of its inhabitants.

In comparison with other places in the Gulf of Kotor, Herceg Novi is relatively young. It was founded in 1382 by King Tvrtko of Bosnia who granted wide privileges in his intention to turn it into a trading port, which would rid Bosnia of its dependence on the Dubrovnik merchants who controlled almost all of the Bosnian trade. This brought an economic standoff between the two in which the reasons of trade prevailed so that the king had to abandon his project. The town was originally known as Sveti Stjepan (St Steven) after the protector saint of the King's dynasty, but was referred to by locals

Herceg Novi on an 17th c. engraving

(and still is) simply as *Novi*, literally "New (Town)". After Tvrtko's death and the collapse central power, the town became a possession of the barons from the Kosača family. Its most prominent member, Stjepan Vukčić (1405-6 behaved like a sovereig and followed Tvrtko's steps, settling the trade and cloth makers into the town and bringing new prosperity to the commune. As Vukčić used the title of Herzog St Sava, his territory go the name Herzegovina and his main trading p - Herceg Novi. The tov new vigor didn't last for long – Herzegovina dwindled under the Ottoman attacks until Herceg Novi, its last bi of land, was captured

The memorable view of the entrance to the Gulf of Kotor

Landing pier in the late 19th c.

1482. The Turks realized immediately the potential of the town's position and fortified it into one of the strongest forts on the Adriatic. From there they attacked Venetian possessions in the Gulf and generally terrorized the trade on the open seas to such extent that in 1538 the coalition of Christian forces was forged to attack the town. Combined forces of Venice, Spain, Papal state and Perast (*see p.) led by the admiral Andrea Doria attacked and after fearsome fighting captured the town, leaving a Spanish garrison to protect it as well as building one more fort. Ten months later the Turks appeared at its walls, two pashas from land and the famous Hayreddin Barbarossa from the sea. After 25 days of bloody hand fighting the remaining 300 Spaniards decided to surrender; astonished by their bravery, Barbarossa offered them to stay in the town as the Sultan's subjects, which fifty of them did, allegedly for the reason that they fell in love with the town and its scenery. Herceg Novi remained in Turkish hands for the next century and a half until 1687 when it was taken by the Venetians. Its capture meant that the Gulf of Kotor was free from the Turks and opened a new era of prosperous trading and seafaring. Today Herceg Novi is a prime tourist destination in Boka Kotorska

offering a perfect blend of sun, sea and culture. It is also known for its many festivals such as the Mimosa festival held in February when this flower first blooms announcing the coming of spring, or the Film festival held in the wonderful setting of Kanli kula fortress.

Joined with Igalo and Topla, the town lacks a real centre (*see map on pp. 60-61*): it is made up of long roads parallel with the seafront and short streets and notorious stairways connecting these and is furthermore soaked in lush subtropical greenery. The heart of Herceg Novi is the area inside the town walls laying in a series of terraces on the precipitous cliffs above the sea.

1. Seaside Fortification

The mighty **Forte Mare** (Italian for "Sea Fort") towering above the seaside promenade is the most notable of the town's fortifications. Its walls were originally built by King Tvrtko but have been reshaped and strengthened by all the subsequent rulers continually until the beginning of the 19th c. when it got its present appearance. Today the Fort houses an open air cinema and a discotheque. A few steps away to the east along the promenade will lead you to **Citadela**, a lone bastion merged with the sea. Built during the Venetian era it sank partially into the sea in the 1979 earthquake.

Majorettes, one of the well-known symbols of Herceg Novi

Steps leading to the Clock Tower

2. Clock Tower

The Clock Tower (*Sahat kula*) is the focal point of the main town square - **Trg Nikole Djurkovića** – with many cafés, shops and institutions around it. Under the tower is a gate through which one gains entrance to the Old Town. Together with the short stairway leading to it, the Clock Tower is the symbol of the town, also seen on the municipal coat-of-arms. It was built in 1667 by the Turks (note the ogee arch of the central double window) but was later reshaped to suit European taste. The clock on the tower still proudly displays time accurately. Inside its gate stands a small statue of Virgin Mary carved by grateful devotees out of an oak blasted by a Turkish cannonball during the 1687 siege.

3. Belavista

The small, stone paved square Trg Hercega Stjepana, popularly known as Belavista, is arguably the most charming place in the town. Old stone buildings encircle the tiny and delightful **Church of St Michael**. Built in 1905-11, this orthodox church is basically neo-Byzantine in style but with many Gothic and Romanesque details, which together with the four palm trees on its corners add to its maritime appearance. In the church there is a fine iconostasis from the same period. Next to the church is the picturesque **Karača fountain**, a rare survivor from the period of Turkish rule true to its original form.

From the square, small streets and stairways spread out leading in all directions. To the east, one reaches a green corner amidst the town walls sheltered by the **St Jerome's Tower**, built in 1687 by Hieronymus Corner, the commander of Venetian troops. Today, the seat of the Town Orchestra is located here. Taking the Stjepa Šarenca then Prve bokeške brigade and in the end Manastirska Street (each lying a bit above the other) will lead you to the pleasant Savinska Dubrava grove and Savina Monastery (*see nr. 12*).

The church of St Michael with its palm trees

Catholic church of St Jerome

4. Catholic churches

In the lower part of the Old Town lies Trg Miće Pavlovića, another pretty square centered around the catholic **Church of St Jerome**. It stands on the site of the main town mosque, torn down after the Christian capture of the town; present day edifice dates back to 1856. Its most interesting item is the altar painting representing the Virgin Mary surrounded by saints, a gift of Hieronymus Corner. The scenery behind the saints is actually the panorama of Herceg Novi at the time. Directly below this church is a small church dating from the same period and built for the use of the capuchin monks. Today it is dedicated to St Bogdan Leopold Mandić (1866-1942), a native of Herceg Novi, canonized in 1983 by Pope John Paul II.

5. Kanli kula

Best observed from the highway but with its entrance facing the narrow stairways leading downwards to Belavista square stands Kanli kula, whose name translates from Turkish as the "Bloody Tower". Built after the Ottoman re-conquest of the town, it is the largest of Herceg Novi's fortifications, dominating the Old Town and offering exquisite views over the Old Town and the entrance of the Gulf of Kotor. Together with its defensive role Kanli kula was also used by the Turks as a prison, with people held in a deep cistern. Following the reconstruction after the 1979 earthquake, Kanli kula has been transformed into a beautiful open air theatre with a view of the sea (*entry €1*), and home to the local film festival. In a calm setting not far to the left of Kanli kula's entrance stands the **West Tower**, another imposing piece of fortification.

6. Španjola

Just across the highway from Kanli kula starts Srbina Street which will lead you to Španjola Fort, the best preserved piece of fortification in the town. Standing on a hill overlooking Herceg Novi this fort was commenced by

Narrow alleys of the Old Town

the Spaniards during their brief rule but was finished when the Turks returned to the town (1539-48). It is square in base with a massive tower on each of its corners and two gates. Above one of the gates an inscription in Arabic about the building of the Fort can be observed. Inside the walls there are ruins of the original buildings used by its garrison.

7. Njegoševa Street

Starting from Trg Nikole Djurkovića and the Clock Tower and leading all the way to Topla and Igalo, Njegoševa Street is the main commercial and traffic artery of Herceg Novi.

After its first part, enclosed by old stone buildings, on your left side open the views of the sea while on your right there is a row of houses and villas from

1 Seaside Fortification		**4** Catholic churc
2 Clock Tower		**5** Kanli kula
3 Belavista		**6** Španjola

and opened in 1908, but was soon accepted as of common value and all the townsfolk helped it develop. Hotel "Boka" perished in the '79 earthquake but the

Mediterranean vegetation in the park of hotel "Boka"

the end of the 19th c. Past the recently renovated "Gradska kafana" café and its classy terrace you will reach the Town Park, spreading downwards in a series of terraces. The park once belonged to hotel "Boka", the most prestigious in the town

park remains with its many exotic trees and bushes, shady paths and a fishpond.

8. Town Museum
Zavičajni muzej

Mirka Komnenovića 9; 031/322-485; open 9-20h (summer), 9-13 (winter); admission €2

Located just above th "Lovćen" beach on the promenade, the town museum is housed in a lovely late baroque mansion dating from the end of the 18th c. The building and much of it artifacts are a donation by Mirko Komnenović (1870-1941) the mayor o Herceg Novi, MP and a minister in the Kingdor of Yugoslavia. The building of the museum lies in a nice park, full with palm trees, agaves and aloes which togeth form an interesting botanical assortment.

In the museum's collection one can see prehistoric jugs from the vicinity, amphorae and parts of cargo of the sunken ships from the classical antiquity, pre-Romanesque reliefs (9th-11th c.) from the ruir of the churches in the hills above Herceg Nov documents on town's history. Also on display is the collection of thirty

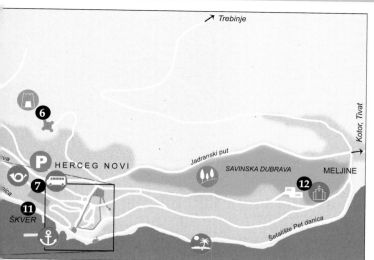

Njegoševa Street

Town Museum

Topla

10 Igalo

11 Pet Danica Promenade

12 Savina Monastery

A 9th c. stone tablet, Town Museum

exhibition of paintings by local artists from the second half of the 20th c.

9. Topla

Up until a few decades ago Topla was a village of its own but is now fully joined with Herceg Novi. The village was known for its mild climate that earned it its name (*topla* meaning "warm") and for its nautical traditions. The importance it held in seafaring is witnessed in the fact that during the Venetian era the seat of the local government was in Topla, not in Herceg Novi. Little remains of old Topla today: its centre used to be around **two orthodox churches** standing in

...ons of the Rafailović-...mitrijević school ...7th-19th c.) with their ...chaic iconography, ...arm naivety and many ...eticulous details. ...he ethnographical ...partment presents ...stumes and jewelry ...om the area, arms, ...ricultural tools and ...ols for processing ...olives as well as ...ditional musical ...struments. In ...dition, there is also an

Njegoševa Street – St George from 1688 and the one dedicated to the Ascension from 1713 - both typical maritime edifices with nice baroque details and an imposing stone gate. Above them is the local graveyard adjoined by a monastic cell in which young Njegoš was tought to read and write by monk Josif Tropović.

In 1964 the noble prize winner Ivo Andrić built a modest house in **Njegoševa St. no. 65**. In this idyllic setting and pleasant climate that did him a world of good Andrić spent most of the time until his death in 1975 writing and hosting many prominent

Bust of Njegoš, Topla

personalities and writers. Later, the house was the seat of the Tribunal founded by Bertrand Russell which gathered prominent intellectuals who investigated American intervention in Vietnam and was in this period visited by Jean Paul Sartre. The house is today used by the writers' club of Herceg Novi. It retains its original look with features of Bosnian rural architecture while inside one can visit a memorial room dedicated to Andrić and his work.

A monument near the Pet Danica Promenade

10. Igalo

Further east from Topla lays Igalo (5km from Herceg Novi's Old Town). Its long beach slopes very gently into the sea so that after 250m the water is still

large hotels are booked mostly by tourists who are perfectly healthy and are here to enjoy its sun and sand.

The area to the west and north of Igalo is called **Sutorina**. Curiously, up to 1930 this was administratively a part of Herzegovina and had a different historical development then the rest of the area. A part of Dubrovnik Republic since the middle ages, it

whole affair took place in order to separate small Dubrovnik from its most serious rival in the Adriatic, Venice. Administratively part of Herzegovina but much more connected with Herceg Novi, Sutorina lived a twin existence. In all the Herzegovinia uprisings against the Turks it was here that the rebels had their safe hideout, helped by their fellow Christians from Novi and Topla. Today the best known locality of this small region is **Njivice**, a small resort laying on the sea just below the Croatian border which has a regular and a nudist beach.

The view of Igalo and its hotels

only a meter deep. The fine sand found here forms mildly radioactive mineral mud with many therapeutic traits in curing rheumatism, bronchitis etc. that has won Igalo its glory. This is the only health resort in Montenegro and the only one of its kind in the entire east Adriatic. Nevertheless, in tourist season its

was ceded voluntarily to Ottoman Empire after the Venetians conquered Herceg Novi and Topla. The same thing was done on the northernmost tip of the Republic at Neum, today Bosnia-Herzegovina's only exit to the sea, and thus Dubrovnik only had borders with Turkey with whom it was in a fair relationship. This

11. Pet Danica Promenade

This long seaside walkway runs from Igalo all the way to the other end of Herceg Novi. It follows the line of the old narrow gauge railway which connected it via Sutorina to Hercegovina and Dubrovnik and which was operational until 1968. It was due to this

avina monastery, hidden in its greenery

lway that Herceg
ovi and its vicinity
came leading tourist
sorts in the Gulf of
tor. A walk on the
omenade will take you
rough several railroad
nnels and past Herceg
ovi's town beaches.
ose to the Old Town
ts most dynamic part
led **Škver** with open
pool, town port and
ite a few cafés and
taurants.

. Savina
Monastery

At the west end
Herceg Novi, in
leasant Savinska
brava grove full of
presses, oaks, laurels,
lms and various
rbal plants lies the
hodox monastery of
vina. According to
dition the monastery
s founded in 1031 but
e oldest of its churches
esn't predate the 13th c.
nat is known for sure
hat it was given new
petus by the monks
o in 1694 settled
re fleeing from the
mous Herzegovinian
onastery of Tvrdoš
ich was destroyed

by the Turks during
troublesome wartime
years. The rest of
Savina's days passed
quietly and the event
best remembered here
was Njegoš's stay during
his schooling in Topla
(*see nr. 9*).

Above the complex
lies the small parochial
church of St Sava from
the 13th c. after which
the whole site and the
monastery was named.

The monastery
complex comprises
two churches, both
dedicated to the feast
of Assumption. The
smaller one is older:
judging from its gothic
features it was built
in the time of Herceg
Stjepan (mid 15th c.).
There are several layers
of fresco paintings on its
walls, ranging from 1565
to 1831. The iconostasis
was done and redone
on several occasions in
the 18th c. The central
"Emperor's Door" and
the crucifix above it
were painted in 1703 by
Dimitrije, the father of
Rafailović-Dimitrijević
school of icon painting.
The **larger church** is
a remarkable edifice

built from 1777 to 1799
following the plans of
Nikola Foretić from the
town of Korčula (today
in Croatia) who skillfully
blended the Byzantine
ground plan and cupola
with the traditional
Romanesque details
and baroque bell tower.
Inside the church you
will see the marvelous
high iconostasis painted
in 1797 by Simeon
Lazović of Bijelo Polje.

The monastery has
a rich **treasury** (*riznica;
free entry*), most of its
valuables brought from
the abandoned Tvrdoš
monastery. Here you
will see the crystal
cross edged with silver
supposedly belonging to
St Sava (13th c.), gilded
enamel server (1648),
silver reliquary from
1759 of a hand belonging
to Jelena, wife of Serbian
Emperor Dušan the
Mighty, gilded ciborium
(1675) made to resemble
the look of Tvrdoš,
epitrachileon of blue
silk (14th c.), shroud
embroidered in silver
and gold thread (1659),
a wooden cross with
intricate carvings (16th c.)
etc. The collection of old

books and documents is equally extensive comprising of the monastic rule of St Sava (transcribed in the 16th c.), charters of Nemanjić kings and dukes of Bessarabia (present-day Romania), hand written Octoechos from 1509 and letters written by the Montenegrin metropolitans.

Enjoying the sun of Herceg Novi

ENVIRONS:

Continuing along the highway from Savina one reaches **Meljine** quickly, a small resort with a sandy beach hidden in lush greenery. On its waterfront one can see the ruins of a Venetian lazaretto (maritime quarantine) from 1732. Immediately after the tunnel you arrive in **Zelenika**, a large village known for its harbour. Close to the last stop of the narrow-gauge railway in 1902 hotelier Antal Magyar from Budapest opened the first modern hotel in Boka Kotorska. The building of his hotel "Plaža" ("Beach") still stands on the waterfront but was until recently off the tourist path, as it was being used by the army. The family Magyar still lives in Zelenika. At the exit towards Kumbor you will notice the church of Holy Trinity (mid 19th c.) standing charmingly on a hill above the highway.

The most interesting antiquity in the surroundings of Herceg

WHERE TO EAT IN HERCEG NOVI

Feral
Šetalište pet Danica 47, 031/322-232; open 08-01h
This is the best of the several fish restaurants on "Škver", center point of Herceg Novi's busy promenade. Surrounded in greenery, with a small terrace and two rustically furnished levels inside it serves an array of fish dishes. Amazingly, almost all of the dishes from its rich menu are always available, freshly prepared and delicious. Prices are slightly high but all the dishes are served in plentiful portions.

Hercegovina
Trg Nikole Djurkovića; 031/322-880; open 07-23h
Adjacent to a butcher's held by the same owner, this eatery next to Herceg Novi's green market gets it's meat fresh and delicious at all times of the year and at good prices. Except for the salads the rest of the menu is grilled meat only. The best recommendation is a regular crowd of locals eating here.

Sport caffe
Šetalište pet Danica 34; tel. 031/322-018; open 09-23h
One of the best seafront establishments, this modern looking place is located by and above the sea of the town harbour. The place gets its name from the dozens of TVs playing sport channels so this is the place to come and watch any kind of sporting event. Though it is mostly visited for its café and excellent cocktails, it also features an elegant restaurant with a view on its upper floor. The food served here is mostly fish and seafood combined with pizzas and pastas.

Krušo
Šetalište pet Danica bb (Igalo); 031/32-32-38; open 11-01h
This waterside *konoba* (tavern) with a covered terrace has modest looks with checkered tablecloths and the usual decoration of fishnets and paintings depicting boats but boasts a good selection of fish specialties and a range of gourmet dishes of national cuisine. The place livens up in the evenings to the sounds of live acoustic music.

Leut
Njegoševa 166; tel. 031/670-157; open 00-24
Situated on the main road to Dubrovnik, this restaurant sunk in pleasant greenery is open non-stop. During the warmer days and evening you can sit on in its airy beachside terrace. On its menu one finds a range of starters, local fish specialties, spit roasts as well as meat roasted *ispod sača*.

Mimoza,
Šetalište (Igalo); tel. 031/322-893; open 09-23h
Located on the waterfront promenade in Igalo, this restaurant has a terrace with a view and an interior with a warm feel to it. It serves a good mix of fish and national dishes at affordable prices.

The old church in the village of Podi

...ovi is the Church of ...ints Sergio and Bakh (*...rkva svetog Srdja i ...kha*) in the village of **...odi**. The village lies ...st above Herceg Novi ...d can be reached by ...road branching uphill ...om the highway at ...eljine, on the main ...ute towards Trebinje. ...e church stands ...ove the road at the ...llage cemetery where ...u will see many nice ...avestones of local ...erchant families who ...nstituted a good ...rt of the prosperous ...rb colony in Trieste. ...is unusually tall ...urch was built at the ...ginning of the 15th ...but is remarkably ...ell kept. It is made ...t of local stone and ...s a round cupola. Its ...le ornaments are the ...ind arches and the ...roque belfry added ... 1769. Inside is a nice ...onostasis done by ...meon and Aleksije ...azović of Bijelo Polje.

❷ Orjen

10 km from Herceg Novi

Orjen (1894m) is the highest mountain of the east Adriatic coast. When seen by sailors from far away the mountain's peak served as a clear guide marking east - *oriens* in Latin. Orjen's massif rises above Herceg Novi, reaches its highest peak just 14km from the sea and descends to the north and west, well into Bosnia-Herzegovina and Croatia. This unkind mountain has the highest precipitation in the whole of Europe due to warm air from the seaside cooling quickly while ascending its sides and forming rain-heavy clouds. The enormous amount of rain falling on its limestone rocks forms the most rugged karst terrain in the Dinaric Alps with countless pits (many with snow on their bottoms all year long), sinkholes and caves which make it a heaven for speleologist especially as most of these formations are unexplored. In winter the mountain looks much more serene as the heavy snowfall covers the coarseness of its surface. Here one can enjoy snow or even ski (though there are no ski lifts) up to the end of May and then go for a swim in the already warm sea. Its southern sides are also used for paragliding with amazing views of Boka Kotorska and the open sea. If planning to hike on this mountain note that the most rainy months are May and October, while in August the weather is sizzling in this waterless area.

The rough terrains of Orjen are easily accessible by the road leading to Trebinje. One of the favorite excursion points for locals is the **mountain**

The peaks of Mt Orjen, seen from the coast

hut **"Borići"** (*see p. 105*), 18km from Herceg Novi, reached by taking the right turn after passing the Kameno village. The mountain hut lies underneath the cliffs of Dobroštica, one of many unassailable ridges of this mountain. "Borići" got its name after a pine (*bor*) forest planted at the beginning of the 20th c. in this barren area. Unfortunately a good deal of it disappeared in

fifty beds and electricity but is not open all year long and you should announce yourself to "Subra" mountaineering association in Herceg Novi (*contact 069/348-600*). The hut is the usual starting place for climbing the peak of **Odijevo** (1571m) on Dobroštica ridge: a marked path leads through a birch forest to Kabao and then along the ridge (2h) allowing

endemic Macedonian pines clinging to the cliffs. One should watch for poisonous snakes, especially in high summer. Subra is the best viewing point on Orjen and on a clear day one can see several ridges further inside Montenegro and Herzegovina, as well as all the islands of the south Adriatic. Underneath Subra opens an amazing stone **"amphitheatre"** where cliffs fall vertically for several hundred meters on three sides.

One of many Austro-Hungarian fortifications on Orjen

a forest fire in 2002. Here one can enjoy a view of Herceg Novi's bay, have lunch or stay overnight (*bed and breakfast €15*). From "Borići" there is a 2km long marked path to the north, over the Vratlo ridge to the **"Za Vratlom" mountain hut**. The path follows the stone road built by the Austro-Hungarian army at the end of the 19th c. towards one of the many fortresses that secured Boka and kept the local populace calm. Real hiking lovers can reach the hut by following a marked route starting from the bus station in Herceg Novi (4h). The hut has

for marvelous views of the Gulf. The most impressive (though not the highest) peak of the massif is **Subra** (1679m) reached from the hut in 2h while passing through heavily karstified terrain with views of

Other point of interest reachable by car is the village of **Vrbanj** (27km from Herceg Novi), on the west side of the mountain, reached by the other branch of the road after Kameno village. In Vrbanj there is a pleasant **motel** of the same name (*bed and breakfast €12; contact 067-805-117*) decorated with many hunting trophies. Otherwise you can use the deserted mountain hut, which is in decent condition. The starting point for the ascent to the highest peak of the massif – **Zubački kabao** (otherwise simply called Orjen) – is the deserted mountain hut on Orjen sedlo (1580m). This point can be reached by a very bad winding road from Vrbanj or from Crkvice above Risan (*see p. 70*). The hut has 12 beds (*contact 069/348-600*) while water can be found in a nearby well (*studenac*). From here to the highest peak of Orjen will take you 1½h. To the east lies the 8km long **Reovačka greda** ridge whose steep sides are a challenge even for the most seasoned alpinists

Exploring the mountain

Bijela

3,800

Bijela (meaning "White", mentioned in medieval Latin sources *Alba*) is a large village lying on the north side of the second bay of the Gulf, facing Tivat. It developed in a field, the largest and most fertile between Herceg Novi and Risan, hence its early development: in the 6th c. it had a basilica, destroyed probably in the Slav onslaught, and in 809 it got a Benedictine monastery, used as a starting point for the conversion of the locals. Although it was an agricultural area it also took part in seafaring, producing a number of famous captains, some of whose houses survive near the waterfront. Its sandy

Fishing boats near Bijela

beach, one of the best you will find in the Gulf of Kotor, is somewhat spoiled by the shipyard next to it. The shipyard continues the tradition reaching from the Middle Ages, and though not as active as before, it still employs a great deal of Bijela's population.

Bijela's most important monument is the orthodox **church of Riza Bogorodice**. It is located in a charming dale about one kilometer inland from the highway. The turn is marked with a sign; the road at one point becomes very narrow and drivers should be wary of the vehicles coming from the other direction. The large stone edifice that we see today was built in 1824 but it incorporates a part of a much older church whose white-washed apse is an unusual addition to its look. This church originates from the end of the 12th c. and is one of the oldest surviving in the whole Gulf, the fact reflected in its simple pre-Romanesque looks. The interior of the church is dominated by the gilded high iconostasis done by the Nicolaos Aspiotis

Church of Riza Bogorodice

from Corfu and a pair of old icons brought by the seafarers from their voyages to Greece. On the floor you can see the outlines of where the old church used to stand as well as its original basis through two glass panels. In order to see its apse you will have to ask the priest to let you behind the iconostasis. The apse of the old church is located considerably beneath the foundations of the new one and is reached by descending steps. Its frescoes date from around 1200 and are the oldest in the Gulf of Kotor. They represent the Divine Liturgy with saints and angels bowing to the Virgin and Christ. In the small niche the unknown patron of the church's fresco painting is represented.

On the high hills above the church stand the crooked houses of the abandoned village of Kruševice whose several churches tell about its past importance. The village is best known as the place of origin of Felice Peretti, who later in his life became pope Sixtus V (1585-90). Peretti's father left Kruševice for Italy after a devastating Turkish raid on the village. It is believed that Felice kept memory of his origin in his surname - *pera* (pear) in Italian being the same as *kruška* in Serbian.

North of Bijela you will pass the village of Kamenari standing at the beginning of the **Verige straits**. This is the narrowest point of the Gulf with its sides closing to merely some one hundred meters. The name Verige ("chains") comes from a legend that the inner bay was closed with chains long ago. Instead of using the chains, during the Venetian era the straits were guarded by the brave mariners of Perast, the town that faces Verige (*see p. 71*). The names of the opposing capes – Turkish Cape (*Turski rt*) and Cape Virgin (*Rt Gospa*) – come from the 16th and 17th centuries when the north side of the Gulf was under Turkish and the south under Venetian control. There is a nice **viewpoint** at the tip of Turski rt just off the highway. From Kamenari the ferry transports vehicles to Lepetani on the other side of the gulf (*see p. 268*).

④ Risan

2,100

Situated on mildly rising slopes on the north end of Risan's bay lays a town with the longest history of all the settlements in the Gulf of Kotor - Risan. Behind it, amidst the bushy Mediterranean vegetation well-known

The marvelous Roman mosaic depicting Hypnos

for its many herbs, one sees the old road twisting steadily into the mountains. It was by this very road that its first known inhabitants, the Illyrian tribe of Rhizonites, descended to the shore and founded the town. First mentioned in the 4 c. BC, it grew steadily in importance and it is quite possible that

it became the capital of Illyrian king Agron and his wife Teuta. The legend holds that queen Teuta, after she was defeated by the Romans in 229 BC, retreated here and decided to commit suicide rather than fall into the hands of her adversaries. In fact, Teuta succumbed to the Romans and was left to rule a small district as a Roman vassal and

thus Risan continued to be a seat of several more kings, one of which minted his money here. Absorbed into the Roman Empire, the town obtained the status of a *colonia* and was named *Iulium Rhisinium*. In those days it was several times larger then today and held such importance that the whole Gulf of Kotor was actually named *Sinus Rhizonicus*, a name by which it was known well into the Middle Ages. In early Christian times Risan became the seat of the bishop. With the coming of the days when strong walls were the only valid protection, most of its populace escaped to the newly founded Kotor. Risan's

WHERE TO EAT IN BIJELA'S VICINITY

Deli Radivoje
Baošići bb; 031/674-181; open 07-23h
This simple roadside tavern is known and visited for its lamb spit-roasts and other grilled dishes at good prices. It has a large terrace shadowed with wine leaves and a rather shabby interior but the locals don't seem to mind as long as they eat well and plentifully.

Porta
Obala bb; Djenovići; tel. 069/041-364; open 08-24h
The beachside establishment lies beneath the orthodox church at the place where Baošići meets Djenovići to its west. The place serves fresh fish specialties as well as international dishes. During the summer it opens its own beach.

e was sealed in 5 AD when it was cked and burnt wn in a raid by racen corsairs. the Middle Ages stagnated and it mains unclear if its me designated a wn or perhaps just group of villages. e Turks captured n 1482 and held until 1687 when e Venetians got ld of it. Although the 18th c. the habitants took to amanship and ve several famous ptains, they kept se ties with the rzegovinian terland by means the only decent ad leading inland m the Gulf of Kotor, ll to be seen winding hill beyond the town. e "Herzegovinian arket" brought in de but also helped ep the old traditions ve, making the locals fer from the other habitants of Boka in ms of dress and unity ideas. This became pecially evident ring the Krivošije and rzegovina uprisings nich they steadfastly pported. The same avery was shown ring the occupation in WII when they led the rising in this region. Risan of our days a township keeping th its own pace d is seemingly not rticularly interested in urism apart from the tel "Teuta" with its rine gravel beach and mall yachting quay. like the situation in ost other places in ka, Risan's central bela Street leads m the shore to the ls. The street is lined th quaint stone houses

Gabela, the main street of old Risan

and paved with multi-colored rocks set in simple patterns.

To the right of the street is a park with **two orthodox churches**. The smaller one is older and dates from 1601, but sits on the ruins of a medieval church. The large one, dedicated to Saints Peter & Paul, was built in 1796 in a restrained baroque style. Its dominant feature is the tall bell tower with a clock and a fine rose window. The most important works of art inside the church are its 16th – 19th c. icons, many of them painted by the local Dimitrijević-Rafailović family that gave eleven artists in five generations. Two centuries of their continuous work saw very few changes in their famous conservative style.

Just a few steps to the right of the park is Risan's best known site, the remains of a Roman country villa with marvelous **mosaics**, all from 3rd c. AD. The freshly built visitors' center treasures well-preserved mosaics with a range of floral and

Rose window on the Saints Peter & Paul Church

WHERE TO EAT IN RISAN'S VICINITY

Ćatovića mlini
Morinj polje bb; 032/37-30-30; open 11-23h
The village of Morinj (6km from Risan) was always known for its many streams and mills. The one belonging to Ćatović family is today a restaurant in an astonishing ambient of babbling water and lush greenery spreading all around the old stone mill securing freshness even in high summer. The lengthy menu is dedicated to fish and seafood dishes prepared deliciously and served in many intricate variants. Excellent, attentive service.

Risan, as seen from the winding road to Nikšić

geometrical patterns; certainly the most memorable among them is the one depicting Hypnos, the deity of sleep and oblivion, which embellished the bedroom of the villa.

A road leading upwards from this point follows the old route to the hinterland. Today it is primarily used as a shortest way to Nikšić. Similar to the "Ladder of Kotor" (*see p. 93*), this road turns quickly into a series of serpentines with stunning views over the Gulf. While driving along it pay attention as it is narrow and very bumpy. The road reaches the new one halfway up the slope but don't be deceived since these good conditions don't last all the way to Nikšić. After approximately 1,5km at a sharp curve take a left turn onto a minor road. This is the area of the **Krivošije** clan, best known for its brave uprising (*see inlay*) and the **village of Crkvice** which has the highest precipitation in the whole of Europe, averaging yearly 5317mm and with the highest rainfall of 8065mm recorded in the year 1937. Unfortunately nearly all of the villagers left for the seaside after the 1979 earthquake and the whole region is virtually uninhabited today. That means that Crkvice (or any other place here) is impossible to recognize. The whole region is sunk in wilderness and is interesting only for adventurous hikers and speleologists.

About a kilometer away from Risan in the direction of Herceg Novi the highway passes above a crag in the rocks, the **Sopot** well. Uninteresting in sunny weather, the well should be visited after the rain when it turns into a wild looking waterfall, spilling huge amounts water into the sea from the height of some 30m.

KRIVOŠIJE UPRISING

Krivošije (literally "Bent Necks") are a clan living in the unassailable mountain hinterland of Boka Kotorska. Though their territory lies close to the sea their ways were more similar to those of the neighboring Montenegrins and they lived with little or no connection to their nominal masters in towns by the sea. In 1869 Austria-Hungary decided to break the old agreement between the clans of Boka Kotorska and the Venetian Republic by which the clans were exempt from serving the army. Krivošije (and other maritime clans such as Grbljani, Paštrovići etc.), who saw this as a breach of tradition and an intrusion on their freedom, unanimously refused to obey and rose to arms. The first smaller army units sent against them did not even manage to reach the clan's settlements. The Empire took to wider preparations and amassed an army several times larger than the entire population of Krivošije. The troops marched uphill in several directions but were attacked in the harsh terrain which offered excellent possibilities for ambush, blocking of narrow roads and hit-and-run tactics. After several days of hard fighting the troops had to retreat. After another offensive was beaten off, the commanding general was dismissed but the next one and his attack from all sides witnessed a similar fate. After four months of fighting with very little results the Empire was forced to give up and sign a peace treaty with its inhabitants settling on their terms! The Empire now decided upon a tactic of slow intrusion, building forts which were not meant to just protect the border but also to keep an eye on the clans. To connect the forts to the seaside and amongst themselves, the Austrians built many roads in very difficult terrain, some of which remain unchanged to this day. When in 1881 the original agreement was broken again the new uprising was dealt with within a few weeks and many of the rebels fled to Montenegro.

Perast

14 km from Kotor
400
Fašinada - 22nd July

Nested at the foot of
eti Ilija Hill (873m) and
cing the Verige straits,
e historic township
Perast appears to
ard the entrance of
e Risan-Kotor bay.
th its rear against the
ep and barren hills of
e mainland, it opens
the sea and plunges
elf towards the two
ets, Sveti Djordje with
e Benedictine abbey
adowed by cypress
es and the man-made
spa od Škrpjela,
oduct of Perast's
domitable residents
e below). The silence
its deserted houses
d the aged stone
eets speaks loudly of
passing greatness:
e town grew quickly
the 16th c. becoming
remarkable place of
mous seafarers and
roque artists but
graded even faster
eady at the end of
e 18th c. As a result,
rast seems to be stuck
time, endowed with a
riously homogenous
chitectural legacy and
air of faded glory.
Though numerous
cheological findings
m the Neolith and
name's association

Perast and the Islet of Sveti Djordje

with the Illyrian tribe
of Pirusti indicate a
settlement of great
antiquity, Perast is
mentioned for the first
time only in the 14th
c. In those days the
township was formally

Perast's coat-of-arms

still a possession of the
Benedictine abbey on the
islet of St George, but
nevertheless operated a
shipyard challenging the
monopoly proscribed by
Kotor, whose primate
Perast disputed with
growing strength.
Building their reputation
in troublesome times of

Turkish conquests, the
people of Perast became
known as brave seafarers
who daringly clashed
with the Ottomans and
the Muslim corsairs on
the seas. Men such as
these were what Venice
needed most and after a
brave defence of Kotor
in 1539 the town's twelve
noble families (called
casadas) obtained an
honour of guarding the
standard of the Venetian
Republic in times of
war. Finally, after its
men fought in the battle
of Lepanto in 1571,
Perast was awarded a
status of an autonomous
municipality in 1584
beginning the era of
prosperity. As it relied
on its craggy hillside and
maritime valor Perast
never built town walls
but only a fort of Sveti
Križ above it. Using
the absence of men, the
North African corsairs
struck in 1624 looting
the town and taking
women, children and
elders as prisoners to be
later dearly ransomed to
their families. Because
in those days Perast
had a fleet of about a
hundred trading and
war ships it was able to
start anew, building in
the following years its
palaces and almost all of
its 17 churches. In 1654
the town was attacked
again by a 6,000 strong

Engraving of Perast at the height of its power

Turkish army but this time not only did it fight the enemy off entirely on its own, but also managed to kill the Turkish commander. By a twist of faith, the Venetian victories over the Turks, supported by Perast as well, were to lead to the town's doom: after the entire Gulf of Kotor passed to Venetian hands, other towns developed their own fleets and Perast lost its importance. Already in the 19th c. it retained only a shadow of its former glory, witnessed in its palaces, resounding names and titles and old traditions. In recent times the subtle charms of Perast were noted by many who bought old houses and refurbished them in luxurious fashion bringing new life to the town's streets.

The church and islet of Gospa od Škrpjela

The view of Perast is embellished with its two tiny islands. To the left is the one bearing the name of **St George** (*Sveti Djordje*), hosting a Benedictine abbey and the old town cemetery shadowed by tall cypress trees. Though

the abbey's history can be traced as far back as the 12th c. little remains of its earliest existence as it has been destroyed many times since, most ruinously in the 1669 earthquake. The present day church was built after that event in a simple style with some details (such as the renaissance capitols) reused from the older edifice. On the tombstones of the cemetery one can see the coat-of-arms of the old Perast *casadas* and other notable families. The abbey is surrounded by walls with loopholes testifying to the times when it was used as a stronghold. During the French occupation here resided a small garrison and amongst them Ante Slović, a sailor from

Dalmatia. During his stay Slović fell in love with a local girl Katarina who lived next to the fort on the hill. In the fighting around it in 1813 Slović had to fire a gun and by mistake hit the house of his lover killing her inside it. The unfortunate sailor took the monastic vow spending the rest of his life in this monastery and was in the end buried beside his loved one.

The **islet of Gospa od Škrpjela** ("Our Lady of the Rocks") is the most important catholic sanctuary in the Gulf of Kotor and the most important one dedicated to Virgin Mary who was highly praised by the local populace, especially by seamen. However impossible it might sound, the islet is completely man-made: generations of Perastians have piled rocks and sunk their old ships or captured Turkish vessels to form it and by now the island has grown to 3000m². The islet still grows once a year when on 22nd July, the festive day of the Lady, a decorated

Sveti Djordje islet with its small abbey

ocession of boats rives from Perast llowed by traditional ngs and beeping of at sirens as each of the rastians throws a stone the water. The legend lds that the icon of other of God was und by two fishermen a small reef; the pious en took it ashore and aced it in the church t during the night it urned to the reef. As s was repeated three nes it was presumed

best baroque artist not only of Boka Kotorska but of the entire east Adriatic coast. The paintings in lower areas represent the prophets of the Old Testament with the sybils, foretelling the arrival of the Savior and his mother, and are of lesser quality. In the upper zone there are four large canvases depicting scenes from the life of Jesus and of the Virgin Mary. The whole ensemble

plaques of all shapes and sizes testifying to the piety surrounding the church. Many of the plaques are donations by sailors representing their rescue from the stormy seas with the help of the Lady. The marvelous high altar of Carraran marble (made in Genoa in 1796) is all baroque except for its centerpiece, the icon of the Lady of the Rocks itself, work of late gothic master Lovro Dobričević of Kotor, made for the old 15th c. church. On the side walls you will notice details of the bridal dress left over for good luck by the couples married in the church. The smaller altar to the right has an 18th c. icon of St Rocco attributed to Tiepolo.

One of many votive plaques on the walls of the Church

at the miraculous icon efers being there and people started the ilding of a stony islet ound the reef. The mple was consecrated 1452 but destroyed the raid of 1624. The gend has it that the on participated in hting off the Turkish ack of 1654 scaring off e infidels. Present y church dates m 1630, with the tagonal cupola in estrained baroque ⁄le and the atypical und belfry added 1722.

In contrast to its stere stone exterior, e **interior** is richly corated. The walls d the ceiling of e nave are covered th 68 masterful paintings, the life g work of Tripo okolja (1661-1713), ative of Perast, nsidered to be the

culminates with the ceiling paintings with scenes from the New Testament, surrounded (in the smaller frames) by angels and still lifes and the painting of the Ascension of the Virgin in the centre. Between the first and the second zone there are more than 2,500 silver votive

The house adjoining the church is home to the small **museum** (*entrance fee €1*) which displays many items related to the history of Perast such as archeological findings, paintings of ships in battle, old weaponry and peculiar items such as the silk needlework representing the main altar of the church, work of Hijacinta Kunić which took her 20 years to finish and during which she almost lost her eyesight.

Contrary to the Sveti Djordje which is off the tourist perimeter, Gospa od Škrpjela is visited by many. In the summer fishing boats ferry to the island at a cost of c. €2, there and back; in the colder part of the year this short trip might be more of a problem: it is best to inquire in one of

"Lady of the Rocks" by Lovro Dobričević

the local taverns if there is someone willing to take you for the same amount of money.

The highway goes around the town while the most important street in Perast itself is the one by the sea also frequented by cars and smaller buses. There is no obvious solution for parking and you should grab the first place you spot. Our tour starts from the northern side of the town and the large **Bujović Palace**, the finest piece of architecture in Perast, enjoying nice views of the coastline and the rest of the town. The palace was designed by Venetian Giovanni Battista Fontana in 1694 for Vicko Bujović (1660-1709), the commander of the town's fleet known for his hotheaded temper and heroic deeds who died in a street duel with a local judge not far from his home. The stately palace has an open

Captain's drawing room presereved in the Town Museum

see a small collection of Roman and Greek tombstones from the vicinity and the town of Risan. On the two upper floors are displayed many documents, gravures and objects illustrating the rich history of the town and its seafarers, with items such as the maritime banners crowned by the Venetian gonfalon (state standard) and the flag presented to Matija Zmajević (*see below*) by

heavy with gold and gems and finally a small cannon used by local youths to practice firing. On the second floor one can see the self-portrait of Kokolja, icons from Dimitrijević-Rafailović school of painting and some of the paintings of the "Gallery of Solidarity" donated by Yugoslav artists to Kotor after the 1979 earthquake.

A few steps to the north of the museum is a residential building marked with a plaque explaining that here at the beginning of the 18 c. operated **"Nautika"**, the school of Marko Martinović where the first Russian captains received a part of their training in naval skills. This was the first naval school in all of the Slav countries.

In the highest row of houses one can clearly notice the ruins of **"Biskupija"** ("the Bishopric"), the grand palace built in 1678 by Archbishop Andrija Zmajević (1624-1694) an erudite, writer and a collector of folk songs. On its façades are proverbs and morals written in Latin, while the inside was once covered in Kokolja's

The renaissance Bujović Palace

loggia on the ground floor and a vast balcony which runs along the whole length of the front decorated with two stone lions holding the family coats-of-arms. Today the palace houses the **Town Museum** (*Gradski muzej; tel. 373-519; open 9-19 except on Sun 9-14; admission €2*). On the ground floor you will

the Russian Tsar Peter the Great, the portraits of Zmajević and Vicko Bujović by Tripo Kokolja and of many other prominent Perastians, as well as a painting (from 1711) depicting Marko Martinović teaching to the Russian seamen, many models of ships, a 15th c. sword with a Cyrillic inscription

A window on Biskupija

urals. Next to the ...lace stands his chapel ...dicated to **Our Lady** ... **the Rosaries** where ...e archbishop was ...ried. This harmonious ...all chapel has a portal ...th the Zmajević coat-...-arms (displaying a ...agon - *zmaj*) and a ...acious eight-sided ...wer.

Back on the shoreline ...s the massive **Smekja** ...lace from 1760 with a ...ulted boathouse facing ...e sea. To its right the ...lace is adjoined by ...e **Church of St Mark** ...740) with sculptures ...Jesus, St Peter and St ...ul on top of its gable.

Passing a small square ...ed with a rare modern ...ilding in Perast we ...ach the centre of the ...wn marked by the

parish **Church of St Nicholas** and its high belfry. The church was built in 1616 while the 55m high **belfry** – the highest in Boka Kotorska - was added in 1691 by the plans of the Venetian architect Giuseppe Beati in the style of late renaissance. The climb to its top (€1) is awarded with excellent views of Perast and the islets in front of it. After the building of the belfry, works were started on a construction of a grandiose new church. However, only a lofty apse and a part of the nave were constructed to the west of the older church when around 1800 the works were stopped due to a lack of funds and left jutting above the old church. On the outer walls of the church you will see several Roman inscriptions as well as one in the local dialect celebrating a victory

over the Turks in 1654. The rich interior of the church with several altars is crowned by an old organ. For the price of €1 you will gain entrance to the church's rich **treasury** hosted in the apse of the never-finished church. Here one can see liturgical objects, church utensils and vestments from the 17th and 18th c,

Parish Church and its high belfry

archbishop Zmajević's renaissance silver cross, a depiction of the 1654 battle on a silver tablet and an oriental

The waterfront of Perast

Arms on the Luković Palace

streets today offer views of many houses of bright white stone. On the right side you will see the **ruins of Visković Palace** built around a defensive tower from c. 1500 with nice ornaments around its portals. A bit further is the **Balović Palace** a typical example of baroque mansions of the 18th c. with two floors and a belvedere. It was here that Njegoš spent the summer of 1844 and wrote his only love song "A Night Worth More Than a Century" (*Noć skuplja vijeka*). At the end of the lane, next to the small marina are palaces Šestokrilović and Bronz

Directly above the highway stands the **Fort of Sveti Križ** ("Holy Cross") built at the start of the 17th c. as the main defense point against Turkish attacks from the land. It stands on the site of the old church bearing the same name and dates from the 9th c. which stood by the Roman road and below which Perast developed gradually. The simple square edifice of the fort housed the small Venetian garrison commanded by a castellan elected by Perastians.

On the other side of the highway is the modern **Franciscan monastery** with the church of St Anthony (*Sveti Antun*) in which one can see some more paintings by Kokolja.

baldachin brought from a battle with the Turks in the 18th c.

On the small square by the church are **three busts** by Croatian sculptor Vanja Radauš representing Matija Zmajević, admiral of the Russian Baltic fleet, Marko Martinović, seafarer and a teacher of nautical sciences, and Tripo Kokolja, a baroque painter.

From this square starts the main town street; it stretches parallel with the waterfront road which was constructed in the 19th c. cutting through the gardens and docks of the palaces. Both

Relaxing at the berth

WHERE TO EAT IN PERAST

Školji
On the waterfront; 032/373-653; open 09-24h
In the centre of Perast, this restaurant enjoys views to the seaside and the islands. A spacious terrace (regretfully, only under sunshades) and a stony interior are equally nice. Fish prepared in a local manner and Montenegrin dishes make up most of the menu but there is also a good vegetarian section.

Otok Bronza
Luka bb (by the local harbor); tel. 069/672-665; open 09-24h
A small patio all in stone and shaded with old vine invites you to this cozy restaurant. The place is renowned for good food, particularly fish and baked dishes.

Conte
Next to the parish church; 032/373-687; open 10-24h
Located centrally, this fine restaurant faces the sea with three terraces around it. Its menu lists seafood dishes, national and international cuisine at prices higher than average but these are compensated by service and ambiance.

⑤ Orahovac

10 km from Kotor

300

These days, Orahovac is just a sleepy fishing village at the top of the Kotor inner bay, but back in the 19th c. it was famous for its sailing ships and captains. After the Krivošije uprising of 1882 (see p. 70), which the people of Orahovac helped with enthusiasm, most of the seamen left for Argentina.

Immediately by the seashore stands a **huge oak**, estimated to be over 500 years old. From the middle of the village there is an ascending road leading to the **church of St George** (crkva svetog Djordja). The church, surrounded by its graveyard, stands in a spectacular position, atop a massive rock. It was built in the Middle Ages and has frescoes from the late 15th c. preserved in its oldest part. From here one can enjoy the view opening all the way to Kotor.

Half a kilometer along the road to Kotor is **Ljuta river**, which depends solely on precipitation in the regions above Boka Kotorska. Visiting it shortly after rainfall you will witness its short stream rupturing from the steep crags and forcefully flowing into the sea after only a hundred meters of a most magnificent display of whitewater fury.

Two kilometers in the direction of Perast is **Dražin Vrt**, a hamlet of Orahovac with whom it shared its nautical fame, having in 1848 thirteen captains out of only 50 inhabitants. The most famous among them was Miloš Vukasović (1842-1908), descendant of an illustrious captains family, ship builder and an organizer of Argentinean steamship corporations. Today, the hamlet is known for two things. One is **Kula Baja Pivljanina**, standing by the highway, the tower-like stronghold of Bajo Nikolić-Pivljanin (see p. 220), who led his daring attacks on the Turks from this piece of Venetian land. The other is a small gravel **beach** underneath the tower, famous for its crystal clean waters.

Church of St George and its cemetery

A local jetty in Orahovac

WHERE TO EAT IN ORAHOVAC

Stari Mlini
Ljuta bb; 032/333-555; open 12-24h
This restaurant enjoys an amazing setting in an old mill (*stari mlini*) at the confluence of the short river Ljuta into the sea. The mill is genuine and over three centuries old while the surrounding with small bridges, ducks and a pier for boats adds to the atmosphere. The menu concentrates on fish and national dishes; try the trout from their own lake or the octopus baked ispod sača. The setting is reflected in the prices and relatively small portions but the real downside to this place is the service which can sometimes be of low quality.

❼ Kotor

🏛 13,600

ℹ Stari grad 328,
032/325-952

🚌 Škaljari, 032/235-809

🎉 St Tryphon's (Feb 3rd)

Kotor's coat-of-arms with its patron saint

Kotor is one of those amazing places so unique in its setting and history that there is nothing like it anywhere in the world. The town lies huddled underneath the rocks of Mt Lovćen at the farthest end of the Gulf of Kotor. Though palms and olives surround it, the high mountains casting their shadows give it a cruel and cold feel. The educated Byzantine Emperor Constantine Porphyrogenitus (10th c. AD) wrote: "Around the town are high hills so that the sun can be seen only in midday during the summer and never in winter". Though overstated, his vision of the town's setting is also true today and you'll be surprised how late the sun comes up above Lovćen and how early it sets behind Mt Vrmac, especially during the winter. The town core, enclosed by walls, is a muddle of constricted streets bordered with tall stone edifices and paved with multicoloured slabs which only reveal their true beauty after the rain. The narrow lanes spread out in all directions connecting the small squares in such a bewildering fashion that no map will help the inexperienced visitor. One of the nicest things to do here is to get "lost" in Kotor's Old Town, finding your own way through layers of its history and discovering interesting details and vistas.

The beginnings of Kotor are covered in darkness. The earliest settlement was probably in Špiljari (*see p. 91*) in a well sheltered gap behind the Fortress, where the remains of a prehistoric settlement are and from where men could descend to the sea to fish or to hunt in the woods above. Their hideout in case of an attack at the top of the hill (today occupied by the Fort of Sveti Ivan) was later fortified by the Illyrians. In Roman times a settlement called *Acruvium* is mentioned and tradition claims it to be the predecessor of Kotor, but this town probably lay on a more fertile area to the south. The present-day location of the town is in consequence to the era of instability, during the time of barbaric onslaughts when good protection was the most important prerogative for survival; the residents of Roman Acruvium took shelter on a small patch of land hidden at the end of the deep Gulf, protected on one side by the sea, on the other by an inaccessible hill, from the north by river Škurda and from the south by the Gurdić spring. These four natural barriers amongst which the town developed were to remain its limits until the 19th c, the turtle's shell to which it would retreat in times of danger during its turbulent history. Kotor was mentioned first as *Dekaderon* in 670 when it was already a bishop's seat. In this early phase the town was sacked by the Saracens in 867 and by

Imposing cliffs overlooking Kotor Bay

e Bulgarians in 1002 t it managed to rise d become again an portant administrative d trading spot on e Adriatic under zantine protection. 1186 it became a part the Serbian state of emanjićs and thus s most prosperous a begun. The town's istocracy which was Roman descent ntinued to rule er all of the town's ternal matters while s merchants received a uaranteed market with otor becoming the most portant trading port

Lion of St Mark and St Tryphon

r Serbia. From Kotor omanesque and Gothic t spread into Serbia but e town also absorbed fluences from the east d its art remained a end of Byzantine and estern influences. The th c. was the golden ge of Kotor when s merchants stood oulder to shoulder ith those of its largest ompetitor – Dubrovnik. he aristocracy secured l the power in its hands d built gothic palaces, ecoming the treasurers the Serbian state d financiers of mines hile its educated ranciscan monks built e most magnificent yal monasteries for the emanjićs. When in 1371 e dynasty ended and arons started quarreling otor was faced with a

crisis: trade was crippled by many internal borders, the Dubrovnik fleet threatened the town and the armies of local barons stood in front of its walls demanding taxes and pledges of allegiance. The town tried to find protection and changed several masters until in 1420 it agreed to accept Venetian rule. This arrangement had a mutual benefit and as all the neighboring lands fell into the hands of the Ottomans, Kotor stood sheltered by its thoroughly strengthened long walls. In the 16th and 17th centuries its walls gave home to a number of renaissance artists while successfully fighting off Turkish attacks from land and the sea. Much more damage to the town was made by the earthquakes of 1563 and 1667 which tore down its old palaces, and by several plagues that wiped out many noble families. When all of Boka Kotorska was freed from Turkish danger at the end of the 17th c, Kotor was faced with much fiercer competition of other communes

and lost its trading importance remaining only an administrative and religious centre for the Gulf. It was also the closest town to Montenegro, the place from where Venetians communicated with the inland, sending money to spread their influence and spies to gather information. By now Latin became reduced to the language of administration and science and when the Venetian Republic was abolished by Napoleon the local Catholics and the Orthodox felt the moment was right to unite with their brethren in Montenegro, as was decided in 1813 in Dobrota, today a suburb of Kotor. In the 20th c. the antiquities of Kotor attracted more and more attention from scientists and tourists alike. When the devastating earthquake hit the town in 1979 this only cleared the road for a thorough reconstruction of its Old Town (*see map on pp. 82-83*) which now enjoys all the amenities of the modern age while not loosing its ancient looks. The town tripled its populace which spilled outside its walls, forming new suburbs and embracing the neighboring communes.

A boat from Dobrota's 19th c. merchant fleet

Sea Gate, the main entrance to the Old Town

1. Sea Gate
Morska vrata

Today visitors see this as the most common entrance to Kotor's Old Town but only two hundred years ago this gate could be approached only on a ship as the whole of the waterfront didn't exist. The current gate was opened to the north of the old one which sank into the sea in the 1537 earthquake. After the successful defense against Hayreddin Barbarossa the Sea Gate got its renaissance decoration in 1555 under the provost Bernardo Renier (note the initials *BR* and the year in Roman numerals). The gate was vandalized after the communists took over in 1945 when the Venetian lion of St Mark was replaced with a five-pointed star and the date of the liberation of Kotor, furthermore the Habsburg coat-of-arms was replaced with the one of socialist Yugoslavia.

Inside the gate is a late 15th c. **relief** of the Virgin Mary flanked with the town's patron - St Tryphon (always shown with the model of Kotor in his hands) and St Bernardino of Siena. Facing it is an inscription in Latin celebrating the Turkish defeat of 1657.

On the outer side of the fortifications, to the left of the gate is a small park with a café and to the right the town's picturesque **green market**, with a variety of fresh products brought in every day.

2. Arms Square
Trg od oružja

The largest of Kotor's squares is also its social centre where most events happen. Its size and an unusual L-shape are due to the clearing of several old buildings and a church during the French occupation. The focal point of the square is the **Clock Tower** built in 1602 on the site of the medieval torture tower, while the clock was added in the

Choosing the right postcard

late 18th c. The ornate obelisk in front of it served as a pillory. The whole west side of the square is taken by the **Provost's Palace** built after the 1667 earthquake in which the old one crumbled. The main decorative element of its 60m long façade is a balcony of almost the same length. The palace is adjoined by the Guards Tower. On its other side is the so-called **Old Town Hall**, given this name due to its function in the late 19th and early 20th c.

Relief inside the Sea Gate

The Clock Tower, the measure of time in Kotor

4. St Tryphon's Cathedral
Katedrala svetog Tripuna

The cathedral church of Kotor is the most important monument in the whole of Boka Kotorska and one of the most important cathedrals in the East Adriatic. The first church dedicated to St Tryphon, a 3rd c. martyr from Phrygia in Asia Minor, was built here in 809 to host his relics, obtained by Kotor merchants from Constantinople. In time, the cult of the saint grew, he became the patron saint of the town and his church the seat of the bishop. The old church was replaced in 1124-66 by the current one. It was built in a mix of byzantine and romanesque styles, with a dome, two high bell towers and a terrace between them, inspired by similar edifices in Puglia (Italy) where the seat of the archbishop was. After the damage inflicted to it in the 1563

en its neo-renaissance çade was constructed. s also known as apoleon's Theatre, as was adapted by the ench in 1810 to become e first theater hall in otor. Across the small ssage is the building the old **Arsenal** where eapons for the town's rrison and fleet were pt and after which the uare was named. Later it housed the military kery. The edifice got present-day look after e 1979 earthquake. ie passage between the leatre and the Arsenal ves way to the **Citadel**, e strongest part of otor's ramparts, and the round Kampana wer.

In the street starting the south side of the uare and leading to e Flour Square at your ght you will notice the lendid stone **portal** in e late Venetian gothic le. The portal features e arms of the Bizanti nily, one of the most portant patrician nilies in Kotor from ʰ to 18th c.

Flour Square
Trg od brašna

This small square kes its name from the ur storehouse that od here. Its main ght is the **Pima Palace**,

built after the 1667 earthquake. Though baroque in conception and with a 16m long balcony on the stylish consoles, it also has renaissance features such as the first floor terrace standing on two archivolts and decorated with the family coat-of-arms. The Pima family was one of the oldest and most notable in Kotor producing several poets during the renaissance and baroque ages. However, the most important family in the city for two centuries were the Bućas, who gave several treasurers of state to 14th c. Serbia and whose gothic palace stood facing the Pima Palace. In time the Bućas became poorer and after the 1667 earthquake could not rebuild their home and instead had to split it into three separate homes, the way it still stands today.

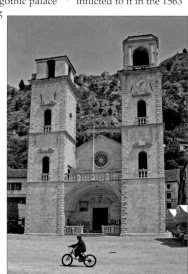

St Tryphon's Cathedral - the heart of the town

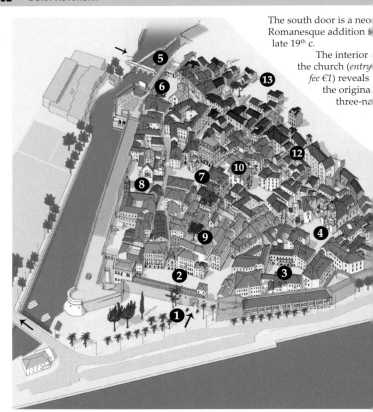

The south door is a neo Romanesque addition ... late 19th c.

The interior ... the church (*entry fee €1*) reveals ... the origina... three-na...

Legend

1 Sea Gate
2 Arms' Square
3 Flour Square
4 St Tryphon's Cathedral
5 River Gate
6 St Mary of the River
7 St Luke's Square
8 Church of St Cla...
9 Church of St Mic...
10 Maritime Museu...

earthquake, the shaken dome was torn down. The large earthquake of 1667 destroyed completely the romanesque bell towers and the west face which was consequently rebuilt in a baroque style, but following the old design. This was the last major modification of the church as the last earthquake of 1979 provided an opportunity for a detailed restoration of the cathedral, uncovering many of the features buried in oblivion during the eight and a half centuries of its existence.

The **west face** from the late 17th c. is unique in its architectural mix of renaissance and baroque, with reminiscences of the romanesque in details such as the rose window. Another notable feature of its exterior is a **three-bay window** on the cathedral's apse, work of local masons in a romanesque-gothic style from the mid 14th c. Almost identically designed windows are to be found on the apses of the Studenica and Dečani monasteries (in Serbia) that were built by the same masters.

disposition. The colum... between the nave and the aisles are of differe... origin and built out of different materials, som... with the Corinthian

A 14th c. fresco from the Cathedral

apitols taken from Roman ruins. On some of the columns as well as in the apse you can see the remnants of frescoes done in the mid 14th c. in the Serbian-Byzantine fashion. The prime feature of the interior is the **altar canopy** (ciborium) from 1362, again in a transitional romanesque-gothic style. The four columns of red stone bear the architrave

11 Šuranj Gate

12 Artisans' Street

13 Fort of St John

which are carved scenes from the life of St Tryphon. Above it rises a crown on three levels each of which is held by small columns and figures of angels, Roman soldiers and citizens. Behind the canopy is the gilded silver **polyptych** from 1440 representing Christ, St Tryphon and other saints, the work of local goldsmiths under the guidance of master Johannes of Basel. Around the high altar are four smaller ones from the baroque era decorated lavishly with marble, silver and gold. In the south aisle is the

tomb of Bishop Tripun Biznati (died 1532) with his effigy.

To the left of the high altar is a door leading to the **sacristy** with chalices, pastoral crosses, monstrances and pre-romanesque reliefs from the ciborium of the 9th c. church. Above it is the **reliquarium** all in white marble, built in 1704-08 from the designs of Francesco Cabianca of Venice. Its main feature is the marble sarcophagus held by kneeling angels and topped by the praying figure of St Tryphon. In the sarcophagus is the silver casket containing the relics of the saint with the scenes of his martyrdom, a Venetian work from the 17th c. Beside the casket the sarcophagus contains the golden reliquary in Gothic style with the saint's head and a crystal cross (16th c.). The other 50 reliquaries here are placed in closets around the room. In the middle of the room hangs a large wooden crucifix in Gothic style. The paintings here include works of local artists such as the gothic master Lovro Dobričević ("Mary and Jesus") and Tripo Kokolja ("Ecstasy of St Francis") as well as of the Italians Girolamo

The magnificent altar canopy

Santacroce ("St Bartholomew"), Bassano ("Crucifixion"), Giusepe Diamanti, Sassoferato and two works of Tician's school ("Three Kings" and "The Finding of the Holy Cross") and Michael Nordlinger. In the end you will also see a cross used to bless the army of Jan Sobieski before its decisive victory over the Turks at the gates of Vienna in 1683.

Adjoining the cathedral to the left is the **Bishop's Palace** with its airy courtyard. This

Gothic windows of the Drago Palace

edifice was endowed in 1327 by Jelena Drago to the bishops of Kotor.

To its left is the **Drago Palace** which is of an "L" shape. The façade facing the square is narrow and has modest renaissance-baroque decoration from the end of the 17th c. To the right of this protruding wing is the passage through the palace decorated with family coats-of-arms displaying a dragon, an early renaissance window with an angel and a splendid two-bay window. The north face of the palace remains the best preserved with its several gothic windows. Today the palace houses the regional institute for the protection of monuments.

5. River Gate
Vrata od Rijeke

On its north, Kotor town walls are additionally strengthened by river Škurda, which springs from the rocks and after a few hundred meters flows into the sea. It branches in two streams forming a river island previously known as the Montenegrin Market, where the highlanders would come to trade their cheese, skins and meat for gunpowder, textiles or simply grain. This was the furthest point to which they could bear arms, their most valuable possession; to enter Kotor they had to turn them over to the guards of the gate. The stone bridge and the gate to which it leads were built in 1540 in memory of the previous year's victory over the Turkish admiral Hayreddin Barbarossa. After taking Herceg Novi, Barbarossa came to Kotor, sailed up the Škurda and attacked the northern walls which were successfully defended after a fierce fight. The bridge, once covered and with numerous loopholes, blocked the approach to the gate from the river. Its last part was wooden and could be lifted in case of attack. The renaissance decoration of the gate displays the winged lion of St Mark, initials of Venetian provosts and dodges from the time of its construction and a short inscription of the 1539 victory.

Square next to the St Mary of the River

6. St Mary of the River
Sveta Marija od Rijeke

This church sits in a square just by the River Gate. Its beginnings are to be found in the 6th c. basilica that served as the original seat of the Kotor bishop. The old, dilapidated church was replaced by the present-day edifice in 1221, which is much smaller than the old basilica but with the apse in the same place. The single-nave church was built with alternating rows of reddish and white stone. Its octagonal dome, blind arches and round apse with a pretty two-light window are all features of the local blend of romanesque and byzantine styles developing at the time in Kotor. The north side of the church was extended with an aisle 1434 while the bell tower was added in 1771. The church is roofed with thin stone tiles, the usual method from the 13th c. repeated in restoration

River Škurda protecting the northern walls of the Old Town

er 1979. The main, ~~s~~tern door is work of modern artist Vasko ~~~~ovac presenting ~~~~nes from the life of ~~~~ssed Osanna who's ~~~~ly decorated coffin ~~~~ in the church and ~~~~ reliefs by Croatian ~~~~lptor Antun ~~gustinčić~~ (1939). ~~~~anna, a shepherdess ~~~~o came to Kotor and ~~~~ame a Dominican ~~~~n, played a crucial ~~~~e in the strengthening ~~~~spirits during ~~~~barossa's attack of ~~~~9. Inside the church ~~~~e can also see the 14th ~~~~tone pieta, a 15th c. ~~~~oden crucifix, several ~~~~oque paintings and ~~~~ly 14th c. frescoes by ~~~~nters from Kotor ~~~~o were mentioned in ~~~~cuments as "pictores ~~~~eci" (Greek painters) ~~~~ their Byzantine style. ~~~~To the back of the ~~~~rch starts the street ~~~~ding to the Fort of St ~~~~n (see nr. 13). Above ~~~~ street is an **arch** with ~~~~ylized winged lion ~~~~ medallion, a Latin ~~~~cription explaining ~~~~t it also once led to ~~~~ town granary and the ~~~~e of its construction ~~~~60). The building ~~~~he right of the arch

Western door - a modern addition to St Mary's Church

is the Grubonja Palace from the late 16th c. On the façade of the first floor is a small **relief,** depicting the Monogram of Christ (*IHS*), a skull with snakes and a mouse, lizard and tortoise beneath it. This is the emblem of the pharmacy that opened here in 1326, amongst the first in south-eastern Europe.

On the other side of the square are stairs leading to the **town walls**. To the right is the Bembo Bastion (1539-40) adapted as an open-air stage, while to the left you pass above the backyards to the Citadel

from where you can descend to the Arms Square (*see nr. 2*).

7. St Luke's Square
Trg svetog Luke

This square in the north part of the city takes its name from the old church dedicated to St Luke which can be seen in its centre. The church was built in 1195 by tradesman Andrea Caccafrangi and his wife Bona "during the reign of Grand *Župan* Nemanja and his son Vukan" as is stated on the plaque above the west entrance. The church was used by Catholics until the mid 17th c. when it was handed over for use by the Orthodox population from the vicinity who found refuge in the town during the war with the Turks. However, the Catholics retained an altar in the church where once a year their service would follow the Orthodox one. This duality lasted until the French occupation (1807-14) when the church was turned over entirely to the Orthodox, who by this time formed the majority of the citizenry

~~T~~he view of the town and its harbour with the large Campana Tower to the left

Church of St Luke with St Nichola's in the backdrop

Ćiril Ivekovi the church h a Byzantine disposition and a large cupola whic rises above t rooftops, wh the details were done ir a romanesqu style. Until i disappeared in an 1896 fi the Dominic church dedicated to the same saint stood here. The unpainted interior is uninteresting except for its iconostasis done by the Czech painter František Ziegler in 19

but could use only this church. The church draws on Byzantine inspiration (cupola) but is Romanesque in details (two-light windows on the west façade and the apse). The chapel of St Spyridon was adjoined to the north side of the church in 1747 and at about the same time the church also recieved its baroque bell gable "on distaff". Inside stands the gilded iconostasis topped by a splendid crucifix, the work finished in 1710 by Dimitrije Rafailović, the father of Rafailović-Dimitrijević school of icon painting. In a niche to the right of the iconostasis is the only surviving fragment of the frescoes painted around the year 1200. The artist painted western saints – St Catherine (left), St Clement the Pope and St Marina (right) – yet in the manner of Orthodox iconography. The floor of the church is made out of gravestones above the collective graves of Kotor citizens, since the church and its yard served as a cemetery until the 1830s. The iconostasis standing in the chapel is a master work of Italo-Cretan

painting from the mid 18th c. with a standing figure of "Christ the High Priest".

To the right of the church stands the **Lombardić Palace**. Built in the mid 18th c, it is a fine edifice with baroque details and a belvedere on the top. It was here that during his many

A centuries old detail on an old house in Kotor

visits to Kotor Njegoš stayed with his friend the parish priest Ilija Lombardić. Njegoš's window was the left one on the first floor and it was underneath it that the Municipal Orchestra, founded one year earlier, played to him in 1843.

The largest edifice on the square is the orthodox **church of St Nicholas**. Built in 1909 according to the plans of

8. Church of St Cl.
Crkva Svete Klare

The first church in this place was run by t Benedictine nuns. Whe

in the mid 14th c. their order faded, the site w donated to the clarissa nuns and the current church edifice was buil In the 16th c. this order was dissolved and the church was taken over by the Franciscan friar The front face of the church got its present day shape in 1708. Inside there are severa altars of which the mo beautiful is the **high**

Splendid altar in the Church of St Clair

...ltar, work of Francesco ...abianca from around ...700. Its centerpiece is ...e byzantine icon of ...e Virgin Mary with ...sus all clad in silver ...nd gold. In front of it ...e figures of St Francis ...nd St Clare while to its ...ar stands the "canopy" ...odeled from yellow ...arble. On its top are ...gures of God the Father, ...hn the Baptist and St ...incent. All around are ...nall angels and cherubs, ...gnifying both divine ...ve and the love of the ...atrons – Ivan Bolica ...d Vincencija Buća – ...ho donated the altar ... honor of their happy ...arriage (as is written ... the inscription). To ...e left of the church are ...e convent's quarters ...gether ...th a small ...oister ...d a large ...rary ...th over ...000 rare ...lumes, ...cluding ...s of ...cunabula. ...e belfry is ...sentially ...manesque, ...th its bell ...st in 1512.

9. Church of St Michael
Crkva svetog Mihaila

The church stands on a small square easily recognizable for its huge poplar tree, which is thought to be over 300 years old. The square is new in origin, having been converted from the yard of a closed down church. Its name - Pjaca od kina - was formed in the same way as the names of the old squares - according to their most important feature, in this case the cinema (*kino*)! The first church standing here, even from before the 12th c, was a pre-romanesque three nave basilica, considerably larger than the present day edifice. It was probably destroyed in some unrecorded 14th c. tremor after which it was reduced to its present day size. Another earthquake, that of 1979, helped to revive its looks since before this date it served as a one storey house, not very different from the neighboring ones. Today on its west façade one can see several medieval reliefs and an inscription; the interior of the church is left without a floor in order to observe the foundations of its predecessor. In and around the apse there are fine 15th c. frescoes by Lovro Dobričević.

10. Maritime Museum
Pomorski muzej

Trg bokeljske mornarice; tel. 032/325-646; open 8-13 and 18-23 except Sundays 9-13; admission €1.50

The museum is situated in the **Grgurina Palace** on the Boka Navy Square (*Trg bokeljske mornarice*). The palace, built in 1732 closes its north side with its wide and well proportioned façade decorated with large stone balconies. The last descendant of the Grgurina family, Bishop Marko Antonije, left his palace for the use of the town council in 1813 and it has served as the seat of the town administration since then. The museum was founded on the second floor in 1938 and was expanded to the whole building after WWII. The interior of the palace has been preserved, with wooden ceilings, floors in red and white stone and a small garden on the first floor terrace.

Grgurina Palace, today housing the Maritime Museum

A ship model, Maritime Museum

The museum is focused on the development of seafaring in the Gulf of Kotor and to the cultural progress of the region. The oldest items are Greek and Roman inscriptions and sculptures such as the head of Emperor Dioclecian, followed by the stone reliefs from the early Middle Ages and the Romanesque period, models of old ships, nautical instruments and equipment, historical paintings, weaponry, traditional costumes of Boka as well as the portraits and period furniture of Kotor citizens. Special attention is devoted to the Boka Navy (*see inlay*) and the mutiny of sailors aboard the Austro-Hungarian ships in 1918.

11. Šuranj Gate
Vrata od Šuranja

The southern approach to Kotor, from the vanished suburb of

Fortifications of the Šuranj Gate

Šuranj is closed by the **Gurdić spring**. This undersea spring is fed by the waters draining through the limestone hills above Kotor and erupts here from the depths of the abyss. Gurdić has a beautiful deep blue colour and is most amazing after rain when it gushes up from its depths, sometimes very forcefully. Above it stands the mighty Bon Tower, a fine piece of fortification from the 15th c. with several relief coats-of-arms built into it.

The Šuranj Gate is actually a system of three gateways from various epochs. The outer one is the youngest and dates from the 18th c. On it you can see metal wheels by which the drawbridge above Gurdić was once lifted. The middle gateway is part of the medieval town wall and probably dates from the 13th c. The third and the strongest is the inner gate, added

DEFENDERS OF THE GULF

The Boka Navy (*Bokeljska mornarica*) is an association of seamen dating from the Middle Ages. Today you will see its members on festive days in Kotor and other towns in the Gulf parading in their traditional black costumes and armed with historic weaponry. Though on most of these occasions you will hear that the Boka Navy will be 1200 years old in 2009, this is an exaggeration since there is no record of it until the 14th c. when it appears as a guild of seafarers formed for mutual aid but also prepared to go to war on their ships. In times of Turkish attacks this warlike aspect became predominant while later the Navy lost its initial purpose and became a patriotic association. It was abolished by Austria in 1848 because of its Yugoslav nationalism while in communist days its religious aspect was deliberately disregarded. Everything connected with the Navy is soaked in ritual - starting from its 1463 statute (though, understandably, much revised since), to its Admiral who is always accompanied by a "young admiral", a boy destined to become the future commander, and to the kolo (circular dance) performed by its members linked by holding handkerchiefs.

n the 16th c. to reinforce he protection of this mportant position. To he left of the gate there s a stairway to the top of he Bon Tower.

2. Artisans' Street
Zanatlijska ulica

This is the longest treet in the Old Town unning from the Šuranj Gate in the south almost ll the way to the River Gate in the north. Amidst the web of small naking streets this is the only one that was long nough to earn a name.

Starting from the Šuranj Gate the first uilding on the right is he sturdy barracks of he fort's artillery. Next ve reach the ruins of the t Francis Monastery. This monastery was riginally situated utside of the walls, in ront of Šuranj Gate, but ad to be torn down n 1656 on the orders f the town authorities n order not to be used y the approaching urkish army as a shelter or their guns. The nonastery still boasts a loister and a tall belfry vith a Romanesque rucifix on it.

A bit further away, on he left side is the **Town Hospital** built in 1769, fter the battle with the

rebellious clans who joined Šćepan the Little, a mysterious Montenegrin ruler (see p. 23). Today the building is used as the seat of the Cultural Centre and is connected to the sea promenade through a small gate made in the walls.

Continuing past the small **Salad Square** (*Pjaca od salate*), from which the alternative climb to the Fort of St John starts, and further behind the back of the cathedral the path reaches the large building of the former **Town Prison**. Built in the mid 19th c. in place of two old churches it served its grim purpose all the way to the beginning of the 1990s and still stands completely unchanged from that time. Except for the imprisonment of criminals, the prison served on many occasions for the jailing of political adversaries: firstly of the rebels in the Krivošije Uprisings (see p. 70), then in 1914 as a temporary concentration camp for the Orthodox population who were then sent to camps in Hungary; in 1918 here were imprisoned the sailors who mutinied against Austria-Hungary - including the four ringleaders who were shot, while in 1948 the jail was

Artisans' Street and the Salad Square

filled with those who took the wrong side in the Tito-Stalin conflict (see p. 32). To the right of the prison building, hidden behind a tall stone wall with only its Romanesque portal visible is the **Church of St Paul** from 1263. Used for centuries by the Dominicans, it was turned into a barracks during the French occupation and then in 1948 into a women's prison when the high wall towards the street was added. The old Romanesque church is closed for visitors and expects to be reconstructed into a conference hall. To the left of the large prison building is the **Church of St Joseph** built in 1631 and used until the beginning of the 19th c. as a Franciscan nunnery. A staircase leads to the southern entrance and the bell tower in which a 15th c. bell still hangs. Inside the church is the high altar by Cabianca and on a side altar a painting by the Flemish painter Peter de Coster (17th c.).

Steps leading upwards from Artisans' Street

Continue along the Zanatlijska St. and take the first alley left to reach the small but incredibly appealing **Church of St Ann** (*crkva svete Ane*). The church was originally dedicated to St Martin and later, when it was maintained by the butchers' guild, to St Veneranda, and got its present day saint-protector only at

Childhood spent on centuries old stones

the beginning of the 19th c. Built probably in the 12th c. it has features similar to those of the churches of St Luke or St Mary of the River with alternate rows of red and gray stone and romanesque two-light windows. Inside of the church are fragments of frescoes done by Lovro Dobričević in the mid 15th c. with the oldest inscription in Serbian in the Boka Kotorska.

13. Fort of St John
Tvrdjava Sveti Ivan

The completely preserved town walls of Kotor, 4.5km in length, are one of the chief reasons that helped Kotor reach UNESCO's list of world heritage sights. This extensive fortification system is even more impressive considering that it climbs up the fearsome hill behind the town surmounting its many cliffs to reach the top at 260m above sea level where the Fort of St John stands. Here formerly stood the Illyrian and Roman strongholds even before the "lower town" (present-day Kotor) developed and in a later era the hilltop was dominated by a Byzantine castle. The walls encircling the town and the hill were finished in the 14th c. except for some sections which were unassailable to such an extent that they needed no protection. The medieval walls got their present day appearance in the 16th and 17th centuries when they were reinforced and strengthened by the Venetians to withstand cannon fire. The fort was used by the army until the end of the Second World War. One of the fort's peculiarities is an endemic species of slug almost black in colour – *Clausilia catharensis* – which lives only amongst its walls.

Climbing to the top of St John's is a must for each and every visitor of Kotor. This 45 minute climb up its stone stairways with a total of 1,350 steps opens aerial views on to Kotor and dramatic vistas along its bay.

There are two places to start the ascent: one leads from St Mary of the River (*see p. 85*) and the other from the Salad Sq (*see p. 89*) along the so called *Scala Santa* ("Holy Stairway"); on both of these you will find post charging €1. As many sections of the fortress are in bad condition you are advised to keep to the beaten path. Twisting in tight curves between the last houses nested on the steep slopes, both roads have two widenings (once used by gunmen) just above the rooftops before they meet at St Joseph point (all the bastions, sections of the walls and forts bear names of their patron saints or of the Venetian commanders who built them). Past the scenic cypresses and five little chapels you will reach the church **Gospa od zdravlja** ("Lady of Health"). Lying half way to the top it was first mentioned in 1518 as the Lady of Rest but was renamed after one of the many plague epidemics that hit the town. Through the wrought iron railing you can see a baroque

The winding fortifications climbing to the Fort of St John

Gospa od zdravlja looking over Kotor

...ar with a silver clad
...on of the Madonna and
...atues of St Tryphon
...d St Jerome. Hence
...veral more serpentines
...d to the north side of
...e walls and the "Small
...rt", a series of strong
...ints. From here a small
...te leads to the village
Špiljari (*špilja* – cave)
...th its small church
...d just one family
...ing off their goats.
...ll hidden, the village
...isted long before
...tor was established.
...recent centuries
...was known for its
...cks and supplied
...tor with meat. A
...w minutes more and
...u reach the **Fort of
John**, the highest
...int above Kotor with
panoramic prospects of
the deepest part of the
bay. On the other side is
a deep gap from which
starts the climb up to
the mountains of Old
Montenegro.

ENVIRONS:

Just to the north of
the Old Town starts
Dobrota, once a separate
township and today
fully joined with Kotor.
For a long time this was
a village in the shadow
of the might of Kotor but
when its brave captains,
who distinguished
themselves in skirmishes
with the Turks, managed
in 1705 to win the status
of a separate commune
Dobrota quickly
prospered from sea
trade and maintained
the largest fleet in Boka
Kotorska, numbering
more than 400 ships.
Since Dobrota lived from
the sea it's no surprise
to learn that it spreads
for 7.5km to the north,
with seven hamlets and
with almost every house
taking a portion of the
coast. Above it looms
a daunting rock called
Pestingrad, where stories
tell of fairies living in its
caves. The gardens and
olive groves of Dobrota
are now covered with
buildings and houses
but the walk along the
coast is one of the most
romantic things to do in
Kotor. The walk starts
by the town's open
air swimming pool.
Here the coast is lined
with 19th c. houses and
several fine restaurants.
Passing two small
beaches you will reach
the promontory with an
old edifice housing the
Institute of Sea Biology,
in front of which stands
a miniature chapel.
Behind it are several
palaces including the
one of the Ivanović
family, in which Njegoš
once stayed. Passing
a number of stately

...brota, pressed between the sea and the cliffs

Baroque Tripković Palace in Dobrota

edifices and among them the grand Milošević palace (early 19th c.) you will reach the **Church of St Mathew** standing on a small rise above the sea and enjoying grand views. It was built in 1670 after its predecessor tumbled down in the 1667 earthquake. Inside one can see the paintings "Madonna and the Child" by Giovanni Bellini and "St Nicholas" of Pietro Novelli. In one of the chapels is the bas-relief depicting the Annunciation by Venetian sculptor Giovanni Bonazza. Next to the church is the **Institute for Tourism** located in the house in which in 1813 the "National Commission" met. Comprised of 9 men from Boka and 9 from Montenegro and presided over by metropolitan Petar I, this body reached a decision on the short-lived unification of the two provinces. Some 2km to the north past the **Tripković Palace** with its rococo gable you will reach the large **Church of St Eustace** (*crkva svetog Stasija*) dating from 1773, the time of the greatest flourishing of Dobrota. Inside you will see seven marble altars, each endowed by one or more local families, the paintings "The Finding of the Holy Cross" attributed to Veronese, "Madonna" by Karlo Dolci and several more works of Alojzije Soliman, the Dalmatian pupil of Tiepolo. On the ceiling are paintings on the life of St Eustace from 1938 and the modernist mosaic on the high altar is by Croatian painter Edo Murtić. The church also possesses a collection of Dobrota needle laces specific in their style and made by the wives of absent mariners. In the treasury are kept a flag and a turban - trophies captured by the Ivanović brothers in their famous clash with Turkish corsairs in front of Athens in 1756.

The walk along the coast on the other side of the Old Town leads past the suburb of Škaljari and then winds north along the coast which now faces Kotor. One kilometer from the Old

WHERE TO EAT IN KOTOR

Galion
Šuranj; tel. 032/325-054; open 10-24h
This fine restaurant lies on the seafront a few dozen meters away from the Old Town. Its warm interior is outshined by the outdoor seating on a terrace above the water with a view across the harbour. It serves delicious fish and seafood dishes at prices somewhat above the average.

Bastion
Old Town, by the River Gate; 032/325-116; open 11-24h
This old-established restaurant of unpretentious interior keeps to its high standards in food preparation and is also one of the rare places where on most of the evenings you'll see the owner working to please his guests. Their famous chef prepares excellent fish and seafood, each tastier than the other. It also has a garden courtyard bordered by town walls.

Tiha noć
Dobrota 151; 032/330-880; open 07-24h
The restaurant sits on the sea promenade in Dobrota, to the north of the Old Town. The furnishings are simple but the atmosphere is hearty. It serves a variety of grill and oven dishes, fish and the lamb spit-roast - the unbeatable specialty of the house.

Ellas
Donji put (Dobrota); 032/335-115; open 08-01h
Contrary to its name, this renowned establishment has nothing to do with Greek cooking but sticks to fish and other maritime specialties, traditional Montenegrin dishes and the usual range of grilled dishes. It is located on the waterfront and enjoys nice vistas from its first-floor terrace but has also seating on the street and in its stony interior.

own you will reach the village **Muo**. This village is one of the oldest in Boka and, interestingly, was never even in a major range of populace. The inhabitants live from times immemorial even fishermen and have even preserved some Greek and Latin words in their fishing terminology. Even today most of the fish on Kotor's market comes from Muo. The row of modest stone houses is overtopped by the **parish church** dedicated to the Virgin Mary, Saviour of the Christians. It was built in a mix of neo-byzantine and neo-romanesque styles in 1864. In it lie the relics of beatified Gracija (1438-1508) who from his native Muo went to Venice as a sailor but then joined the Augustine monks there, spending the rest of his

life in sanctity, feeding the poor and helping the needy. His body was brought back to Muo in 1810.

Kotor was always the starting point for the climb into the hills of Montenegro. Here travelers and diplomats would stack up on supplies of necessities not found further inland, find a good guide who also served as a guard and begin up the small dirt path starting from the River Gate and the Montenegrin Market (*see p. 84*). As this "road" was nothing more than a track used by men and cattle, the Montenegrin prince-bishop Njegoš took on the building of a better road. Though better than the last one, this road could also be covered only on foot or by donkey and was so steep that it was named the **"Ladder of Kotor"**. This historic road is shamefully neglected and therefore dangerous in some sections but can still be covered by experienced hikers. In 1879

Austria-Hungary started the construction of a new cart-road to Montenegro. Most of the Montenegrins were against this fearing that the road might bring cannons and troops more easily up into the mountains but were convinced by Prince Nikola, to whom transport of any kind (even of furniture or a piano) was a pain staking effort. The construction of a road on such harsh terrain, a great engineering accomplishment, was completed up to the Montenegrin border in 1884. The road still serves as the only connection between Kotor and Cetinje. It climbs up to the Trojice point marked with a small Austrian fort and a couple of curves later reaches the steep slopes of Lovćen which it surmounts with 25 serpentines, looming one above the other, each with a view a little better than the last. The road is a fascinating experience whether you cover it by car, bicycle or on foot. It is also the place where car and bicycle races take place every summer.

Village of Muo and its parish church

A flower amidst the stones

❽ Prčanj

5km from Kotor
1,200

Prčanj is a pretty township at the foot of green Mt Vrmac, spreading four kilometers along the water's edge. The place was famous for its mariners: first mentioned in the 16th c., they prospered quickly and already at the beginning of the 17th c. the Venetian Republic assigned them with postal service around its Adriatic and Ionian possessions. Prčanj reached its prime during late 18th and all through the 19th c. when, together with Dobrota across the bay, it had the largest number of ships in Boka Kotorska. The number of inhabitants was twice as high as today, and many of them were rich and well educated promoters of culture. With the end of the era of sailing ships Prčanj declined and sunk to a level of a large village whose past glory is reflected in many historic monuments.

The township enjoys a favorable climate, especially in summers when its rich greenery and shades of precipitous Mt Vrmac keep it pleasantly cool.

Coming from the south one first encounters a small gothic palace known for its unusual three-part shape as **"The Three Sisters"**. The palace was built in the 15th c. as a summer house of the Buća family from Kotor, whose members rose to the ranks of the state treasurers of Serbian Empire. The legend says that here lived three sisters who all fell in love with the same seaman who went on a long trip and never returned. The sisters waited faithfully, refusing marriage proposals; when the first died her window was walled, when the second one died her window was nailed with a wood cover; the third one never saw her beloved one either, but by then there was no one left to close her window.

Continuing northwards there are several nice views of centre of Prčanj to be enjoyed. Next comes the tiny church dedicated to **Our Lady of Carmen**

A small harbour on the way to Prča...

built in 1652 by Tripo Luković, admiral of the Boka Navy (*see p. 88*), whose family coat-of-arms can be seen above the entrance. The stately **Church of St Nicholas** dates from 1730 and was used by the Franciscans as their monastery. The adjoining building, actually a cloister, was for a period home to a private naval school but is best known for the episode from revolutionary 1848 when, on June 13th, representatives of Boka communes gathered in its courtyard and reached the decision to unite with other South Slav provinces, an idea which succeeded 70 years later.

The centre of Prčanj is marked by the **Parish Church**, standing on a 20m rise above the rest of the houses. Dedicated to the Nativity of Virgin Mary, it is the largest church in the whole Gulf of Kotor (35 by 23m and 31m high). It was started in 1789 on the plans of the Venetian

"The Three Sisters" House

Stairway of Prčanj's Parish Church

Štrosmajer (work of famous sculptor Ivan Meštrović) and Frano Ućelini-Tice, both promoters of South Slavic unity, archbishop Andrija Zmajević, an 18th c. forerunner of this idea from Perast, don Niko Luković, vicar in Prčanj and connoisseur of Boka who wrote many books on the subject, Ivo Visin (*see below*) and Njegoš (*see p. 192*). To the back of the church there are several old tombstones and various stone fragments built into the wall. The interior is plain but appealing with most of the decoration consisting of fine stone masonry. The main altar of particular baroque shape was made in Venice in 1744 by Giovani Maria Morlaiter while the icon of Mother of God constituting its central feature was done in the 14th c. in a late Byzantine fashion. To the right is the side altar dedicated to Our Lady of Rosaria (sculptured in 1746 by Morlaiter) and to the left an early baroque altar dedicated to the Holy Family. The choir of the church is adorned with two more paintings - the large oil-on-canvas representing the Annunciation done by a late 17th c. follower of Veronese and a small gothic Virgin with young Christ (15th c.). The sacristy of the church has been transformed into a small museum keeping church vessels and dresses as well as a number of works of art, mainly by various 20th c. Yugoslav artists.

Continuing further along the shore one first comes to the **Visin House**, home of captain Ivo Visin who sailed around the world in 1852-59 on his ship "Splendido" with a crew from Boka. Visin is often mistakenly described as "the first South Slav to sail round the globe", while this was already achieved by Stevan Vukotić in 1823-26. However, Vukotić was in service of the Russian Emperor and remained relatively unknown, whereas Visin sailed under the flag of Austria, who proudly publicized the success of the first citizen of Austria to accomplish such journey. Lining the

architect Bernardino Maccaruzzi and financed enthusiastically by local captains who even transported the needed stone from the island of Korčula free of charge. The lower portion, in a distinctively Palladian style, was finished by 1806 when the Napoleonic wars hindered trade. The upper parts, together with the cupola, were done in the course of the [19]th c. but closely follow the original late baroque design. The church was finally consecrated in [18]09 after the completion of the works on its exterior, while the imposing double stairway leading to it took four more years to finish. In front of it are busts of prominent people connected with history of Prčanj and the Gulf of Kotor: bishops Josip Juraj

The new parish church by the sea and the old one in the hills

shore alongside this house stand a number of similar, stoutly built stone houses.

Returning from the Parish Church back in the direction of Kotor, take the first path leading uphill. Initially you will pass the orthodox cemetery and in it a chapel built in 1982 as a replica of the old Njegoš chapel which once stood at the top of Mt Lovćen (*see p. 190*). At the top of this track you will reach the **old parish church** of Prčanj, dedicated to the same feast as its newer counterpart by the sea. This old church

ENVIRONS:

On the north edge of Prčanj is **Markov Rt** point, possibly the nicest beach of the inner Kotor bay.

Two kilometers further starts **Stoliv**, another settlement with a nautical tradition. The part lying by the sea, with tiny beaches and lots of flowers, is known as Donji (Lower) Stoliv. It is much younger and more populated than its upper equivalent Gornji Stoliv, high above in the greenery of Vrmac. Directly by the seaside stands the **Church of the Name of**

Gornji Stoliv, high in the hills of Vrmac

Peaceful end to a day in Donji Stoliv

sunk in the vegetation slowly overwhelming it was mentioned already in 1399. The octagonal chapel with a cupola is an addition from 1740. Inside are two baroque altars from the end of the 17th c.

Mary from 1774, with an opulent baroque main altar decorated with figures of Saints Peter and Paul.

Gornji Stoliv, up to the 18th c. the only Stoliv, is located high above the gulf, in a position from which an approaching enemy

could be seen from afar and which offered much more protection. Today this peaceful hamlet comprises only a few houses lost in vegetation, all with a fantastic view across the Gulf. The walk to it (30min) starts from the highway some hundred meters before the church (in the direction of Prčanj). It will lead you past the small village graveyard and the olive groves and through a lush chestnut wood. In the hamlet is a large **Church of St Elijah** from 1553. Though somewhat deteriorated it is still in service and its old clock regularly strikes the hour. In its courtyard you will walk over many old tombstones with representations of the deceased. If you're lucky enough to find it open, inside it you will see a fine triptych with scenes from Christ's life (Josip Tominc, 1853) and two side altars from the 19th c.

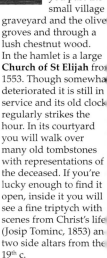

● Tivat

● 9,500

● Palih boraca bb, 032/672 620

● + 382 (0)32/671-337

● Palih boraca 8; tel. 032/671-324

● Bowling Olympics (July)

Tower of the Buća-Luković Palace

Tivat, "the youngest town of Boka kotorska", is set at the foot of Mount Vrmac, on the edge of a fertile plain opening to the south and to the wide bay that bears the town's name. Sheltered from the north winds by Vrmac and open to the south, it enjoys a favorable climate that made the plain in which it lies from time immemorial into a wine and fruit growing region. This copious area attracted settlers such as the Illyrians and Romans, but remained pastoral, with several smaller villages scattered around. The name of the present day town is mentioned first "only" in the 14th c. when the noble families of Kotor built here their summer houses, small castles from which they could gather their feudal duties in crops, which were later owned by the wealthy captains from Perast and Prčanj. It was only after 1898 when Austria-Hungary built its naval arsenal here that Tivat grew rapidly, becoming the largest town in the Gulf until the mid 20th c. when it was surpassed by Herceg Novi and Kotor. Today Tivat and its surroundings are an attractive resort, with many hotels and boarding houses. However, except for a few, the beaches here are small and those in Tivat itself are all concrete.

A fairly modern town, Tivat doesn't offer too many tourist attractions but makes a good starting point for visiting places in its close vicinity. The main historic sight in the town, and one of only a few reminders of patrician villas erected here, is the **tower** of the Buća-Luković summer house. The tower with logia on its top, built in 1548 by a local builder, is the only remaining part of the house. It is located on the street parallel to the coastal promenade and is today part of the Town Gallery. In a closed yard next to the tower is a small chapel from the same period, dedicated to St Michael. Slightly northwards from the tower is Tivat's **Town Park**, the largest in the Gulf of Kotor. Its tradition was started by the seafarers who used to bring tropical and sub-tropical plants from their journeys. Today it is just a shadow of its former glory, with only the old trees surviving the neglect. In the park there is a **monument** to naval officers Milan Spasić and Sergej Mašera, who in April of 1941 heroically blew themselves up together with their ship "Zagreb" in order not to fall into Italian hands.

On the other side of the town centre is the small and pretty Kaliman port.

ENVIRONS:

Heading north along the coast one passes through several settlements that have blended into one with Tivat. Directly behind the closed down shipyard is **Rt Seljanovo**, a point of land that juts into the gulf and has a long sandy beach. Adjoining it to the north is the village of **Donja Lastva**, earlier also one of the sites that attracted the patricians of Kotor. Its waterside is lined with nice 19th c. stone houses ending with the Church of St Roch (1901) whose most valuable possession is the 17th c. icon of St Tryphon, work of Greek painter Ilias Moschos.

Much older than its lower lying counterpart is **Gornja Lastva**, located 3km uphill in Vrmac.

Boats docked at the Tivat's promenade

Church in Gornja Lastva

Today almost deserted this old village is topped by a fine catholic **church** from the 15th c. and thoroughly renewed in 1715, whose size tells of the prominence of the village at the time. In contrast to the unassuming exterior, its interior is much more baroque with the main altar made of colorful marble from 1720 which previously stood at the Gospa od Škrpjela church (*see p. 72*). Its painting of the Nativity, to which the church is dedicated, is a work of Angelo Trevisani, a Venetian artist from the early 18th c. The rest of the village is partially covered in lush vegetation. High above the village, at the top of a hill overlooking the Verige straits stands the small church of St Vid, built at the beginning of the 14th c. It enjoys views of Tivat and its bay on one side and Mt Lovćen on the other. To reach it take the road above the large church and then a path to its left before the last houses in the village. If walking in nice weather be very cautious of snakes. The road climbing from Gornja Lastva will take you to the top of **Vrmac**, past its highest peak Sveti Ilija (785m) and then along the ridge of the mountain and down to the Kotor-Budva highway.

Back on the main road, which now follows the coastline closely, one reaches **Lepetane** from where the ferry crosses in a short ride to the other coast of the gulf, to Kamenari village. Lined along the seaside, Lepetane was always

To the south of Tivat lies a group of three islands tailing one another. Closest to the land, and actually for centuries joined with it by a small dyke, is **Prevlaka**, also known by its tourist name Ostrvo cvijeća ("Island of Flowers"). To reach it get off the highway to Budva, past the gas station before the airport and then follow it to the end. This small island (200 by 300m) with nice gravel beaches had a huge historical importance since the 9th c. when the Benedictine abbey dedicated to St Michael was built here. In 1219 the monastery became eastern-orthodox

Lepetane, a village at the Verige Straits

famous for its seafarers. In the village there is a small catholic church of St Anthony with an 18th c. painting of the Tiepolo school on its main altar. Behind Lepetane are the famous Verige straits (*see p. 68*).

and the seat of the bishop of Zeta was located on it. When in 1420 the island fell to the hands of Venetians the monastery had a difficult time and was barely tolerated by the catholic prelates. Soon afterwar the monks supported the rebellion by peasants of Grbalj against their masters in Kotor; the Venetians responded by poisoning the entire fraternity and razing the monastery to the ground. Today, the island looks seemingly unburdened by its legacy given that at the beginning of the 1980s it was turned into a holiday resort for the Yugoslav army, with dozens of small cottages dispersed in greenery and flowers which served as the island's trademark. The flowers are still here but the gayety of the resort is gone since for over a decade the island houses no tourists but is home to Serb refugees from Croatia and Bosnia. The remains of the famous monastery are located at the far end of the island. The work to restore it is on its way but for the time being one can only observe the foundations of this 21m long three-nave basilica. Facing the ruins stands a small church built in 1833 by Countess Katarina Vlastelino-vić from Herceg Novi, who sold her property to buy the island and donate it to the Orthodox Church.

The islet of Otok with its Franciscan monastery

Second in line is an island that is known by many different names but today mostly referred to as **Sveti Marko** (St Mark). The elongated island covered in thick wood was purchased in the 1980s by the "Club Mediterraneo" and turned into an exclusive resort where its members spent their holidays in Polynesian-style wooden bungalows. Since the start of the war in Yugoslavia it saw no tourists but remains off limits to visitors.

The third one is known simply as **Otok** or *Island* and is home to a small Franciscan monastery. Originally dating from the 15th c, it was destroyed by a lightning in 1844 and restored in 1901 by Bishop Frano Učelini-Tice of Kotor. The island is off the tourist map.

Immediately to the south of Prevlaka is the **Soliosko polje** field that takes its name from salt flats (*solilo*) that used to operate here in the middle ages, making it an object of many aspirations. Abandoned long ago, the salt-works are now a marshy field washed by the sea, in which many bird species found their home and which has recently been promoted to a bird sanctuary.

'Island of Flowers', otherwise known as Prevlaka

❿ Luštica

Tivat -Rose 20 km

Luštica is a name of a fairly large peninsula lying between the Bay of Tivat and the open sea, connected with the mainland by the 1,5km wide isthmus. The whole of peninsula is dominated by its highest peak - Obostnik (586m) and is covered in thick Mediterranean copse and, in spite of its size, it has little fertile land. The coast of Luštica towards the bay is dull and almost straight in line, while the one facing the sea is set thickly with bays and coves of all sizes. On the peninsula there are two groups of small villages – Krtoli and Luštica. The six villages of Krtoli lie on and around the isthmus, where there is more arable land. Apart from crop growing, Krtoljani (as the inhabitants are called) were known to produce clay objects. Approaching Luštica by the only road from Tivat, after the airport one cannot fail to see the closed down brick factory which continued that tradition in the socialist period. The eight villages of Luštica lie on the peninsula itself and were known

for the abundance in olive groves and for its seamanship, giving many famous sea farers throughout the centuries. Today Luštica is known for several excellent beaches, certainly the best in Boka kotorska, some of which are very busy while the others are well hidden and less frequented.

Luštica basically has one road that circles around Mt Obostnik with several smaller

Church of St Luke on the hilltop of Gošići village

roads branching off to the villages and coves. Taking it will allow you to enjoy a well balanced combination of beaches, desolate shrub-covered scenery and small inland villages. If coming from the direction of Tivat

take the right turn after the airport, and then pass the Soliosko polje swamps (*see p. 99*). The road follows the coastline with many summerhouses and pensions and than forks the right branch goes to Krašići and Rose at the tip of Luštica, while the left leads to **Radovići**. The largest of the villages in the Krtoli group, Radovići has several well supplied shops which are open whole day (in contrast with those in most of the other villages) and makes a good starting point for the tour of the peninsula in a clockwis direction. Radovići has a fine **church of Sveta Gospodja** (from 1843) located on a rise close to the road on the right hand side. In the village of Gošići that has nowadays melded with Radovići is the church dedicated to **St Luke** (*crkva svetog Luke*), which stands on an impressive hilltop that can be seen from afar. To reach it, follow the sign and continue along the main road to the end in spite of all it

Detail of the old stone house on Luštica

Waters around Luštica are popular for a variety of water sports

curves. The present day orthodox church was built in 1776 on the place occupied in the middle ages by a Benedictine monastery and even earlier by an Illyrian stronghold. The church enjoys spectacular views of the vicinity and of both sides of the isthmus. At the exit of the village, a road splits to the left leading down to the **Pržno beach**. The beach lies in front of the "Plavi horizonti" Hotel and is well maintained. Pržno is a small cove in a large Trašte bay that has a fine sandy beach descending very gradually into the sea. Its fine sand is thought to cure rheumatism.

Back on the circular road, one embarks on a ride through the secluded south side of Luštica. Passing the small Mrdari and Begovići villages, from which there are several dirt roads descending to small coves facing the open sea and several locations attractive to divers, you reach the looking curve leading to Žanjica cove. The road slides down through delightful Mediterranean vegetation and then splits into two. To the right is **Žanjica**, a wide pebble beach

with several cafés and restaurants and a camping site. Due to its clear turquoise waters it is one of the favorite beaches of Boka and is visited often especially by boats arriving from Herceg Novi. The same boats continue their trip (*every half hour, €2*) to **Plava spilja**, a cave hardly reachable from the landside. This cavern filled with seawater is known for its spectacular blue colour (that gave it its name) and for the play of sunlight in its waters contrasting with the dark ceiling, creating an experience

that attracts many tourists to enjoy a swim here. The fee of €2 usually includes visit to the island of Mamula (*see below*). The left branch of the road leading to Žanjica takes you on the other side of the small cape to the **Mirište beach**, smaller and more intimate than Žanjica. The rocky coastline continues towards the open sea with several more bathing spots, past the small island with a recently restored 12th c. orthodox monastery surrounded by defensive

View of Žanjica and Mirište beaches

walls, to the **Fort of Arza**, at the very tip of dry land. Arza is one in the system of three forts built by the Austrians in the 1850s to guard

The cave of Plava spilja

The fortification of Arza

the entry to the Bay of Kotor. The second fort is situated on the top of Rt Oštro Cape, in present day Croatia, while the third occupies almost all of the small island of Mamula, lying between the two. Arza's massive 2m thick walls stand almost untouched by the passing of time but the interior is in a pitiful condition and is somewhat dangerous for visiting. The **Fort of Mamula**, beautifully isolated but still seemingly within an arm's length, changed the look and importance of the island so radically that it gave it its name. Earlier known as Lastavica, for the last one and a half centuries the island is known by the name of the man who supervised the fort construction, Austrian general and governor of Dalmatia Lazar Mamula, one of many Serbs from the Military Border in Croatia who faithfully served the Habsburg emperor. This strong fort of low silhouette and round base never saw any major fighting but was instead used as notorious prison during the First and the Second World War. The island, still abandoned by all but the seagulls, is covered in inhospitable low bush and plenty of agave but has a small rocky beach on its north side frequented by tourist boats on their way to Plava spilja.

Back on the circular road, one passes the hamlet of Zambelići, from which originates Luštica's most famous seafarer Petar Zambelić (1849-1903), explorer of the Strait of Magellan and Tierra del Fuego in South America. On a sharp curve behind this hamlet stands the orthodox church of the **Radovanići** village, certainly the most imposing in the whole of Luštica. This 19th c. edifice is nicely set on a gentle slope and encircled with tall cypresses. The scene is especially picturesque from the old stone well across the field to the west of the church. The road continues through aged olive groves to the village of **Mrkovi**, whose church of St Peter (to the left of the road), built in the year 1596, boasts a nice ensemble frescoes from the period but one can rarely find it open. After passing the Klinci village there is a crossroad where the main road continues

Mamula fortress on the island with the same name

The idyllic village of Rose

The circular road continues a bit further up, reaches its highest point and starts its lengthy descent offering grand panoramas of the Gulf on its left. It reaches the coastline in Krašići village that has grown into a large and well-visited tourist spot with several smaller beaches. Before reaching our starting point and the fork to Radovići, the road passes **Bjelila**, two scenic groups of old houses jutting into the sea.

...o the right while the ...adly marked left one ...eads to Rose in a long ...escent.

Rose (pronounced *...w-seh*), today not ...ore than a small ...ourist village, is ...ctually one of the ...ldest settlements ...n the Gulf of Kotor, ...ating back to the times ...f the ancient Greeks. ...he site was chosen ...or its small harbour ...ell protected from ...he south winds and ...till within easy reach ...f the open sea. In ...oman times a small ...own prospered here, ...urviving until 841 ...D when it was burnt ...own in one of the ...aracens' raids that ...pread terror in all of ...outh Adriatic. From ...en on Rose continued as a fishing village, gaining again some importance from the 18th c. onwards when it was an obligatory station for all ships sailing into Boka Kotorska to be left here for quarantine. In recent times its relative isolation, interrupted only by visitors' boats arriving from Herceg Novi, attracted relaxed, bohemian residents but this is changing quickly as a new hotel will soon grow next to it. Rose's charming harbour at the foot of a steep hillside has a couple of restaurants.

A scene from Bjelila

WHERE TO EAT ON LUŠTICA

Mirište
Mirište cove next to Žanjica; 067/515-485; open 09-01h
A smart restaurant spreading over several terraces overlooking the sea. The place dishes up excellent fish and seafood but also has a wide range of starters.

Dobreč
Dobreč cove; 069/331-554; open 08-24h
If you get the chance to visit this idyllic cove reachable only by boat don't miss its excellent restaurant. The atmosphere on its open terrace is relaxed and friendly. Restaurant's imaginative menu lists such items as "stone soup", tartuffe di mare, sea eggs and sea urchins. Open only from 20th April to 20th October.

Aragosta
Rose waterfront; open 09-24h
This is the best and the most frequented of several restaurants in Rose and has a lovely terrace just a few steps from the sea. It dishes fish specialties the traditional way and offers some local wines as well.

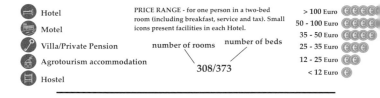

- Hotel
- Motel
- Villa/Private Pension
- Agrotourism accommodation
- Hostel

PRICE RANGE - for one person in a two-bed room (including breakfast, service and tax). Small icons present facilities in each Hotel.

number of rooms   number of beds

308/373

> 100 Euro
50 - 100 Euro
35 - 50 Euro
25 - 35 Euro
12 - 25 Euro
< 12 Euro

HERCEG NOVI: Vila Aleksandar ★★★★

16/35

- Save Kovačevića 64
- + 382 (0)31 345 806
- www.hotelvilaaleksandar.com

Though just bellow the old enwalled town of Herceg Novi and on the main town promenade this hotel is surrounded rich Mediterranean vegetation. It has its own restaurant with a large dining hall and a terrace with views across the bay; l music in the evenings. Furthermore, it has a small swimming pool and a large roof terrace ideal for sunbathing. All of rooms have a safe deposit box.

HERCEG NOVI: Plaža ★★★

286/625

- Herceg Novi
- + 382 (0)31 346 151
- www.hercegnovi.cc

This large glass-paneled hotel built in the 1980s has still not been fully reconstructed, with rooms in block „A" being co siderably better than the rest. Its main plus is its beautiful position right on the beach and near the Old Town.

HERCEG NOVI: Hunguest Hotel Sun Resort ★★★★

230/459

- Ul. Sveta Bubala bb
- + 382 (0)31 355 000
- www.hotelsunresort.hunguesthotels.com

Hotel resort of the Hungarian Hunguest chain in Herceg Novi features several buildings, amongst them the luxuric villa and bungalows but the majority of its beds are in the large hotel building. The hotel has a sizable swimming pool a a wellness centre whose use is included in the price of the room. The work on full renovation of the hotel is underway. T refurbished rooms are of high standard.

HERCEG NOVI: Kukoljac ★★★

24/100

- Njegoševa 111a
- + 382 (0)69 345 845
- www.montenegro.com

This large apartment complex is situated between Topla and Igalo, immediately by the sea and „Krušo" restaurant whi has a small private beach. Rooms facing the sea enjoy excellent views across the bay. Room furnishings are a bit older b solid.

HERCEG NOVI: Villa Galija

8/22

- Šetaliste pet Danica 76
- + 382 (0)31 345 731
- www.apartmanigalija.com

Located in Savina, a few minutes walk from Herceg Novi's Old Town, these apartments lie on the seaside promenade. The offer good rooms, a small private beach with crystal clear water just across the walkway and their own fine restaurant.

HERCEG NOVI: Pansion Savina ★★

21/55

- Šetaliste pet Danica 99
- + 382 (0)31 345 808
- www.pansionsavina.cg.yu

Located below the Savina Monastery, this private pension enjoys sea views and has its own concrete beach. The place h a modest appearance and simple furnishings.

HERCEG NOVI: Porobić ★★★★

12/36

- Braće Grakalića 36
- + 382 (0)31 345 333
- www.montenegro.com

This family run accommodation is located 50m from the sea and is a five minutes walk from Herceg Novi's Old Tow The apartments are spacious, well-equipped, tastefully arranged and cleaned every day. All of them enjoy grand views the Gulf.

Herceg Novi: Villa Palma ★ ★ ★ ★

- ✉ Šetalište pet Danica 62/A
- ☎ + 382 (0)31 345 952
- ⓦ www.montenegro.com

🔑 4/12

Set on the Herceg Novi's promenade close to the Old Town, this nice villa has its own tiny but pleasant beach and well fitted rooms with a sea view. In the basement a fine fish restaurant „Copas" can be enjoyed.

Herceg Novi: Planinska kuća Borići

- ✉ Vrbanj bb
- ☎ + 382 (0)67 805 117

🔑 6/15

This mountain hut lies some 20 minutes of driving uphill from Herceg Novi. At the foot of Mt Orjen, surrounded with pine woods, it offers a relaxed atmosphere and enjoyment of snow with vistas over the Herceg Novi's sunny bay.

Herceg Novi: Đaković ★ ★ ★ ★

- ✉ Braće Grakalića 53 a
- ☎ + 382 (0)31 346 400
- ⓦ www.montenegro.com

🔑 5/12

This pension is located some 80m from the sea in a quiet Savina quarter. The rooms are basically furnished but tidy and with views of the sea.

Herceg Novi: Laban ★ ★ ★ ★

- ✉ Braće Grakalića 77, Savina
- ☎ + 382 (0)31 348 008
- ⓦ www.laban.cg.yu

🔑 7/15

Nicely set and spacious these apartments enjoy views of the sea. It has a comfortable lobby and a very nice, privately owned beach.

Igalo: Centar Igalo ★ ★

- ✉ Sava Ilića 7
- ☎ + 382 (0)31 338 422
- ⓦ www.centar-igalo.com

🛏 262/558

This is one of the old hotels in Igalo and you will find its curious 1980s interiors almost fully preserved. The same retro look goes for its rooms but they are kept clean and tidy. It has its own medical center with various rehabilitation and spa programmes. The hotel beach is rather small and unappealing.

Igalo: Metalurg ★ ★

- ✉ Norveška 2
- ☎ + 382 (0)31 331 888

🛏 139/404

Although at first sight the hotel might seem unattractive with its tower building, lively adaptations to the details of its interior have removed most of its downsides. Each room features a terrace, most of them with a view of the sea.

The resort of Igalo with its several large hotels

IGALO: Mediteranski zdravstveni centar Igalo

Sava Ilića 5
+ 382 (0)31 658 555
www.igalospa.com

420/840

This is a large center for spa treatments which runs its own physiotherapy and nursing college and as such is the center of medical activities and healing in Igalo. Olympic size indoor pool, sauna, sports grounds and similar facilities are on offer, not to mention the famous mud application and other wellness treatments. Most of the rooms have large balconies facing the sea.

Hotel "RR" in Meljine

MELJINE: RR ★★

Braće Pedišića 4, Meljine
+ 382 (0)31 348 123
www.hotelrr.cg.yu

20/50

Adapted from a spacious stone building, this hotel's terrace and beach jut into the sea. Since this private beach is just a concrete strand you can opt for a long beach just next to it, the best Meljine can offer. The rooms are clean and have good furnishings.

KUMBOR: Xanadu ★★★★

Kumbor bb
+ 382 (0)31 684 666
xanadu-hotel@cg.yu

41/86

This new hotel is located at the Kumbor straits, some 5km from Herceg Novi. It's rooms are large but not too imaginative. It has a small gym and a sauna but its best features are its large terrace facing the sea and an open-air swimming pool.

ĐENOVIĆI: Milinović

Djenovići bb
+ 382 (0)67 301 658
www.montenegro.com

3/9

Just a few meters from the sea these nice 4-bedded apartments are very nicely furbished and comfortable, all with a tiny balcony towards the bay.

BAOŠIĆI: Max ★★★

Obala bb
+ 382 (0)31 674 063
www.hotelmaxhercegnovi.cg.yu

14/41

This unassuming hotel has simple rooms, two restaurants, both connected with its own well-kept beach. The hotel insists on safety with a supervised parking lot with a night watch, video supervision of the whole complex and a safe deposit at the reception.

ELA: Jadranska Straža ★ ★ ★ ★

✉ Bijela bb

☎ + 382 (0)31 671 408

🛏 420/840

his old villa lies in a beautiful green park close to the sea where it has its own beach. Intimate and quiet. The rooms are er small and with somewhat older furnishings but are tidy and clean. The income from this hotel is used to support the l „Mladost" orphanage.

ELA: Villa Azzurro ★ ★ ★

✉ Bijela bb

☎ + 382 (0)31 671 606

🛏 28/70

Ⓦ www.azzurro.co.yu

tuated on the very coast this hotel has basically equipped rooms. The guests have three private beaches at their disposal ther with chairs and parasols and a kids' slide. Hotel also organizes water skiing and banana riding, rents jet-skies and vides speed boat excursions around the Gulf of Kotor.

ELA: Delfin ★ ★

✉ Bijela bb

☎ + 382 (0)31 683 400

🛏 120/420

Ⓦ www.hotel-delfin.net

ecently refurbished, this hotel is a cornerstone of tourism in the resort of Bijela but this also means that it is often visited chools and sport clubs. It has its own small port, several large terraces with nice vistas, a fine restaurant and, most impor-ly, its own beach, probably the best in Bijela. Rooms are basically furnished.

Hotel "Delfin", Bijela

ELA: Regina

✉ Bijela bb

☎ + 382 (0)31 682 132

🛏 18/50

his pleasant newly built hotel has comfortable, modern rooms with nice balconies. Not far from the seafront but enjoying uiet setting. In the basement are a pizzeria, a bar and a small souvenir shop.

OSTANJICA: Vila Kostanjica ★ ★ ★

✉ Kostanjica bb

☎ + 382 (0)32 373 232

🛏 7/14

Ⓦ www.montenegro.com

 small hotel in a quiet corner of Boka Kotorska which blends well with the surroundings. It has modern, well appointed ms, a restaurant and its own beach.

Kostanjica: Vila Vujović ★ ★ ★ ★

Kostanjica bb

+ 382 (0)32 301 099

www.apartmani-montenegro.com

4/8

A fine new pension located on the very seafront. Elegant and well equipped rooms, all with a view. It has its own priva beach and a small swimming pool.

Perast: Vila Milinović

Obala kapetana Marka Martinovića bb

+ 382 (0)32 373 556

www.milinovic-perast.com

8/16

This pleasant hotel is located in an old stone house in central Perast. The rooms are large and clean and there is a goo restaurant on the premises.

Perast: Polcer

Perast bb

+ 382 (0)32 373 602

www.montenegro.com

8/30

This small pension is situated near the sea. Its large and tastefully furnished rooms all have balconies. It has its own ca park and water supply system

Orahovac: Amfora ★ ★ ★ ★

Orahovac bb

+ 382 (0)32 305 856

www.hotelamfora.cg.yu

12/42

This small hotel lies in a peaceful setting. Luxuriously furnished, it has its own small wellness centre and a restaurant ser ing international cuisine. Though plainly furnished the rooms are comfortable and well-appointed.

Kotor: Cattaro ★ ★ ★ ★

Stari grad 232

+ 382 (0)32 311 000

www.cattarohotel.com

20/43

VISA MasterCard

This smart hotel is situated in a historic edifice inside the enwalled Old Town of Kotor. Its good-sized rooms combin period details with all the modern amenities

Kotor: Sind ★ ★ ★

Muo bb

+ 382 (0)32 301 400

www.sindcentar.cg.yu

16/36

VISA MasterCard

This lovely small hotel is situated in Muo and faces the Old Town of Kotor. It has simply furnished, good-sized rooms wi all the necessary amenities as well as a conference hall.

Kotor: Marija ★ ★ ★

Stari grad, Kotor

+ 382 (0)32 325 062

17/40

VISA MasterCard

Located in a stone house characteristic of Kotor's Old Town, this hotel has small cozy rooms and friendly service.

Kotor: Palazzo Radomiri ★ ★ ★ ★

Dobrota bb

+ 382 (0)32 333 172

www.palazzoradomiri.com

10/15

VISA MasterCard

This luxurious small hotel occupies an old seaman's palace in Dobrota, several kilometers to the north of Kotor. Stylish decorated rooms reflect much of its past looks while providing everything a guest needs.

Kotor: Vardar ★ ★ ★ ★

Trg od oružja, Stari grad

+ 382 (0)32 325 084

www.hotelvardar.com

23/47

Recently refurbished, this luxurious hotel is situated at the heart of Kotor's Old Town. It's modern and attractively fu nished rooms are comfortable and well-apointed. The hotel also posseses a small meeting hall and a wellness centre.

Kotor: Villa Duomo

✉ Stari grad 385

☎ + 382 (0)32 323 111

🅦 www.villaduomo.com

 13/33

 VISA

Located in the Old Town centre, these luxurious apartments have hand-made period furniture, jacuzzis and hydro-massage baths en suite as well as all the other technical equipment necessary to ensure you a pleasant stay.

Kotor: Tianis – Tomčuk ★ ★ ★ ★

✉ Tabačina 569

☎ + 382 (0)32 302 178

🅦 www.montenegro.com

 4/12

Situated just outside the walls of the Old Town with views onto Kotor's impressive ramparts. The rooms are well furnished and brightly decorated.

Kotor: Villa Panonija ★ ★ ★

✉ Dobrota bb

☎ + 382 (0)32 334 893

🅦 www.vilapanonija.com

7/14

This pleasant small hotel is located to the north of the town centre. It has large and airy rooms with simple furnishings.

Kotor: Spasić Mašera

✉ Dobrota bb

☎ + 382 (0)32 330 254

🅦 www.hostelkotor.com

 125/230

 €

This, the only hostel in Kotor, is actually a students' hall of residence and is fully vacated only from late June to mid September. During the other seasons you might check out the availability but the prices are likely to be higher. The hostel restaurant offers lunches and dinners at attractive prices. Though rather far (2km) from the Old Town of Kotor, the hostel is very near the sea.

Kotor: Babilon ★ ★ ★

✉ Dobrota 232

☎ + 382 (0)32 333 375

 5/16

 VISA MasterCard Maestro

This pleasant pension fuses together the charm of the old days with the modern facilities of its apartments, each having a view of the sea. It also has a restaurant with outside seating surrounded by lush greenery.

Kotor: Bogdanović

✉ Dobrota

☎ + 382 (0)32 308 600

🅦 www.bogdanovicapartmani.com

6/20

These nice apartments are located about one kilometer north from the Old Town of Kotor in the quiet surroundings of Dobrota. They are well equipped and excellently appointed, caring for all the needs of their guests. The pension is particularly well suited to families with small children.

Kotor: Forza Lux ★ ★ ★

✉ Stari grad 483

☎ + 382 (0)67 376 508

6/12

Luxurious apartments located in a historic edifice of Kotor's Old Town. Stylishly furnished, well equipped and with lots of details reminiscent of the town's glorious past.

Prčanj: Splendido ★ ★ ★ ★

✉ Glavati bb

☎ + 382 (0)32 301700

🅦 www.splendido-hotel.com

43/103

VISA MasterCard Maestro

This fine hotel enjoys a lovely location in the middle of the Kotor bay, at the entrance to the historic townlet of Prčanj. Lying on the seafront, the hotel has an open-air swimming pool and a good Italian restaurant. The rooms are well furnished and have a warm feel about them.

Prčanj: Villa Prčanj ★ ★ ★

✉ Prčanj

☎ + 382 (0)32 373 232

🅦 www.montenegro.com

6/13

A small hotel in the centre of Prčanj, right on the waterfront. The rooms are smallish and very simply furnished but tidy.

Prčanj: Vrmac

✉ Markov rt
☎ + 382 (0)32 338 009
🌐 www.rehabilitacija.com

181/210

This hotel caters mostly for guests taking in its rehabilitation programmes and health spa. It is located at the entrance Prčanj, on one of the nicest beaches in the whole of the Gulf of Kotor. Apart from the rooms in the main building a simi number of rooms are in adjacent bungalows. The rooms are modest but clean.

Lepetane: Vučinovic

✉ Lepetane bb
☎ + 382 (0)32 686 042

3/9

A private pension hidden in the lush greenery of its garden, some 100m away from the beach. The rooms are nicely fitt and confortable.

Tivat: Plavi horizonti ★ ★

✉ Radovići bb
☎ + 382 (0)32 677 066
🌐 www.primorje.cg.yu

330/660

Set in a beautifull bay filled with greenery, in front of an excellent beach with fine sand. The rooms are nice and comfortab each with a terrace. The hotel restaurant has outdoor seating in the shade of pine trees as well as a beach bar.

Tivat: Aurora ★ ★ ★

✉ Kalimanj bb
☎ + 382 (0)32 671 651

44/75

An interesting hotel next to the Tivat's picturesque Kaliman marina. It has a marvelous garden with plenty of seating. T quality of the rooms varies, with some having outdated furnishings, but overall it is satisfying.

Tivat: Palma ★ ★ ★

✉ Pakovo bb
☎ + 382 (0)32 672 288
🌐 www.primorje.cg.yu

122/250

Located in the heart of Tivat, this fine hotel has well-equipped rooms, a conference hall and an excellent restaurant. Spec attention is paid to disabled guests who will find this hotel very welcoming.

Tivat: Mimoza ★ ★

✉ Moše Pijade bb
☎ + 382 (0)32 672 250
🌐 www.htpmimoza.com

72/166

A town hotel in central Tivat only 20m from the beach. The rooms are simply furnished but spotless while its restaura serves good meals. It also has a 100-seat conference hall.

Tivat: Vizantija ★ ★ ★

✉ Kaludjerovina
☎ + 382 (0)32 680 015
🌐 www.vizantija.com

12/26

The hotel is situated in quiet surroundings some 10km from Tivat. Its nicely furnished rooms enjoy stunning views ov the bay. It also has a small swimming pool and a fitness gym. Rich buffet breakfast.

Tivat: Villa Royal ★ ★ ★ ★

✉ Kalimanj bb
☎ + 382 (0)32 675 310
🌐 www.hotelvillaroyal.cg.yu

12/30

This pension lies on the main road from Tivat to Budva, just a few minutes stroll from the town centre. The rooms a spacious, well furnished and equipped.

Tivat: Pine ★ ★ ★

✉ Obala bb
☎ + 382 (0)32 671-305

26/66

Located on Tivat's town promenade, this medium-sized hotel is set in an modernized old stone building. The front roo enjoy nice views but get noisy on summer evenings. The hotel has its own restaurant, pastry-shop and cafe.

Tivat: Apart hotel Samardžić

✉ Obala Djuraševića

☎ + 382 (0)32 670 170

16/60

This small hotel offers luxuriously furnished appartments with all the ammenities, including a private beach.

Tivat: Kamelija ★ ★

✉ Donja Lastva bb

☎ + 382 (0)32 82 684 587

🌐 www.htpmimoza.com

162/446

This hotel is located in pleasantly green surroundings 1,5km north of the town centre, directly on the waterfront where it as its own private beach. It has several sports grounds, swimming pools and its own diving club. Room furnishings are a bit lder but in good condition and the place is kept very clean.

Tivat: Jovičić ★ ★

✉ Komat bb

☎ + 382 (0)32 671 060

4/8

A family-run pension of simple furnishings which is located 100m from the beach and about one kilometer from the entre of Tivat.

Tivat: Fazo ★ ★ ★

✉ Kalimanj bb

☎ + 382 (0)32 338 009

3/9

A small pension with basic facilities only 15m from the beach. Parasols and deck chairs are provided by the owners.

Tivat: Zornija ★ ★ ★

✉ Donja Lastva

☎ + 382 (0)32 684 572

5/14

The pension is situated at the seafront, conveniently close to the Opatovo beach and some 3km from the centre of Tivat. oom furnishings are very simple.

Rose: San

✉ Markov rt

☎ + 382 (0)69 367 951

16/70

These are actually bungalows set around the ruins of the old fort in the lovely fishing village of Rose. On the waterfront e hotel has a restaurant and a quay for smaller boats and yachts. The location is popular with the local divers who also offer eir services to the guests of the hotel. Open only from the beginning of May to the beginning of October.

e idyllic cove of Rose

THE LITTORAL

For all those who yearn for sun, ...a and beaches this is the part ... Montenegro to come to. From ...antamuni Point just north of ...udva to Bojana River, which forms ...e border with Albania, you will ...nd views across the open sea, ...ild climate, olive groves and all ...her things one associates with the ...editerranean.

Most of the Littoral (*Primorje*) is a ...arrow strip of land between the sea ...nd the steeply descending mountains ...ith just a few small plains, the largest ... which have now been taken by the ...ties of Budva and Bar. Other towns ...e pressed into the sea, with new ...otels, villas and apartments at their ...ck and old villages draped on the ...ountainsides above them. Once

The beauties of this area have drawn attention from people throughout the ages. The oldest cities – Budva and Ulcinj - were founded already by the Ancient Greeks as trading outposts with the inland tribes. Roman presence left a mark much deeper than the few ruins and mosaics remaining to this day: after the downfall of their Empire and the barbaric invasions the Roman population withdrew to the fortified maritime towns keeping their Latin language and close ties to Italy. During the course of centuries the population was slavicized and the Roman Catholicism gave way to Orthodox Christianity. The Latin and Catholic legacies have survived due to the rule of the Venetian Republic

The picturesque Praskvica Monastery set in the hills above the sea

...e rural part of the Littoral was as ...portant as the urban one, but today ...ost of its inhabitants have moved ... the urbanized coast. Furthermore, ...e towns of the Littoral receive a ...eady influx of people from all of ...ontenegro due to the good possibility ... finding work and a favorable ...mate. Recently the newcomers are ...ned by Russians, English, Irish and ...hers buying property and building ...eir homes here. All of these novelties ...d the orientation of the region ...wards tourism have drastically ...anged the regions appearance and ...e places untouched by commercial ...velopments are becoming more rare.

which ruled a lion's share of this region from the mid 15th c. The towns of Ulcinj and Bar were taken by the Turks in 1571 and changed their character completely, which is evident to this day, but Budva and its environs remained in the grasp of the Venetians. Montenegrins liberated Bar and Ulcinj in 1878 winning access to the sea for their small principality the, while the rest of the Littoral was joined with Montenegro in 1918 when Yugoslavia was formed.

The northernmost town in the region is Budva, the undisputed capital of Montenegrin tourism. On the elegant stone streets of its walled Old

...w of Sveti Stefan and the Budvan riviera

Town and in its refined restaurants one will find tourists throughout the year, but it is in high summer when the city is visited by the young, enjoying its beaches and nightlife that Budva becomes dreaded by many. The Budvan riviera around the town is a series of large and small beaches served by a multitude of hotels and apartments-to-let. The first one is Bečići with its long beach and many top-class hotels. Sveti Stefan is an old island village turned into an exclusive apartment-hotel and surrounded with some of the most beautiful beaches in east Adriatic. Close by is Petrovac, smaller and much calmer than Budva, but equally nice in terms of nature and tourist commodities. Further to the south is Bar, the largest city of the Littoral; surprisingly, it is not a tourist spot at all but a modern city centered around its large harbour and shipyard. However, nearby is its historical predecessor, Old Bar (*Stari Bar*), with its fascinating ruins of the medieval town amidst its strong walls. The strip of coast south of Bar equals in beauty the one of Budva but lacks the picturesque small towns and is cluttered by summer houses and auto camps. Ulcinj differs from the rest of the Littoral as the only town with ethnic Albanian majority and a strong oriental character. This is reflected both in its mosques and other monuments of the Ottoman era as well as in the general atmosphere of trading, small coffee houses and kebab restaurants. The scenery changes as well: the last hills are in Ulcinj and from here on opens a coastal plain with many villages still focused on agriculture. The coast forms into a single 13km long beach, deservedly called the Great Beach (*Velika plaža*). At its southern end lies Ada Bojana, an unusual natural feature – a river island at a confluence into the sea, which uses the best of both the sea and the river Bojana. Ada is a naturist-only resort but is also known for the excellent fish restaurants and peaceful apartments lining the banks of the river Bojana.

The Adriatic Highway (*Jadranska magistrala*) runs the full length of the region following along the coastline. Though it becomes quite hectic in the summer, the drive along it is an experience in itself with different views of the coast opening after every curve. Smaller roads branch off from it leading on one side to numerous coves and beaches, the smallest of which are impossible to see from th highway, and on the other to the monasteries and rarely visited villages imbued with peace of the olden times.

Dusk on the sands of Ada Bojana

Podgorica

Cetinje

Tuzi

Golubovci

Košmač

Virpazar

Crmnica

SKADARSKO LAKE

Bar

Shkoder

Dani Mrkojeviča

ADRIATIC SEA

Tirana

Ulcinjske solane

Ulcinj

1. Budva
2. Sveti Stefan
3. Praskvica Monastery
4. Reževići Monastery
5. Petrovac
6. Gradište Monastery
7. Sutomore
8. Bar
9. Ulcinj
10. Ada Bojana
11. Svač

BEACHES OF THE LITTORAL

Jaz entered history in May 2007 when the Rolling Stones held their concert on this beach, north of Budva. The best way to reach it is to take the highway towards Tivat and then,

A view of the beach of Jaz

after 2,5km from Budva, look for the sign for a left hand turn, which can be quite tricky with a lot of traffic around. The beach is sheltered from the surroundings by low hills and, for better or worse, still retains the atmosphere of unrefined spontaneity. The 800m long beach consists of large pebbles descending into the turquoise sea. A third of the beach to the east is reserved for nudists. There are several bars and a modest restaurant at Jaz; rooms for rent are also to be found here but the majority of its users come from the large caravan site behind

it, accommodating some two thousand people. If you continue behind the camp you will reach **Trsteno**, a deep inlet of dark blue sea with a 200m long sandy beach. Due to the bad road leading to it, this beach is a bit more secluded and quieter, though this rule does not apply to the high season.

A short walk along a narrow foot path from Budva's central hotel "Avala" takes you to the **Mogren** beach, a narrow strip of fine sand lying under precipitous rocks. Its two parts are joined by a tunnel cutting through the rock-face. This is a hotel beach and there is a charge to enter. Due to the steep descent, the bright blue sea quickly changes to deeper colours.

There are two small beaches right in the centre of Budva. **Brijeg od**

Budve lies underneath the walls of the Old Town, next to the square in front of the Land Gate. The hundred meter long pebble beach is almost always packed and is the location for many TV beach shows. The other one is **Pizanica**, no more than a bar of stone and sand sheltering the town marina, its main advantage being that it's less crowded.

The main place for enjoying the sea in Budva is the long **Slovenska plaža**, stretching 1600m from the town marina along the bay to Hotel "Park". The beach is lined with restaurants and serves as a promenade and the place where all the action takes place which, on the other hand, means lots of people and noise. Facing Slovenska plaža lies the isle **Sveti Nikola** with its own beach (*see p. 126*). Next in line is **Guvance**, a tiny, 80m long beach lying beneath the foot path leading to Bečići; well sheltered by thick vegetation it is one of the rare intimate places in Budva.

After passing the sand heaven of **Bečići** (*see p. 126*) one reaches

Beach volleyball at Bečići

Crystal blue waters at Kamenovo

Kamenovo (6km from Budva), easily accessible from the highway. This is a 330m long sand beach with crystal clear waters. Facing south, it enjoys sunshine almost all day long. 500 meters along the highway there is a turn towards **Pržno**. Once a small fishing village, today Pržno is dominated by the Hotel "Maestral" and dotted with villas and apartments, though some of the old olive groves still survive. The beach here is 260m long with sandy and rocky sections and is served by several restaurants and cafés. A short walk through the woods from its southern tip is **Kraljičina plaža** and behind it **Miločer** (see p. 129); both are

hotel beaches and therefore entry is charged. Bordering these two is **Sveti Stefan** (*see p. 128*) where one side of the sandbar leading to the island is a hotel beach while the other one is open to the public. Both are sandy and together are more than 700m long. Though quite busy, these two are never noisy or annoyingly overcrowded.

Not far away is the nudist camp **Crvena glavica** (9km from Budva) with seven beaches of different types and sizes but all with their backs to the reddish rocks and thick groves.

Next to it is **Drobni pijesak** in a well sheltered cove of idyllic appearance. The beach is 240m long and covered with yellowish-white sand. On the beach there is a spring of drinkable water and a small restaurant.

To reach **Perzića do** you will need to take a right turn just before the Reževići Monastery, followed by a steep descent and then another one on foot from the car park to the beach. The small sandy beach is sheltered on all sides by high cliffs and lush vegetation. The works in progress on hotel "As" will considerably widen the beach.

The town beach (*gradska plaža*) of **Petrovac** is located in a cove around which the town developed. 600m long and with fine reddish sand it is

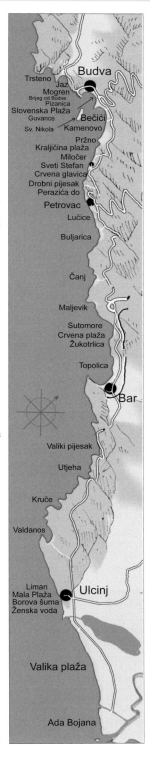

Feeling the sun all over at Crvena glavica nudist camp

Pebble beach in Bar

rather narrow and gets busy in high season but is otherwise clean and tidy.

The next inlet to the south of Petrovac is **Lučice**, 500m on foot from the town and its beach. Sheltered by a verdant hill on each side, it is 220m long with red sand. Several bars and cafés operate here during the season.

Buljarica (2km from Petrovac) is one of the largest beaches of the Montenegrin seaside (2400m). Until recently it was wild and with no infrastructure but this is changing fast and hotel development is expected here as well.

The 1800m long beach of the **Čanj** tourist resort is sometimes called Biserna obala ("Pearl Coast") for the pebbles in the water scattered on multi-coloured sand. An outcrop of hills divides it into two parts: the smaller side

called Kraljeva plaža is isolated and quiet. To the back of the larger side are several large hotels, cheap restaurants, sports grounds and a campsite. Though popular with families, it lacks varied entertain-ment for young

Perazića do is well known for its secluded beach

people. Chaotic parking near the central part of the beach and scattered rubbish ruin the whole effect.

Maljevik is a small strand of shingle with crystal clear waters in a lovely setting of

Mediterranean greenery. Until last year quite secluded, the whole of the locality has now been bought privately and construction of a smart tourist resort is expected.

Sutomore is a substantial tourist resort with hotels and apartments for rent to the back of its golden sand beach. On the other side of the small green hill to the south of Sutomore is an extension of this beach called Zlatna obala after the hotel of the same name. The place gets overloaded on weekends when the residents of Podgorica arrive here by train in swathes.

The dark red colour of the sand gave **Crvena plaža** ("Red Beach") its name. Located just outside the city limits of Bar it is small but with clean water and lots of greenery and gets very popular especially with the younger crowds who enjoy the loud music from the beach bar.

At the northern outskirts of the town of Bar is **Žukotrlica**, a kilometer long shingle beach. Towards its southern end there are lots of smaller restaurants and cafés.

Topolica is the name of the beach in central town area of Bar. A part

Sunbathers at the Crvena plaža

it is pebbly while the ...ddle part is covered ...th shingle. Due to the ...oximity of the town ...rbour the water here is ... dubious quality.

Some 10km to the ...uth of Bar and a short ...le through olive and ...k groves you will ...ach the stony **Veliki** ...esak beach. It is 300m ...ng with very clear ...ter but isn't too well ...pt. Most of its visitors ...me from a nearby ...ttered settlement ...bre Vode.

Near by to the south ...Utjeha, lying directly ...neath the highway. ...rrounded with olive ...oves and two craggy ...pes it is covered in ...ge white pebbles. ...e sea is clear and its ...ltiness is diluted by ...derwater springs. To ...e back of Utjeha is a ...w of small groceries, ...ops and rather loud ...fés.

Kruče beach shares ...name with the ...uristy village above ...e highway. It is 600m ...ng with a surface ...mbined of shingle and ...bbles. The mud from ...e bottom has healing ...alities in the treatment ...rheumatism. The

place is also known for the visits by Roman Abramovich to a secluded villa owned by his brother.

The cove of **Valdanos** (5km from Ulcinj) is well sheltered from the winds and thus served to anchor ships. Until recently it was in the possession of the Yugoslav army whose bungalows and restaurant still dominate

Windsurfing at Velika plaža

the scenery. The shingled beach is 600m long and ends on both sides with rocks. To the back of it are vast olive groves with centuries old trees.

From the beaches of Ulcinj, the most obvious Mala plaža is

not recommended because of the crowds and dirt (*see p. 140*) but nearby, bellow the walls of the Old Town is the small **Liman** beach with fine sand. On the other side of Mala plaža is a series of stony capes, two of which – **Borova šuma** and **Ženska voda** – are adapted to suit the needs of bathers. At the south end of Ulcinj

is the beach of the hotel "Albatros" with a section for nudists.

The two most important beaches in the Ulcinj riviera are **Velika plaža** (*see p. 141*) and **Ada Bojana** (*see p. 142*).

An enchanting cove south of Ulcinj

❶ Budva

👥 11,100

ℹ️ Mediteranska 4, 033/402-814

🚌 Popa Jola Zeca, 033/456-000

🎭 Grad teatar, mid July to mid August

With its excellent sandy beaches, multitude of hotels and a scenic walled old town Budva, including the surrounding area, is the single most important summer resort in Montenegro. The old town lies at the cape of Budva's spacious bay, while the rest of the flat terrain around it is quickly being filled with houses and apartments gaining ground each year. During the beginning and at the end of the season Budva is very pleasant if you don't mind the prices which remain high all year long. From mid June the crowds arrive and in high season Budva is not to everyone's liking, with its traffic jams, lack of parking, noisy nightclubs and almost inevitable water shortages.

Budva is one of the oldest settlements on the Adriatic. The legend holds that it was founded by the Theban king Cadmus, (*see inlay*) while the written sources tell us about the Greek colony *Buthoa* already in 4th c. BC. The town existed quietly throughout the Roman era but was plundered in 841 by the Saracens. It recovered as the Romans embraced the Slavic and Avar populations who settled locally and gradually mixed with them. In the period of Nemanjić Serbia it was a sizable merchant town, but lingered far behind the importance and wealth of Kotor. The town acquired a statute (whose text is preserved) that regulated its autonomy and all the important communal questions

Budva's coat-of-arms

as well. For the house of Balšić it served as the main port both for trade and for sending ships to war with the other nobles. After changing masters several times, Budva decided to accede to Venice in 1443. Bit by bit, the Turks closed in on its walls leaving Budva cut off from its surroundings and dependent on Venetian help. However, Venice proved to be too far away when in 1571 Turkish pirates from Ulcinj captured and burnt down the town. It was wrestled back the following year but took a long time to recover to its former condition. The town was damaged by an

CADMUS AND THE ILLYRIANS

Cadmus was a son of the Phoenician king Agenor. When Zeus kidnapped his daughter Europa, Agenor sent his sons to find her. During his search Cadmus came to the Delphi oracle where he was advised to give up and instead establish a town at the place where a cow with a half moon on both sides of her thighs lies down exhausted. Cadmus did so and founded Thebes on that spot. After he killed the serpent guarding the nearby spring he sawed off its teeth from which sprang armed men who started killing each other until only five remained, from which descended the noble families of Thebes. However, the dragon was sacred to Ares and Cadmus had to return the favor by serving the Olympian gods for eight years. After finishing this he was given Harmonia (daughter of Ares and Aphrodite) as a wife. Hephaestus was enraged since Harmonia, the daughter of his wife and her lover, received so much attention from the other gods. He therefore presented her with a necklace which brought many misfortunes to Cadmus and his family in future years. In the end Cadmus decided to leave Thebes for Illyria, a barbaric land to the north of Greece. Seated on an oxcart Cadmus and Harmonia reached the tribe of

Enheleans who, as advised by Dionysus, chose them for their rulers. Under their leadership the Enheleans overcame other Illyrian tribes and Cadmus became their king and also founded several towns, amongst them Buthoa, modern-day Budva (supposedly named after the oxen – *bous* in old Greek - that brought them there). Reflecting on his life, Cadmus one day lamented that if the gods were so vengeful of him killing a serpent, he would like to become one himself. This wish was granted to him and he was turned into a black snake with blue spots. Harmonia decided to follow her husband and in their honor Illyrians built a temple where snakes were worshiped.

A view of Budva from the early 19th century

...rthquake that rocked ...e southern Adriatic ... 1667. With the fall of ...e Venetian Republic ... 1797 Budva began a ...rbulent period in its ...story. The aristocrats ...ted for the Habsburgs ...d the citizens and ...e peasants for ...ontenegro; the latter ...rty prevailed and ...etropolitan Petar I ...ministered ...for several ...onths until the ...ustrian army ...rived. After ...eir defeat at ...usterlitz, the ...ustrians ceded ...dva and ...her towns of ...ka Kotorska ... joint forces ...ade up of the ...ontenegrins ...d the Russian ...driatic fleet. ...e French ...tempts to ...pture the town ...ere fought off and ...e joint government ...otracted until Tilsit ...ace was signed ... 1807. The French ...ministration was ...athed for its clashes ...th the neighboring ...ans who rebelled ...ainst its attempts ... conscription, and ...e liberation in 1813 ...v the Montenegrins ...as met with relief. ... 1814 Budva became ...part of Austria. The ...ustrian attempts to ...obilize men for its

army was met with two insurrections, in 1869 and 1882. In 1915, during World War One, Budva was briefly liberated by the Montenegrins during which period many people joined the Montenegrin army. These volunteers returned victoriously in 1918 leading the Serbian army and unifying their town into the new state of Yugoslavia. Tourism flourished already in the 1930s when the first modern hotels were built. In 1979 a strong earthquake reduced Budva to rubble. The recovery of the walled town took many years but when it was finally finished Budva shone like never before.

The hub of Budva is its **Old Town** (*see p. 122*) which became

too small for its population only in the second half of the 20th c. The reconstruction following the 1979 earthquake purged it from several newer buildings and brought back fully its medieval character with narrow zigzag streets and tiny squares. This is also the main shopping district in the town with many small boutiques, jewelers and souvenir shops, but it is also home to many fine restaurants and cafés.

Budva's Old Town from the pathway to Miločer beach

1. Old Town Walls

The Old Town is enclosed by sturdy town walls that stand in the place of the medieval ones but date mostly from the renewal following the 1667 earthquake. The entrance to it is gained through six gates: the main Land Gate from the spacious square facing north, the small Sea Gate towards the small beach and four others from the direction

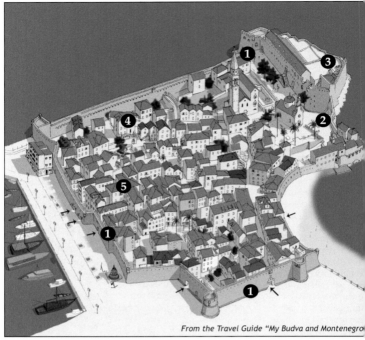

From the Travel Guide "My Budva and Montenegro"

1 Old Town Walls

2 The Square Between the Churches

3 The Citadel

4 Municipal Museum

5 Stefan Mitrov Ljubiša Memorial Home

of the yachting marina. It is possible to climb up the walls in three places and walk along the ramparts from the Land Gate to the Citadel. Above the **Land Gate** stands the winged lion of St Mark, the symbol of the Venetian Republic. Further up is a tablet commemorating the liberation of Budva in 1918 by the Serbian army, led by many volunteers from Budva. From the Land Gate starts **Njegoševa St.**, the main street of the Old Town, which leads to the Trg pjesnika (Poets' Square) with an info point and the tiny Sea Gate to its right.

2. The Square Between the Churches

Two small snaking lanes connect the end of Njegoševa St. with Trg izmedju crkava, a square with many street cafés and the four churches of Budva. Leaning on the walls to your right is the **Santa Maria in Punta** ("Saint Mary in the Cape") named after its prominent location. It was built in the year 840 for a Benedictine monastery but was later taken

over by the Franciscans who used it until the abolishment of their order by the French in 1807 when it was converted into an armory. Next to it is even smaller (only 5 by 3m!) **church of St Sabbas of Jerusalem** (*Sveti Sava Jerusalimski*, not to be mistaken with St Sava Serbian). It was

A narrow alleyway in the Old To

...ilt in 1141
...d used by
...e Orthodox
... to the 16th
...when they
...ere forced to
...are it with the
...anciscans. In
...e middle of the
...uare stands
...e beautiful
**...urch of Holy
...inity** (*Crkva
...etog Trojstva*)
...ilt with
...terchanging
...ws of red
...d white
...ck modelled
...er the one in
...e Podmaine
...onastery (*see
...124*). It was
...ected in 1804
... which time
...e Orthodox
...pulation
...came a
...ajority and used
...e fall of Venice to
...in religious equality
...th state-sponsored
...atholicism. Inside it
...a splendidly gilded
...onostasis from 1864
...inted by Nicholaos
...piotis from the
...eek island of Corfu.
...front of the church
...the modest grave
... Stjepan Mitrov
...ubiša (*see below*).
...e church with the
...l belfry is **St John's**
...*rkva Svetog Ivana*),
...til 1828 the seat of
...e Catholic bishopric
...hile today it is
...ly a parish church.
...unded in the 7th c. it
...re witness to many
...anges, destructions
...d reconstructions
...til it got its present-
...y look in the 17th
...The belfry, one of
...dva's landmarks,
...s added in 1867
...hile the adjoining
...shop's residence was
...modelled in a neo-
...thic style in 1903.
...side this three-nave

Rooftops of the Old Town with a belfry of St John's

basilica several icons of Byzantine style are displayed, the most important amongst them stands in the marble altar and is called Santa Maria in Punta (brought from the church of that name after its closing), revered as the patroness of the town. Next to this church you can see the foundations of the oldest church in Budva, a large **basilica** from the early Middle Ages, built probably in the 5th c.

3. The Citadel

At the highest point in the Old Town rises the Citadel, sheltered on all sides by high walls. It stands in the place of the Hellenic acropolis. Its present-day looks date from the time of the Austrian adaptation in 1836. One enters the Citadel through its barracks (*entrance fee €1*). Its courtyard is adapted for the performances in the "Grad Teatar" Festival when the best theatrical plays from Montenegro and the region are performed on this stage. The ruins of the Church Santa Maria di Castello can also be found here, of which only one wall with medieval frescoes remains.

Roman flasks, Municipal museum

4. Municipal Museum

Muzej grada Budve; tel. 086/453-308; open in summer Tue-Fri 10-22, weekends 14-22, in winter 9-21 every day except Mondays; fee €2, children €1

The museum is situated in a stately stone edifice in south-eastern corner of the town. The ground floor is dedicated to temporary exhibitions, the first and second floor present the archeological findings from the era of the town's founding, the Roman and medieval period, while the exhibits on the last floor depict the life of town families and of peasants from the surrounding area. The most important of the exhibits are surely those from the Greek and Roman eras such as their jewelry, pottery, extraordinarily well preserved flasks of all types and a coin collection.

rose to the position of the head of the Dalmatian parliament, and became one of the most influential figures amongst both the Orthodox and the Catholics in Boka Kotorska and the rest of the littoral. He is even

later era about his life and work.

Next door to the Memorial Home (up the steps) is the Gallery of **Modern Art** (*Moderna galerija*) which houses temporary exhibitions of contemporary Montenegrin artists.

Small boats in the Budva marina

5. Stefan Mitrov Ljubiša Memorial Home

Spomen dom Stefan Mitrov Ljubiša; Cara Dušana 15; tel. 033/452-060; open 8-14 and 18-22, Saturdays 18-22; entrance free

Ljubiša (1824-1878) was a writer and a Serb patriot who

better known as a writer of stories dealing with subjects of local history and coloured strongly by local folklore and language. The exhibition in the house where he was born presents copies of archival documents on his life, original editions of his works as well as news articles and testimonies from the

6. Ancient Necropolis

During the digging of the foundations for "Avala", Budva's first hotel, in 1938 the workers came across a foundation of a Roman necropolis. Later excavations showed that it lay above the Illyrian-Greek one, while the oldest layer is a burial sight from the neolith. The best preserved tombstones found here and a large Roman mosaic can be seen in the green area between hotels "Avala" and "Mogren" facing the Land Gate.

At the beginning of Slovenska obala, a promenade parallel to the coast, stands the **bust of Stefan Mitrov Ljubiša**, a work of Slovenian sculptor Lojz Dolinar from 1935. After their defeat in Brajići above Budva in July of 1941, the Italian occupying forces first

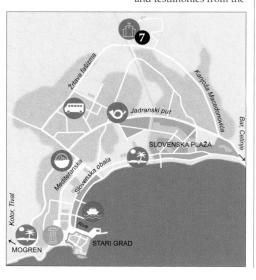

West portal of the Podmaine Monastery

the main character of Njegoš's "Mountain Wreath", spent here his last days; his body lay here until 1856 when it was carried to Cetinje and buried on Orlov krš (*see p. 188*). It was also one of the residences dearest to Njegoš who wrote here several of his books. The Austrians used it as a barracks and a prison.

Podmaine has two churches. The large one standing in the middle of its stone-paved courtyard was built in the mid 18th c. by metropolitans Sava and Vasilije. It is built in rows of white and reddish stone and has a large cupola with small windows. Its west face has a richly decorated portal while above it stands a nice rose window. The interior is decorated with new frescoe paintings. The older church is actually a small underground chapel beneath the monks dwellings and was constructed at the time of the monastery's renewal in 1630. Inside it one can see quite damaged frescoes from the period of its construction. On the other side of the dwellings is a large terrace with a view of the fields of Budva, built on the level

...remonially shot the bust ...d then pulled it down.

Podmaine Monastery

Until a decade ago ...is monastery stood ...lemnly on the slopes ...the first hills to ...e west of Budva ...t due to the ...pid expansion ...the town today ...s well inside ...limits. To reach ...is monastery by ...r it is best to take ...tava fašizma St. ...d (if coming from the ...est i.e. the Old Town) ...er crossing the bridge ...er the small Grdjevica ...ver to turn left at the ...st intersection; proceed ...lowing the wooden ...gns.

The monastery ...ternatively also called ...dostrog) and the ...rrounding area ...longing to Maine ...an were the spurt ...Montenegrin ...rritory closest ...Budva until ...37 when Njegoš, ...llowing many ...ars of pressure, ...ld it to the ...strians and ...us regulated the ...rder with the ...absburg Empire

which was then reestablished on top of the first mountains. It is not known who or when founded this

monastery but we know that it was renewed in 1630. Enjoying mild, Mediterranean climate it was popular with metropolitans of Cetinje, especially during winters. V*ladika* Danilo,

Sveti Nikola Isle in front of Budva

with the monastery's walls. On the west side there is a small tower and a stone well decorated with reliefs of a two headed eagle, a lion and a cherubim's head.

8. Sveti Nikola Isle

The isle, called after a church of St Nicholas standing on its west promontory, is a wedge like piece of rock closing the bay of Budva. The side facing land has several small coves but the ground then steeply rises to the highest peak of 120m above sea level, from where one can enjoy a panoramic view of the whole of the Budvan riviera. Practically the whole of the isle is covered in lush greenery known for many rare plant species, among them a unique kind of wild lily called *Lilium buthuense*. It is inhabited by doves and mouflons. The small St Nicholas church is first recorded on a drawing of Budva from the 16th c. but it is possible that it predates this portrayal. Until 1836 the graveyard of Budva lay here and many old gravestones can still be seen around it. The vicinity is much merrier: the lone dock

and restaurant "Hawaii" whose name is now synonymic with the whole island. The elongated beach in front of the church is attended by boats coming from Slovenska plaža and other parts of Budva (*ticket €2*).

The imposing walls of the Kosmač Fortress

ENVIRONS:

South of Budva and almost joined with it is the resort of **Bečići** known for its sea of fantastic blue colour and a long sandy beach that has been voted as one of the finest in the Mediterranean as far back as 1937. At the side closer to Budva is a group of hotels, led in grandeur by the recently renovated "Splendid". On the other side of the beach is the tourist **village of Rafailovići** with old stone houses adjoined by hotels

and several well-known restaurants. On the bea there are facilities for water sports and tennis courts.

After final demarcati with Montenegro in 1841, Austria decided to secure its maritime possessions with a seri

of fortifications. One of most impressive among these is **Kosmač**, locate in the village of Brajići (11km from Budva), on the highway towards Cetinje. The derelict for was built with large sto blocks with loopholes for cannons. Kosmač was attacked in the 186 insurrection by Brajići but was never taken. Th importance given to it c be seen from the fact th it was visited in 1875 by Emperor Franz Joseph.

Bečići with its numerous hotels

RESTAURANTS IN BUDVA AND VICINITY

Demižana
Slovenska obala 3; 033/455-028; open 12-24h
Friendly setting on the main promenade with its small terrace hidden in flowers and with a tastefully decorated interior. Seafood at its best, including such delicacies as crabs and octopus served by attentive waiters. Just a tad overpriced.

Aquarius
Zmajeva 6; 033/453-419; open 09-01h
This restaurant in a small hotel of the same name not far from the post office has a cozy interior and a few tables in the shades outside. It offers fresh fish and seafood as well as succulent cuts of meat, all washed up with a fine selection of wines.

Stari grad
Njegoševa 14, Old Town; 069/082-794; open 12-01h
Very centrally located, this restaurant actually has outdoor seating that spills out to the beach outside the town walls. It offers a fine range of seafood from cold (octopus salad, scampi cocktail) and hot starters (scampi, mussels) to main dishes, with a choice of a few steaks too. Live acoustic music.

O sole mio
Slovenska obala 15; 033/457-713; open 08-01h
Large restaurant on the main Budvan walkway with an interesting stylish décor of vivid colours, open on all sides except for the rear. The cuisine here is touristy-oriented with a mix of Italian, fish and some local specialties prepared in a modern style. Live music in the evenings.

Jadran – Kod Krsta
Slovenska obala 10; tel. 033/451-028; open 09-02h
This well known restaurant facing the town marina serves fresh fish, tasty grills and Italian specialties prepared in a distinctive manner. Its main feature is huge outdoor seating.

Galeb
Vrzdak
Old Town; 033/456-546; open 11-01h
Tucked in a quiet alley of Budva's Old Town, "Galeb" has a warm feel to its old interior and small garden under the vine to its rear. It serves a variety of fish and seafood dishes as well as standard grilled items.

Porto
Town Marina;. 069/331-424; open 09-01h
Right in the marina, with most of the seating outside. It offers a good range of tasty fish, seafood, grill and steaks. One of the best choices for grilled squids or fried crabs.

Hot Moon
Njegoševa 32, Old Town; 069/332-682; open 10-01h
A romantic terrace in the heart of the Old Town with dimmed lights and candles. It serves imaginative snacks (mostly Mexican or pastas) and salads to go with their fine cocktails.

Tri ribara
Rafailovići; tel. 069/267-467; open 08-24h
Seafood restaurant with a long tradition run by the three fishermen, brothers Rafailovići. The menu consists exclusively of fish freshly taken out of the sea and therefore varies according to what is caught. Relaxed, friendly atmosphere with only music being the waves.

Velji mlin
Radanovići; tel. 067/513-323; open 08-24h
10km north of Budva lies the village of Radanovići and this famous restaurant readapted from the old mill. The restaurant is widely known for its succulent lamb and veal *pod sačom* - baked in clay pots in hot ashes, a must try if here. For starters try their Grbaljski soft cheese with fennel along with the freshly baked bread.

❷ Sveti Stefan

5 km from Budva
👥 500

The panoramic view of Sveti Stefan is surely one of the most memorable sights along Montenegro's coast, photographed so many times that it is almost impossible to imagine a promotional brochure or video without

of the twelve families had a house while jointly they built a church dedicated to St Steven which gave the name to their settlement. The attack indeed came and was later repeated many times, but the island fort withstood them all, serving as a refuge for all the clan members during the worst of times. Gradually more houses were built in this

of the sailing ships. Wh in 1954 the number of inhabitants fell to just 21 it was decided to resettl them and turn the islan into an apartment hotel.

The coast facing the island boasts a fine sand beach, several small hotels and all the touris practicalities one might need. The only approac to the former island is b the isthmus, built in 190 in place of the seasonal sandbar. To enter the town-hotel and disturb the peace of its wealthy dwellers the entry fee is € and includes a coffee or juice on the terrace of its restaurant. Ju by the heavy town gate is small church dedicated to the Transfiguration fr

Sveti Stefan, a playground for the rich and famous

its enchanting look. This miniature island is dotted with stone houses and joined with the mainland by a narrow sand isthmus which the sea currents have built during the ages. It is an exclusive tourist resort visited by rich and famous with each house serving as a separate luxurious apartment.

The history of Sveti Stefan goes back to 15th c. when Paštrovići clan helped the besieged Kotor by attacking the Turks from their rear. Returning from this victory, Paštrovići learned that the Turkish fleet is harboured near Budva. The surprise attack was a success and great booty was obtained from the sunken ships. Expecting the Turkish reprisal, they decided to use the loot to build a fort on this craggy island. On the island each

stronghold by Paštrovići merchants and by those who turned to attacking the Turkish ships and the small town soon became an unofficial capital of the clan. At the beginning of the 19th c. the "smallest town in the Adriatic" grew to 400 inhabitants but shortly afterwards it started to decay due to the demise

1693 with the remains of the frescoes from that period. The narrow crooked lanes lead to the highest spot on the island which is crowned by two churches, both dedicated to St Steven. The smaller church was founded with the town in the 15th c. while the larger dates from 1885. The larger later served a

---

WHERE TO EAT IN SVETI STEFAN

Famelja Kentera
Slobode 24; 069/231-922; open 08-03h
A picturesque little place facing the Sveti Stefan isle, large terraces with unbeatable views of this resort. Fresh seafood and Italian dishes a la card as well as inexpensive "tourist menus".

Langust
Pržno, Obala 34 (next to Hotel "Maestral"); 033/468-369; open 11-24h
A beachfront restaurant in Pržno, 20 minutes on foot from Sveti Stefan, serving fish and seafood at prices slightly above average. In summers one can enjoy food on one of their three terraces nex to the beach and in winter in a closed one with views of the sea.

More
Pržno, Obala 18; 033/468-255; open 12-23h
This old tavern on the beach of Pržno offers a fair selection of delicious seafood specialties. The authentic interior has an especially warm feel to it.

PAŠTROVIĆS AND THEIR BANKADA

The Paštrović clan is the largest and the most important one on the Montenegrin coastline. Also it is very old, being first mentioned in 1355 when some Paštrovićs were noblemen in service of Serbian Emperor Dušan. From the beginning of the 15th c. we have records of the 12 families of Paštrovići united into one clan. In 1422 they decided to accept Venetian supremacy and to wage war for her between Kotor and Shkoder but on conditions that the Republic should guarantee their trading rights and a wide autonomy in dealing amongst themselves. This meant above all that the Paštrovićs settled the conflicts between their clansmen in their own court called "zbor" ("gathering"), "bankada" (from Italian *banco* – "table") or "the Place of Justice". In dealing with civic disputes the court used the Code of Emperor Dušan and common law while in deciding on questions of common interest for the clan every man had a right to speak out. The Bankada was made up of four judges and 12 "nobles" who were elected for a one year term on Vidovdan (28th of June), a very important Serb holiday. The court's patron saint is St Stevan Štiljanović, a late 15th c. duke of the Paštrovići, who had to flee from Venetians to Hungary where he became a Serb despotes (leader of the nation). The Bankada initially convened at the Drobni pijesak beach but later also in Sveti Stefan and in the Praskvica monastery. Although the Paštrovići were stripped off their rights, first by the French and later by the Austrians, the Bankada traditionally continued to meet for another whole century, until 1926. It was renewed in 1999 and nowadays again resides on Vidovdan in Drobni pijesak. Today the Bankada's main concerns are preserving the old traditions, religious festivities, economic development of the Paštrović area (from Budva to Sutomore) and protection of historical monuments.

...d yet its courtyard ...th lots of flowers and ...drinking well seems ...world away from the ...ustle and bustle of the ...aches. The monastery

Davidović, as stated on the inscription above the entrance. Its interior is entirely covered in wall-paintings, work of the famous priest Strahinja

were given in contrast to his saintly life.

The third church, dedicated to the **Dormition of the Virgin**, stands on a mound with a small cemetery. Very small (6 by 4m) and without any outer décor, it is typical for the old village churches of the coastland. The interior was painted by priest Strahinja on the same occasion when he worked on the church of St Nicholas. Strahinja seemed to prefer smaller, intimate spaces since he made a better disposition of scenes and characters here, producing a harmonious whole ranked as his best work. Among the ecclesiastical themes we encounter once more the busts of the Nemanjić rulers.

A view into the complex of Gradište monstery

...mplex consists of ...ree churches. The one ...osest to the entrance, ...dicated to **St Sava**, ...the youngest; it was ...ilt in 1863 on the spot ...an older temple from ...e 15th c, but with its ...erchanging rows of ...d and white stone fits ...perfectly with the ...ole. Inside there is an ...teresting iconostasis ...ade by Greek painter ...cholaos Aspiotis. ...The unusually ...entated Church ...St Nicholas was ...ilt around 1618 by ...oniosije and Stevan

of Budimlje and the painter Jovan in 1620. The frescoes represent episodes from the Old and New Testaments, the Dormition of the Virgin, the Nemanjić rulers and the large bust of St Nicholas. The fine iconostasis was carved and painted by Vasilije Rafailović of Risan in 1796. On one of the icons you will notice a dog-headed saint, which was actually a usual depiction of St Christopher in Eastern Orthodox iconography, where his beastly looks

The dog-headed St Christopher

⑥ Sutomore

📖 1,850

ℹ️ 030/373-257

🚌 030/72-128

If you turn to the left after coming out of the Sozina tunnel the first place you will come across is Sutomore. This favorable connection with the hinterland makes it a preferred one-day excursion spot for people from Podgorica, for whom it is only a 45min train ride or even less by car. Its train connection also makes it very popular

Sutomore's long gravel beach

with people from Serbia and elsewhere from Montenegro. Sutomore has a 1,250m long sandy beach, several hotels and numerous houses that offer rooms for rent. The pleasant scenery is highlighted by the sides of Mt Sozina (805m) towering steeply behind it.

The area surrounding Sutomore, known as Spič, was once characterized by small country churches used by both Orthodox and Catholics. The Orthodox formed a large majority but during the Venetian and later Austrian domination no matter how few Catholics lived in a village the service had to be held regularly, and therefore many

village churches were shared by these two confessions. The only remaining example of this phenomenon is **St Tekla**, to the east of Sutomore. This modest edifice in the middle of the local cemetery was built in the 13th c. Inside the church, on the left hand side is a small iconostasis for the Orthodox and on the right the altar for the Catholics.

ENVIRONS:

On Ratac, the first promontory to the south of Sutomore, stand the ruins of the Benedictine abbey known as **Bogorodica Ratačka** ("Our Lady of Ratac"). The monastery was founded at the beginning of the 11th c. by Italian Benedictines who originally dedicated it to St Michael. It soon became one of the most important sacral sites of Duklja and was often visited by its rulers, but more importantly it was also a prominent place of pilgrimage. Its already large estates were further expanded in the 13th c. by the Serbian queen Jelena and from then

onwards the monastery held control of most of Spič and a good part of Paštrovići as well. The illustrious abbey met its end in 1553 when the Turks sacked it; the imposing edifice was la to ruins in the fighting betweens Venetians and Turks in 1571. The last destruction came in WWII when a part of it was adapted for Italian bunkers. Today, its extensive ruins testif to its former grandeur. The most notable amon the ruins are those of th main church, 27m long, with its walls in rows o red and white stone and three apses.

The ruins of **fortress Haj Nehaj** stand on a lone and inaccessible hi (225m above sea level) the north of Sutomore. To get to it, take the roa for Zagradje village; the hill and the fortress are your right and, as the p ascending from the roa is not marked, you shou ask the locals for directi on rely on your own estimate. The steep clim passes through a forest and ends up in front of the gate of Haj Nehaj. T impressive stronghold was built by Venetians mid 16th c. as the main defensive point for Spič The most interesting among many objects in ruins here is the Church of St Demetrios standin on the highest point of the fort. It predates the fort for several centurie and was in Venetian da readapted for use of bo the Catholics and the Orthodox.

WHERE TO EAT IN SUTOMORE

Izvor
Obala Iva Novakovića bb; 030/373-821; open 07-24h
By far the best of several establishments on the seafront of Sutomore, this simply decorated restaurant offers fish and seafood, grills and the usual range of national cuisine specialties that com plentifully and at good prices. Open all year long. In summers you can choose between the beachside seating or the first-floor terrace with a view of the sea.

⑦ Bar

🔢 13,900

ℹ️ Obala 13. jula bb, 030/312-912

🚌 030/346-141

🚉 030/301-615

🎪 Barski ljetopis, July-August

Bar was founded in 1878 when the Montenegrins acquired this region in a war which devastated the town of Old Bar (*see below*). Its original name was Pristan ("Anchorage") as it was Montenegro's first harbour. It developed rapidly after WWII when it got a new modern harbour which was in 1976 connected with the Bar-Belgrade railway, to which gravitated all of Montenegro and all of Serbia. Bar is also the only maritime town in Montenegro with a regular ferry line connecting it to Bari in Italy (*see p. 267*). Today, the town serves as an important traffic centre, second only to Podgorica and there is barely anything touristy about it as it consists most exclusively of socialist era apartment blocks.

North from the harbor lies the pleasant **Topolica Park** and on its edge, facing the sea and the promenade is the **Palace of King Nikola**. This nice villa was built in 1885 and is adjoined by a chapel and a winter garden. The palace houses a **local museum** (*tel. 030/313-810, open 8-14 & 18-22, entrance €1*) presenting numerous

A scene from the port of Bar

archeological findings, the vivid traditional dresses of Orthodox, Muslims and Catholics from the local area and a section devoted to the narrow gauge railway Bar-Virpazar, the oldest in Montenegro (1908). Around the palace are planted many exotic trees and shrubs, gifts to

King Nikola from around the world. In front of the palace is a long beach, the only one in the town itself, but the proximity of the harbour makes you wonder whether the water is clean.

In a small green spot close to the corner of the main street – Jovana Tomaševića – and Branka Ćalovića St. are the excavated foundations of a large **trefoil church**, in fact the first cathedral of Bar. It was built in the 6th c. by an unknown bishop whose grave can be seen in the northern leaf of the cathedral.

As a town of considerable size, Bar is a good place to stock up on supplies and the best place to do so is its **green market** (*pijaca*), probably the most picturesque one in Montenegro. This comes not only from the variety of fresh Mediterranean products on sale but also from the boisterous vendors and elderly ladies often adorned with details from the local folk dress.

The palace of King Nikola, today the local museum

A view of Stari Bar, with a backdrop of Mt Rumija

ENVIRONS:

The most important tourist sight in Bar is its predecessor, **Stari (Old) Bar.** It is located to the southeast of the town, on the first slopes of the imposing Mt Rumija. The old, walled part is a ghost town turned into an open air museum. Underneath it huddles the inhabited part immersed in oriental legacy.

The hill occupied by the walled town was settled in prehistoric and Illyrian times but was abandoned during the Roman era when it was moved to the coast, to the same location where modern Bar stands today. With the Avar and Slavic invasions in the 6th c. the Roman population left the shore for the safety of this hill which they encircled with walls. As the situation settled Bar became the most important centre of Duklja, often visited by its princes and kings. In 1089 it became the seat of the archbishopric, which still exists to this day. Its name comes from Latin *Antibarium* – "Facing Bari", the town in

southern Italy to which it was closely connected by religious affairs and trade. The town reached its heyday during the rule of Nemanjićs when it doubled in size and population. Later on it

Fragments of Bar's history in the monument to Prince Nikola

was squabbled over by several feudal lords until in 1443 the townspeople decided to take on the protection of the Vene-

tian Republic. The protection worked well for more than a century during which Bar became a isolated commune, encircled from all sides by Ottoman possessions. Veneti rule ended in 1571 when Bar fell to the Turks. Soon, the churches were turned into mosqu and the remaining population became Muslim. Three hundred years later the town was besieged and taken by Montenegrins in 1878, after which it gradually lost its importance to its coastal namesake. Careless stocking of gunpowder by the Montenegrin army led to two large explosions (1881 & 1912 which destroyed many of the old monuments. After additional damag inflicted by the 1979 earthquake the enwalle town is gradually being repaired and renovated

To reach Stari Bar follow the sign from the road to Ulcinj, take the first left and then the fir right. The steep road wi lead you to a spacious parking lot in front of th captivating ruins. Next to the parking lot is an unusual **monument** to the "knightly liberator" prince Nikola, assemble in 1881 from an array of

The high street of Stari Bar

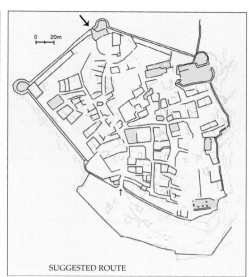

SUGGESTED ROUTE

interesting fragments found in Stari Bar – Roman, medieval and Venetian inscriptions, coats-of-arms of local families, columns and capitals, all crowned with a gun shell. The main street begins with a small green market followed by several shops and kebab grills. The street continues steeply uphill and follows the line of the town walls whose slanting appearance dates back to the 16th c. Venetian renovation when they were adapted for defense against cannons. Entry to the inside of the walls is gained through an imposing gate near the upper tower. This spacious gate was, until the Venetian renovation, a church standing by the town walls; today it contains a relief of St Mark's lion and a huge olive press. Facing the entrance there stands the Omerbašića Mosque, a small structure from 1662. The domed structure next to it is the tomb of Dervish Hassan. In front of the whole complex stands a dry drinking well displaying

an Arab inscription. To explore the town further you will need to purchase a ticket (€1). The first building to the left of the ticket office is a 15th c. **customs office** turned into a small museum with archeological material and photos of Stari Bar from before and after the earthquake. Further uphill you will reach the **Tatarovica citadel**, whose oldest layers date back to the 10th c., but which has

been continually rebuilt all the way to the 19th c. and was even used by the Italians in WWII as a prison. From its walls you can observe the Turkish **aqueduct** and the old road following the stream Rena deeper inland. In front of the citadel gate stand several surviving walls of the Church of St Francis and on one of them there are 14th c. **frescoes** of two saints. To the left of the citadel you pass the **old**

Omerbašića Mosque with its dry well

Some of the surviving edifices inside the walls of Stari Bar

town gate: the part remaining behind you is a 13th-14th c. enlargement while you now enter the original town core. On what used to be a small town square stands a modest church and a two-storied **bishop's palace**, a late gothic edifice renovated to its original appearance. Behind it is the 14th c. **Church of St Veneranda**. The path leads you to the southern plateau where the cathedral dedicated to St George, the patron of the town, once stood. The main street descending downwards passes the former **Church of St Catherine** which used to stand on the vaults above the street. In the middle of the ruins of Stari Bar are the 17th c. Turkish baths. The Turkish **clock tower** (late 16th c.) is close to the place where the southern town gate used to be. By the western tower the 15th c. **Duke's Palace** (in ruins) and the unidentified church can be found.

The area around the town of Bar is an olive growing region and has been since time immemorial. A living monument to this useful tree and the craft of its cultivation is the **old olive tree** (*stara maslina*) in the suburb of Mirovica. It is estimated that it was planted around the time of Christ's birth, which makes it one of the oldest olive trees in the world. The remarkable thing is that although cracked and curved it still bears fruit. The tree has grown into one of the symbols of Bar and

The two millenia old olive tree in Mirovica near Bar

the area around it has been smartened up. To reach it from Stari Bar take the first turn left after the descent, continue straight along the road, cross the bridge and carry on for another several hundred meters.

8 Ulcinj

10,900

26. novembra bb, 030/412-595

26. novembra bb, 030/413-225

The southernmost town on the Montenegri coast has a distinguishin Oriental flavor and feel it, partly because of the long Ottoman presence here (till 1878) and more due to the fact that this is the only coastal town with a Muslim Albanian majority. This makes Albanian the first language here and most of the signs are (at best!) bilingual. In spite of the town's imposing history there aren't many old things to see here: the old ways of life and the old houses surrounded by gardens are quickly giving way to the new distasteful commercial apartments and shops that seem to sprout erratically without any planning.

WHERE TO EAT IN BAR

BB
IV proleterske brigade 34; 030/353-902; open 07-24h
Hidden in the green of its yard this restaurant dishes excellent se and lake fish, various shrimps and mussels, as well as abundant portions of grills. For starters take their *Zakuska BB* made up of dried ham, cheese, olives and salty sardines.

Samba
Jovana Tomaševića 41; 030/312-025; open 08-24h
A friendly restaurant offering tasteful grill and national dishes a good prices.

Ulcinj one of the oldest cities in the Adriatic: it was probably founded as a colony of the ancient Greeks from the town of Colhis (in present day Georgia). The Romans captured the town 167 BC. Destroyed in the barbarian onslaughts, the town was rebuilt by emperor Justinian in the location of the today's Old Town. In the middle ages it was a bishopric and an important trading centre, exporting wood and salt from the surrounding area. In the time of the Serbian Nemanjić dynasty it was often visited by heirs to the throne and queen mothers whose presence made it into a sort of unofficial capital. Later on it was an important stronghold of the Balšić family. In 1422 it came under Venetian "protection" which lasted until 1571 when it was conquered by the Ottomans. Soon afterwards, in 1580, the town was captured by Uluz-Ali, Algerian pirate and later viceroy of the province. His rule began a period of more than a century in which Ulcinj was the dreaded seat of pirates, who with their light vessels attacked not only Venetian or other Christian traders but also Turkish ships in the Adriatic. The local pirates were known far and wide, acquired

Arial view of Ulcinj's Old Town and its Mala plaža beach

vast wealth in valuables, especially from slave trading. It is speculated that the famed Spanish writer Cervantes was sold as a slave to Algerians in Ulcinj when he fell captive. The corsairs also kept good connections with other parts of the Ottoman Empire and especially with their "colleagues" from Africa. In this way, in Ulcinj also settled a number of black slave families and if you're lucky you might even see some of their mulatto descendants. This era was ended in 1737 after the Sultan banned corsairs in the Adriatic and destroyed their fleet. In 1878 the town was taken by Montenegrins

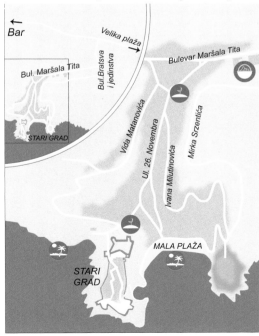

THE FALLEN MESSIAH

Sabetha Zwi (1626-1676) was the best known and most successful of the Jewish "messiahs" of the 17th and the 18th c. He was born in Smyrna and spent his youth in Jerusalem and Saloniki but later moved to Germany and Poland. This adventurer studied kabala and led an ascetic life preaching in poor Jewish communes and eventually pronouncing himself to be a messiah. He profited from the art of printing, sending his pamphlets across Europe, causing an unknown frenzy among many Jews. His prophecy marked the year 1648 as the Second Coming, but when this turned out to be incorrect he announced that the world will end in 1666. That year he hired a boat in Hamburg and with a group of followers set off for the Holy Land (Palestine). A part of his scheme was to be crowned the King of Jews by the Ottoman Sultan. However, the Ottomans seized him and convicted him as a false messiah. He and his men were offered to die or save their lives by accepting Islam. They opted for the latter forming a specific Muslim sect with many elements of Judaism. Under his new name Mohamed-effendi Zwi spent his last years in house arrest in Ulcinj, making the town the seat of his sect and famous in Jewish history.

becoming a valuable harbour for their previously land-locked state.

The city wraps around and climbs a hill standing in its midst; the centre is behind it, away from the sea while the area most visited by tourists is around the Mala plaža (Small Beach) and the adjoining Old Town. The **Small Beach** is a 360m long sandy cove between two promontories. Painfully full throughout the tourist season and not very clean, the beach is visited mostly by the locals. On its northern side rises the cliff on which stands the **Old Town**, a muddle of small streets framed by both old and new houses. The tall Venetian walls are its best preserved part and make a dramatic impression atop the high cliffs. There are two entrances inside its walls, one ascending from the cove and the other from the top of the hill. Close to the latter is the former Slaves' Square, where the unfortunate were sold to their masters. In it stands a pretty **drinking well** from 1749 with an Arabic inscription. Enclosed by a fence is the local **museum** (*tel. 085/421-419; open 9-13 and 17-23, closed on Mondays; entry fee €1*) which is housed by several buildings. Th[e] shapely medieval **churc[h]** was built in the early 13th c. and was converted into a mosque in 1693 as demonstrated by the ruins of the minaret found next to it. The archeological collection with the Greek red figu[re] vases, Venetian cutlery and Turkish jugs is displayed in the church[.] Of special interest are the 9th c. ciborium from Ulcinj, a sacrificial altar dedicated to Artemis Elafavolis, patroness of deer hunting (5th c. BC), and a cameo with a depiction of Athena. In the former Bishop's Palace (13th c.) is the ethnographical collectio[n]

Cloudless blue sky over the medieval corner of Ulcinj's Old Town

Minaret of Namzgah Mosque and the Clock Tower

church of St Nicholas, built in 1890 on the site of the medieval monastery and surrounded by a pleasant olive grove. Further down you will find **Pasha's Mosque** built in 1719 with Turkish baths next to it. At the top of the long 26. novembra Street stand the **Namzgah Mosque** (1828) and the 18th c. **Clock Tower**.

th varied costumes of cal ethnic groups. To e right of the entrance the building the **Venetian stoms fice** which is day used by e museum anagement; side it one n see the ale model the town. sing next the church the 15th c. lšić tower on hose top floor sided Sabetha vi (*see inlay*) d where two wish altars still nd preserved. The wer leans on the walls the inner citadel. Just outside the city alls lies the orthodox

On the other side of the Small Beach is a headland descending to the sea in a cascade

One of these is the so-called **Women's Water** (*Ženska voda*) that got its name after the sulphuric mineral spring that assumingly helps infertile women.

ENVIRONS:

The road south of the town leads across the **Milena Canal** (named after King Nikola's wife), leading to the vast Ulcinj saltpans. On the canal one can see *kalimere*, traditional fishing devices with the net on the end of a long pole designed to catch fish. From here stretches the long **Great Beach** (*Velika plaža*). With the length of 12 km of fine gray sand it is the largest in Montenegro. Its two

Kalimera fishing devices on Milena Canal

of flat rocks turned into small beaches. Further to the south stretches a series of similar rocky inlets shaded by a wonderful pine forest.

main disadvantages are that the water is very shallow and on windy days, when the waves are high, it is forbidden to swim here. The beach can be reached by a number of roads branching off from the highway. Several small hotels behind the highway and cafés on the waterfront have their own parking lots; otherwise parking is a bit chaotic. The sand of the Great Beach has therapeutical traits, especial helpful for curing rheumatism and similar ailments.

HERE TO EAT IN ULCINJ

šića dvori
ri grad; tel. 030/421-457; open 10-01h
ough a somewhat obvious solution this old restaurant is a good ace to savor some of the local specialties like okra (*bamje*). It oys a prime location in an old stone house in Ulcinj's Old Town erhanging the seaside but this is also reflected in its prices.

arinero
ala plaža; tel. 030/423-009; open 08-23h
is simple eatery with a warm atmosphere lies in the heart of cinj's tourism, on the Little Beach. The place attracts mostly als but the welcoming staff will make you feel at home. The enu lists a little bit of everything from fish and seafood to grills d pastas.

❾ Ada Bojana

15km from Ulcinj

This unusual river island (*ada*) lying between the two branches of River Bojana is the southernmost point of Montenegro. It is a heaven for nudists and off limit for all those who don't want to adapt to their ways. Yet, a little bit of nudity is bountifully rewarded with its untamed nature and

mouth of river Bojana; gradually the wreck collected sand around it until the river was forced to split its course. The result is a sand island covered in low shrub except for the sides close to the river that have more verdant vegetation. Ada's beach is 3km of fine sand washed by the high waves that are given impetus by the ever present breeze. This fact makes it popular with wind and kite surfers, although their

You can roam around the island dressed but to bath on the beach you will have to undress. Possibly the nicest spot for swimming is at the northern tip of the beach where fresh river water mixes with the salty sea forming brackish water that attracts not only swimmers but also a colony of sea gulls.

The only approach to Ada Bojana is from the Ulcinj side where a bridge linking it to the mainland stands. On both of its sides there is a number of seafood restaurant rendered by many a the best in Montenegro, not only for their fresh fish but also for the special kind of easygoing clientele. Amongst this merry group of eateries

The long nudist beach of Ada Bojana

feeling of isolation from the world which leaves a permanent impact on all those who visit it.

There are two tourist objects on Ada Bojana: bungalow apartments and an auto camp. All those who are not staying in these are admitted to the island only after 5 p.m. This is not as bad as it sounds as this is possibly the nicest time of the day on Ada, often ending with an enchanting sunset.

The island's origin is an interesting story in itself: it came to being after a merchant ship sailing in 1858 towards Shkoder sank in the

clubs are located on the southern tip of the Velika plaža beach. However, the number one sport here is beach volleyball played for fun by almost everyone, either on the sand or, due to the very gradual descent into the sea, in knee-deep water.

many are built on stilts above the river and som have *kalimera* fishing nets. There are also several houses that offer rooms for rent. If staying on Ada Bojana in the evenings be sure to have a mosquito repellent.

WHERE TO EAT IN ADA BOJANA

Miško
069/022-868; open 09-02
This is the oldest and best known (one may add for a reason) of restaurants lining river Bojana. The best way to enjoy its position is on its terrace overlooking the river. It specializes in fish and seafood with always fresh fish soup a range of seafood salads and the taverns specialty - dried fish (*sušena riba*).

Riblja čorba – Kod Marka
Bojana riverfront; 030/411-517; open 9-02
This friendly riverfront restaurant serves fish fresh out of sea, has excellent fish soup from which it got its name and tasty simple meals such as grilled squids.

Sunset on Ada Bojana

⑩ Svač

22km from Ulcinj

The ruins of this medieval town lie some 2km NE of Ulcinj, in the direction of the Sukobin border pass with Albania. When you reach the village of Vladimir (named after St Jovan Vladimir who reigned in this region, *see p. 172*) take the right turn at the main crossroad and follow the road that leads towards the Šas village. Look for the ruins on a hilltop on your right or for a black stone monument by the road, this is the best place to leave your car. The walking path leads to the top of the hill and it will take you some 10 minutes to cover it.

Svač was mentioned already in the 8th c. as the seat of the local bishop. It was less known in times of Duklja but prospered in Nemanjić Serbia. The town was destroyed in 1242 when fierce Mongolians swept through the Balkans looting and pillaging, however it was quickly rebuilt soon after, particularly due to the help of Serbian king Uroš and his queen Jelena who came from the catholic background of French Anjou family. The city's fortifications remained weak and in times of feudal petulance and against the Turkish advance they provided little protection. The town dwindled in size and importance and already at the beginning of the 15th c. it was recorded as a village. Its existence was ended when in 1571 the Turks captured and destroyed it, never to be rebuilt again.

On your way up you will first reach the remarkable ruins of the **Church of St Mary** which was once a part of the city's suburbs. It was built as a part of a Franciscan monastery in mid 14th c. The surviving western façade and the square apse have gothic windows while the portal is of Romanesque style with small decorative heads on the consoles. On the top of the hill the most notable ruins are those of the **Cathedral Church** dedicated to St John, which was built in the year 1300.

On the other side of the hill lies the **Šasko Lake**. It is connected by a small canal to Bojana River and is 1,5 by 3,2km in size

Water-lilly on Šasko Lake

during the summer but in the winter it doubles its size expanding to the surrounding hills. The lake is rich in fish (carp, perch, mullet) attracting birds which are at their most numerous during autumn migrations to the south.

Ruins of Svač cathedral near the Albanian border

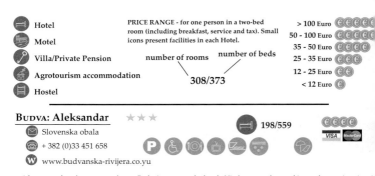

Hotel

Motel

Villa/Private Pension

Agrotourism accommodation

Hostel

PRICE RANGE - for one person in a two-bed room (including breakfast, service and tax). Small icons present facilities in each Hotel.

number of rooms   number of beds

308/373

> 100 Euro
50 - 100 Euro
35 - 50 Euro
25 - 35 Euro
12 - 25 Euro
< 12 Euro

Budva: Aleksandar ★ ★ ★

Slovenska obala

+ 382 (0)33 451 658

www.budvanska-rivijera.co.yu

198/559

A large complex of apartments close to Budva's most popular beach. Nicely arranged around its good open-air swimming pool, the apartments are pleasant and well-appointed.

Budva: Blue Star ★ ★ ★ ★

Mainski put bb

+ 382 (0)33 423 100

www.montenegrostars.com

22/54

An attractive hotel situated in the centre of Budva catering both for businessmen and holidaymakers. Bright, large rooms are tastefully furnished and there is a range of facilities including a conference hall.

Budva: Aquamarin ★ ★ ★ ★

Podkošljun, Budva

+ 382 (0)33 460 269

www.aquamarin-hotel.com

24/68

Situated conveniently close to both Slovenska plaža and Bečići beaches, this fine hotel offers a number of services including a sauna and a small restaurant. Friendly service

Budva: Astoria ★ ★ ★ ★

Njegoševa 4

+ 382 (0)33 451 110

www.hotelastoria.cg.yu

12/38

A luxury boutique hotel in an attractive location right in the heart of Budva's Old Town. Pleasant, attractively furnished rooms are equipped to suite all your demands. One of hotel's highlights is its charming roof terrace.

Budva: Kangaroo ★ ★ ★

Jadranski Put bb

+ 382 (0)33 425 100

www.kangaroo.cg.yu

32/86

Situated in the town centre, the hotel has a spacious roof terrace and a restaurant garden behind a screen of greenery. The rooms are simply furnished and lack character but are well-sized and clean.

Budva: Max Prestige ★ ★ ★ ★

Žrtava fašizma bb

+ 382 (0)33 458 330

www.hotelmaxprestige.com

19/50

This new hotel has well equipped rooms, a sauna, jacuzzi, laundry, children's' playground, a small pool and full video surveillance. It also has its own power and water supply. The main downside is its relative distance from the sea – 700m.

Budva: Šajo ★ ★ ★ ★

Jadranski Put bb

+ 382 (0)33 460 842

www.sajohotel.com

26/55

This hotel is located close to the town centre, some 300m from the waterfront. Its rooms are bright and spacious and its elegant restaurant offers excellent international cuisine.

Budva: Mogren ★ ★ ★

Mediteranska bb

+ 382 (0)33 451 102

49/112

The hotel is situated just outside the Old Town, on the town promenade where it has a popular cafe. It also has a congress and banquet hall. The rooms are rather small and the furnishings are past their best.

Slovenska plaža beach with the appartements complex of the same name

BUDVA: **Slovenska plaža** ★ ★ ★

Slovenska obala

+ 382 (0)33 451 654

www.budvanska-rivijera.co.yu

754/220

A complex of one- and two-storied apartment blocks organized in a self contained resort centered around a promenade and open-air pool. Though their furnishings may be a bit outdated, the rooms of this hotel are pleasant and comfortable.

BUDVA: **Zamak Pobore** ★ ★ ★ ★

Pobori bb

+ 382 (0)33 464 601

www.hotelzamak.com

36/80

This unusual hotel is located on a hill above Budva, on the road to Cetinje, at an altitude of 550m. Its rooms, restaurant and conference hall are characterized by rustic furnishings and modern facilities.

BUDVA: **Katić** ★ ★ ★

Zakulac bb

+ 382 (0)33 462 423

5/17

This pension is located 60m from the seafront. The rooms are furnished simply but are of decent size and comfortable.

BUDVA: **Villa Memidž** ★ ★ ★ ★

Četvrta 18

+ 382 (0)33 453 675

www.memidz.budva.com

15/56

Located close to the Slovenska plaža tourist resort, some 300m from the sea, this pension offers nicely furnished rooms.

BUDVA: **Hippo**

IV proleterske 37 (Podkošljun)

+ 382 (0)33 452 206

www.hippohostel.com

4/24

The only hostel in Budva, „The Hippo" is a place where comforts and luxury are replaced with friendliness and easy-going atmosphere. It has three simply furnished dorms and one double-bed room. Breakfast included in the price. Its main downside is the relative distance from the beach and the Old Town.

BUDVA: **Vukićević** ★ ★ ★

Žrtva fašizma bb

+ 382 (0)33 465 278

13/39

A nicely furnished pension in a quiet part of Budva with its own water supply. Each room has a balcony.

Bečići: Mediteran ★ ★ ★ ★

- Mediteranska 23, Bečići
- + 382 (0)33 471 845
- www.hotelmediteran.info

230/547

A very large hotel with a variety of facilities at the guests' disposal – health spa, two swimming pools, congress hall, sport grounds and an aqua park. It's elegant rooms are large and well equipped.

Bečići: Montenegro ★ ★ ★ ★

- Bečići
- + 382 (0)33 773 773
- www.montenegrostars.com

172/352

This is one of the finest four star hotels in the region. At the front it has a verdant garden leading to the private beach. T modern and large rooms have all the possible amenities.

Bečići: Queen of Montenegro ★ ★ ★ ★

- Narodnog Fronta bb
- + 382 (0)33 662 662
- www.queenofmontenegro.com

233/466

A new hotel in Bečići with its own casino, congress hall and two smaller swimming pools. The rooms are spacious, all wi a balcony and a nice view towards the sea.

Bečići: Splendid ★ ★ ★ ★ ★

- Bečići
- + 382 (0)33 773 777
- www.montenegrostars.com

341/682

Probably the most luxurious place to stay in Montenegro, this gigantic hotel has an extensive spa and wellness centre, t biggest conference facilities in the country and several exclusive penthouse suites that have already housed many famo visitors to Budva. Other facilities include four restaurants, a pool bar, night club etc.

Bečići: Iberrostar Bellevue ★ ★ ★ ★

- Bečići
- + 382 (0)33 425 100
- www.iberostar.com

578/1200

This extensive hotel complex lies directly on the beach but also has a swimming pool in its large gardens. Its rooms a spacious, all with a balcony and a sea view.

Sveti Stefan: Villa Montenegro ★ ★ ★ ★ ★

- Vukice Mitrović 2
- + 382 (0)33 468 802
- www.villa-montenegro.com

11/29

Elegant and luxurious, this small hotel overlooks the beach and the resort of Sveti Stefan. It possesses all the amenitie a top-class hotel – a garage with elevators, swimming pool, fitness gym, jacuzzi, its own power and water supply etc. 7 rooms are spacey and comfortable, each with a terrace and a sea view.

View of Sveti Stefan and its fine beaches

Sveti Stefan: Maestral

★ ★ ★ ★

📧 Pržno bb
☎ + 382 (0)33 410 100
🌐 www.maestral.info

180/334

This large hotel has recently been renovated and its spacious, bright rooms, almost all with a sea view are pleasantly furnished and well equipped. The hotel has a casino, a large conference hall, several different saunas, closed and open-air swimming pools.

Give yourself the best!

MAESTRAL, Resort & Casino
žno, 85315 Sveti Stefan
: +382 (0)33 410 108, 410 109
tel@maestral.info
ww.maestral.info

MAESTRAL
RESORT & CASINO
Budva, Montenegro
hit holidays

Sveti Stefan: Romanov

★ ★ ★ ★

📧 Sveti Stefan
☎ + 382 (0)33 468 452
🌐 www.hotelromanov.com

22/42

A luxury small hotel additionally benefiting from its proximity to the beach. Its stylish rooms are comfortable and well quipped.

Sveti Stefan: Kažanegra

📧 Obala 13
☎ + 382 (0)33 468 429

6/24

€€€€

private pension sunk in greenery just a few dozen meters from the sea and the center of life in this small resort. Each of the asantly furnished and neatly cleaned rooms enjoys a sea view.

Petrovac: W Grand

★ ★ ★

📧 Vrulja bb
☎ + 382 (0)33 461 703
🌐 www.wgrandpetrovac.com

50/120

€€€€

This fine new hotel has large, elegant rooms with modern facilities, a fine restaurant and a lovely rooftop terrace. It also udes a jacuzzi, sauna and a massage salon.

Petrovac: Palas

★ ★ ★

📧 Petrovac
☎ + 382 (0)33 421 000
🌐 www.budvanska-rivijera.co.yu

175/336

€€€

large hotel located on the very beachfront in Petrovac, it has a closed and open-air swimming pool and a sauna. The rooms e standard furnishings and facilities.

Sutomore: Korali ★ ★ ★

🛏 353/783

✉ Obala b.b.

☎ + 382 (0)30 373 465

🌐 www.korali.org

A huge hotel complex close to the Sutomore resort with a spacious sandy beach in front. The hotel which has retained i interesting 1980s retro-looks awaits renovation.

Sutomore: Sozina

🛏 31/78

✉ Obala b.b.

☎ + 382 (0)30 373 322

🌐 www.korali.org

An old hotel on Sutomore's promenade, located a few steps from the beach. The interiors still retain their old looks, but th rooms are spacious and well equipped.

Sutomore: Mirela ★ ★ ★

🛏 19/40

✉ Mirošica 2

☎ + 382 (0)30 374 737

🌐 www.hotel-mirela.de

With lots of shady greenery around it, this hotel leaves a nice impression boosted by the friendly and attentive staff. Th rooms are cosy and well equipped, most of them with large balconies. Its main downside is the 600m which separate you fro the beach but they organize transport to the nearby beaches as well.

Sutomore: Nikšić ★ ★ ★

🛏 104/274

✉ Obala Ive Novakovića bb

☎ + 382 (0)30 373 422

🌐 www.htponogost.com

A large hotel in the centre of Sutomore whose interiors are drowned in socialist decoration from days long gone. All room have balconies but not all of them look out on to the sea. Can get quite noisy in the evenings.

Sutomore: Čaković ★ ★ ★

🔑 4/13

✉ 20. jula br.18

☎ + 382 (0)30 372 102

A pension located some 150m from the sea catering to holidaying families.

Sutomore: Ostojić ★ ★ ★

🔑 6/18

✉ Mirošica 1/10

☎ + 382 (0)30 373 972

This pension located 250m from the sea offers comfortable and well appointed apartments.

Čanj: Vila Babović ★ ★

🛏 50/130

✉ Čanj bb

☎ + 382 (0)30 350 480

A medium-sized hotel in a booming neighborhood of Čanj. The hotel has basic facilities, a rooftop terrace and is some 200 away from the beach.

Čanj: Zec ★ ★ ★

🛏 7/25

✉ Plaža bb

☎ + 382 (0)30 377 068

🌐 www.apartmanizec.com

This pension is located at the very seafront where it has its own private beach equipped with all the amenities including jetty for small boats. In the basement there is a restaurant and a pizzeria.

Utjeha: El Mar ★ ★

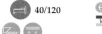

✉ Pečurice - Utjeha
☎ + 382 (0)30 458 363
Ⓦ www.binex.com

40/120

A small hotel situated in the lovely Utjeha cove some 16km north from the town of Bar. Just 50m from the sea, the hotel also possesses two tiny swimming pools as well as sports grounds

Utjeha: Vidikovac ★ ★ ★

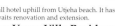

✉ Utjeha, Bar
☎ + 382 (0)30 458 253

20/70

A small hotel uphill from Utjeha beach. It has a huge terrace with a view on to the sea and two small swimming pools. The hotel awaits renovation and extension.

Dobre Vode: Villa Rezidencija ★ ★

✉ Nišice
☎ + 382 (0)30 364 478

3/12

Located at the very seafront, this pension has a large terrace overlooking the sandy beach and small, simply furnished rooms.

Dobre Vode: Elite ★ ★ ★

✉ Marin ploča
☎ + 382 (0)30 364 580

10/28

A small pension on two beaches. Rooms are clean and simple. Beach accessories are free of charge.

Bar: Princess ★ ★ ★ ★

✉ Jovana Tomaševica 59, Topolica
☎ + 382 (0)30 300 200
Ⓦ www.hotelprincess-montenegro.com

135/294

Recently renovated to new heights of luxury, this is by all means the classiest hotel in Bar and the vicinity. Spa and therapy treatments are an outstanding feature accompanying a large swimming pool, three conference halls and cozy rooms. A short walk through the luxuriant greenery will take you to the town promenade and the beach.

BAR: Sidro ★ ★

Obala 13 jula bb

+ 382 (0)30 312 200

www.lukabar.cg.yu

98/211

A fairly large hotel in the centre of Bar popular with sportsmen who use its extensive sports grounds. On the whole the hotel is not bad but some of its facilities are rather old. Note that the amenities in the older part of the hotel are of much lower quality.

BAR: Adriana ★ ★

4. proleterska Partizanska 50, Žukotrlica

+ 382 (0)30 305 585

www.hoteladriana-bar.com

20/46

This small hotel lies on the outskirts of Bar, just a few meters from the sea and a nice gravel beach. The rooms and the interior generally are simple to the verge of sparseness but very neat and tidy.

BAR: Pharos ★ ★

Topolica III

+ 382 (0)30 302 708

www.hotel-pharos.com

15/45

Hidden amidst verdant Mediterranean greenery in a quiet neighborhood of Bar, this hotel is still only a short stroll from the centre town and the town beach. The rooms are very simply furnished but spacious.

BAR: MD

Šušanj - Ilino

+ 382 (0)30 305 124

www.hotel-md.com

16/40

A brand new hotel close to the centre of Bar. The rooms are nicely furnished and equipped. The approach to the nearby beach (200m) is spoiled by the highway which passes close to the hotel.

ULCINJ: Aida ★ ★ ★

Mirka Srzentića bb, Pinješ

+ 382 (0)30 401 460

www.hotelaida.net

13/40

Each of the hotel's apartments has its own small kitchen and enjoys a sea view. A fully equipped fitness gym and sauna are at the guests' disposal.

ULCINJ: Dvori Balšića ★ ★ ★

Stari grad

+ 382 (0)30 421 612

www.realestate-travel.com

20/64

A hotel situated in the heart of Ulcinj's Old Town with excellent views to the sea. All of its apartments are large and airy, nicely furnished and with all the needed facilities. The hotel also has a fine restaurant and a smaller conference hall.

Dusk, Ulcinj's Old Town and its "Dvori Balšića"

LCINJ: **Bellevue** ★

✉ Velika Plaža

☎ + 382 (0)30 455 059

🌐 www.ulcinjska-rivijera.cg.yu

381/770

A large hotel complex to the south of Ulcinj, facing the Velika plaža beach. The rooms are simple but have all the modern amenities.

LCINJ: **Imperial**

✉ Velika Plaža bb

☎ + 382 (0)30 455 288

🌐 www.hotel-imperial-montenegro.com

44/120

A newly built hotel overlooking the Velika plaža beach. The rooms are rather simple but comfortable and clean.

LCINJ: **Velika Plaža** ★★★

✉ Velika Plaža bb, Štoj

☎ + 382 (0)30 413 145

🌐 www.velikaplaza.com

130/450

This hotel complex offers rooms and bungalows spread around enclosed green surroundings 250m from the Velika plaža beach.

LCINJ: **Olympic** ★★

✉ Velka Plaža bb

☎ + 382 (0)30 412 382

🌐 www.ulcinjska-rivijera.cg.yu

130/252

This large hotel near the Velika plaža beach has good sports facilities, a nice swimming pool and simply furnished rooms.

LCINJ: **Mediteran Resort** ★★

✉ Mujo Ulcinjaku bb

☎ + 382 (0)30 403 124

🌐 www.hotel-mediteran.com

100/306

Recently refurbished, this large hotel now has nicely-fitted modern rooms and good facilities, including a conference hall with 300 seats. The staff are efficient and friendly. The surroundings are relatively quiet, most rooms enjoy a view to the sea and over the town, while the beach is some 150m away.

LCINJ: **Ada** ★★★★

✉ Ada Bojana

☎ + 382 (0)30 455 059

🌐 www.ulcinjska-rivijera.cg.yu

250/500

A nudist resort on an island bounded on two sides by the River Bojana and on the third by the sea where it has a long sandy beach. Quiet and with unspoiled surroundings. The hotel's facilities are old but its rooms, both in the main building and in the bungalows are comfortable.

LCINJ: **Adriatic Apartments**

✉ Velika Plaža bb

☎ + 382 (0)30 404 030

🌐 www.adriatic-apartment.com

14/30

Located at the south exit from Ulcinj, only 30m from the beach these newly built apartments have modern furnishings and offer excellent value for money.

LCINJ: **Vila Hot** ★★★

✉ Ivana Milutinovića bb

☎ + 382 (0)69 674 966

27/80

Located in the centre of the town, 200m from the Small Beach. Basically equipped, comfortable and clean.

LCINJ: **Milla Apartments**

✉ Meraja 26

☎ + 382 (0)30 401 304

9/34

Located close to Ulcinj's Small Beach, these simply furnished apartments have all the basic amenities.

CENTRAL MONTENEGRO

The central part of the country is a distinctive whole easily recognizable for its mild climate, rough karst terrain and lack of woods, different from both the lush seaside and the cold north and east. Yet, Central Montenegro is itself a mixture of several smaller regions that differ both in landscape and history.

The Old Montenegro (*Stara Crna Gora*) is a kernel from which present-day country started its growth in the beginning of the 19th c. It lies directly above Boka Kotorska and the town of Budva, behind the first ridge of high mountains, spreading from Čevo in

National Park with magnificent, untamed vistas of dark woods and jagged rocks as well as the views of the nearby seaside. Below Lovćen lies the historic village of Njeguši, birthplace of all Montenegrin rulers. The only part of Old Montenegro which differs significantly from this rough picture is its southernmost county, Crmnica. With Virpazar as its market town it produces wines, fruits and vegetables known for their quality throughout the country.

The lower part of Crmnica lies on the shore of Lake Skadarsko, a huge water surface forming a border with

Waterfalls of Cijevna River at their most thunderous in early spring

the north to Virpazar in the south. Historically it was divided into four counties (*nahije*) and 22 small clans, some not bigger than a single village but all ripe with heroic personalities and tales of battles from the past centuries. The largest part of it is a barren muddle of shrub, rocky hills and smaller woods with many small villages clinging to their scrap of arable land. Today, most of the villages are cut off from the modern world and the development it brings, and it's the region's few roads that form the arteries through which life flows. The centre of Old Montenegro is Cetinje, previously the capital of the country, a preserved 19th c. town with many historic buildings bearing witness to its harsh history. Next to it is Mt Lovćen

Albania. Around the lake are many small fishing villages with preserved rural architecture as well as small orthodox monasteries, many of them isolated on their tiny islets.

North of Lake Skadarsko is the plain of Zeta with the capital city Podgorica lying in its middle. Approaching the city one can observe rural Zeta as it once was, with houses hidden in the greenery of fig trees and with poplars standing by streams and rivers that irrigate Zeta and spill into Morača, the largest of its rivers. The plain of Zeta is also the place where huge vine and fruit plantations are located. Podgorica has suffered greatly in WWII and is essentially a modern city, unburdened by history and willing for the reshaping of its looks.

...ts lined up in front of the fishing village of Vranjina on Lake Skadarsko

River Zeta springs in the vicinity of Nikšić but after only a dozen of kilometers disappears underground and then continues steadily south east towards Podgorica. Near to the site where it reappears is Ostrog Monastery in the fantastic setting high up in the forbidding rock which from afar seems impossible to reach. Fertile fields and small groves lie around the slow waters of river Zeta, whose banks offer a place of refreshment in the heat of long summers. Half way to Podgorica is the administrative and economical centre of this valley, the town of Danilovgrad. Its rectangular street plan reveals that before the capture of Podgorica the town was intended to become the capital of the country.

Thanks to the vicinity of the sea the whole of the region enjoys sub-Mediterranean climate with long summers and fairly cold winters. In summers Podgorica and the plain of Zeta live through sizzling heat waves with temperatures rising as far as the low 40^{0}Cs that wipe out the greenness of the area while the upper regions, including Cetinje, are enjoyably fresh. Winters see more rain than snow but can get quite chilly.

Cetinje monastery, the heart of Montenegrin history

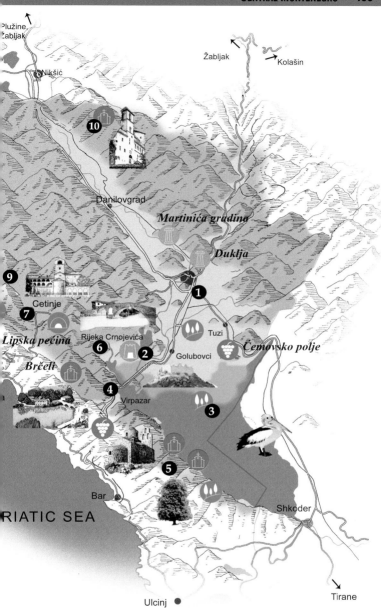

1 Podgorica
2 Žabljak Crnojevića
3 Lake Skadarsko
4 Virpazar
5 Kraijna

6 Rijeka Crnojevića
7 Cetinje
8 Lovćen
9 Njeguši
10 Ostrog

❶ Podgorica

👥 140,000

ℹ️ Ulica Slobode 47, 020/667-535

✈️ Golubovci (14km), 020/242-916

🚌 Mitra Bakića 5, 020/620-430

🚆 Trg goloootočkih žrtava 7, 020/63-36-63

🎭 The Night of Podgorica (18th December)

Podgorica is an administrative and commercial capital of Montenegro, a modern and rather uninteresting city often overlooked by tourists. Yet, for anyone traveling through Montenegro it is almost impossible to miss as all major roads meet here. With its wide selection of hotels and other necessities, Podgorica also makes an excellent starting point for visiting most of the central Montenegro in one day trips.

The town lies in the plain of Zeta, the largest flat piece of land in the country, with an average height of just 44m above see level and only an hour's drive from the sea. This lowland is notorious for unusually warm weather caused by the lack of refreshing sea breeze and circulation of air, both prevented by the surrounding mountainous terrain. In the summer the heats are unbearable, but Podgorica therefore enjoys mild winters allowing all but few of Mediterranean plants and fruits to prosper, giving it a specific look of a maritime town without the sea. The plain is traversed by rivers Zeta, Cijevna and Ribnica which merge with the larger Morača and continue southward as one, spilling into the nearby Skadarsko Lake.

Favourable climate and abundance of fertile soil and drinking water made the plain of Zeta an attractive place for human settlement. The first recorded settlement on the sight of present day Podgorica was *Birsiminium*, a Roman way station living in the shadows of the city of *Doclea* (its ruins lie 3km to the north of Podgorica, *see below*). During the early Middle Ages the Slav settlement called Ribnica grew on the confluence of Ribnica and Morača. While it served as a stronghold it allowed for the artisans and traders to inhabit the other shore, under the stumpy hill Gorica, thus forming Podgorica ("Bellow Gorica"), mentioned for the first time in 1326. The Turks captured the town in 1474, rebuilding and strengthening its fortress. In the following centuries Podgorica had two roles: in times of peace it was the marketplace for the surrounding Serb and Albanian clans, while during the unstable years (which greatly outnumbered the troublefree) it was resisting attacks by fierc highlanders. The town remained in Turkish hands until 1879 when it was acquired by Montenegro. Unlike in many other towns, the local Muslim townsfolk did not move abroad, and Podgorica remained and important commercial centre. The town grew slowly and steadily, acquiring a

Scattered Roman gravestones at Duklja archeological site

❶ Stara Varoš

❷ Sastavci

w rectangular street
an for the present day
wn centre and first
uropean style edifices.
e progress continued
the Kingdom of
goslavia, with the
wn population
aching some
,000 (the largest in
ontenegro) but still
gging in many aspects
hind the regional
pital Cetinje. In WWII
dgorica suffered
om the bombings,
st by the Italians
d later much more

devastatingly by the
Anglo-Americans,
reducing the town to
rubble. Amidst the
skeleton of old Podgorica
the new communist
power holders started
the construction of a
new, modern town
renamed as Titograd
(after the leader of
Yugoslav communists
Josip Broz Tito), the
name it retained until
1992. Soon after the first
wounds were healed the

communist authorities
broke with tradition and
in 1948 transferred the
seat of government from
Cetinje to Podgorica.
Thus the town started
its economic and
population boom
fueled by the economic
enterprises such as the
aluminum factory and
by the rise of educational
and cultural institutions
such as the university
(est. 1974). After the
break during the gloomy
1990s, the town is again
developing quickly, with

1 Nova Varoš

5 Novi Grad

7 Municipal Museum

Gorica

6 Contemporary Arts Centre

modern architectural edifices changing its appearance one more time.

Most of Podgorica is a curious mix of old and new. Post-war urban development ate almost the entire city centre, while the suburbs made of small cottages with gardens and vineyards, reminiscent of the old Podgorica, spread to the edges of the Zeta plain. The old centre - Nova or Mirkova Varoš - lies to the east of Morača. The other side of the river ("preko Morače") was until recently home to only a few institutions but is now experiencing a construction boom that is soon going to equal its importance with the other riverbank.

1. Stara varoš

This is the oldest preserved quarter of Podgorica, dating back to the Ottoman rule. It is a muddle of several narrow streets and ending at the bank of river Morača. Though almost all of the houses have been readapted, the area still has an

Old Turkish bridge at Sastavci

undeniable oriental feel for its gardens behind high walls, mosques but also for its neglect and dirt. The most prominent sight here and one of the town's landmarks is the **Clock Tower** (*Sahat kula*) standing at the edge of the quarter and facing the socialist apartment blocks across the street. This modest stone edifice was built in the latter part of the 18th c. by a local Muslim Adži-paša Osmanagić as a good deed for his town. Around the Clock Tower spreads a small square lined with a couple of old cafés. Here you can also find the modest **Natural History Museum** (*Prirodnjački muzej; 081/633-184; www.pmcg. cg.yu; open for scheduled visits*) presenting flora and fauna of Montenegro. A few steps away to the left of the tower, almost hidden behind the hotel "Boja Tours", stands the nicest piece of Ottoman architecture in the town, the **Čubranović**

House. Dating from 1630, today it is home to the "Dvor" national cuisine restaurant. In the central street of Stara varoš one will find **two small mosques** from the mid 18th c.

2. Sastavci

Sastavci or Skaline, as it is known to younger people, is the name for the confluence of Ribnica and Morača. The sight is uncared for but remains very picturesque with a small Turkish bridge over the Ribnica. Above the confluence stand barely visible ruins of the fortress of Ribnica. These are usually known as *Nemanjin grad* as it was here that in 1113 Stefan Nemanja was born, who subsequently founded the Nemanjić dynasty which ruled Serbia (and thus the territory of Montenegro as well) for two centuries. What can be seen today dates from the time of the Turkish rule, when the fort was rebuilt and strengthened

3. Nova varoš

Nova varoš was laid out in 1886 as a rectangular grid of streets under the orders of Prince Nikola's son Mirko and was therefore also known as Mirkova

Clock Tower in Podgorica's oldest quarter

varoš. The new street plan made a break with the oriental Stara varoš across the river and quickly became the centre of administration and commerce.

One of its main streets is Svetog Petra Cetinjskog, running parallel to river Ribnica. On this street the National Parliament and the National Bank are located. Facing the former is the equestrian **monument to King Nikola**, work of Risto Radmilović from 2005.

The Millenium Bridge over the Morača

The new monument to King Nikola

From Svetog Petra Cetinjskog St. starts the main town street Ulica Slobode. It passes the recently renovated Trg Republike square with its fountain and continues to the foot of Gorica Hill (*see below*). Hercegovačka ulica is a popular pedestrian zone and its intersection with the equally busy Njegoševa Street is the centre of cafés and nightlife.

At the end of Hercegovačka St. opens the view of the **Millennium Bridge** (*Milenijumski most*) to the right. This boldly envisioned piece of architecture, work of architect Mladen

Uličević from 2005, has already become the new symbol of the city, mark of its modern growth and hopes for a bright future. A walk beneath its only pylon, a slanting metal arm that seems bent by the twelve cables with counterweighs arranged in a semicircle, is particularly nice, opening a number of appealing angles for interesting views and photos.

4. Gorica

The "Small Hill" under which the town originated and which gave it its name is a squat mound with its peak at 133m. Ulica Slobode leads to the town stadium "Pod Goricom" used by the FC Budućnost, the undisputed ruler of the Montenegrin football throne. To its right starts the main

walkway approaching first the **Church of St George** (*Crkva svetog Djordja*), certainly the most interesting sight in the town. Its unwieldy western part is a 19th c. addition but behind it stands the original edifice dating from the 11th c. This pre-Romanesque church has a square apse and a short blind square cupola with three niches on each side. St George is the southernmost of about a dozen more churches with these specific features, others can be found only in south Dalmatia. The interior was fresco painted around 1670 by an unknown artist of modest skills. The iconostasis dating from 1881 is the work of Macedonian Djinoski brothers. In the corner of the churchyard stands the monument to the two victims of King Nikola's autocracy.

Church of St George at the foot of Gorica Hill

The walkway continues through the abundant Mediterranean vegetation, crosses a small bridge and leads to the **Monument to the Partisan Fighter** (*Spomenik partizanu borcu*). This marvelous piece of socialist memorial architecture is reminiscent of an antique mausoleum. At its entrance stand statues of two colossal partisans, communist fighters from WWII. Between them is represented the medal of National Hero, the highest honor in socialist Yugoslavia, which was also bestowed upon the city of Podgorica for the

A mix of architectural styles at the Church of Resurrect

Soc-realist Monument to the Partizan Figther

courage and martyrdom of its inhabitants in WWII. The monument is a central spot of the Statehood Day celebration on every 13th of July.

5. Novi grad

This part of the town, more usually referred to as "preko Morače" ("across Morača") was laid out after WWII and until recently held little interest in tourist itineraries. The new construction boom can best be observed here

with several modern apartment blocks where prices for flats match those of much bigger cities. This development lures the capital's elite, closely followed by posh shops and restaurants. The main sights are equally recent but are dedicated to linking this modern quarter to the history of Montenegro. The first one is the **Church of Resurrection** (*Hram Vaskrsenja Hristovog*), the new orthodox cathedral of Podgorica. This monumental structure (Predrag Ristić, 1993) strives to unite all the different styles of ecclesiastical architecture of Montenegro in one edifice – the dome of the medieval Raška style churches, the side bell towers like those of St Tryphon in Kotor, and the central belfry "on distaff" to be seen in the 18th and 19th c. churches - to note just some of the

reminiscences. Though still not completely finished, the church is open for service. One block to the left of here, in front of the Podgorica University head offices, stands the **monument to St Peter of Cetinje** (*see p. 23*), unveiled in 2006. With its height of 6.8 meters, this grandiose work of sculptor Nenad Šoškić seems fitting for Petar as a ruler but seems a bit odd for the remembrance of a saint.

6. Contemporary Arts Centre
Centar savremene umjetnosti

Kruševac bb; 020/225-043; op Tue-Fri 9-21h, weekends 9-14, admission free

The centre is located in the compound of Prince Nikola's winter residence called Kruševac. The compound consists of the palace, court chapel winter garden, music pavilion and life guard

Contemporary Arts' Centre in Kruševac park

ESTAURANTS IN PODGORICA

vor
alja Nikole 36; 020/622-265; open 08-24h

is restaurant is located in the oldest house in Podgorica, a dignified Ottoman edifice from 1630. It
s a pleasant front yard while the main dining area is in the basement. The menu lists many national
shes, which are very tasty though some might be a bit insufficient for those really hungry. Mid range
ices. Live music on some evenings.

aša
etog Petra Cetinjskog 31; 020/224-461; 07-24h

restaurant known to everyone in the city for
 top service and food. Bright, airy interiors
th modern décor and a large outdoor seating
vered with shades. The accent of the menu
on imaginatively served international dishes
d seafood but there are plenty of local special-
s too choose from as well. Prices well above
e average.

Giardino
mski trg 29; tel. 069/313-313; open 8-24, weekends
-24h

well known Italian restaurant frequented
ostly by business people. Cozy interior and
vement seating which is closed in the winter. A lengthy menu of sophisticated Italian dishes with
mething for anyone.

alabria
arka Miljanova 61; 020/622-577; open 08-24h

ough it sounds outright Italian this restaurant offers not only the classic choices of pizza prepared in
ood-burning ovens but cherishes also many local variations of pizza, prepared with a taste of Monte-
grin national dishes. Its menu also lists tasty grills and exceedingly abundant salads.

lvador Dali
đordza Vašingtona 87; tel. 020/234-567; open 08-01, weekends 09-01h

uch more posh than surrealist, this restaurants aims to become Podgorica's top one. The food range is
om pastas and seafood to a splash of national cuisine, all served up stylishly by the responsive staff.
ices fit the glamorous setting.

Mareza
Mareza bb; 020/268-722; 09-01h
Located 5km to the north of the city, the
restaurant sits in the middle of a field
soaked by the waters of river Zeta and
smaller streams which keep its spacious
terrace pleasantly cool. The restaurant is
known far and wide for its home-grown
trout and the always warm spit-roast
lamb.

Posejdon
Stanka Dragojevića 8; tel. 020/665-449;
open 09-24h
A cozy little restaurant with a nautical
theme but serving both a long list of fish
and seafood as well as the usual range of
pastas and grills, all reasonably priced.

aterna
arka Miljanova 41; tel. 020/232-331; open 09-24h

he restaurant is located in an old stone house on one of downtown Podgorica's busiest streets but its
m interior with bare walls and simple wooden furniture will take you worlds away from the traffic
ns. Pizzas, pastas, seafood and delicious grills - all good value for money.

d volat
g Bećir-bega Osmanagića; tel. 069/66-66-22; open 07-24h

 great little kebab grill with a large shady courtyard and a leisurely atmosphere, ideal for observing
e locals. The menu consists of a short list of usual grilled dishes but you can't really miss by choosing
y of them.

aballero
iljana Vukova 21; tel. 020/230-180; open 7-24h

 quiet old restaurant in the centre of the city with several rooms with different settings. The range on
e menu is usual for Podgorica, from national dishes to fish and Italian specialties accompanied by an
undant selection of wines.

quarters, all finished in 1891, and located in a fine park decorated with several statues. The Centre was formed in 1995 inheriting the funds from the Gallery of Non-Aligned Countries "Josip Broz Tito"; this fact explains the variety of the collections which include works of art from Africa, Asia and Latin America as well as the works by prominent Yugoslav and Montenegrin sculptors.

7. Municipal Museum

Muzej grada Podgorice

Marka Miljanova 4; tel. 081/24-25-43; open Tue-Fri 9-21h, weekends 9-14h; entrance fee €1

The museums collections are divided in four departments. The first one is archeological with a valuable assortment collected from prehistoric sites in the town's vicinity and especially from Roman Doclea. The second department is

ethnographical department exhibits many nice folk costumes and objects used in everyday life.

ENVIRONS:

One of the most fascinating sights in the vicinity of Podgorica is certainly **river Cijevna**. The river springs at the northernmost tip of Albania, runs 32km through Montenegro and merges with Morača next to the Golubovci airport. In its upper flow it builds a canyon almost 1000 meters deep and then gradually shrinks until east of Podgorica, in the plain of Zeta, Cijevna becomes merely a crack in the ground. With some parts narrowing to just 2-3 meters wide it reminds of a pipe ("cijev"), the

Waterfall of the River Cijevna

river is quite fast and boasts several attractive waterfalls. Its banks are the most popular places for a quick refreshment in Podgorica, the most prominent being the one called "Niagara" for its tall waterfall. To reach it take the road to Tuzi, then turn off to the right in front of a bridge that spans Cijevna and head straight for roughly another kilometer.

The remains of the town of **Duklja** are the most important archeological site of Podgorica, standing at its northern outskirts. The town was founded by Illyrians at the point where river Zeta meets Morača at the beginning of the 1st c. AD but was captured by the Romans only a few decades later. In their hands Doclea (as was its Latin name) prospered reaching the number of some 10,000 inhabitants and had all the features of a pleasant provincial town – temples, urban villas, triumphal arch and baths. The city rose in importance after in 297 it became the seat of the

Ornamental women's belts, Municipial Museum

dedicated to the memory of Božidar Vuković (1465-1540), a native of Podgorica who printed in Venice Serb books of utmost artistic value. The third section deals with cultural history of the area, displaying books, icons, money and old maps. The

appearance of which is described in its name. In this low lying part of its flow its stony bed filled with crystal clear blue water is in sharp contrast with the desolate grassland of almost desert-like appearance. Although seemingly calm, the

The plan of the Duklja archeological site

ewly founded province f Praevalitana and soon fterwards the bishop's eat. Its prominence as crushed a century ater when in 401 the Vestern Goths sacked it. This raid was followed y another in 486, hen it suffered from e hands of Eastern oths and finally by a evastating earthquake 518. After a short vival in the time of mperor Justinian, the lavic invasion forced e remaining Roman opulace to retreat to a illside fort at Martinića radina (excavation te on the road from odgorica to Nikšić) hich was more suitable r defense and Doclea ll into ruins. The cho of its importance found in the fact at one of the newly rmed Slav states was

named Duklja. The best way to reach this site is to take the first turn right immediately after you have crossed the Millennium Bridge to the side of Novi grad and follow this road until the second bridge appears on your right. Additional attention is needed here as the approaches on both sides of the bridge are one way roads. After crossing the railway line the site appears at your left. Since the whole of the excavation area is unattained and unmarked you can only enjoy walking amidst the scattered ruins, the most interesting being those of the town's forum. Here there are many fragments of pillars, consoles or tombstones lying around while on the north side are the walls of the curia (courthouse).

Medun is a village 12km northeast of the city in the area of Kuči clan and is interesting for two reasons – the ancient fort and the house of duke Marko Miljanov (*see inlay on p. 164*), turned into a museum. To reach it follow the road signs towards Belgrade; after passing beneath the railroad go

straight (the main road continues to the left) through Skopska and Djuke Jovanova streets. Weather permitting, the ridge climbing to Kuči offers memorable views of the whole of Podgorica. At the top of the ascent in front of you opens a slowly rising plateau with a much more pleasant climate and an almost incessant light breeze. The sign will lead you to Miljanov's home, a large stone building on a ridge overlooking the village. Miljanov built his house inside the walls of the lower town which remains from the Middle Ages when Medun was a castle controlling the road from Ribnica (Podgorica) to Plav and Peć. In the courtyard stands the bust of Miljanov while his house has been turned into a **museum** (*open Wed-Sun 11-16 h, previous announcement on 020/242-543 advisable; entrance 5€*) displaying weapons, flags and pictures from Miljanov's era, costumes and household items illustrating the life of Kuči as well as Miljanov's manuscripts (note the naivety of his handwriting) and first editions of his books. A short climb uphill takes you to the village church, built at the start of the 18th c. with the

Remains of the Roman presence in Duklja

THE BRAVEST AND MOST HUMANE OF ALL WRITERS

Marko Miljanov Popović was born in 1833 in Medun into a distinguished family which held for generations the role of the head of the Kuči clan. His life and career followed the usual lines: he fought against the Turks, joined Prince Danilo's personal guard and as an intelligent and loyal man in 1862 he became a judge in Bratonožići clan; soon he rose to the ranks of the Montenegrin Senate and in 1876-79 war commanded his troops with distinction and great bravery. However, in 1882, after a disagreement with Prince Nikola, he was forced to retire from the affairs of state and return to seclusion of his native village. Spending his days in Medun, Miljanov – although already 50 years old - decided to learn how to read and write so that he could immortalize the brave deeds of many Montenegrins and Highlanders he saw during his life. With no formal education or knowledge of literature Miljanov took to writing the same way as he would narrate, with no pretensions on leaving a polished work of art but of recording history he witnessed. However, being a man of words, a natural born story-teller, his works turned out to be masterpieces of simplicity, stripped of any learned style but rich in fresh expressions and figures of the common people. His main work, the one that he felt obliged to write for posterity, is the "Examples of Humanity and Bravery" (*Primjeri čojstva i junaštva*). Describing many brave acts and uncovering morals in them, he defined that bravery is to defend yourself from the other while humanity is to suppress one's anger and defend others from yourself, thus remaining honourable and with a clear conscience. In this book he wrote about others and did not mentioned himself even once, although he was known as one of the greatest heroes of his time. Miljanov died in 1901, a few months before his first book was published in Belgrade. Subsequent reading of his works revealed the value of his writing, both in terms of style and in deep introspection of the customs and beliefs of the era.

money brought by the clan's head from Russia. Next to it lies Miljanov's grave (the smaller tombstone erected by his wife and the larger slightly later by his clansmen) surrounded with half-ruined walls from where you can enjoy the views of the vicinity. This prominent position has been a hill fort from times immemorial. Here stood the acropolis (upper town) of Meteon, the enwalled town of the Illyrian tribe of Labeati, founded not later than the 3rd century BC. It was here that in 168 BC the Romans captured the brother and family of king Gentius, the leader of the Illyrian tribes, ending their resistance to the Roman Republic. Although rebuilt several times, the ruins of Medun still have parts of the original so-called "cyclopic" walls and steps cut into rock dating from the Illyrian period.

❷ Žabljak Crnojevića

20 km from Podgorica

Žabljak (with an addition "of the Crnojevićs", not to be mixed with the one near Mt Durmitor) is a well preserved medieval castle with a small village underneath it at the edge of the Skadarsko Lake.

Though it is almost certain that at this same place stood the fortified centre of an early medieval Slav shire of Podlužje, the castle of Žabljak as we see it today is the work of Crnojevićs from the mid 15th c. when they turned it into their principal residence. However, neither its mighty walls nor the exquisite position could save it from the relentless drive of the Ottomans and it was taken in 1478 by Sultan Mohammed the Conqueror forcing Ivan Crnojević to move his seat to Rijeka Crnojevića (*see p. 172*). The Turks kept a large garrison here which first operated against the Venetians and later kept the nearby Montenegrin clans at bay. The Montenegrins captured the castle from the Turks for the first

A fishermen engaged in his daily pursuits

Castle of Žabljak Crnojevića and the Malo blato lake

ne in a surprise attack 1852, an incident that d to a war with the ttoman Empire. After e Turks finally lost e castle in the 1878 ar, Žabljak's defensive le disappeared and it adually turned into ruin.

The only way to ach Žabljak Crnojevića from Golubovci: ading in the direction Petrovac, take a right rn at the only traffic ght in the town; after short drive you will ass across a narrow idge and then you ould take a left turn; ere follows a longer de and another bridge ltogether 9 km from olubovci). In front of u emerges a view of solemn hill covered ith small houses d crowned with a stle. Beware that in ringtime the high vel of the Skadarsko ake's water may enclose turning the hill into d island and forcing u to negotiate a boat ive from the locals. In ont of the parking area

lays a Turkish bridge that used to connect it on these occasions. The scenic ensemble is ruined by the recent concrete and brick additions to its small stone houses. Apart from a couple of shanty bars operating during the season the site is largely neglected. A steep climb passes the village church and the ruins of a mosque and leads to the castle walls which are up to 14m tall and two meters thick. Next to the castle's only gate stands the round tower still hanging onto its machicolations (openings for shooting downwards from the top of the wall). Inside the clutter of its ruins stands the monument to the Montenegrins who died capturing it. From here there are excellent views across the plain with Malo blato Lake to the north and Lesendro and Vranjina (*see p. 167*) to the south.

❸ Lake Skadarsko

Vranjina village, 020/879-103

Lake Skadarsko (*Skadarsko jezero*, often referred to as Lake Scutari) is the largest lake in the whole of the Balkans, some 40km long and 14 wide. It lies on the Zeta plain in the south of Montenegro, very close to the sea from which it is divided by a strip of land roughly 15km wide and dominated by Mt Rumija. From afar the Lake is an imposing sight with high hills and rocky islands rising from its tranquil surface. The lake forms a natural border with Albania: two thirds of its surface including the whole of its north and west coast are in Montenegro, while the other third which includes the east and the south coast are in Albania. Shkoder (*Skadar* in Serbian, *Scutari* in Italian), which is in Albania, is the

Water lillies covering the Lake

only substantial city on its shores and gives the lake its name. The lake receives its water from river Morača and underwater springs, but also has a constant outflow through river Bojana to the Adriatic Sea. These conditions make its size very variable – from 530km² during the snow-melting period in springtime, to just 370 km² in late summer and early autumn. In the dry season many of its islands join with the mainland, vast areas are turned into shallow marshes and parts of it become separate lakes. The whole lake is a crypto-depression – a natural phenomenon in which the lake's surface stands above sea level while its depths are below it. The lake is generally only 5-8m

deep but has some 30 underwater springs (called locally *oka* – "eyes") which reach the depths of 60 meters! The lake's coast in its Montenegrin part is ragged with many small coves, peninsulas and around 50 isles, locally called *gorica* ("small hill").

On its shores stony inlets interchange with small bays covered in thick reeds, while its surface is covered

in water lilies or such natural rarities as *kasoronja*, the floating water nut, which does in fact contain an eatable part, a rare delicacy you can try in some restaurants. On its shores one can find many small flowers, wild pomegranate trees, laurels etc. The waters of Skadarsko Lake are rich in fish, both the freshwater kind of which most common are carp and bleak, and the sea fish such as eels and striped mullets that swim upstream along the river Bojana. The abundance of fish and favorable nesting

Diverse birdlife in unspoiled marshland scenery

conditions attract as many as 264 indigenous and migrating bird species. Amongst them the most numerable are cormorants, the grey herons are becoming a rare sight while the most interesting are the large Dalmatian Pelicans who nest here. Numerable flocks of ducks and geese spend their winters on the lake. Together with the rest of the Zeta plain and Podgorica, Skadarsko Lake has mercilessly warm summers when the lake's water warms to 28°C; in contrast, during winter its shallower waters freeze. Due to al

Boys playing on the lake

ese remarkable
atures Lake
kadarsko is
otected as a
ational Park.
Lake Skadarsko
equally
teresting for its
storical heritage
om various
ochs. Around
spread small
wns such as
jeka Crnojevića (*see p.*
2) or Virpazar (*p. 168*)
d many small fishing
llages such as Vranjina,
aruč or Dodoši which
ve retained their
aditional looks with
nall stone houses
cked in together. In
em one can enjoy the
clusion and the slow
ace of a fisherman's
e. **Karuč** and **Dodoši**
e best reached from
e Podgorica–Rijeka
rnojevića road or
ternatively continuing
rther from Žabljak
rnojevića (*see p. 164*).
he route through the
ajina region on the
ake's west coast leads
rough a number of
enic villages and
ast the medieval
onasteries standing on
eir *gorice* (*see caption*
. 5).
The main route
rough this region is
odgorica-Virpazar
hich can be traversed
 both car and train.
oth the highway and
e railroad pass across
e lake through a dike
hich separates the
ke into two parts, the
aller part being to
e north of the dike.
he dike first reaches
e **island of Vranjina**,
 fact the largest of all
ontenegrin islands
cluding those on the
aside! Close to the
ad lies a large fishing
llage of the same name
ith a preserved look
 the old days, nested

A typical old house in Vranjina village

around a small bay and now almost completely closed off by the dike. The seat of the National Park authorities is located here with its small **visitor's centre** (*open during the summer*

Fortress of Lesendro mirrored in calm waters

every day from 8-19) where one can learn more about the park. Next to Vranjina is the small **isle of Lesendro** dominated by a fort of the same name. As the control over the island also meant the control of the trade to and from Montenegro, during the early 19th c. the fort witnessed long standing

disputes between the Turks and the Montenegrins, on all occasions being resolved through fighting. As it is impossible to park near Lesendro it is best to leave your car near the restaurants on the west tip of Vranjina and walk along the highway to the fort. The sides of the dike are lined with fishermen enjoying in the abundance of the lake's fish. To join them you will need a permit from the National Park authorities

(€5 per day).

The best way to enjoy Skadarsko Lake is on one of the boats which can be seen cruising on it. Most of them start from Virpazar, some from Plavnica complex on the north shore while less often boats sail out from the local villages.

WHERE TO EAT IN THE LAKE SKADARSKO AREA

Jezero
Vranjina; tel. 067/619-603; open 10-22h
This modernly refurbished restaurant is under management of "Plantaže", the greatest wine producer in the country. Its main feature is a terrace that looms over the lake and enjoys magnificent vistas of most of it. Apart from wine the accent here is on fish, though the grilled dishes are not to be underestimated either.

Plavnica
Plavnica bb; 020/443-700; open 09-01h
This popular excursion spot has recently been enriched with several luxurious objects, including a prestigious restaurant set above the waters of the Lake. The menu lists dishes ranging from international classics to local specialties.

❹ Virpazar

330

Festival vina i ukljeve, 3rd weekend in December

Virpazar is a tiny town on the road from Podgorica towards the coast. It lies on the place where rivers Crmnica and Orahovštica meet and immediately flow into Skadarsko Lake. During springtime the high levels of the waters turn Virpazar into an island joined to the mainland by its three old stone bridges. The town is the centre of Crmnica, a fertile region with a climate favourable for growing vine, olives and all kinds of fruits and vegetables. Virpazar is also the starting point for

the town became the most important trading point in Montenegro, visited by traders from Podgorica and Shkoder. It's role during this time left a permanent mark on Vir adding *pazar* ("marketplace") to its name. It had a lively port and in 1908 was connected to Bar by a narrow-gauge railway, the first in the country. Virpazar is also famous for the insurrection on the 13th of July 1941 when, upon hearing the news that the quislings and Italian occupiers have pronounced the "independence" of Montenegro, the men from local villages attacked the Italian garrison and liberated the town, starting an

The drinking well in Virpazar

miss the sharp left turn leading to the town immediately after crossing the bridge. The houses of Virpazar are arranged in a circle with their fronts towards the wide town square and their rears to the water. In the middle of the tree-shaded square is a nice old drinking well and around it there are three restaurants and a tourist info point. On most days you will find people selling local produce such as the famous Crmnica wines and *lozova* grape brandy, but the best day to come for shopping is Friday, the local market day. Across the old bridge leading southwards, atop of a high rock stands a memorable **monument** to the 13th of July Uprising.

One of Virpazar's three bridges

most boat excursions on Skadarsko Lake.

The place of Vir was first mentioned in 1242 and it is quite possible that it was a small trading hub for the local villages even at that time. In the 15th c its strategic location was capitalized by the Turks who built the Besac castle which still stands above the town (*see below*). After the Turks were banished from the castle at the beginning of the 18th c.

uprising against the Axis powers in Montenegro.

Virpazar is well connected to Podgorica with a highway and a railroad. If coming from the direction of Podgorica one should be very careful not to

A short walk further along this road will lead you to a path leading uphill to the **Besac Castle**. This well-preserved fortification

WHERE TO EAT IN VIRPAZAR

Badanj
On the main square; 020/712-509; open 10-23h
This small rustic restaurant has a view of the quiet river and one of Virpazar's stone bridges. The core of the menu consists of river fish but on weekends they prepare lamb in milk. After lunch you will be served gratis pancakes with home-made honey or *patišpanj* cake.

as built by the Turks 1478. Between o world wars it as used as a police ation and during e Italian occupation their stronghold. esac has lower outer alls sheltering a large ourtyard and a citadel ith a round tower on ch of its four sides. is possible to climb its top from where e can enjoy views Virpazar and the rrounding marshy ea.

Fort of Grmožur, in the middle of Lake Skadarsko

Krajina

Days of ecology, tourism and culture, Donji Murići, first week of August

Krajina is a name of e region on the west ast of Lake Skadarsko retching from Virpazar the north to the lbanian border in the uth. Bordered on one de by the Lake and on e other by Mt Rumija, forms a natural whole d was treated as an dministrative unit ready in the Middle ges when it was an nportant region in the ate of Duklja. Today, n the 22km long road om Virpazar to Ostros llage you will pass rough numerous amlets with preserved ral architecture and e many remnants of ncient times. It is also sited by many nature vers for its interesting enery, plants and bird ecies. Note that the ovementioned road is arrow and very curvy ith many blind corners o one should pay ecial attention while riving on it.

The village nmediately to the uth of Virpazar is odimlje. The first

turn to the right will take you to the village cemetery with its old church. From here one can observe the oldest and best preserved part of the village, a cluster of stone houses hanging on the hill facing towards you. The houses are built close to each other with thick walls and arched entrances, all of which are influences of Mediterranean architecture. Godimlje is famous for its red wine so be sure to sample it or buy it if you come across some.

Opposite the village is a tiny islet of **Grmožur** with a fort that covers almost the whole of it. Built by the Turks and taken by Montenegrins in 1878, it was consequently used as a prison for serious violators. As the first institution of this kind in Montenegro the prison had its own book of regulations, which

proscribed that all the detainees as well as their guards should be non-swimmers and one of its most peculiar rules was that if someone escaped the guard responsible for it should have had served the rest of his sentence. The only residents of Grmožur today are numerous cormorants and pelicans who nest in its walls.

The next village you will reach is **Seoca**. While the centre of this village enjoys an agricultural setting seemingly far from the lake, its nearby hamlet of Raduš is an interesting example of a small fishing community. It nests above the "oko" (*see p. 166*) of the same name, which with its depth of 60m is the deepest spot in the Lake and a protected spawning place of bleak.

Donkeys are still cherished in the region of Krajina

The beach in Murići

After Seoca the road continues high above the shore with nice views of the coast and its many small islands, called locally *gorica* ("small hill"). This is also where the Christian villages end and Moslem ones start, with Albanians as a predominant population.

The village of **Murići** is divided into two – Gornji, above the road and Donji, closer to the Lake. The latter has a long pebble beach, which is probably the best place for swimming in Lake Skadarsko if you don't mind the muddy colour of the water and the algae around you. On the beach you will also find a restaurant, one of the rare places to eat along this route. Facing Murići are two isles with orthodox monasteries. To visit them one should negotiate a price with the locals for a boat ride; the price varies on your haggling skills and the season but should not exceed €35.

The monastery on the **isle of Beška** directly in front of Murići consists of two churches. The larger one (still in ruins) is the endowment of Djuradj Balšić from the end of the 14th c. and has a central cupola and the belfry "on distaff". The smaller one was built by his widow Jelena, daughter of the Serbian Prince Lazar, a well educated noblewoman that left behind several poems and built many monasteries in Zeta. In the narthex of the small church, above the door, stands carved the original inscription about its construction which took place in 1438, while inside it is the grave of the church patroness. The monastery, still being renovation, is inhabited by friendly and welcoming nuns. If offered, try their pomegranate juice (*sok od nara*), the refreshing

specialty of Murići and the adjoining region.

A bit further to the north is the smaller **isle of Starčeva Gorica**. It dates from 1378 and was founded by the monk Makarije, famous spiritual leader, hermit and practitioner of hesychasm, a technique of meditation popular in the 14th c. throughout the Orthodox world. In bond to this tradition the monastery is today inhabited by a solitary monk, a true loner reluctant to communicate with tourists. The monastery

Church on the isle of Beška

is famous for the grave of the printer Božidar Vuković (*see p. 162*) who was buried here with his wife in accordance to his last wish.

To the south of these two is the **isle of Moračnik**, also giving home to a monastery. Negotiating a trip to it will almost double the sum you pay for seeing just Beška and Starčeva Gorica. The monastery was built by Balša III, son of Djuradj and Jelena, prior to first mention in 1417. Today on this small isle stands

---

WHERE TO EAT IN KRAJINA

Plaža
Murići village; open only from March to October 09-22h
A restaurant on the very shore of the Lake with most of the seating under the shade of an old tree. Most of the things served in this family run place are home made, locally produced or freshly caught from the lake. Their grilled carp is a must try. Friendly and attentive service.

Starčeva gorica isle with its small monastery

n equally tiny domed church of the tree-leaf type, next to it a bulky tower four floors tall and, to complete the setting, a small monastic dwelling.

Continuing southwards along the road will take you through wild and desolate scenery of rocks and shrubbery. After several kilometers the road starts to take a more inland course and the inhospitable terrain is replaced by increasingly more fertile grounds and greener surroundings where people still practice agriculture and hang to their old ways. Especially nice are the old trees of oak and chestnut, an example of which is one by the road in the centre of Livari. Before and after the large

and dispersed village of **Kostanjica** you will pass through two **chestnut woods** that gave the village its name (*kostanj* in Old Church Slavonic

An orthodox nun goes shopping

is a chestnut, modern word is *kesten*). Here the fascinatingly large trees, all several hundred years old, overhang the road and dim the sunlight even during the sunniest

of days. These natural rarities are remains of much larger forests that existed here and give you some idea how the area looked in the time of Duklja and its Prince Vladimir. Between these two lies the center of the village, a fertile dale in which many of the inhabitants grow tobacco.

The last interesting place along this road is **Ostros**, a large ethnic Albanian village with a restaurant (with rooms to rent), supermarket and bakery where you can stock up on your

supplies. The village is at its nicest on Wednesdays when peasants from the surrounding villages come and offer their produce on the local market. Half a kilometer

Chestnut woods in Kostanjica village

Ruins of the Prečista Krajinska monastery

⑥ Rijeka Crnojevića

🏘 450

🎪 Riječki pazar, mid July

Rijeka Crnojevića is a name of a very small town on the waterfront of the river of the same name. The sleepy townlet constitutes of a single street and the recently renovated embankment both extending along the river. The town's origins lie on the hill on the other bank where in 1478 Ivan Crnojević transferred his seat to the castle of Obod. Today it place is taken by a small monastery and several houses. The first houses in Rijeka Crnojevica were built at the beginning of the 19th c, as the river which is navigable all the way from its mouth in Skadarsko Lake was the easiest way to bring

after the centre of the village, look for a stone tower to the left of the road. These are the **ruins of Prečista Krajinska** monastery. Founded in the mid 10th c. it gained its glory as the burial sight of St Jovan Vladimir (*see inlay*). For a brief period in the 15th c. it was a seat of the orthodox Zeta bishopric before it was transferred to Vranjina and then to Cetinje. The monastery was laid to ruins in one of the punitive expeditions by the pasha of Shkoder in the late 17th c. Today we see walls of the original church, which are a few feet high, and a narthex with a high belfry, an addition from the time when the church became the seat of the bishopric. On the last level of the belfry you can see the apse of a tiny chapel. The whole sight is neglected and disgracefully polluted.

The road continues further to the Stegvoš pass and then descends to the village of Vladimir and beyond.

SACRED LOVE OF VLADIMIR AND KOSARA

Duke Jovan Vladimir succeeded his father Petrislav at the throne of Duklja while still of a very young age. He lived a life of a pious Christian ruler, building churches and taking care of his people. Due to being an ally of Byzantium he was attacked by the mighty Tsar Samuil of Bulgaria. However, not wishing to shed blood, Vladimir retreated with his people to the hill of Oblik near Svač (*see p. 143*). His people suffered from venomous snakes and Vladimir asked God for help; from then on, the legend tells, no snake on Oblik was ever poisonous again. As the siege became drawn-out, Vladimir decided to sacrifice himself for his people and surrendered to Samuil, who took him as a captive to his capital on Lake Prespa in Macedonia. The Tsar had a daughter Theodora Kosara, equal in virtues to the young duke. While washing everyday the feet of her father's prisoners she fell in love with Vladimir and managed to persuade her father to let her marry him. Thus Vladimir was not only allowed to return to Duklja as a ruler but received from his father-in-law the province of Travunija as well. After Samuil's death in 1014 his nephew Jovan Vladislav was eager to get rid of his uncle's ally and take control of his lands. In 1016 the new Tsar sent a priestly envoy to Vladimir asking him to come and swearing on a cross that no evil will come to him during his visit. The treacherous Vladislav organized his men, dressing them up as bandits he ordered them to ambush Vladimir and kill him, but his attempts failed as they reported that the duke was guarded by an angel. Enraged by Vladimir's arrival to Prespa, Vladislav lost his temper and ordered him to be killed immediately. The killers found him praying in a church and beheaded him as soon as he came out; in his hands he was still holding a cross with which he was lured into the trap. That

same night the dead body radiated with light and Kosara had no problems persuading her relative to give her the body. Duke Vladimir was buried in his capital, in the church of Prečista Krajinska where Kosara spent the rest of her life as a nun and was eventually buried by his feet. Tsar Jovan Vladislav met his demise the following year. Vladimir's body was taken in the 13th c to Elbasan (Albania) where it remains to this day, revered as a relic. The cross from his hands is kept by Mrkojevići clan who are settled in the vicinity of Bar. On every Pentecost the procession of Catholic, Orthodox and Muslim believers carries the cross to the top of Mt Rumija always arriving before dawn.

The old stone bridge in Rijeka Crnojevića

...oods to Cetinje and ...e rest of Montenegro. ...e locality became ...marketplace for the ...djacent villages and ...eveloped quickly. ...lthough the town was ...ughly of the same size ... it is today, it ...as Montenegro's ...cond largest ...d second ...ost important ...til 1878 and ...e liberation of ...e lowlands. ... had a regular ...oat connection ...ith other ...aces on Lake ...adarsko, a royal ...mmerhouse, ...o hotels and ...any merchant ...ores but all of ...is disappeared after ...cond World War when ...ceased to be the seat of ...e local administration ...d the boat traffic ...came less important. ... All that remains from ... heyday are several ...cturesque old houses ...t its main attractions ...e surely the **two stone**

bridges. The older one is a particularly picturesque sight with its asymmetrical looks and two wide arches. It was built by Prince Danilo in 1852 at the place of a wooden one which was the work of his predecessor Petar II. The house next to it was used as Danilo's dwelling when he stayed here. The new bridge dates from 1900 and looks much more sober. The road passing across it leads to Virpazar, 24km of winding track through

thick shrub and several small villages. A few meters away from the old bridge stands the **house of St Peter of Cetinje**, possibly one of the first houses in the town. Renovation has removed almost all the markings of its antiquity except the unusual design that survives, but you will easily recognize it for the cross above the entrance to the yard. The house is used as dwellings for the local monks. It was here that in 1873 a sawmill was founded as the first industrial enterprise in Montenegro.

Curves of Rijeka Crnojevića River on its way towards Lake Skadarsko

The river Rijeka Crnojevića is one of the rare waterways in the world which is navigable after only a kilometer of its flow. Many of the boats tied to the shores offer rides to Virpazar and around Lake Skadarsko.

WHERE TO EAT IN RIJEKA CRNOJEVICA

Stari most
Rijeka Crnojevića; tel. 041/239-505; open 10-23h
A fine restaurant with an outdoor seating on the waterside of Rijeka Crnojevića serving mostly fresh fish caught in the river itself and Lake Skadarsko. The house specialty is their home-smoked carp grilled on its own or cooked in sauerkraut, all accompanied with freshly baked corn bread. For a starter you should try fried smoked bleak (*dimljena ukljeva*).

Poslednja luka
Potpočivalo bb, Rijeka Crnojevića; tel. 041/239-527; open 12.30-21h
A short distance away from the centre of the town, this small tavern serves succulent fish dishes (try their grilled trout) with good home-made white wine adding to the atmosphere. The only consideration are the prices which are above the average fare.

❼ Cetinje

18.500

Baja Pivljanina 2,
041/230-250

041/21-052

International Folklore
Festival (August)

Cetinje, the old historic capital of Montenegro, is a pleasant small town with harmonious architecture and an undoubted sense of pride for its heritage, which is best observed in its museums that are amongst the richest in the country. Tourist season or not, the town enjoys its own slow pace with barely anyone outside during hot summer days, the situation which abruptly changes in the pleasant fresh evenings when both young and old get on the streets for a walk or to sip a drink or two. Located close to the coast, Cetinje attracts many tourists on one day visits from the nearby Budva or Kotor but to be fully explored it certainly deserves more time.

Cetinje lies in the middle of an elongated karst field ringed with barren mountains. Before the mid 15th c. it was a mere *katun* (a seasonal shepherds' dwelling) in the middle of nowhere but the advancement of the Turks forced Ivan Crnojević to move his seat deeper into the mountains and in 1482 he decided to build his court here. Two years later he brought an orthodox bishop as well and established a monastery next to the court. The monks operated the printing

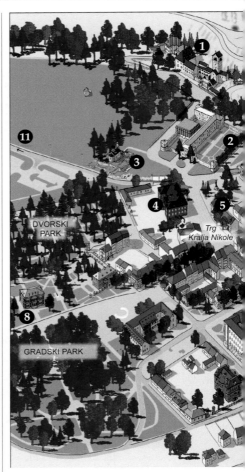

DVORSKI PARK

Trg Kralja Nikole

GRADSKI PARK

❶ Cetinje Monastery

❷ Biljarda

❸ Ćipur

❹ Museum of King Ni

❺ Ethnographic Muse

❻ House of the Gover

press famous for the production of the oldest Serb and indeed the oldest South Slavic incunabula. However, the new capital never lived to become a town as the Turks conquered the site in 1496 and the last of the Crnojevićs had to flee to Italy. Their court was destroyed but the monastery was left alone. In the region of highland mountain villages settled by shepherds

the monastery served not only as a spiritual refuge but much more as the only authority they really respected: whether they rebelled against the Turkish taxations or when they quarreled over the fields and pastures they looked to the bishop for solutions. The monastery's influence slowly increased until i became their unofficial centre and thus Cetinje became the capital

6

7

7

Balšića pazar

10

, Budva

Bulevar Crnogorskih junaka

Bajova ul.

hostile clans. The first step in the transformation of Cetinje to a town was made in 1838 when Njegoš built his fortified palace in front of the monastery. The men needed at the palace, the guards and the first senators soon built their houses next to it. The further development of state authority and administration brought to Cetinje its first clerks, doctors, shop-keepers and workers for the state printing house.

These were followed by many clan leaders who held important state functions and who started spending more time in the capital than in their native villages. The town grew even faster when in 1878 Montenegro became an internationally recognized country. Around the court of Prince Nikola formed a circle of well-known personalities, such as the Serb writers Laza Kostić and Simo Matavulj and the Russian geographer Pavel Rovinski, who instigated the cultural

7 Njegoševa Street	**10** Vlaška crkva
8 The Blue Palace	**11** Orlov krš
9 Zetski dom	

before it even became a town. In those harsh days the history of the Cetinje Monastery, the hub of all the resistance to the Turks, became one with the bloody history of Montenegro which consisted of endless rebellions and wars (*see caption 'History', p. 16*). The Turks knew this well and the monastery was burnt down and destroyed several times while the field of Cetinje was the place where

the few Turkish armies that were successful in making it this far tried to impose peace on the

Postcard of Cetinje from the beginning of the 20th century

A market day in Cetinje in 1904

and intellectual life of the capital by running the literary magazine, founding the reading room and the first theatre. By the end of the 19th century Cetinje grew to around 400 houses and 2,500 inhabitants. It acquired a form of a very small but orderly town with court and government buildings, foreign legations, parks and even such excesses as the skate-ring. On the other hand, it still was a capital of a poor warrior nation, and presented a curiosity to the outsiders with its male inhabitants, from innkeepers to MPs, carrying weapons and with sheep and cattle lurking just around the corner from the Royal Palace. Cetinje managed to escape the destruction of WWI but witnessed a bloody day of fighting on Orthodox Christmas in 1918 when the town was unsuccessfully attacked by the adherents of the disposed King Nikola. In Yugoslavia the town remained the seat of the regional administration but the local governor could hardly match the pomposity of the exiled King. In

the Second World War the town was occupied by the Italians who tried in vain to promote it into a capital of their puppet state of Montenegro. The town was liberated by communist partisans in 1944 but already in 1948 the capital of the new republic was transferred to Titograd (Podgorica). Cetinje gradually fell into slumber and was kept alive only by its museums and its two factories. This was changed during the last few decades as more institutions as well as two faculties were transferred here, bringing with them educated and young people to the town. The inhabitants of Cetinje proudly cherish memories of the town's importance and in the last decade played an important role in the

revival of Montenegrin nationalism and the roa to independence.

1. Cetinje Monastery
Cetinjski manastir

The oldest surviving edifice in Cetinje is its monastery around whic the town grew. The present day monastery was built in 1701 by metropolitan Danilo following the destructio of the old complex (*see no. 3*) by the Turks in 1692. For the sight of his new monastery Danilo chose the place previously occupied by the court of Ivan Crnojević which was easier to defend with its back and sides sheltered by rocks and with a high wall needed on just one side. He chose wisely as the monastery had to be defended several times during the 18th c. The las occasion it was looted and burnt down was in 1785 which was the last time the Turkish forces made it to Cetinje. As the metropolitan was also the ruler of Montenegro the monastery was the center of spiritual and political life of the country. In 1838 Njegoš moved to his newly erected Biljarda court (*see no. 2*) where he continued to preforme

The complex of the Cetinje Monastery

is state duties. In 1851 the roles of bishop and of prince were separated and the monastery remained a seat of spiritual authority over the whole of Montenegro remaining so to this very day.

The monastery complex is an unusual cluster of edifices which were all built with local stone. Its central feature is a church dedicated to the birth of Virgin Mary with a high bell-tower at its farther end and an apse jutting towards the approaching visitor. In the middle of the nose one can see the plaque with the two-headed eagle, coat-of-arms of the Crnojevićs, which originates from their old court. To the right of the church is the covered graveyard of the Petrović-Njegošs. By the main entrance to the complex are a drinking well and the grave of Janko Vukotić, the commander-in-chief of the Montenegrin army in World War One.

In the stone clad courtyard there are several more tombs, the most notable ones being of metropolitan Sava (1735-82) and of metropolitan Mitrofan Ban whose main achievement was the unification of bishoprics under his jurisdiction with other orthodox-serb ones in the newly formed Kingdom of Yugoslavia, hence forming the united patriarchate of Peć. The entrance to the monastery church is gained through a small narthex and a door above which stands

a carved inscription about the founding of the monastery in 1484, brought here from the destroyed old monastery. The interior of the church is unpainted but has a high iconostasis,

Crnojević coat-of-arms set in to the walls of the Cetinje monastery

a work of anonymous Greek painter from the mid 19th c. To the right of it is a casket with the **relics of St Petar of Cetinje**, the most venerated saint of Montenegro, because of which this monastery is also sometimes referred to as the "Monastery of St Petar of Cetinje". Inside the church are also the graves of Prince Danilo and of grand

duke Mirko, father of King Nikola.

The central part of the monastery is comprised of monks' cells which lie behind the arched porches with short columns whose capitals display two-headed eagles and come from the old monastery.

On the other side of the courtyard is the entrance to the **treasury**. As it contains innumerable wealth it can be visited only in a guided tour, available until 2 p.m. every day. The monks will take no less than three persons and no more than ten inside; with the price fixed at €20 you are advised to form a larger group to reduce your expanses. This should not present a problem as the monastery is visited by many tourists during the season but pay attention that, depending on the group's choice, the tours are either in Serbian, English or Russian. The treasury is the richest in Montenegro and one of the richest in all of Serb Orthodox monasteries. It contains many ornamented vestments and richly embroidered bishops' robes (one especially splendid

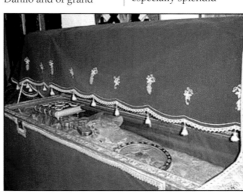

Relics of St Petar of Cetinje

associated with St Sava), scepters, the church flag from the time of Balšićs and two old mitres, one supposedly belonging to King Stefan Dečanski (14th c.), the other to metropolitan Visarion Borilović from the 16th c. Amid the liturgical objects the most interesting is the intricately carved wooden cross framed with gold (1637). Of special interest are books kept here such as the hand illuminated Divoš's Gospel (13th c.), Piva Gospel and Cvjetni Triod (both 17th c.), then the valuable incunabula (first printed books) – Krakow Breviary - the first Slavic printed book from 1491, Psalter from the Crnojević printing-house (1494) with its excellent woodcut illustrations in the spirit of renaissance, as well as

An old photo of the monastery with Tablja tower above

the 16th c. books printed in Venice by Božidar Vuković and his son Vićentije and Jerolim Zagurović in Kotor. Of special interest is the founding charter of the Cetinje Monastery guarded throughout the centuries by the monks, the seal and a the staff of Ivan Crnojević. There is also a special chapel keeping the splinter of

Illumination from the 13th c. Divoš's Gospel

the True Cross and the right hand of St John the Baptist, two relics of utmost value (*see inlay on p. 184*).

Right in front of the monastery stands the **threshing floor** (*gumno*) reconstructed in our times to the likeness of the original one constructed by metropolitan Savo in the mid 18th c. Its diameter is the same as the Tsar-bell in Moscow's Kremlin, which Sava visited. The threshing floor of the monastery, as well as the other village ones from the region, was used not only for the purpose of finishing field work but also as a convenient place for gatherings of people in which important community

matters were debated. This one was especially important as the making of all state decisions and the elections of the metropolitans happened here. A good part of Njegoš's "Mountain Wreath" is set here as well.

Taking the road to the right of the monastery will lead you to a small plateau where until 193. stood **Tablja**. This was a large tower which was built in 1835 by Njegoš for defensive purposes but it was soon discovered that it was not suitable and its construction was abandoned. Instead, it became a place where the cut-off Turkish head were displayed until thi habit was abandoned in the latter part of the 19th c. Later on it was used as a place from which important guests were greeted and important news announced with cannon fire. After 1873 when the foundry of Laza Urošević from Zemun (Belgrade) donated a large bell with a weight of 1631kg Tablja served as a bell-tower of the monastery. The tower was pulled down with an intention to construct the new episcopal church (mode

f which can be seen
the treasury of the
onastery) in its place
ut this never happened
ue to WWII. Its bell was
arried to a small belfry
anding above the site.

The large cavity seen
n the west side of the
lateau is one of the
ntrances to **Cetinjska
ave**, a little explored
atural phenomenon
680m long and with a
small stream at its
ottom. Because it is not
dapted for visits the
ve is out of reach to
urists who can only
enefit from a constant
ream of frosty air
owing outside it.

Biljarda

*jegoš's Museum; tel. 086/230-
0; open 9-16; entry fee €3*

This stately stone
difice of unusual design
as built in 1838 by
jegoš as a first step in
parating his duties
a metropolitan and
s duties as a ruler.
he money for the
onstruction as well as
e architect – emissary
akov Oseretskovsky
came from Russia,
om which Njegoš just
turned. With its walls
d a round tower at
ch of its four corners
looked more like a
astle than a residence,
e sign of the time

*"Inspection of arms" by Cato Woodville
(National Museum of Montenegro)*

when a potential Turkish
attack was still a grim
reality. Initially called
just the "New House",
the edifice got its present
day name after a billiard
table brought by Njegoš
from Kotor to shorten
his long days. With its 25
rooms it was the largest
edifice in the country.
For the Montenegrins of
the period whose houses
only had one or two
rooms it was enormous
and instead of saying
"many" a term "as many
as Biljarda has rooms"
became widely used.
Contrary to popular
belief, Njegoš used just
two of its rooms, one as
a bedroom and other
as a living room; all

others were
intended for
various state
institutions,
rooms for
his personal
guards and
guestrooms
for any
important
foreign
visitor
coming to
Cetinje. One
of the rooms
was also
used to store
the trophies
from wars
with the
Turks, the
core of the current
historical museum.
Biljarda was also used
by prince Danilo,
during whose reign it
experienced its hardest
and most glorious
hours (see p. 26) - and
then by prince Nikola
until 1867. After the
princes moved out,
Biljarda housed almost
all the institutions
of the young state at
various times, from
printing house and
seminary to high school
and ministries who
used it until they got
their own buildings.
In accordance with
new needs the corner
towers were torn down
and Biljarda's look was
drastically changed.
This was
reversed in
1951 when
it got its
original
looks back
for the
celebration
of a sentinel
of Njegoš's
death. A
few years
later a
museum
opened here
displaying
the items

Njegoš's residence - **Biljarda**

connected with the life and work of Njegoš.

Today there are two permanent exhibitions to be seen here, included in a single ticket. On the ground level is the one on the **development of Montenegrin army** with many interesting uniforms, insignia and old photos to be seen. On the upper floor the items of the **Njegoš Museum** are displayed. Only a few of the exhibits were used by Njegoš himself but there are a number of objects from the period. Of Njegoš's personal belongings the most interesting is the armchair whose legs had to be extended to fit his giant stature! Also to be seen here are many weapons, captured Turkish flags, portraits of Njegoš and the pictures of famous Montenegrins of the period, the original manuscript of the "Mountain Wreath" and many editions of the work, his and a personal library of his uncle Petar I, Njegoš's letters and notes and at the end his testament. Many works of art inspired by his personality and his literary works are also displayed here.

A separate feature of the Museum is the large **relief map of Montenegro**, which takes up a lion's share of Biljarda's courtyard. It was made in 1916/17 during the Austro-Hungarian occupations by their army geographers and had a strategic use. Done in 1:10,000 scale it is accurate in every detail and offers a perfect chance to examine all of Montenegro from a birds-eye view with roads and towns as they were almost a century ago.

Ćipur Court Church amidst the ruins of the original Cetinje Monaster

3. Ćipur

In 1890 Prince Nikola built a new church on the ruins of the old Cetinje Monastery founded in 1484; dedicated to the old church's feast, the Nativity of the Virgin, the church served as a court chapel. You can explore the remaining foundations of the original monastery but the most interesting trace of its existence are the four columns at the front of the church entrance, each with a double-headed eagle depicted on its capital. The original church in the monastery was a stately edifice built by craftsmen from Dubrovnik and was the first (and the last!) among Serb churches to have details of renaissance style incorporated in its design. The court church of 1890 is a singl nave edifice with a six sided cupola and the typical front belfry "on distaff". Inside one can see the high iconostasis which was, as well as many other icons on its unpainted walls, created by masters from St Petersburg. On the floor can be seen the grave memorials of Ivan Crnojević as well as of King Nikola and his Queen Milena, whose earthly remains were brought here in 1989 from the Russian Churc in San Remo (Italy) where they died in exile

4. Museum of King Nikola

Trg Kralja Nikole; tel. 086/230 555; open 9-16h; admission €3

The museum is located in the edifice of the New Court to which prince Nikola and his family moved when the left Biljarda in 1867. Thi non-pretentious one-floor building looked even plainer before if got its present day look with a balcony and a gable in 1910. Though done in European style, the dark-red painted building with grey roof and white details

Royal Palace, today the Museum of King Nikola

...as a certain rough, mountain simplicity that makes it unmistakably Montenegrin. The building was used as a court until Nikola's departure from Montenegro in 1916. From 1926 it served as a museum.

The court preserves all the original interiors and decoration from the time when the royal family lived here. On the ground floor is the study of King Nikola with his personal clothes, uniforms and weapons. Next to them state flags and arms, a set of Montenegrin currency *perper* (in use only from 1906 to 1916) and postage stamps (from 1874) are displayed. The medal collection includes both the decorations of Montenegro including the "Medal of Obilić" named after the legendary hero of the Kosovo Battle, where the portrait of Obilić was modelled on Njegoš's appearance), and the ceremonial one presenting all the members of the house of Petrović-Njegoš from vladika Danilo to King Nikola, as well as a range of foreign medals amongst them

the most peculiar being one from the Turkish Sultan awarded to King Nikola during a brief period of peace between these two nations. The smaller rooms to the right contain a court library with many valuable and rare volumes including the books from the Crnojević printing house, old charters, originals of the international agreements and codes of law of Montenegro.

The rooms on the first floor retain fully the style they had while they were used by the royal family, with the large dining room, several salons, the reception rooms and the bed chambers. The most interesting items here are many portraits of Nikola's family and their relatives from other European royal courts. There are many of these as Nikola married five of his daughters to various kings and dukes thus gaining the nickname of "the father-in-law of Europe". Among the historic paintings the best known is the "The Evacuation of Montenegrin Court" by Czech Jaroslav Čermak which depicts the soldiers evacuating paintings from the Montenegrin court through the waist-high snow due to the arriving threat of the Turks, and Vlaho Bukovac's "Montenegrins Around a *gusle*-player".

The main feature of the square at the front of the Court is a small park with a **monument to Ivan Crnojević**, the founder of Cetinje, work of Ante Gržetić from 1982 when the town celebrated five centuries of its existence.

To the left of the museum stands the building of the **Bulgarian Legation**, today housing the "Gradska kafana"

"Montenegrins around a gusle-player" by Vlaho Bukovac (National Museum of Montenegro)

A monument to Ivan Crnojević

by various artists, mainly from Montenegro.

5. Ethnographic Museum

Trg kralja Nikole; tel. 041/230-310; open 9-16; entry fee €3

The house in which the museum is located was built in 1883 as a wedding gift from Prince Nikola to his daughter Zorka who married Petar Karadjordjević, the pretender to the throne of Serbia. The couple lived here for some years and it was here that their son Aleksandar, future King of Yugoslavia was born. Zorka died before her husband became the next King of Serbia in 1903 and hence the house was listed as Petar's property, which he donated to his state at the beginning of 1914 to establish the legation of Serbia in Montenegro.

As the large collections of the Ethnographic Museum can not fit into the few rooms of this modest building here stand displayed only the long-lasting temporary exhibitions. The current one is named "From Thread to Fabric" and presents the traditional textile handiwork, tools and techniques as well

restaurant. The house was built in 1910 by architect Fernando Balacco who was finishing the reconstruction works on the court building at the time. However, Bulgarian diplomats stayed here only for three years as in 1913 diplomatic ties between the two countries were severed when Montenegro joined Serbia against Bulgaria in the Second Balkans War.

Next to it stands the house on whose ground floor the **Atelier "Dado"** is located, named after painter Miodrag "Dado" Djurić who worked here for a period of time. Today one can see here permanent exhibitions

as parts of the national costumes from various parts of Montenegro.

6. House of the Government
Vladin dom

When the construction work on this building started in 1909 the rumor was that Montenegro was at a brink of something huge. In 1910 Prince Nikola announced that on the 50th anniversary of his rule he decided to assume the title of the King and to bestow the constitution to the country and organize its first elections. The young parliament and its government were housed in this brand new edifice, a tasty mix of neo-renaissance and neo-baroque. However, the building was still spacious enough to host the post and telegraph office as well as the state printing house.

Today this is the seat of the National Museum of Montenegro which incorporates all the museums in Cetinje and is a home to the Historical Museum and the Gallery of Modern Art.

The ground floor is occupied by the **Historical Museum** (*tel. 041/230-310; open 9-16; entry fee €3*). The first room deals with prehistory, antique and the medieval state of Duklja, displays the Greek vases from Budva, archeological findings from the Roman town of Doclea and reproductions of medieval documents and frescoes. Second room is dedicated to the Balšić and Crnojević dynasties that ruled parts of Montenegro in

Ethnographic Museum

Fine italianate decoration of the House of the Government

the 14th and 15th c. Their period is illustrated by the coins they minted, the jewelry, copies of pages from the first printed books etc. The third room illustrates the period of Turkish domination and the fight for liberation with many old manuscripts and books and items belonging to the first bishop-princes. The fourth room displays the items from the time of Petar I and his successor Petar II (Njegoš) with the most interesting exhibits being the old Turkish and Montenegrin flags, including the Montenegrin war flag from the battle of Vučji Do (1876) pierced with innumerous bullets, then the various arms from the period as well as the death-mask of Kara Mahmud-pasha Bushatli, taken from his cut-off head after his defeat at Krusi in 1796. Similar display of varied daggers, dervish axes, north African knives and flags captured in the battles against the Turks is the main feature of a smaller room dedicated to the 19th c. The sixth room focuses on the period of the Kingdom

(1910-18) with various state insignia, coins and banknotes to be seen. The next room deals with the inter-war period, mainly with the Christmas Uprising against the dethronement of King Nikola and with the work of the Communist Party, with photos, documents and, of course, guns used in the fighting. The last room illustrates the events during the WWII when the territory of Montenegro saw bloody fighting between various

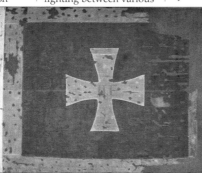

Montenegrin flag from Vučji Do battle (National Museum of Montenegro)

fractions fighting for or against the occupying forces.

The first floor houses the **Gallery of Modern Art** (*tel. 086/230-310; open 9-16; entry fee €3*) which, in spite of its name, has also a collection of icons and some academic

works of art. Its first room features the works of fine art from the territory of the former Yugoslavia from 1890s to 1970s with works of the famous painters such as Vlaho Bukovac and Sava Šumanović or sculptors such as Toma Rosandić. The collection of Milica and Svetozar Vukmanović is more modern and abstract and has works of art of Yugoslav artists such as Mića Popović and Milan Konjović as well as the few smaller works of Renoir, Picasso, Chagall and Dali. The next room is dedicated to the icons and religious paintings whose prime exhibits are the icons of the Dimitrijević-Rafailović school from the Montenegrin coast, "The Execution of the St Genevieve" a late medieval work by an unknown master from north Europe and two representations of the Holy Family, one by Giovanni Battista Pittoni and the other by Tripo Kokolja, the greatest baroque painter from the territory of Boka Kotorska. A special room, coloured in mystic dark blue light is left especially for the icon of Our Lady of Philermo, one of the holiest in the whole of Christianity (*see inlay on next page*). Next is the Montenegrin collection which gives you an overview of the fine arts in Montenegro from its beginnings with Anastas Bocarić (late 19th c.) and Pero Poček

"Night in Montenegro" by Petar Lubarda

(first quarter of the 20th c.) via modernists to the especially rich post-modern group of paintings by Dado Djurić and Vojo Stanić. One room is dedicated to the works of Milo Milunović (1897-1967) who during his lifespan passed through the phases of impressionism, neoclassicism and, most notably expressionism inspired by the colours and light of the Mediterranean ("Fruits of the Sea", 1954). The exhibition of works by Petar Lubarda (1907-1974), certainly th... most important figure in Montenegrin art, includ... several of his famous landscapes inspired by rugged Montenegrin ka... including the antholog... almost abstract "Night in Montenegro" (1951) and the large canvas with a theme from national history "The Kosovo Battle". Next room presents the work... of Branko Filipović "Filo" (1924-1998) a full... abstract artist whose ma... medium was colour. Th... last room hosts the wor... of Dado Djurić (b. 1934)... a surrealist who paints apocalyptic visions and creates sculptures twist... in many mutations.

MIRACULOUS TRAVELS FROM THE HOLY LAND TO CETINJE

When St Luke the Evangelist came to Sebastia to take the body of St John the Baptist, the people would not let him take it because of their belief in its miraculous workings and he had to settle for his right hand. St Luke took the hand to Antioch from where it was later transferred to Constantinople and kept as the holiest of the relics in the church of Hagia Sophia. St Luke is also attributed to have painted the icon of Madonna while looking at the Virgin Mary. The icon was brought during some unknown age to the Byzantine isle of Rhodes where it was highly venerated in the church on the hill of Philermos. In 1309 the island was conquered by the Knights Hospitaller and the icon's veneration was successfully adopted by the Order who proclaimed it as its patroness. Some years after the taking of Constantinople the Turkish Sultan gave the hand of St John to the Knights as a diplomatic gesture while somewhat later the French king Louis XII presented the Knights with the splinter of the True Cross; thus all three relics found today in Cetinje were finally united in one place. It was believed that the miraculous Icon protected the island and the Hospitallers and helped them fight off several Turkish attacks until the siege by Mahomet the Conqueror in 1522 when the Knights had to leave the island. The Order rambled around Europe in search for a patron for seven years carrying with it its most precious sanctities. In the end Emperor Charles V gave them the island of Malta after which they were named the Knights of Malta. Around the relics of St John's hand grew the island's cathedral and in the cathedral a chapel, dedicated to Madonna of Philermos, which obtained great wealth through donations by the Knights and pilgrims. In 1798 Napoleon conquered the island and took these treasures to finance his expedition to Egypt but let the last Grand Master take with him the Icon (though stripped of its golden frame), the Hand and the Splinter. The Knights lost their home once again but were warmly welcomed by the Russian Tsar Paul I who gave them shelter. In gratitude the Knights presented their most valuable treasures to the Tsar who took the title of the Grand Master and ordered the Icon to be framed in gold and gems, the ones that we see today. Paul's successors had different opinions about the Order and it moved from St Petersburg to Rome but the holy objects remained with the Romanoffs until 1919 when the Russian priests managed to take them out of the reach of the Bolsheviks and gave them to the Empress-Mother who escaped to Denmark. On her deathbed Maria Fyodorovna conferred in 1928 the relics to a priest who took them to Berlin and eventually to Belgrade, where the exiled seat of the Russian Orthodox Church was. The Russian patriarch gave them to his benefactor King Aleksandar of Yugoslavia who stored them in his palace. When the Nazis attacked Yugoslavia in 1941 the relics were taken by the underage king Petar II and his government to Nikšić. The young king and his government flew from the improvised airport to London but left the relics in the nearby Ostrog monastery where they were hidden well. Searching for the treasures left behind by the royal dynasty, the communist secret service of Yugoslavia found the three objects in 1952 and took them in its keeping during which the largest of the gems from the Icon was stolen. In 1978 the icon was donated to the Museum in Cetinje as an object of artistic value while the hand of St John and the splinter of the Holy Cross were given to the metropolitan of Montenegro.

. Njegoševa Street

The central street of etinje stretches from e Presidential Palace the north across the ralja Nikole Square the hotel "Grand" in e greenery of Cetinje ommons. This was d still is Cetinje's gh street with many ops and important stitutions lined ong it. But its many staurants and cafés ive it its essence and in e evenings transform it to a lively promenade here one comes to roll and meet his iends.

Starting in the left irection from the point

Colourful old houses in Njegoševa Street

forms one side of the Balšića pazar. Returning back to Njegoševa St. one reaches the **Djukanović House**, the first edifice on the right following a small patch of green. The house, a real miniature

Legation. It was built in 1908-10 following the plans of architect Paul Goudet in a modern style where vertical and horizontal lines are of equal importance and with a minimalist decoration mainly in ceramics. The building today houses a part of the National Library. Across the street is the **Vukotić House** (1914), whose plain façade, round windows at the top floor and reinforced concrete construction mark the first surfacing of modern architecture in Cetinje.

Second building to the right of the Vukotić house is the **Presidential Palace**, by whose entrance stand the ceremonial guards in their showy red uniforms. This monumental palace was built in 1934 following the plans

Djukanović House

here Njegoševa St. eets Kralja Nikole quare there is a line f houses from the first alf of the 20th c, most of em modest one-floor ouses with shops on the round floor and living uarters on the upper ith a few exceptions of nore recent origin. The rst corner to the right akes you to **Balšića azar**, a nice square which used to serve as a narketplace, with a nice ld fountain with lions' eads spitting water in s middle. Present day reen market (*pijaca*) of Cetinje lies behind the ow of houses on Baja ivljanina St. which

palace with interesting neo-baroque sculptures, was built in 1910 by Marko Djukanović, the state engineer of Montenegro.

At the following intersection stands the building of the **French**

The main entrance to the Presidential Palace

of Bogdan Nestorović from Belgrade as the seat of the branch of the State Hypothec Bank. Especially nice are the two figures standing by its entrance representing a man and a woman from Montenegro in their national costumes. Across the street is the edifice formerly belonging to the **Bank of Montenegro,** still displaying its name in several languages on its façade even though it was built in 1910, four years after the introduction of the new

8. The Blue Palace
Plavi dvor

At the lower end of Njegoševa St. the most memorable edifice is the Blue Palace, named after the colour of its exterior. It was constructed in 1895 for the use of the heir to the throne, prince Danilo. Today it serves as an exhibition space of the National Museum. In front of it is a recently unveiled bust of painter Petar Lubarda. To the right of the Palace is the modest building of the British Legation adapted from local houses in

Bust of Vuk Mandušić i Gradski Park

Sarajlija and the other Ljuba Nenadović, a writer who accompanie Njegoš on many of his journeys and later recorded his recollections.

9. Zetski dom

"The House of Zeta" is a popular name given to the first theatre building in Montenegro celebrating the glory of the medieval state of Zeta, the precursor of Montenegro. The work on providing a temporary stage to the amateur theatre group which included almost the whole of the intellectual elite of the town started in 1884. After the rough works were finished the

Blue Palace, once the seat of the heir to the throne

Montenegrin currency, the *perper*.

This is where Njegoševa Street ends and the broad Boulevard of Montenegrin Heroes (*Bulevar crnogorskih junaka*) starts. The boulevard will lead you to the bulky buildings designed for the clerks of the regional Zetska banovina administration (*see no. 9*). On the other side of the road leading towards Mt Lovćen stands the **Italian Legation** from 1910 with a large garden that once included tennis courts, a favored pastime of foreign diplomats living in Cetinje in those days. Today the legation serves as the seat of the National Library.

1912-14. To the front of the Palace is the Town Park, laid out towards the end of the 19th c. for the pleasure of the growing middle class of Cetinje, while to its back lies the Court Park, once enclosed by a wall. At its further end are two busts erected during the marking of the sentinel of Njegoš's death in 1951, the one representing his teacher Simo Milutinović

Traditional Montenegrin dance performed in the Zetski dom theatre

*The imposing **Banovina** building*

a Serb from the province of Vojvodina who, like many others, came to Cetinje to help the small princedom and was one of the founders of the town's reading room, first high school and a theatre becoming a minister of education in the process.

To the right of the theatre stands the bulky **Banovina** building (Nikolay Krasnov, 1930-32) that got its name after the administrative seat of the Zetska banovina, one of the nine regions into which Yugoslavia was divided in 1929. Today this building serves as the seat of the local assembly of Cetinje but this is also where the national assembly meets on significant occasions, promoting the town as

the historical capital of the country.

The first street to the right of the Banovina will take you to the building of the **Russian Legation**, the most beautiful among the buildings of the foreign missions in Montenegro. This work of architect Corradini completed in 1903 is enclosed by decorative railings with two sentry boxes, has a rich ornamentation on its main façade and a pavilion and a fountain in its garden. Today the building is used by the faculty of Fine Arts.

10. Vlaška crkva

This church is the oldest building in the Cetinje Field but for a long time was not considered as a part of Cetinje which grew from the direction of the monastery. It was erected as a wooden edifice in the mid 15th c, before the establishment of the court and monastery of Ivan Crnojević, by the cattle breeders (*vlasi*) who formed a special

uilding was opened ith the drama "The alkans Empress" *Balkanska carica*) by rince Nikola but the orks on the interior rotracted all the way 1896 due to a lack f funding. Except for e theatre stage, it was so the seat of the state brary and museum nd it was here that ost of the sessions the Montenegrin arliament took place. the courtyard of etski dom stands the ust of Jovan Pavlović,

category of population in medieval Serbia and Zeta. Torn down and rebuilt several times, it obtained its present looks in 1864. Though seemingly quite usual, its fence is actually made from 1544 barrels of Turkish guns captured in 1876-79 wars. The church used to stand in the middle of the graveyard with many *stećak* tombstones (*see p. 224*) but as these were later used as building material only two survive to this

ship was torpedoed in January 1916 close to the Albanian coast and they all drowned. The sculpture of the "fairy" and the reliefs on its sides illustrating the event are work of the sculptor Risto Stijović.

Proceeding northwards by the way of Baja Pivljanina St. after the next four blocks you will reach the **Austro-Hungarian Legation**. This was the first among the buildings of the foreign missions

used by the Institute for the Protection of Monuments of Montenegro.

11. Orlov krš

"Eagle's Crag" is the name for a steep, rocky hill that surmounts the town from the south east. The walk to its peak is popular with the people of Cetinje due to its proximity to the town's centre and an orderly track leading to it where one can see the mausoleum of

Chapel of the Austro-Hungarian Legation

vladika Danilo and enjoy memorable views. The small mausoleum was envisioned by princess Jelena, wife of King Emmanuell of Italy, and then designed in detail by the French architect Frouchet. It has a form of a grave covered by a baldachin with a coat-of-arms on each of its sides – the first is of the state, second of the ruling dynasty, then the old arms of Montenegro and in the end one of the Cetinje metropolitan diocese. In addition to the view of almost all of Cetinje lying beneath you, on the other side open great prospects of the Lovćen Mountain.

day, standing by the gate of the churchyard. Other gravestones are newer in origin, some very decorative. Inside it is an iconostasis painted in 1878 by Djinoski brothers from Macedonia.

On the square at the front of the church a monument known as **"The Fairy of Lovćen"** (*Lovćenska vila*) stands tall. It was erected in 1939 to the memory of 350 men from Montenegro, Boka Kotorska and Hercegovina who left America and headed to help Montenegro in its efforts in WWI but whose

to be constructed – the building of it started in 1896 and was finished two years later. The catholic chapel in the style of small churches of the Adriatic coast adjoining the legation was consecrated in 1899. Today the building is

Vladika Danilo's Tomb on Orlov krš

3 Lovćen

20 km from Cetinje

Mount Lovćen is the utmost symbol of Montenegro, symbol of its defiance to its enemies and of its permanence. If one bears in mind that its wooded slopes served as the last retreat for Montenegrins in times of war while its high stone peaks were the first glimpse of the country a visitor would see coming from the sea, the mountain's symbolic value is clearly understood. Furthermore, Lovćen in all probability the "Black Mountain" that gave Montenegro its name. The highest peak is Štirovnik (1749m) topped by a TV transmitter, but it is its second highest Jezerski vrh (1657m) that holds more importance as the last resting place of the country's national hero – Njegoš.

The area around the principal peaks constitutes the Lovćen national Park. The whole of its karst scenery is dotted with fissures and pits giving it a distinct look. Due to the height difference on its deeply ascending sides

A stunning expanse of panoramic views from the top of Mt Lovćen

there are several zones of different plant habitation here. One more reason for the variety of plant life on Lovćen is the influence of both the Mediterranean and the sub-continental climate. Around 60% of it is covered in forest with birch dominating, while on the north face of the mountain grows the rare Bosnian pine (*Pinus heldreichii*). In contrast to the plant life there are very few animal species here, mainly due to the mountain's lack of streams and lakes; of mammals one encounters rabbit and fox and with regards to birds mostly partridge, quail and wild pigeon, also there is a number of reptiles and snakes living here.

The most usual way to reach the national park is by a long, winding road from Cetinje on which you will be charged one Euro for the entrance to the perimeter of the park. The hub of tourist activity is **Ivanova korita** (14km from Cetinje), a wavy upland known for its

Ivanova korita with the view of the Jezerski vrh peak

exceptionally clean air and water, the latter is mentioned in one of the most popular folk songs of Montenegro. A small hostel for schoolchildren, a mountain hut, restaurant and the visitors' centre are located here. By the visitors' centre is a group of **busts** representing all the rulers of Montenegro from the Petrović-Njegoš dynasty. Nearby is also a large threshing floor and a humble chapel erected by King Nikola.

By far the most important monument of the national park is the **Njegoš Mausoleum** atop the Jezerski vrh (*21km from Cetinje, open from May to October from 9 to 18h*). Already during his life Njegoš decided upon the idea of being buried here, at the top of a magnificent mountain he watched many times from Cetinje and where he often came to contemplate the world and his life. He built here a small round church in 1844 and pleaded with the Montenegrins to disregard tradition and take his body here after

An exhilarating walk towards the Njegoš Mausoleum

his death. His wish came true only in 1855 due to the high snows in the winter of his death and the war with the Turks the following spring. The church remained undisturbed by all but rare pilgrims visiting his grave until WWI when it was damaged in the fighting. The occupying Austro-Hungarian forces decided to destroy this symbol of Montenegro and build here a giant statue in remembrance of their victory but they failed to carry out this plan. In 1925 King Aleksandar of Yugoslavia rebuilt the church with some minor additions. However, in the late 1950s a new initiative appeared to tear down the "Aleksandar's Chapel" and build a mausoleum worthy of Njegoš's importance. The controversial plan met

A breathtaking view of Boka Kotorska from the circular road around Lovćen

ith fierce opposition nd started the heated iscussions that lasted r years. Finally, the urch was pulled down nd the present day ausoleum was open 1974.

found his inspiration in the style of antique shrines. Its first part is an atrium of black marble with a symbolic well in the middle. This is where you can purchase the ticket (€2)

pose of reflection, with an eagle sheltering his back. Directly beneath the monument is a small crypt with the Njegoš's grave, approached from behind. On the other side of the mausoleum is a path snaking along a forbidding precipice leading to a round viewpoint. On a clear day one can see for hundreds of kilometers from here, as far as the coast of Italy. All around you is the rocky landscape of Montenegro, waves upon waves of hills and crags, with a brief glimpse of Boka Kotorska.

The statue of Njegoš in black marble and gold setting

The farthest point eachable by car is a very mall parking beneath e top which can often e overcrowded. Next it is a small souvenir op and a restaurant hile above begin e 461 stairs leading rough a tunnel to the p of the mountain. he author of the ausoleum, Croatian culptor Ivan Meštrović

and browse through some more souvenirs. Facing the entrance of the atrium stand two giant caryatides dressed in the national costume of Montenegro. Behind them one enters the mausoleums highlight – the gold-covered room with the grandiose monument to Njegoš (weighing 28 tons!), who stands represented in a

After a short ride down from Jezerski vrh take the first road to the right leading around Štirovnik. Following the next few curves you will reach the side of the mountain facing Boka Kotorska with excellent viewpoints from where all representative photos of this magnificent bay's perplexity have been made. The road ends at the western edge of the Njeguši village.

❾ Njeguši

📖 250

This historical village lies nested in a small karst field directly underneath the northern foot of Mt Lovćen. Approaching the village from the Bukovica pass from the direction of Cetinje you can see almost the whole of the Njeguško polje field, a green patch of fertile ground in a hollow of grey rocks and dark woods, whose lowest point stands at 850m above sea. Looking from the same location, one can distinguish some of the ten little hamlets of Njeguši clan, still counted as separate villages by statisticians

Njeguši village in their karst field

but otherwise connected by the main road into a one whole. Njeguši is only a stone throws away from the seaside which can be seen from the edge of the field, but this proximity is deceiving as the descent to Kotor takes three hours on foot. As this route was also the shortest way from the seaside to Cetinje, Njeguši was a spot that could not be avoided by any traveler coming to Montenegro. This extraordinary position on the brink of two

A WARRIOR-POET AMONGST HIS BARBARIANS

Njegoš was born in 1813 in the house of Tomo Petrović, a member of the family which for several generations provided Montenegro with its bishops. Baptized as Radivoje, short Rade (by which name he remained known to Montenegrins throughout his life) he spent his youth much alike the other children from his native village of Njeguši, taking care of sheep and learning to use a gun and a sabre. Due to his natural brightness and strong constitution his uncle vladika Petar noticed early on that he could be his likely successor. Rade was sent to prepare to be a monk and got some basic education in orthodox monasteries of Montenegro and Boka Kotorska. His main teacher, however, was Simo Milutinović of Sarajevo, a Serb romanticist poet who acquainted Rade with great European writers inspiring him with love for verse and writing. But above all, Milutinović made him appreciate folk poetry and it was under this influence that Rade started writing his first poems. In 1830 metropolitan Petar died and, though only 18, Rade took the monastic vows (taking the new name Petar) and was consecrated as the new bishop-prince of Montenegro. Thus his youth was abruptly ended and he was faced with many problems affecting his small country. On one side were the Turks who never recognized the independence of Montenegro and on the other internal bickering between the clans. Njegoš took the burden of ruling the small state courageously and became a warrior and a judge. Of imposing stature with his two meters height and possessing wise counsel for the problems of his poor and uneducated people, he played his role well but within him remained a free spirit, a philosopher and a poet who stoically obeyed the fate given to him. Ruling the country from his ascetic seat in Cetinje monastery, he was condemned to spend his life in a land where there were only a few men who could read and write. This painful knowledge combined with his talent and the cruel destiny of his people gave impetus for the creation of brilliant works such as the philosophical "Light of the Microcosm", drama "The False Emperor Šćepan the Little" and poems on Montenegrin wars "Slobodijada". But his true masterpiece remains the world-renowned "The Mountain Wreath", a drama that became popular with the educated for its subtleness and also with the common folk for its use of the style of folk poetry. Witnessing the wealth and education of other nations during his trips to St Petersburg and Vienna, Njegoš tried to meld the painful barbarity of his people by founding schools and bringing a printing press to Cetinje. Tired by his obligations he fell ill of tuberculosis and died in 1851, leaving behind him works that seem as fresh as when they were first written and the status of a hero amongst all Montenegrins.

worlds was
so important
previous
nturies as
om here the
Iontenegrins
uld easily
mmunicate
ith the
enetian
thorities
nd this is
hy both the
ling family of
trović-Njegoš
nd their most
rious rivals
e guvernadurs
adonjići (see p. 22)
riginated from Njeguši.
fter Montenegro lost
s independence and as
etter roads to and from
etinje were built, the
nportance of Njeguši

The birth house of Petar II Petrović Njegoš

period, and *kaštradina*, dried mutton. There are several families who produce *pršut* in Njeguši; do not hesitate to knock on their door and ask them to take a

its history, scenic road to Kotor and the fame among the gourmets, there are several fine restaurants in the village visited by passers by.

The principal sight in Njeguši is the **birth house of Petar II Petrović Njegoš**, the famous ruler and an illustrious poet. It lies directly by the road in the middle of the village; the whole complex was closed by a decorative iron railing during the reign of King Nikola who also built here his austere palace intending to make the sight into a royal compound. The old birth house of Njegoš is

One of the rooms in Njegoš's birth house

windled even though
s name still causes awe
nong all history buffs.
owever, the village is
est known today for its
xcellent food products,
r example *njeguški*
šut - a dried ham
hich owes its specific
avour to the mix of
igh mountain air and
e warm air coming
om the seaside and
so to the wood which
burned underneath
. Other specialties here
iclude *njeguški sir*, a
ieese dried for a long

peak at their producing facilities, smoky rooms in which dozens of hams hang high from the rooftop. Capitalizing on

---

WHERE TO EAT IN NJEGUŠI

Kod Pera na Bukovicu
Cetinje road; 041/760-055; open 07-22h
A legendary inn with a tradition dating from 1882, a real rarity in Montenegro. Though more a drinking place, it also offers fine snacks and lighter meals.

Njeguška sijela
Njeguši village; 041/239-801; open 7-24h
An old restaurant in the centre of the village offering all the specialties of the area from cheese (*njeguški sir*) and smoked ham (*pršut*) to dried mutton (*kaštradina*) and mead (*medovina*). There is a choice of souvenirs to buy here as well.

Drying the famous Njeguši ham

a simple stone building housing a modest **museum** (*open every day 9-17; tel. 067/807-522; admission €2*). The house was built around 1780 by Njegoš's uncle and his predecessor Petar I as a dwelling for his extended family (*zadruga*), with one family living in each of its three large rooms, each with a separate entrance but all connected to each other. Inside the house you will see the simple wooden furnishings from the period, then pictures of well known personalities from the period and some of the editions of Njegoš's works. Beneath the living quarters is a basement where farm animals and primitive farming tools were kept.

Directly across the road is **St George's**, one of several old churches in Njeguši. This one dates from 1856 and is typical for the region – a modest stone edifice with the belfry "on distaff". In front of the church stands the attractive bell donated by King Aleksandar of Yugoslavia, a grandson of King Nikola.

⑩ Ostrog

15 km from Nikšić
50 km from Podgorica

St Vasilije of Ostrog, May 12th

By far the greatest pilgrimage sight in Montenegro, this twin orthodox monastery is besieged by sick and needy no less then by groups of religious tourists. These all come to bow in front of the miraculous relics of St Vasilije of Ostrog (*Sveti Vasilije Ostroški*), a 17th c. orthodox bishop of Herzegovina and founder of the monastery who performed many miraculous deeds during his life. As well as for its religious importance the upper monastery is known equally for its unique setting. One can see it from afar rammed in the vertical cliff high above the valley of river Zeta that emerges beneath it. It was founded in 1656 by bishop Vasilije Jovanović as he fled from his seat which was destroyed by the Turks. Here he spent the rest of his days living in ascetic poverty and performing miracles for Orthodox, Catholic and Muslims alike. The monastery's position close to the place where the sides of the nearby mountains draw nearest brought with it a turbulent history: it is here that the Montenegrins blocked

Barefooted pilgrims on their way to Ostrog Monastery

*t Vasilije of Ostrog on an
ld icon*

...e passage between
...ikšić and Podgorica on
...any occasions when
...ey waged war against
...e Turks. In these battles
...strog, itself a fort of
...kind, was destroyed
...everal times, but the
...oly relics were always
...idden in safer places.

The local road
...ranches off from
...e Podgorica-Nikšić
...ighway for the village
...f Bogetići. From the
...illage to the monastery
...e road is 8km long
...ut seems much longer
...ecause of its poor state.
...Vinding above the
...bysses, it is very narrow
...nd badly secured, not
... mention the heavy
...us traffic on it, so one
...hould be extremely
...areful here.

The road first reaches
...e **Lower Monastery** in
...ont of which is a large
...arking lot surrounded
...ith souvenir shops
...nd a few restaurants.
...he church of the lower
...onastery dates from
...824 and is a modest
...one edifice with a high
...elfry. The frescoes in it
...re quite recent in origin
...ut interesting for the
...ramatic scenes they
...epict from the life of
...t Vasilije and his many
...ealings.

The **Upper Monastery**
...an be reached by a

short drive up the
serpentines (this section
of the road is in perfect
condition), or by a half
an hour climb through
the woods, the path that
many of the believers
cover bare footed. In
front of the monastery
is a plateau from
whose edge one enjoys
spectacular views over
the Zeta valley. Here
there is also a hostel
for visitors, where one
can spend the night for
only one Euro (in ascetic
conditions though).
The white monastery
complex, which seems
stuck onto the rock, is
approached through a

small gate. Directly in
front, on the lowest
level, is a tiny cavern
church where the
miraculous relics are
displayed. Its walls
are depicted with
frescoes dating from
1665 which are barely
visible from the thick
soot of the ever lit
candles. Stairs lead to
the highest level with
a terrace on one side
and another small cave
church on the other.
This one contains
frescoes from 1667
done by painter Radul,
which are regarded as
his best work.

Upper Ostrog monastery embedded in solid rock

WHERE TO EAT IN THE VICINITY OF OSTROG

Koliba
Bogetići (8km from Ostrog); 069/603-986; 8-24h
Located in the centre of the village, on the beginning (or the
end) of a painstaking tour to Ostrog, this restaurant is almost
always jam-packed. Nevertheless, the hurried waiters manage
it all and you will promptly be served with a plate from a
wide choice of national dishes, some of which are more than
enormous.

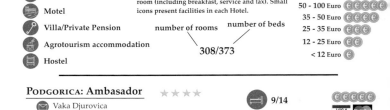

PRICE RANGE - for one person in a two-bed room (including breakfast, service and tax). Small icons present facilities in each Hotel.

> 100 Euro
50 - 100 Euro
35 - 50 Euro
25 - 35 Euro
12 - 25 Euro
< 12 Euro

Hotel
Motel
Villa/Private Pension
Agrotourism accommodation
Hostel

number of rooms   number of beds

308/373

Podgorica: Ambasador   ★ ★ ★ ★

Vaka Djurovica

+ 382 (0)20 272 233

www.ambasador.cg.yu

9/14

This small, prestigious hotel lies on the bank of the River Morača in a quiet part of the town just a few minutes walk from the town core. One of its most notable features is its cascaded terrace reaching to the edge of the water. The rooms and apartments are elegant and the service efficient.

Podgorica: Ambiente   ★ ★ ★

Cetinjski put 34

+ 382 (0)20 235 535

www.poslovnivodic.com/ambiente

12/18

This tiny hotel lies on the main road towards Cetinje, a location that can get noisy due to the traffic. The rooms are spacious and comfortable although simply furnished.

Podgorica: Boja Tours   ★ ★ ★ ★

Mirka Vešovica bb

+ 382 (0)20 621 240

www.montenegrohotels.org

20/24

This hotel is situated within arms' length of the town centre. Contrasting with its dull exterior, the inside is brightly coloured, well furnished and equipped including a large gym and a sauna. The rooms are quite small and follow a pattern of classical design; those facing the street should be avoided due to the traffic noise.

Podgorica: Evropa   ★ ★ ★

Orahovačka 16

+ 382 (0)20 623 444

www.hotelevropa.cg.yu

30/50

The hotel lies in a shanty neighborhood round the corner from the bus and train station, this being its main plus. The rooms are, nevertheless, comfortable and clean but the rest of the place seems more like a restaurant than a hotel.

Podgorica: Podgorica   ★ ★ ★ ★

Bul. Svetog Petra Cetinjskog 1

+ 382 (0)20 402 500

www.hotelpodgorica.

44/85

The hotel has a lovely setting overlooking the river Morača and though it is very close to the city centre one is amazed by its tranquility. Recently renovated, it's rooms are comfortable in their minimalist style and all rooms have large terraces with views. The staff is more than friendly and helpful. The large restaurant terrace offers excellent food.

Podgorica: Eminent   ★ ★ ★ ★

Njegoševa 25

+ 382 (0)20 664 646

www.eminent.cg.yu

13/26

This smaller hotel lies in the very centre of the city, the hub of cafes and nightlife and as such lacks peace and intimacy. The rooms are also small with furnishings that tend to be arty but the service is efficient and welcoming.

Podgorica: Crna Gora   ★ ★ ★ ★

Bulevar Svetog Petra Cetinjskog 2

+ 382 (0)20 443 443

www.hotelcg.com

138/200

Podgorica's oldest hotel, this legendary place where history was made during the communist era now eagerly awaits renovation. For the moment it is a mix of retro designs covered clumsily with boisterous transition-era luxury. The room quality varies heavily with category (economy, standard or lux). The local casino and nightclub can get annoying for those wishing for rest and relaxation.

Podgorica: Kerber ★ ★ ★

Novaka Miloseva 6

+ 382 (0)20 405 405

www.hotelkerber.cg.yu

20/38

The hotel lies on the upper floors of a small shopping centre in the very heart of the city. Catering to many different visitors, the hotel (and especially its restaurant and gym) is overly constricted but clean and cheerfully looking. Rooms are simple and small but very comfortable.

Podgorica: Lovćen ★ ★ ★

Petrovački put, Zabjelo

+ 382 (0)20 625 219

www.hotellovcen.cg.yu

23/41

This small hotel lies outside the city on the road towards the airport and the seaside. The surroundings are unpromising but with its tiny garden, a spacious parking lot, simply furnished and clean rooms the hotel manages to rank itself in the decent lower end of budget hotels.

Podgorica: Garni hotel Holliday ★ ★ ★

I Proleterske 11

+ 382 (0)20 611 411

20/32

This mid-range hotel on the north-eastern outskirt of the city lies in a bleak setting bordered with a road and a railroad track. On the whole it is quite comfortable, with large rooms and functional bathrooms with showers, but its public areas are diminutive.

Podgorica: Kosta's

Bohinjska 1

+ 382 (0)20 656 702

www.hotelkostas.cg.yu

14/46

Located in an dismal residential district not far from the bus and railway stations, this simple hotel has basically furnished rooms that lack style but not facilities.

Podgorica: Best Western Premier Montenegro ★ ★ ★ ★

Bulevar Svetog Petra Cetinjskog 145

+ 382 (0)20 406 500

www.bestwestern-ce.com

48/79

This brand new up-market hotel is conveniently situated in the business centre of Podgorica and therefore has excellent conference facilities. The large, comfortable rooms are enhanced by elegant and efficient service.

PODGORICA: Plavnica

✉ Plavnica bb
☎ + 382 (0)20 443 700

🛏 4/8

This interesting tourist complex stands by the waters of Lake Skadarsko, some 20km from Podgorica. It has an excellen restaurant and well appointed rooms. Here one can rent boats, kayaks and pedal boats, while their landing pier makes it a usual stop for those cruising around the Lake. Organized boat tours on the Lake are also available.

CETINJE: Hotel Grand ★ ★ ★

✉ Njegoševa 1
☎ + 382 (0)41 242 400
🌐 www.hotel-grand.tripod.com/cetinje

🛏 220/420

The only hotel in Cetinje is situated in a pleasant park just south of the city centre. Its oversized facilities are somewhat run down but still offer by far the most comprehensive service.

CETINJE: Zicer

✉ Obilića polje bb
☎ + 382 (0)41 234 630

13/29

This brand new hotel is focused primarily on accommodating visiting sportsmen. Conveniently situated next to the bus station and very close to the city centre.

CETINJE: Bungalovi Ivanova korita

✉ NP Lovćen, Ivanova korita
☎ + 382 (0)41 231 570
🌐 www.nparkovi.cg.yu

5/20

These five bungalows are situated in a forest near the visitors center, in the heart of the „Lovćen" national park. Each has two rooms, a kitchen and a bathroom as well as a small terrace.

Lovcen, "Ivanova korita"

CETINJE: Martinović

✉ Ivan-begova 22
☎ + 382 (0)69 055 473

4/5

A private pension within an arm's length of the major attractions of Cetinje. The two-bed rooms are clean, airy and comfortable.

VIRPAZAR: Pelikan ★

✉ Virpazar bb
☎ + 382 (0)20 711 077
🌐 www.pelikan-zec.cg.yu

🛏 7/16

A small hotel in an old building in Virpazar, with the well-known restaurant of the same name on the groundfloor. It also has a small souvenir shop and the owners organize tours around Lake Skadarsko.

Virpazar, "13. jul"

VIRPAZAR: 13.jul ★ ★

✉ Virpazar bb

☎ + 382 (0)20 711 120

🌐 www.korali.org

25/52

This hotel is located in the townlet of Virpazar and is an ideal starting point for tours around Lake Skadarsko. Simple but comfortable, the rooms all enjoy vistas of the Lake and are excellent value for money. Note that the hotel is open only from April to November.

DANILOVGRAD: Glava Zete ★ ★

✉ Glava Zete

☎ + 382 (0)40 212 666

30/75

The hotel lies in a peaceful setting 7km from the Podgorica-Nikšić road and close to the hydro plant on the River Zeta. The rooms are spacious but basically furnished. The hotel also has several sports' grounds.

DANILOVGRAD: Pejović ★ ★ ★

✉ Ćurilac bb

☎ + 382 (0)20 810 165

6/12

A small hotel along the highway near Danilovgrad. It has all the basic tourist amenities.

Plavnica complex on Lake Skadarsko

NORTHERN MONTENEGRO

The north of Montenegro consists of contrasting sights carved and arranged to their magnificent perfection by nature. The high mountains are joined by vast tablelands and deep river canyons, all mixed in a memorable array of experiences. The ideal example of this is Mount Durmitor, which together with the small town of Žabljak is the capital of hiking and mountaineering in Montenegro. More than forty of its craggy peaks rise above 2,000 meters, among them Bobotov kuk (2523 m), the highest in the country. Facing the massif lies the contrasting highland plateau of Jezera that got its name after innumerable smaller and larger lakes.

Further, both Durmitor and Jezera are bordered by river canyons of Tara, Sušica and Komarnica. The canyons of this region are world renowned above all the one of Tara. With its

other was transformed into a long lake of staggeringly blue colour. There are many fascinating but relatively unexplored mountains in this region such as Maglić at the very border with Bosnia-Herzegovina, a charming place with its Trnovačko jezero Lake just below its peak, Sinjajevina with its vast pastures above the forests, or Ljubišnja in the very north with its small villages unchanged by civilization. The region around the mining town of Pljevlja is somewhat different. Here the scenery is taken by rolling hills, larger villages and orchards, unthinkable of in the higher regions.

The whole of this region is scarcely populated and there are many wild and desolate places, left to nature and to wild animals. Knowing that one cannot survive on his own in the wild, the peasants of the north are always willing to help and will gladly treat

Adventure seekers on the River Tara

300m from its overlooking mountain tops to the river it is the deepest in Europe and second only to the Grand Canyon in the whole world. Rafting in its magnificently clean waters, passing virgin forests, giant pines and innumerable waterfalls is a once in lifetime experience. The other two canyons also hold records: the initial part of Komarnica canyon, called Nevidio ("Not Seen") is so narrow that no living man passed it until 1965 when fully equipped mountaineers disclosed its mysteries. The canyon of river Piva has been cut in two by the high dam in Mratinje – one side of it remained the inhospitable canyon, while the

you to their modest houses and tasteful dairy products.

The climate is harsh and uncompromising: the winters start early and last until May, with lots of snow which leaves many of the places cut off from the rest of the world for months. To prepare for them people need to work hard, stacking hay for the cattle and piling wood for heating. The pleasant summers are to some extent hotter only in the vicinity of Nikšić where the hot air from Zeta climbs to its wide field. Nikšić, the second largest town in Montenegro, is the cultural and economical hub of the North. It is known for its ironworks, the brewery and numerous old bridges traversing the rivers that get lazier in this wide field.

Historically looking, this is a part of old Herzegovina, named after the 15th c lord Herzog Stefan, whose seat was the Soko-grad above the confluence of Tara and Piva, on today's border with Bosnia. It is also the hub of the East Herzegovinian dialect spoken from West Serbia to Croatia, whose resounding beauty captures attention whether in everyday speech or in traditional singing accompanied with *gusle*, the Serb national instrument which is still played by many here. Due to Vuk Karadžić, linguist and reformer of Serb alphabet, this dialect has from the middle of 19th c. been taken as the basis for the literary Serbo-Croatian.

The historical monuments in this secluded area are scattered in its wild scenery and sometimes hard to find. Surprisingly, most of them come from the era of early Turkish dominance (16th c.) when many people ran to the security of the places sheltered by mountains and forests. Here they built new monasteries, the most beautiful of them being those of Piva and Sveta Trojica close to Pljevlja. Though today there aren't many Muslims left here, Husein-pasha's Mosque in Pljevlja with its 42 meters high minaret remains the most beautiful monument to the long presence of the Ottoman Empire in Montenegro.

An earned rest after a travel over harsh terrain

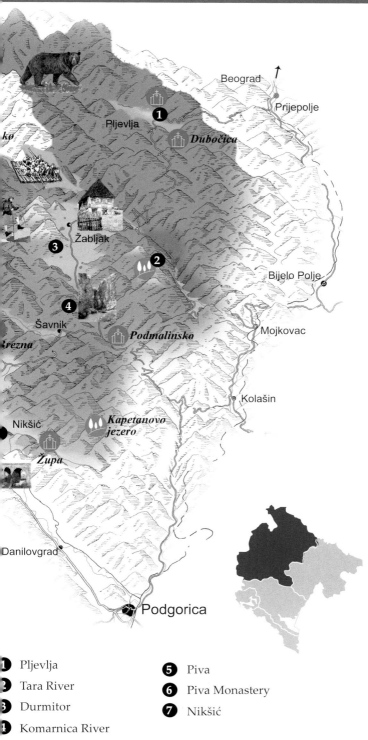

Beograd

Prijepolje

1

Pljevlja

Dubočica

ko

Žabljak

3

2

Bijelo Polje

4

Šavnik

Mojkovac

rezna

Podmalinsko

Kolašin

Nikšić

Kapetanovo jezero

Župa

Danilovgrad

Podgorica

1 Pljevlja

5 Piva

2 Tara River

6 Piva Monastery

3 Durmitor

7 Nikšić

4 Komarnica River

❶ Pljevlja

👥 21,400

🚌 Miloša Tošića bb, 052/23-040

🏛 November festivities (15-20th Nov)

The northernmost town of Montenegro is the most important industrial and mining centre and contributes almost the entire coal produced in the country. That coal is used to supply the country's only thermo power plant that in itself accounts for half of Montenegro's total electrical production. Regrettably, the high chimneys seen from every part of town make Pljevlja also the most polluted town in Montenegro.

The pleasant and fertile area around the confluence of river Breznica and river Ćehotina has been settled since time immemorial. During the Roman rule, in the village of Komini not far from Pljevlja, developed the most important town of continental Montenegro. No record of the town today

known only as "Municipium S" can be found amongst the written sources. Its incomplete name has been discovered on the fragment found during archeological excavations that revealed its size and significance. In the middle ages the settlement called Breznica grew in the place where several caravan roads from the coast merged. The name Pljevlja is first mentioned in 1430 and comes from the word *pljeva*, "chaff". Soon after this – in 1462 - it fell into Turkish hands. Retaining its trading role the place furthermore became the seat of the province of Herzegovina, eventually growing into a prosperous oriental town. Fortunes changed for Pljevlja in the 19th c: in 1818 a great fire devoured almost the whole of it and in 1833 the provincial administration was

Husein-pasha's Mosque, the pearl of Ottoman architecture

moved to Mostar. The impoverished Pljevlja became in 1878 the seat of a large Austro-Hungarian garrison but maintained the Turkish civil administration. The town was liberated in 1912 and became a part of Montenegro but most of the Muslims could not bear the change and left for Turkey. This reduced the town's population to half of its pre-war size. After WWII, Pljevlja with its ore rich hinterland became the motor behind the industrialization of socialist Montenegro and the face of the town was rapidly changed to its present day image.

There isn't much left to witness the town's rich history. The old quarters are oriental more in character than in monuments, while the principal streets are lined with apartment blocks of strange inspiration reminiscent of the pagodas. The very centre of the town is marked by the elegant **Hussein-pasha's Mosque** (*Husein-pašina džamija*),

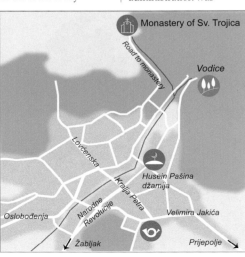

Monastery of Sv. Trojica

Road to monastery

Vodice

Lovćenska

Husein Pašina džamija

Kralja Petra

Narodne Revolucije

Oslobođenja

Velimira Jakića

↓ Žabljak

Prijepolje ↘

the most beautiful oriental monument in Montenegro. This gem of Ottoman architecture labeled as a "mosque worthy of an emperor" by the Ottoman writer Evliya Celebi in his 17th c. travelogue, was constructed around 1580 based on the orders of Hussein-pasha Boljanić. Born in the vicinity of Pljevlja, he climbed to the top ranks of the Ottoman Empire holding the title of vizier and positions such as the administrator of Egypt and the governor of Baghdad. It is assumed that its architect was Hayrudin who also built the famous Mostar Bridge. The approach to the mosque's yard is by the covered fountain, used for ritual cleaning. The mosque has a square base with a large central cupola and two decorative ones at its rear. The open porch stands on the stone columns ending in ogee arches while covered with three smaller cupolas and brightly painted. Next to it stands

a slender minaret which was rebuilt in 1911 after it was destroyed by a lightening. With its height of 42m it is one of the tallest in the whole of the Balkans. The interior distinguishes itself with many colorful floral and geometric paintings of which the most imposing are the ones covering the cupola and the one of the mihrab niche. The courtyard also contains the clock tower

Church and dwellings of the Monastery of Sveta Trojica

built simultaneously as the mosque and several Muslim and Roman tombstones.

Not far from the mosque is the **Milet bašta** (Turkish for "People's Garden") a park with a restaurant of the same name where you will be served by

the pupils of the local waiters' college.

Another pleasant recreational area in Pljevlja is **Vodice** to the east of the town centre. The sight rightfully deserves its name since water (*voda*) is everywhere: a small lake is fed by a fast brook crossed by a couple of bridges.

At the outskirts of the town, 1,5km from the centre, lies the

Monastery of Sveta Trojica (Holy Trinity). To reach it, pass the Milet bašta and head uphill and to the right, passing the large wooded area. The monastery was founded around 1535 by Visarion, a wealthy merchant from Pljevlja who decided to spend the end of his life as a monk. For his endowment he chose the rocks at the end of a quiet vale surrounded by a forest, which seemingly appears many miles away from any settlement. During an

Splendid arabesques in the mosque's dome

A colourful 16th century frescoe

extensive renovation in 1592 the original church was widened with a narthex and a cupola. In this and the following century here operated a small but enduring transcribing school which left behind an extensive array of beautifully painted manuscripts. In the 19th c. the monastery got its present look with an outer narthex added to the church and large buildings of monks' dwellings. These are excellent examples of folk architecture while their details are heavily influenced by the orient. Built into the outer walls of the church there are several 19th c tombstones, while on the side hangs a *klepetalo*, a wooden board that replaces the bells during the observation of the fasts. The interior of the church is covered by colourful if somewhat rustic frescoes by priest Strahinja of Budimlje from 1595. Apart from the usual cycles such as the extensive Passion of Christ we find here also the procession of ten Nemanjić rulers, which reflects the atmosphere of national discontent and insurrections against the Turks. Sveta

Trojica has one of the richest treasuries in the country. A part of it is available for viewing but

A gold-plated book cover in the monastery's treasury

you'll have to specifically ask to see it (*Smijemo li pogledati manastirsku riznicu?*). The admission is charged €0.50 per person. Amongst many worthy items the most valuable are the two late 16th c. icons by Andrija Raičević (St Stephen and the Three Hierarchs), an inlaid monastery door of oriental inspiration, several 16th c. liturgical objects influenced by the gothic style, and finally several relics, such as the staff that allegedly belonged to St Sava as well as his left hand. There is a possibility to stay at the monastery in the adapted monks' cells (€10 *per night*), idea for those who prefer the experience to comfort.

Pljevlja also has a **Local Museum** (*Zavičajni muzej, Trg 13. jula bb; tel. 089/322-247 open 9 a.m. – 3 p.m.*), situated diagonally from the Hussein-pasha's mosque in the Hall of Culture where it shares its premises with the public library. The museum has a valuable archeological collection consisting of the finds from the "Municipium S". Amongst these stands out the glass vase of diatretum type, one of only a few examples preserved in the whole world.

RESTAURANTS OF PLJEVLJA

Milet bašta
Prvog decembra bb; tel. 052/554-332; open 09-23h
This legendary restaurant is located in the park of the same name, very close to the town centre. Although there is plentiful seating in the shade outside, it is often crowded as many celebrations take place here, some of them are often really boisterous which could be considered as its major downside. As this is the favorite venue for the locals and their guests it is pointless to emphasize that the food is very good and reasonably priced.

Oaza
Ratnih vojnih invalida; 069/084-829; open 07-24h
Hidden away from the centre, this small restaurant has a cozy atmosphere that comes as a surprise in Pljevlja. The set of food choices is classic and all the meals are plentiful.

Tri šešira
Njegoševa 26 (Moćevac); 052/352-005; open 09-23h
This restaurant is hidden in a quiet residential street above the centre of the town and is popular with the locals. The menu lists all the usual meals with the house specialty being the selection of three domestic cheeses of different maturity, smoked ham and, of course, the inevitable spit-roasts.

❷ Tara River

052/360-228

With its length of 150km, Tara is the longest river in Montenegro. Its headwaters are two brooks descending from the peaks of Komovi, then the river rapidly presses northwards in a long bow and ends at the other end of the country at Šćepan polje

Clouds rising from the depths of the River Tara canyon

where it joins with Piva and forms River Drina. However, a feature that transcends national borders and rings awe around the world is that in the second part of its course Tara has cut an astounding canyon, whose sides are up to 1,300 meters high and rank as the highest in Europe and second in the world, the first of course being the Grand Canyon in Colorado. If beauty could be measured Tara and its canyon would be the top competitors as well: clear green water that becomes turbid only after heavy rains, interchanging gorges and fields, marvellous woods of birch and pine, numerous waterfalls and white waters famous with rafters. The uttermost

recognition of its beauties came in 1977 when Tara Canyon was added by UNESCO to the list of the world's ecological biosphere reserves.

The first part of Tara's course that passes through Kolašin and Mojkovac, though also beautiful, is overshadowed by its canyon. Traveling north from Mojkovac the pleasant meadowland dotted with houses and orchards slowly grows narrower while the mountains rise higher. The canyon formally starts at the entrance of the Durmitor National Park, 15 km north of Mojkovac. Close below the small hotel "Ravnjak" is the confluence of fast and noisy Bistrica and Tara. Not far from here, immediately after the first rapid, is an interesting wooden bridge at **Djavolji laz**, one of the narrowest points of the canyon. The first two kilometers upon entering the national park the road winds thorough **Crne podi**, a pristine wood of centuries old black pines. These giants rise up to 50m high and close above the road blocking the sunlight and clinging incredibly to the steep rocks high above the river.

The village of Gornja Dobrilovina lies nested in a widening at the end of the woods. It is best known for the **Monastery of Dobrilovina** a few hundred meters to the right of the road. The modest monastery church was built in 1602 but has since been ravaged several times by the Turks and nothing of the original interior decoration has survived. On the other side of the road starts a forest path leading to Lake Zabojsko (5 km away) hidden in the woods on the slopes of Mt Sinjajevina. The road continues steadily northwards; a good place to rest is the **Ćorbudžak spring** that bursts strongly just below the road. Some 10 kilometers further down the road is **Splavište** (sometimes also called

Church of the Dobrilovina Monastery

Djurdjevića Tara bridge hanging over the precipice of the Tara Canyon

Šljivansko), a starting point for many of the rafting tours with a small camp alongside. One kilometer further along the roadside stands the **memorial to vojvoda Tripko Džaković**, who died here in the 1875 war while not allowing the Turks to cross the river. Next, the road crosses the rocks from which springs **Ljutica** ("Fearsome") a river only 170m long but rumbling a dazzling amount of water, some 1000 liters per second, which makes it one of the most buoyant springs in Europe. The road now leaves the river and slowly ascends up to the **Djurdjevića Tara Bridge**, probably the most memorable point in the canyon. The bridge was constructed in 1937-40 according to the plans of engineer Mijat Trojanović and at the time presented an admirable constructional achievement. Its total length is 370 meters with the largest of its arches spanning 116 meters. In the middle of this arch the bridge rises 151 meters above the river. From this location open dramatic views over and along the canyon. The bust of Lazar Jauković on the western end of the bridge stands as a

reminder to a sad story about a life irreversibly connected with this fascinating construction. Jauković, born in the vicinity, was one of the engineers who built the bridge. Just a few years later, in 1943, he was entrusted by communist partisans to blow it up and to prevent the arrival of enemy forces. Jauković did the job well and blew up only the smallest arch. For this act he was later captured by the nationalist *četnik* forces and shot on the bridge.

From this point the road leaves Tara, on one side continuing to Pljevlja and on the other climbing to the Jezera plateau and to Žabljak. The rest of the sights described from here on can only be reached by those rafting down the river.

Some five kilometers further down the river stands the **Greek Bridge** (*Grčki most*), where the old road crossed the river since

Roman times and which was very busy continuously up to 1937 and the construction of the new bridge. On the right bank of the river there is also a small medieval cemetery with *stećak* gravestones. Not far from here, deeper in the woods, are the remains of the **Roman sanctuary** dedicated to god Mithras. The path that branches to the right from the bridge leads to the **Arhangel Monastery** which following centuries of lying in ruins has been renovated recently. Continuing down the river one comes to the Bijela vrela ("White Springs"), a natural phenomenon. These springs funnel water through underground tunnels from Žabljak for ten kilometers, passing unusu

An exciting way to travel

lly, under the riverbed of Tara and emerging on its right bank! After the oncoming two rapids Tara reaches **Lazin kamen**, its narrowest and deepest point: here the river shrinks to just 4 to 6m wide, while its depth reaches 12m. **River Draga** is the most important tributary of Tara in its flow through the canyon. It descends from the Ljubišnja Mountain with a gradient of 88m per kilometer forming a small canyon 6km long, known for its large number of eagles' nests. Next comes **Radovan luka** (24 km from Splavište), the sandy beach on the left bank; behind it is the flat terrain that gives home to a camp and a small motel, a usual overnight stop for rafters (see p. 228). While the right bank remains steep, the left one gradually opens forming a wide amphitheatre in which rests the **village of Tepca**. It lies more than a thousand meters below the rest of the terrain to the south and enjoys an unusual form of solitude. At the side where this amphitheatre closes, the canyon is at its deepest measuring 1343m from the river to the Veliki Štuoc peak rising above the left bank. Further down one reaches **Sige Bajlovića**, cascading waterfalls descending into Tara from the height of 35 meters. Its waters originate from a still unexplored cave some 100 m uphill that has a small lake in it. **River Sušica** (see p. 215), that has also carved an attractive can-

yon, flows into Tara from the left. The **Nozdruć** spring and waterfall on the left side mark the exit from the area of the Durmitor National Park. **Sige Jovovića** also on the left is the largest waterfall in the canyon with a fall of 40m. Some five kilometers down the river lay the **Brštanovica**

the Tara, longer and shorter, and on different crafts. Those that include passing through its most spectacular part start from Splavište; a one day tour goes as far as Radovan luka, two days will take you to Brštanovica and three days to Šćepan polje. Apart from the ordinary rubber boats

Streams, waterfalls and crystal clear waters of the river

and Encijan camps (the latter being on the riverbank that formally belongs to Bosnia-Herzegovina), 50km of rafting from Splavište. These two camps, and the one in Grab which also provides lodging in cottages, are the most common places for those preferring the shorter (and several times cheaper) rafting. From here it is a few hours ride to the **Šćepan polje** where Tara's green-gray waters unite with Piva's dark blue in a foaming whirlpool that ends their long runs, forming the River Drina.

There are several ways to descend down

one can also take a real wooden raft. These are made to the likeness of the old crafts used historically to transport the logs down the river in earlier times. Here, all the work is done by skillful rafters while the guests sit in the middle of the raft. Since all of these tours include taxes to the national park they are more expensive. The cheaper option is to start from Brštanovica (10 km from the confluence) or Grab camps (5 km from the confluence) and still enjoy Tara's clear green waters, the magnificence of its canyon and some of the river's wildest rapids.

WHERE TO EAT IN THE REGION OF TARA

Ravnjak
18 km from Mojkovac along Tara, 050/472-144, 00-24
This small but cozy hotel lies in a dazzling setting of pristine nature at the very entrance to the Tara-Durmitor national park. Rivers Tara and Bistrica which pass directly beneath it give it an always pleasant freshness as well as providing it with fresh trout. Local cheese, ham, polentas, spit-roasts and grill are also on the menu.

❸ Durmitor

052/360-228

052/61-318

Ski & Snowboard competitions (January)

The mountain massif of Durmitor is a cluster of 48 rocky peaks above 2,000 meters, crowned by a 2,523m high Bobotov kuk, which is the highest point in Montenegro. Its exceptionally stunning looks are due to the fact that its rocky sides rise suddenly from the high tableland of Jezera and Pivska planina and have granted it a nickname of *Soa nebeska* – "The Pillar of Heavens". The 20 by 10 kilometers massif is one of the largest in the Dinaric Alps and its furrowed scenery contains several exceptionally beautiful mountain lakes and ponds, called by the locals "mountain eyes" (*gorske oči*). In summer, Durmitor offers many opportunities for walkers, hikers and alpinists while as a winter resort it attracts many skiers. The canyons of Tara and Sušica rivers on the massif's north and west side separate it from the rest of the world. Mount Sinjajevina leans to its south and the serene grasslands of Jezera ("Lakes"), where most of the villages are, spread to its east.

The lower regions of the massif are covered in fir, pine and partly beach while the only trees above 1800m are low mountain pine and juniper. In some places you will see an interesting feature, an inversion of forest cover in which shrubs of birch appear above the level of conifers. In the fields and clinging

Vast grasslands of the Jezera plateau

to the rocks there are many interesting and endemic flower species to be found, such as Nikola's violet or Tara bellflower. In contrast to the abundance of flora, the wildlife is rather scarce: chamois is the most common, there is a fair number of fox and rabbits and rarely a wolf or a bear. On the other hand, birdlife is faring better so you are likely to see a grouse, a partridge or such giants as the grey mountain eagle and whiteheaded vulture.

Lots of water in lakes and ponds and excellent grazing pastures at higher altitudes made this area attractive for sheep and cattle breeding even in the driest of summers. This can be witnessed even in name "Durmitor" which deriv from the Latin *dormire* and *dormitorio* and is connected with spending summers sleeping in the mountains, a method used by the shepherds to this day. Today, the surroundings of Durmitor are settled mostly by the Drobnjaci clan who has expanded here from their original grounds further to the south. Durmitor was almost unknown to the

Durmitor emerging from the clouds on an early autumn morning

Žabljak with the massif of Durmitor

...uter world until 1880s when it was described by scientists from Russia and Serbia. The first man to climb Bobotov kuk as an alpinist was Austrian Oskar Baumann in 1883 but tourism on Durmitor started only after the mountain was visited in the 1920s by mountaineers from Belgrade and Zagreb. Their delighted reports about its beauties spread rapidly and soon more followed in their steps. After a successful 1932 German-Yugoslav movie "The Phantom of Durmitor" commercial tourism started and the first hotel was built in 1940. The area was declared a National Park in 1952 and in 1980 it was listed among UNESCO's World Heritage sites.

The centre of Jezera plateau and tourism on Durmitor is the town of **Žabljak** (pop. 1,930), keeping its olden looks with many nice wooden houses and steep roofs. The logs stocked at the front of the houses warn about the winter colds and the snows that can reach height of several meters. The town is young in origin: it came to being in 1870 when in the place of an old caravan stop a school, a church and the home

of the clan captain were built. Scattered around its modest centre are old and new hotels as well as groups of weekend homes. The town's main sight is the white stone **mausoleum** rising from the cemetery overlooking the town. It

A stuffed chamoix at the natural history collection

was built in memory of 2441 men and women from the area who gave their lives in WWII, amongst them four were honoured with the title

of National Heroes, whose busts you can see inside; behind them is a relief by Rade Stanković depicting the uprising against the occupation. Rising just to the south of the town is the peak Javorovača (1529m), with two ski-lifts leading to its top from where you will enjoy a panoramic view of Jezera plateau.

Walking towards the mountain you will pass the seat of the National Park administration (the building with blue tin roof) located just in front of the car ramp. In it is housed the **natural history collection** (*Prirodnjačka zbirka; open daily 9-18; entry fee €1*) presenting the flora and wildlife of Durmitor; it also has a nice souvenir shop. Behind the ramp you enter the zone of highest protection in which you will be charged a €1 ticket by roaming stewards. The ticket is valid for the whole year, so be sure not to lose it.

A few minutes walk from here you will reach the shores of **Crno jezero** ("Black Lake") whose colour is due to its depth (49 m) and thick forest surroundings. This beautiful lake lies at the foot of the massif making a picturesque

Rowing boats on Crno jezero Lake

sight, especially in nice weather when the steep Medjed and other peaks mirror on its calm surface. The lake consists of two parts – the large one (in front of you) and the "Small lake" connected by a narrow strip of water which breaks in dry summers. On the shore of the Black Lake is a restaurant and a gift shop as well as two spots where you can rent boats by the hour (€8). The water in the lake is very refreshing even in the hottest summer days and never rises above 22°C. The best way to enjoy Black Lake's many beauties is to take the circular route around it (lasting roughly one hour). Another pleasant route is a half-hour walk from Black Lake along Mlinski potok stream through thick pine and fir woods which will take you to **Zminje jezero** ("Snake Lake") . This lake of dark green colour is abundant in marshy vegetation and surrounded with tall firs and spruce, some over 300 years old. In its clean waters one can find trout and triton – a rare species of amphibian.

A one-and-a-half hour walk along the road to Tepca village to the north of Žabljak

An exciting climb to the Savin kuk peak

will guide you through inspiring pastures and woods and to the **Ćurovac viewpoint**. On the road keep going right until the fourth fork where you should turn left. From the road there is a marked path to Ćurovac (20 min). Watch your step for in front of you opens suddenly a 1,100 m deep abyss with stunning views of river Tara. Far below to the left is the village of Tepca, nested in the only widening in the canyon; though it might seem within a stone's throw it is actually more than an hour by foot.

From Black Lake and its restaurant there is a two-hour walk through the woods to the foot of **Savin kuk**. This is the focal point of skiing in winter but in summer it is interesting for a ride with the ski-lift (€7) to

Savina voda spring at 2200 m. The legend tells that water appeared in this strangely high place when St Sava made a cross with his stick with a request to God to drench the thirst of the pupil he climbed with. A short ascend will take you to the top of Savin kuk (2330 m) from where one enjoys views of almost the entire massif.

For those who come to Durmitor by car there are several interesting spots to visit, all within a short drive on the Jezera plateau. Driving on the road south toward Šavnik take the first sharp left turn. This will lead you to **Vražje** (Devil's) **and Riblje** (Fish) **lakes**, with their grey waters contrasting with green marshland and golden grassland surrounding them. The legend has it that a winged horse lived in Vražje Lake and would come out at night to make love to mares; after finishing the act he would kick them in the belly so that they could not have an offspring like him. When Vojvoda Momčilo, a hero of epic songs,

A perfect shot of Tara Canyon from the Ćurovac viewpoint

Stećak tombstones near Riblje Lake

...eard about this he ...nuck up to the lake one ...ight, waited patiently ...ntil the stallion did his ...vork and then suddenly ...imped on the mare ...nd escaped. The mare ...ave birth to the winged ...orse Jabučilo who ...erved his master in his ...nany adventures. Above ...iblje Lake stands ...rčko groblje, ... necropolis ...vith several ...iteresting stećak ...ombstones (*see* ... 224) covered in ...olourful moss. ...he name ("Greek ...emetery") is ...iisleading: the ...rm "Greek" ...vas used by ...ie locals for all ...iings very old, ...vhich they didn't ...inow to whom ... belonged. If ...ou liked this ...ne you might want to ...ee another necropolis ...vith the same name) ...ne kilometer further ...i Bare Žugića village. ...eturning on the

southbound road towards Šavnik you will reach the village of Donja Bukovica with its **Roman Bridge** standing across the river Bukovica. It is a single span bridge, whose stone is almost untouched by two millennia of its existence. Its height of ten meters depicts the force of the river in springtime. Departing westward from the road to Šavnik you embark on a road towards Plužine, which slides behind the west face of the massif, the unknown and rarely visited side of Durmitor. First you will pass the fantastic shape of Stožina hill and then the **Valovito**

several *katuni* (seasonal shepherds' dwellings) still in function. The road improves from Lokvice where you will find an interesting restaurant run by the local cooperative; here all produce is fresh and drinks are cooled in the wooden trough filled with snow and ice from the mountain. The road continues further across the Piva plateau (*see p. 218*).

One hour ride to the NW of Žabljak via restaurant "Momčilov grad" will guide you past some stunning views and to the **village of Crna Gora**. This village stands isolated in a triangle of land bordered on two sides by the canyons of Tara and Sušica and on the third by the mass of Durmitor. On all three sides one enjoys excellent views; additionally there is a number of wooden houses with steep shingled roofs, which are fine examples of local architecture. Note that these houses were

A peaceful spot above Valovito Lake

jezero Lake found in the depths underneath the stone peaks; after the Sedlo pass you will enter the green vale of Dobri do, with

built entirely with wood, without using even one nail.

By far the most beautiful way to enjoy Durmitor is to hike

Bobotov kuk peak rising above the ever-blue waters of Škrčko Lake

through its massif. There are numerous well marked paths crisscrossing it, two mountain sanctuaries for those surprised by rain or nightfall (one in Lokvice and other by the Debeli namet) and two mountain huts in Škrka valley and Sušica canyon, on the west side of the massif. Be sure to take with you a detailed map, enough water and warm clothes as weather can change rapidly. We recommend several interesting tours but there are a number of possibilities to combine on your own. The easiest one is to the quaint **Jablan jezero lake** and then to the top of the **Crvena greda** clif (2164m) and back. The tour to Obla glava by Stari katun, one of the vales with summer homes of shepherds (*katun*), will allow you to descend to the **Ledena pećina** ("Ice Cave") in which snow

Inside the Ledena pećina ice cave

and ice melt only in the warmest of summers. The return is around Čvorov bogaz ridge and through Lokvice. Our third recommended tour will take you steeply up **Medjed** ("Bear") ridge with an excellent view of the Black Lake lying directly underneath you and the middle of the rocky massif. The gently ascending ridge tour will take you from Mali Medjed (2170m) to Južni vrh (2287m, 3½ h to this point) after which the path descends to **Debeli namet**, a patch of everlasting snow, the last remains of mighty

glaciers that shaped the looks of Durmitor. The route returns to Black Lake via Struga and Mioč poljana. The latter is also along the way of our next route, whose first part takes you to the foot of Savin kuk (*see above*). The ascent to its top is either on foot or by ski-lift. The route to **Šljeme** (2455m), the third highest peak in the whole massif, has a very dangerous section - the climb through Kotao, and afterwards continues along the ridge. The return is via Čista strana. The fifth tour leads us past the Zminje jezero (*see above*) through Donja and Gornja Ališnica to the top of Planinica (2330m, 4 hours in all) commanding views of the glacier circ valley of Škrka and two **Škrčka Lakes**. A one hour descent will take you to its mountain hut (*open from 1st June to 1st October; overnight*

Snowbording on the challenging slopes of Durmitor

❹ Komarnica

Žabljak - Nevidio 30 km

Rivers Komarnica and Piva are often considered as one waterway with two names due to the fact that at the place of their confluence Komarnica is several times larger than Piva but the latter is the one that gives the name to the joint flow. From its source on the south side of Mt Durmitor to the Piva monastery where it changes its name, the flow of Komarnica is characterized by abrupt changes in appearance and direction. It starts as a small stream running from north to south through a wide valley, continues bursting thorough the magnificent Nevidio Gorge, then as a sizeable river through a wide canyon towards the north, gently turning into a calm lake. In its

...ay in bed without ...nens €5, with linens ...12; prior announcement ...hrough National Park ...uthorities advisable). ...his valley makes one ...vith the canyon of river ...ušica to the north. ...he river starts from ...he **Sušičko Lake** and ...ontinues northwards ...o Tara disapearing ...ndergorund several ...mes. Both river and ...he lake got their name ...fter their occassional ...rying up (*suh* - "dry"). ...he tour to Bobotov kuk ...rom the side of Žabljak ...s very long and takes ...½ hours one way, ...o those who are not ...n excellent condition ...limb it from the west ...ide of the massif, either ...rom the mountain hut ...n Škrka (3 h) or from ...rdeni do, to which you ...an drive. Starting from ...he latter you will pass ...**areni pasevi**, a natural ...henomenon where ...ou can see numerous ...eological layers brought ...o the surface by tectonic ...noves. On the other side ...ou see **Zupci** ("Saw ...eeth"), a series of very ...teep peaks. After Zeleni ...ir pool starts the heavy ...scent first to Djevojka ...nd then to **Bobotov ...uk** (2½ h in all) with ...ewarding panoramic ...iews to all sides.

Skiing in Durmitor is centered in the foothill of Savin kuk where there are seven ski-lifts and several pistes. In winter on every hour there is a bus going from the centre of Žabljak to the foot of Savin kuk. There are two more ski lifts on Javorovača, closer to the centre of the town.

RESTAURANTS OF DURMITOR

Javorovača
Javorovača bb; tel. 052/360-236; open 08-23h
This restaurant lies close to the centre of Žabljak, under the hill of the same name where several ski-lifts operate. It treasures the richness of traditional cooking of Montenegrin mountains. The restaurant has a wide-ranging menu in which even those who spent a lot of time here will find something new worth trying. Open fireplace, woolen cloths with folk motives and clay and wooden dishes in which food is served all add up to its very cozy atmosphere. As a real rarity in Montenegro, "Javorovača" even has a section for non-smokers and access for the disabled.

Crno jezero
On the Black Lake; tel. 052/361-474; open 09-23h
This fine old restaurant lies on the shore of the Black Lake, in the heart of the national park of Durmitor. It has a large wooden terrace and a pleasant interior with a warm feel to it. The food here is based on national cuisine from the region and its moderate prices come as a surprise for such a prime location. Here one can also drop by for a drink or a snack, such as *priganice* or *krompir ispod sača*.

In the depths of Nevidio Canyon

229). From this idyllic setting one can follow several marked trekking paths to Mt Vojnik (1997m), ride a bicycle across this wide tableland or enjoy excellent viewpoints over the canyon, whose depth reaches to 600 meters. The other side of the river is rather

widest and deepest part between Nevidio and Piva its steep eroded limestone walls divide mountain Treskavac in the north from Vojnik in the south, presenting a considerable natural obstacle between the Drobnjak and the Piva clans.

The best starting point for exploring the canyon and its south side is the "Etno selo Montenegro" huts in the village of Gornja Brezna (24km south of Plužine, see p. 229).

inaccessible for all those without a 4x4 vehicle, as there is no road. One can descend to the calm waters of the lake via Rudinice village and even climb to the other side to the Borkovići village, but that's where the asphalt road ends.

The most fascinating part of Komarnica is its **Nevidio Gorge**. The name roughly translates as "not seen", faultlessly explaining the phenomenon. Here the stream cuts its way

between two vertical rocks whose sides draw ever closer and almost meet at the top – at their narrowest they are just a few meters apart, giving an impression that one can leap to the other side. If one didn't know this gap in the terrain several hundred meters deep could easily be overseen (therefore the name). This incredible wonder of nature has since its creation remained unseen by the human eye and was the last gorge in Europe to be explored: the first men to pass it were a group of local mountaineers and speleologists in 1965. Even to this very day only a couple of hundred people have passed its 3,5 kilometers of rocks and water, where the temperature drops and the sun rarely breaks through creating a vegetation specific only for this micro region. To embark on this adventure one needs mountaineering equipment, experience and a guide. Those less adventurous can enjoy its mysteriousness best at its beginning near the village of Komarnica.

Boljske grede, the south face of Durmitor

One arrives here from the direction of Šavnik or Žabljak passing two memorable villages, **Petnjica and Pošćenje**. The former is best known as the place of Vuk Karadžić's (1787-1864) family origins. Vuk was the reformer of Serbian alphabet and collector of folk songs and stories, whose father moved to Serbia from here. The peasants from Petnjica still treasure the memory of their illustrious compatriot. The adjacent Pošćenje lies on the slopes next to two green lakes and has a fine collection of *stećak* gravestones scattered around its church. Just round the next curve the scenery changes dramatically: the wide view of the Komarnica valley merges ending with a precipitous wall of Boljske grede cliffs. Taking the left branch of the forking road will lead you to the short bridge over Nevidio, with fantastic views of its depths. The right branch descends into the valley passing the Skakavac waterfall, being the highest in Montenegro with its 65m, but existent only during the season of the snow melting. From this side the unequipped tourists can approach the beginning of the Nevidio gorge.

⑤ Piva

Village fair in Trsa (2nd of August)

Piva is a name for a river, a region and a clan that lives on both sides of the river. Though the name sounds very similar to *pivo*, i.e. beer, the correlation is only accidental while the name actually meant "drinkable" in Old Slavic. River Piva is officially only 34 km long - from the Piva monastery (*see next*

Surreal blue of the Piva Lake and the crossing towards Plužine

caption), where its source was, to the convergence point with Tara at Šćepan polje where they form Drina. However it was dammed in 1976 at approximately half of its course and became one with river Komarnica, forming an exceptionally elongated lake (40km) of incredible turquoise green-blue colour which seems to change from moment to moment depending on the light. The forming of the Pivsko Lake changed the life of this area dramatically: the water flooded the most fertile ground and a part of the Piva canyon became a deep lake (up to 188m) expanding into

neighboring valleys, while the climate changed to a milder one.

The centre of the region is the tiny town of **Plužine** (pop. 1,500), built simultaneously with the dam and therefore totally new. From here the road splits in two directions, one continuing along the lake to the north and the other ascending sharply to the Pivska planina, a vast tableland backcountry of raw wilderness (*see below*). The town is also where the canyon begins and the last place to fill in your tank for the next 60km which are uninhabited. Plužine also has a hotel, several restaurants and is a good base to enjoy the lake, with locals organizing boat rides and excursions such as the one to the Velika pećina cave.

The **Piva canyon** is one of the most staggering places in the country. The road hacks its way along the lake, pressed on the other side by sheer rocks of sun-shadowing heights or passing through a multitude of tunnels. After 16km one reaches the **hydro-electrical power plant "Piva"** (also known as "Mratinje" for the village that lies above it). The dam is 220 meters high, the highest in Europe, and presented a huge engineering success at the time of its construction. Its tall wall crossed by a road makes a sharp distinction with the calm waters on one side and the chasm with a small river at its bottom on the other. From here on the experience is even more astounding as you can view the real proportions of the canyon that reaches the depth of 1200 meters. The journey climaxes with the 122m long single span **Kostova greda bridge**, an astonishing feat of engineering that seems to fly over the abyss at the height of 145 meters. Soon afterwards the canyon wanes though the wilderness of the deep forests is still there. Rivers Piva and Tara join at **Šćepan**

The untouched wilderness of the Piva Canyon seen from the Kostova greda bridge

polje, where the border crossing with Bosnia-Herzegovina is situated. If you're going rafting on the last part of Tara, you will have to pass the border contr as if you are leaving the country but will take only the road that forks immediately to the righ from the check-point (th sign reads "Crkvičko polje") and leading to Brštanovica, Grab and other camps popular with rafters.

Pivska planina is a desolate tableland with an average height of 1200m from which rise peaks of up to 2500m. C three sides it is framed l canyons: to the west of Piva, to the north of Tar and to the east of Sušica The scenery is moonlike a limestone terrain dotted with sinks and with just a few forests. Surprisingly, there are 1 villages in this uninvitir and unique region, all of them living from

RESTAURANTS OF THE PIVA REGION

Sočica
Baja Pivljanina bb, Plužine; open 09-23h
You can reach this restaurant with a short descent downwards from Hotel "Plužine". During the cooler days the interior is warmed by a fireplace and in summers there is a spacious terrace within a peaceful setting. Apart from the usual dishes (grill and international plates) one can also try their trout from the Pivsko lake.

Milogora,
Trsa village, tel. 069/537-541; open 07-24h
One of rare places for eating in Pivska planina, this modest inn serves always fresh lamb in a number of varieties (steamed, in milk or baked in coals) as well as other highland specialties. To go with these try their mead (*medovina*).

Zadruga "Bajo Pivljanin",
Lokvice (3 km south of the Pišče village); open 07-21h
This small eatery belonging to the village cooperative of Pišče seems lost in the wild surroundings of Piva tableland. Here all products come fresh from the adjoining farm and are served in a rustic wooden interior. The menu lists a variety of cheese and ham starters as well as main dishes, all of them being modest local specialties of cream, potatoes and lamb. All of this comes at very affordable prices.

arming, mostly sheep. The village of **Trsa** has central position. The chool, "Milogora" n and the shop are n the road while the ouses lay behind the rst hill. Together with ne camp houses (*see p. 28*) these make Trsa a ood starting point for urther exploration. To ne south and bit higher is **išče**, whose emetery by ne church olds a umber of ld stećak ombstones ith ntriguing ymbols (*see 224*). To ne north f Trsa the oad leads cross the vooded rise f Milogora o the **village f Nedajno**. This scenic illage lies at the edge of ne amazing Sušica river anyon, a deep, always reen scar between the vo plateaus. From here ne enjoys superb views ver the Sušica and ara canyons and the illage of Crna Gora at ne other side of the gap, eemingly just a couple f hundred meters away ut actually 15 km far.

⑥ Piva Monastery

8 km from Plužine
51 km from Nikšić
Assumption
(28th of August)

The 16th c. Piva monastery has for centuries represented the hub of clan life in Piva, while its spiritual and artistic importance radiated further away. The sober, stone complex is today located just by the Nikšić-Plužine road. However, its original location was more concealed, lying in a forest next to the source of the Piva River. To preserve it from being flooded, while the building of the dam (*see p. 217*) was being carried out, the monastery

Moved and re-assembled church of the Piva Monastery

church was disassembled and relocated uphill to its present position. The whole process was very sluggish due to the complications of pealing off and putting up the 1260m² of the monastery's precious frescoes. In the end, the works lasted 13 years (1969-1983), exactly as long as it took the 16th c. builders to complete the original construction! The only reminders of the relocation process are the numbers preserved on every single block of stone by which they were identified and put in their original place.

The monastery was built in 1573-86 by Savatije Sokolović, the metropolitan of Herzegovina and a member of the family that gave several heads to the Serb orthodox church - Savatije himself became the Serb patriarch in 1687. For the people of Piva the monastery became their holiest place which they guarded from the Turks, generation after generation donated to it as much as they could until the monastery grew to be the greatest landowner in pre-socialist Montenegro.

Living in harmony with nature on Pivska planina plateau

Nothing of that wealth survives: after WWII all of the land was nationalized and, as most of it disappeared under the waters of the lake, there is no hope of its retrieval. Today the fraternity in the monastery consists only of an abbot and one monk.

The church was erected at a supposed place where St Sava, at the time still prince Rastko Nemanjić, decided to join a group of Russian pilgrims and go to Holy Mount Athos to take his monastic vows. For his endowment Savatije chose experienced builders from the Adriatic coast who were familiar with the Romanesque style, popular with the Nemanjić rulers, which the metropolitan wanted to imitate. The result is one of the largest Serb churches built under Turkish domination, a simple three-nave basilica of white stone skillfully cut into rectangular blocks. The plain and unornamented exterior seems like it was designed to hide the

Fresco of St Sava in front of the Virgin Mary

wealth and opulence of its interior.

It took some years until this huge church was fresco painted, but the artists chosen for the job were among the best masters of fresco-painting one could find at the time. The first space into which one enters from the west is the elongated **narthex**. Its ceiling and upper zones were painted by priest Strahinja of Budimlje in his naïve style; however, the most beautiful frescoes - the ones in the three lower levels – are not his but the work of painter Jovan, completed in 1626. These rank as top achievements in orthodox art by this accomplished painter

and of the whole epoch. Amongst them the most memorable is the one to the left of the door leading to the nave where we can see St Sava in front of the Virgin and Christ renouncing earthly powers (symbolized by the crown and the ruler's belt cast underneath his feet). To the right and up of the entrance is a painting of Saint Kosmas the Hymn-Maker binding a book shown with precisely drawn book-binding tools.

Entering the **nave** one passes the beautiful wooden door inlaid with ivory arranged in fantastic shapes. Most of the nave walls were decorated in 1604-6 by

BAJO PIVLJANIN

Bajo Nikolić Pivljanin (early 17th c. – 1685) is one of the best known personalities in Serb epic poetry, a proto-type of a brave outlaw fighting against the Turks. He was born in village Rudinice in Piva from where, barely out of his teens, he had to flee after killing a Turkish landlord in the place now called Bajovo Polje. He gathered around him a group of men who waged a silent guerrilla war on the border of Venetian possessions in Boka Kotorska and Dalmatia with the Ottoman Empire. They attacked Turkish caravans, robbing their lords and burning down their border forts. From their bases in Boka they would infiltrate Turkish territory where they looted for their livelihoods, while also defending Perast and Kotor from Turkish raids. Nominally under Venetian rule, Bajo's and groups similar to his were very useful in times of war but a menace in times when the Republic tried to keep good relations with the Sultan, since they knew nothing else but to fight. After a debacle in trying to settle them in Istria, Venice found a good use for them in the new war during which Bajo lived his most glorious days, fighting across Dalmatia and Herzegovina. When in 1685 pasha from Shkoder raised his army to punish Montenegrins and Highlanders for their rebellion against the Turks, Bajo's company came to help and this is where he heroically met his end on Vrtieljka, on the threshold of Cetinje.

Opulent interior of the monastery church

...a company of Greek painters. By the south door are two portraits, one of metropolitan Savatije holding the monastery church in his hands, while the other is a mysterious representation of a "Turk", possibly of Savatije's relative Mehmed-pasha Sokolović who at that time held the position of the Grand-vizier of the Ottoman Empire. While during his life Mehmed-pasha made possible the building of the monastery of this size, later on his portrait saved the monastery from Turkish wrath on several occasions. In the middle of the nave hangs a splendid chandelier of inlaid wood and decorated additionally with ostrich eggs and two-sided hanging icons by master Longin (these being just the copies, the originals are kept in the treasury). The splendidly carved and gilded iconostasis is considered to be one of the most beautiful of its time, especially the lofty central crucifix for which alone, the legend says, the unnamed carver got 25 pairs of oxen. The iconostasis was completed in 1638 when Longin painted the last of its outstanding large icons depicting (from left to right) St Demetrios, Mother of God, the Assumption, Christ and at the end St Sava and his father St Simeon, which was scratched during one of the Turkish raids of the monastery. In front of the iconostasis stand tall marble candlesticks with lions' heads as their base which, once again, draw their inspiration from the Romanesque models.

The monastery's **treasury** is equally rich; to view it you have to specifically ask the abbot (*Smijemo li vidjeti riznicu?*). Here one can marvel at the church utensils such as the silver ciborium and *petohlebnica* created in fantastic gothic shapes, the crosses with meticulous wood carvings and the abbot's throne of inlaid wood. The original icons by master Longin include also the Assumption of the Virgin, famous for its handling of colours (note the blue angles darkened by Christ's red shine). Also displayed are the silk *sakkos*, a vestment worn by the bishop – a fine Venetian work, and the metropolitan's crown stripped of almost all of its jewels during the hectic times of communism. The Psalter printed in 1494 at the Cetinje printing-house is one of the first Serb printed books. The exhibition ends with two items not related with the church but with local history – the bag and the powder cartridge once owned by Bajo Pivljanin, famous for fighting the Turks in 17th c. (*see inlay*).

Assumption of the Virgin, masterpiece of painter Longin

❼ Nikšić

- 59,000
- Bulevar 13. jula bb, tel. 040/213-602
- Ivana Milutinovića 10, 040/213-262
- Guitar festival (mid July)

Montenegro's second largest city is situated in a large karst field, a feature that made it an important place and a crossroad throughout its history. A late Roman era town of *Anderva* stood here until it was destroyed during the barbaric invasions. In the 5th c. AD Eastern Goths, who wrestled the area from the Byzantines, built a fortress here calling it Anagastum, probably after one of their leaders. The Goths soon departed for Italy and their place was taken by the Slavs who adapted the previous name to Onogošt. In the Middle Ages the location was an important stop on the caravan routes from the Adriatic to the hinterland and was visited by several kings of the Nemanjić dynasty. With Turkish onslaught a demographic change occurred witnessed in the change of the name, the old Onogošt became known as Nikšić after a clan that settled in the area. Turks captured the town in 1465 but less than a century later had to wage constant battle with the surrounding Herzegovinian clans who attacked the city regularly. In the end, the Turks decided in 1703 to rebuild the medieval fortress and surround the town with walls. Frequent attacks and sieges by Herzegovinians and Montenegrins finally found success in 1877 when Nikšić fell to Montenegro. The Muslim population left and the fortress fell into decay while the city's new masters laid out a practical radial street plan, built European styled edifices and started the first industrial enterprises of which the best known is the brewery, established in 1896. However, the real boom that made the town what it is today followed WWII when it became the seat of several large factories, most importantly the ironworks. The demand for workers was grave and the town's population rose tenfold from 1945 to 1985. With the founding of several faculties during the 1990s Nikšić also became the centre of learning. Today students are its

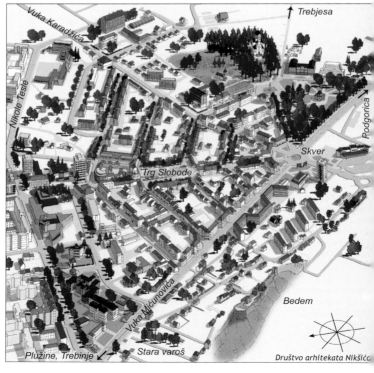

Palace of King Nikola, today the local museum of Nikšić

second most important feature, the undisputable first being *Nikšićko pivo*, a very palatable beer popular well beyond the borders of Montenegro.

The main attractions of Nikšić are suitably grouped at the entrance from the direction of Podgorica. Facing the bus station is a fine park with **Turkish baths** in its middle; interestingly, the baths were built after the Turkish departure and in European style. Behind the park lies the **Palace of King Nikola**, built in 1895 by architect Josip Slade, the chief engineer in Montenegro at the time, who also drew the above mentioned plans for the laying out of the Nikšić streets. This neo-renaissance edifice nowadays houses the local **museum** (*open Tue-Sat 9-13 and 17-20h, on Sundays 9-12; entrance fee €1, students €0.50*). On the ground floor is a permanent exhibition of paintings by Ilija Šobajić. The upper floor presents the history of the town and vicinity, era by era. It begins with archaeological findings, continues with fine Illyrian and Roman collections, the Middle Ages and the 19th c, which are followed by a large collection of folk costumes and armoury from the period and ends with a large section depicting battles waged in WWII.

Next to the museum, elevated on a small hill, stands the grandiose **Church of St Vasilije of Ostrog**. Before climbing up the steps to its entrance, take a minute

The western portal of the Church of St Vasilije of Ostrog

to examine several stećak tombstones (*see inlay on next page*) lying scattered at the foot of the hill. The Church was built in 1900 with the funds donated by the Russian Emperor.

The architect of this grand temple was also a Russian - Mikhail Preobrazhensky, who mastered the style of the local churches. The church was built in memory of the Montenegrins and Herzegovinians (Nikšić being the most important town in Herzegovina acquired by Montenegro) who fell in the 1875-78 wars for the liberation of this area. Until a decade ago this was the largest church in all of Montenegro. The airy interior is unpainted but boasts a fine iconostasis.

In the square at the front of the church stands a high **column** with a statue of the Virgin Mary, the latest in the series of Russian donations to Nikšić.

To the left of the church is the **Old Cemetery**, nicely kept and with many interesting 19th c. tombstones which are

WHERE TO EAT IN NIKŠIĆ

Portun
Njegoševa bb (courtyard); 040/212-336; 08-23; open 08-23
The restaurant is located in a quiet courtyard linking pedestrian Njegoševa with the local market. Its interior and its porch with outdoor seating have modern wooden furnishings which give it a rustic feel. The main plates on offer - fish, spit-roasts, grilled meat or specialties of the house - are abundant and reasonably priced.

STEĆAK TOMBSTONES

Stećci (pl. of *stećak*) are medieval tomb-stones found in Bosnia, Herzegovina, West Serbia, South Dalmatia and North Monte-negro (historically a part of Herzegovina). These are large stone blocks standing above graves, most of them with carvings and some with Cyrillic inscriptions. The oldest date from the 11th c. and by then already have all the distinctive features that endure until their end in the 15th c.: large tablets, single stone blocks - some in a shape of a sarcophagi, decorations depicting crosses, rosettes, swords, shields and bows with ar-rows, scenes of tournaments and hunt (characterizing the noble rank of the deceased), saints, geo-metrical patterns, wines, sun, moon, stars, people dancing *kolo* or the figure of the deceased with one hand raised in greeting. The inscriptions on them remind the reader about the deceased and warn him about the transience of life, cursing those who dare to desecrate his grave. Though an art form characteristic for medieval Bosnia and its immediate surroundings, stećaks are wrongly associated with the so-called "Bogomils", a Christian sect active in medieval Bosnia. In fact they were also created by the Bosnian Orthodox and Catholics and later even by the first converts to Islam. Most stećaks in Montenegro are to be found in old cemeteries and the most interesting necropolises are in Nikšić, Grahovo, Velimlja, in Pivska planina and Sokol above Šćepan-polje. They are usually located in old graveyards or on higher grounds.

decorated with folk motives. In its centre is the **Church of Saints Peter & Paul**, a modest edifice dating from the 15th c. In its interior there are remains of slightly younger frescoes. You can see some more *stećci*, most of them with a colonnade design, scattered around the church (some fragments are even built in its walls) and indeed all over the cemetery.

In the backdrop behind the church and the museum one can see the wooded **hill of Trebjesa**, with its walking and bicycle tracks. Upon reaching halfway up the hill, a motel which shares the same name can be found from whose terraces one can enjoy the pleasurable view of the town.

On the other side of Nikšić stands the old fortress, called **Bedem** ("Wall") by the locals. In fact, its upper fort resembles a long wall which lies along the full length of the low elongated hill. Once, there was also a lower fort where the Turkish Nikšić used to be, but today it is hardly noticeable amongst the private houses and their yards. What can be seen today was built in 1703 by the Turks at the same location where the medieval fort and the one built by Eastern Goths used to stand when they founded the city. Seemingly its design is not too different from the forts of the earlier era, but a closer inspection reveals that its towers have been built to house cannons. Sadly, this most valuable monument in the town has been ruined by amateur reconstructions and adaptations and, even worse, nowadays stands neglected and left to decay. As it became pray to hooligans and a venue for drug addicts today it is locked and guarded. To enter it you will need to find one of the guards and ask him to let you in (*Da li bi nas mogli pustiti u tvrdjavu?*).

The centre of the town is the **Trg Slobode** and the streets around it, combining one-storied houses with the social realist buildings of the post WWII era. The central feature of the square is a new equestrian **monument to King Nikola** (M. Živković, 2006). Continuing along Njegoševa St. you will reach a colossal **"House of the Revolution"** (*Dom

Nikšić Bedem fortress overlooking the town

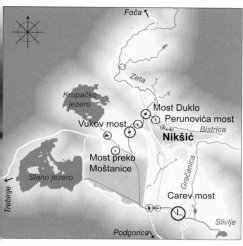

bridge is behind it, close to the houses. Taking the road from the centre of the city towards Foča/Srbinje will lead you across **Duklo Bridge**. This bridge which stands over Zeta after its convergence with river Bistrica, was built in 1807 by Hajji Ishmael, a rich Turk from Nikšić. The unusual feature of this bridge is that its arches are of different height, one of them being significantly lower.

The road to Foča will also take you to the village of **Vir** ("Whirlpool") that got its name after an interesting natural phenomenon. A 94m deep hole filled with water is linked by a small stream with the nearby river Zeta forming the Europe's largest **estavelle**. The estavelle sometimes discharges water from its spring through a stream

Revolucije), a grandiosely envisioned project by the local communists; the works on it started in 1975 but faltered due to its sheer size and were never completed. To the left of it Radoja Dakića St. will lead you to the 19th c. mosque, one of the rare Islamic places of worship in Montenegro that survived even when it lost its congregation.

The surroundings of Nikšić are unusually rich in **old stone bridges**. Several streams and rivers that flow through its fields are bridged by approximately a dozen of them. Taking almost any road from Nikšić you are bound to cross some of them. The largest among them is **Carev most** ("Tsar's Bridge"). It lies on the old Nikšić-Podgorica road streaming the river Zeta, which is now reduced to a canal but was once a much mightier river judging from the length of 269 m and 16 arches of this imposing structure. It was built in 1894 again from the donation of the Russian

Emperor, therefore its name, although its imposing size could give inspiration to this name as well. To reach it, start in the direction of Podgorica and than follow the road going straight for Kličevo. The oldest and the most interesting amongst

A Roman bridge still crossing Moštanica

old stone bridges is the so-called **Roman Bridge** over Moštanica River, whose unusual openings testify to its antiquity. It is assumed that it was built in the 8th c. AD on the road from Dubrovnik to Nikšić. To reach it take the road towards Trebinje; after passing parallel with another old bridge – **Vukov most** – take a left turn to the sports airport; the

into the river and on other occasions receives water from the river, depending on its water level.

To the west of Nikšić lie two large man made lakes – Krupačko and Slansko. The former is a popular place for refreshment during the summer heats and its "Sky" bar offers possibilities for various water sports.

Hotel

Motel

Villa/Private Pension

Agrotourism accommodation

Hostel

PRICE RANGE - for one person in a two-bed room (including breakfast, service and tax). Small icons present facilities in each Hotel.

number of rooms   number of beds

308/373

> 100 Euro €€€€€
50 - 100 Euro €€€€€
35 - 50 Euro €€€€
25 - 35 Euro €€€
12 - 25 Euro €€
< 12 Euro €

PLJEVLJA: Pljevlja ★★

Kralja Petra bb

+ 382 (0)52 323 140

38/68   €€

This old socialist hotel of unusual appearance lies in the centre of the town and offers a large number of rooms with basic comfort and catering.

PLJEVLJA: Gold ★★★

Marka Miljanova bb

+ 382 (0)52 323 102

12/20   €€
VISA MasterCard Maestro

This small hotel is a smarter alternative for a stay in Pljevlja. Though its interior furnishings are rather kitsch the rooms are comfortable and clean.

ŽABLJAK: Bjelobor ★★

Tmajevci, Žabljak

+ 382 (0)52 361 635

www.durmitor.com/motel_bjelobor.php

32/100   €€€

A basic hotel at the approach to Žabljak from the direction of Pljevlja. The rooms, all with central heating, are simply furnished.

ŽABLJAK: Enigma ★★★

Tmajevci, Žabljak

+ 382 (0)52 361337

www.durmitor.com/enigma.

18/49   €€€
VISA MasterCard Maestro

This new hotel on the eastern outskirts of Žabljak offers pleasant, cosy rooms. At the guests' disposal are also a restaurant, a room with a fireplace and a night club. Transport to the ski centre is organized.

ŽABLJAK: Žabljak ★★

Trg Durmitorskih ratnika 1

+ 382 (0)52 361 300

www.hm-durmitor.com

23/54   €€€
VISA Maestro

Located in the very centre of Žabljak, the hotel has small and plainly furnished rooms. Its main plus is its location and the large terrace overlooking the main town street.

The old hotel "Žabljak"

Hotel "Planinka" on the Jezera plateau

Žabljak: Planinka ★ ★

- Narodnih heroja bb
- + 382 (0)52 361344
- www.primorje.cg.yu

146/324

€€€
VISA MasterCard Maestro

This, the largest hotel in Žabljak, also has a proportionately-sized restaurant serving local specialties, a congress hall with ?00 seats and a night club.

Žabljak: Javor ★ ★ ★

- Božidara Žugića 8
- + 382 (0)52 361337
- www.durmitor.org.yu

6/12

€€

A small hotel in the centre of Žabljak with comfortable and spacious rooms. Also on offer are two houses with several .partments, just next to the hotel. The hotel also has a restaurant serving national cuisine.

Žabljak: MB ★ ★ ★

- Tripka Džakovića
- + 382 (0)52 361 601
- http://mb-hotel.com

14/44

€€€
VISA MasterCard Maestro

A small hotel next to the town centre. Its wood paneled rooms are tastefully decorated and comfortable. Except for the fine 'estaurant offering specialties of the local cuisine there is also a small conference room.

Žabljak: Golubović

- Drobnjačka bb
- + 382 (0)52 361 521

6/14

€

This pension is conveniently situated both to the centre of Žabljak and to the Javorovača ski piste. Each of its comfortable 'ooms has a TV with a DVD set.

Žabljak: Vila Talia

- Žabljak
- + 382 (0)69 543 210
- www.zabljak.org

3/8

€€€€€€

This smart pension is located in the serene surroundings of pine woods around the Black Lake. It has three bathrooms, .inder-floor heating and a fireplace.

Žabljak: Brvnara Šarović

- Savin kuk
- + 382 (0)67 832 686

3/7

€€€€€

This pension designed like a mountain shack lies underneath the Savin kuk peak, in close proximity to the major skiing 'pistes of Durmitor. The pension has a bathroom and a kitchen at the guests' disposal.

TARA: Radovan luka

 Radovan luka

 + 382 (0)69 504 236  **19/50**

This small motel lies in the middle of the impressive canyon of the river Tara, some 24km from Žabljak. Camping facilities used mostly by rafters, are available next to the hotel. The rooms are plain but sufficient.

TARA: Kamp Grab

 Kamp Grab, Šćepan Polje

 + 382 (0)67 255 200   **11/54**

Ⓦ www.tara-grab.com

This camp at the bank of the River Tara caters mostly for rafters of its spectacular whitewaters but is also a good place for a peaceful rest far from civilization

ŠAVNIK: Šavnik ★ ★ ★

 Šavnik

☎ + 382 (0)40 266 227 Ⓟ **29/47**

The hotel in Montenegro's smallest town is located favourably for all kinds of excursions to the nearby natural attractions Its rooms are basic but comfortable and it also has a national cuisine restaurant.

ŠAVNIK: Boan ★ ★

☒ Boan

☎ + 382 (0)40 268126 Ⓟ **18/46**

This hotel lies in a mountain setting at the foot of Mt Sinjajevina. It is mostly visited by junior sports teams for its isolation, volleyball, handball and mini football sports grounds. The rooms are equipped very basically.

PIVA: Piva ★ ★

☒ Baja Pivljanina bb, Plužine

☎ + 382 (0)40 271 132 Ⓟ **19/45**

The hotel lies at the edge of the beautiful Piva lake, just a few steps from the centre of Plužine. It is spacious and tranquil but far from any kind of luxury.

PIVA: Eko kamp Milogora

☒ Trsa **7/18**

☎ + 382 (0)69 537 541 Ⓟ

This is the only accommodation between Žabljak and Plužine, lying high up on the Piva tableland. The five huts that lie near the centre of the village are simply furnished. The owners are more than willing to organize all kinds of mountain adventures for you.

NIKŠIĆ: Onogošt ★ ★ ★

✉ Njegoševa 24

☎ + 382 (0)40 243 608

Ⓦ www.htponogost.com

178/256

This large old hotel lies conveniently in central NIkšić. It has a tavern, a pastry shop, a restaurant serving national cuisine and an interesting relic from the old days – a "milk restaurant" reserved for non-alcoholic beverages. The rooms on upper floors enjoy nice views of the town.

NIKŠIĆ: Trebjesa ★ ★ ★

✉ Trebjesa bb

☎ + 382 (0)40 731 144

Ⓦ www.htponogost.com

8/16

A small hotel on the wooded hill in the centre of town. Close to all amenities and quiet. It has a well known restaurant serving decent national cuisine and game.

NIKŠIĆ: Sindčel ★ ★ ★

✉ Danila Bojovića bb

☎ + 382 (0)40 213 655

13/25

A simple hotel with basic furnishings.

NIKŠIĆ: Vučje

✉ Vučje, 21 km from Nikšić

☎ + 382 (0)67 641 213

15/66

Starting from 2008, this mountain chalet will be opened throughout the year. For the time being they cater mostly for families and skiers at the nearby pistes. Convenient for trips to Kapetanovo jezero Lake, Nevidio Canyon and other natural beauties of the area.

NIKŠIĆ: Etno selo Montenegro

✉ Village of Gornja Brezna, 30km north of Nikšić

☎ + 382 (0)67 209 049

Ⓦ www.etno-turizam.com

17/41

A group of bungalows and a nearby house in the pastoral setting of the Brezna village make a good starting point for hiking, cycling and excursions to its beautiful natural surroundings.

The old-styled dining room of "Etno selo Montenegro"

EASTERN MONTENEGRO

Except for a few locations, this part of Montenegro is off the tourist map for foreign travelers. One may add, unjustly, as it abounds with natural beauties, such as fast rivers and high mountains but also monuments from the previous centuries and scenic old villages. Most of these attractions are unexploited and visited only by an adventurous few. This is mostly due to the relative isolation of the region - most of the tourists pass along the Podgorica-Belgrade road never bothering to wander further afield. The second reason lies in the fact that the large part of the region ranks amongst the poorest in Montenegro

downstream from Berane) that makes it popular with rafters. With modern roads built across the mountain ridges the valley has lost some of its former importance but in previous centuries it represented a distinctive whole and played an important agricultural and commercial role. In the early Middle Ages it was a hub of the Serbian state and there are several monuments bearing witness to this era such as Djurdjevi Stupovi monastery close to Berane or the church of Saints Peter & Paul in Bijelo Polje. Later on the region was taken by the Ottoman Empire for which it was an

The secluded church of Podvrh monastery

with underdeveloped infrastructure and derelict industrial facilities.

The region's main artery from times immemorial is the river Lim which spills out from Plavsko Lake, flows northwards passing Andrijevica, Berane and Bijelo Polje and continues further into Serbia. Most of its flow passes through a valley, not particularly wide but wide enough to constitute the flattest piece of terrain in the whole of this mountainous region. The river has its other face too with several sections where it speeds up and rushes through several small gorges (the best known of which is Tifran some 5km

important transit zone towards Bosnia. The Ottomans remained here until 1912 and their influence is still widely encountered, most importantly in the numerous Slav Muslim population (Bosniaks) but also in many mosques of a specific mountain type that imitate the pattern of local houses with their steep shingled roofs. The area of Plav and Gusinje in the south of the region is an alpine looking valley at the foot of the Prokletije Mountains. Once prosperous trading spots, these two towns were plunged into bare survival by new borders which left them at the dead end of the road.

...ouful flowery meadows of Grbaja valley leading to the heart of ...kletije mountains

Alongside Durmitor, Prokletije are the most fascinating mountain ridge in Montenegro: their sides rise steeply from the surrounding fields capped by hostile stone peaks which attract many mountaineers and alpinists.

Much more spectacular than Lim is river Morača. In its first part it descends quickly between Mt Sinjajevina and mountains Žurim and Stožac forming a pleasant but narrow dale crowned by the impressive Kapa Moračka ("Hat of Morača") peak towering at 2226m. After passing Morača monastery, an excellent piece of art from the 13th c, the cliffs rise higher announcing the beginning of the forbidding Morača canyon. The motorway and railway which run along the whole length of it provide stunning sights of its peaks and chasms. Equally impressive is the canyon of river Mrtvica which joins Morača from the right, impenetrable until a few decades ago and now one of the favourite routes of seasoned hikers.

Between the rivers Lim and Morača flows Tara with towns of Mojkovac and Kolašin on its banks. The latter lies bel-low Mt Bjelasica and is quickly developing into a mountain and ski tourism centre. Bjelasica is widely known amongst nature lovers for its Biogradska gora National Park with beautiful Biogradsko Lake and deep pristine woods around it.

At the far east of the country lies the small town of Rožaje populated almost exclusively by Muslim Bosniaks. With several good hotels the town offers possibilities for hiking in high mountains such as the imposing massif of Hajla (2403m) and even better for winter sports at its improving (and potentially huge) skiing resorts.

Žabljak

Nikšić

Tifran rapids of the River Lim

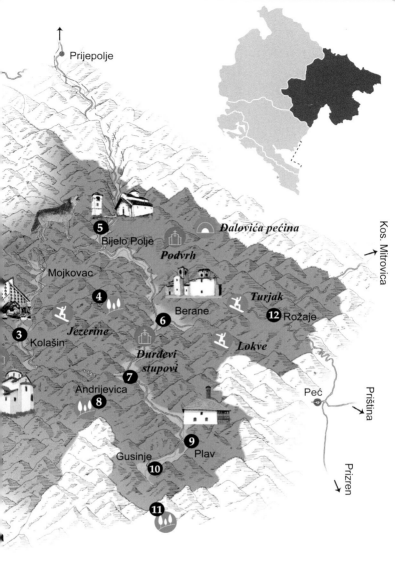

1. Mrtvica
2. Morača
3. Kolašin
4. Bjelasica
5. Bijelo Polje
6. Berane
7. Andrijevica
8. Komovi
9. Plav
10. Gusinje
11. Prokletije
12. Rožaje

❶ Mrtvica

49km from Podgorica
32km from Kolašin

Mrtvica River is the chief tributary of Morača, flowing in from the west near the village of Medjuriječje. The small but potent Mrtvica forces its way between the steep sides of mountains Maganik (2,139m) and Stožac (2,226m) forming a 9 kilometers long canyon. The average depth of the canyon is around 600m; however, if measured from the peak of Mt Maganik which lies just 4km from the river, the canyon depth excels even the one of River Tara. This hostile ravine has remained virtually inaccessible up until the mid 1980s when the army drilled through the rock in its side making it possible to track its flow for the first time in history. Since then, the spectacular canyon of Mrtvica has become one of the most visited mountaineering tracks in Montenegro but has remained unknown to the wider audiences due to its isolation.

With its richness in trout and sprout the river also attracts the attention of anglers. The experienced ones claim that angling here demands a lot of knowledge and patience since the fish is very wary.

The wilderness surrounding the canyon of Mrtvica is captured in the very sound of its eerie name (mrtvo – dead). There are several explanations for it, all coming from the associations flared by its hostile looks, but the most convincing one is connected with the change of water

Refreshing waters of Mrtvica River

quantities in it: though during springtime and early summer the river is very abundant in water fed by the snow melting in the mountains, as soon as this season is over (at the beginning of July) the river suddenly "dies" turning itself into a stream not larger than a brook or even dries completely in its upper course. More vivid answers to the question are given by local legends. One tells that the river got its name after many dead bodies ended in its waters following a battle with the Turks, another that a great flood carried away everything from the village of Velje Duboko, even the dead in their graves.

To reach the starting point for hiking from the direction of Podgorica one should pass the sign announcing the Medjuriječje village on the Podgorica-Belgrade road and then look carefully for a red sign that directs you to the left. Be very cautious since the turn is of a sharp angle and has to be made at a busy road. The same turn is much easier from the direction of Kolašin.

The walk through the canyon takes some 5 hours in one direction. The marked path starts from the confluence of the two rivers, both remarkable for their clean, cold water. After some 15 minutes through the rich vegetation one reaches the **Danilo's Bridge** (*Danilov most*), built by Prince Danilo in 1858 "for the soul of his mother Krstina", as it is commemorated in large

The immaculately clean waters of Mrtvica before the storm

Cyrillic letters on a stone tablet. With its two arches high above the enchantingly green waters of the Zeleni vir ("Green Whirlpool") it is certainly one of nicest packhorse bridges in the country (not being wide enough for a cart), not least for its unique setting.

A narrow path carved in the rock of Mrtvica's canyon

The bridge is a part of an old track that avoided the canyon and used to be the only connection for several villages deeper in the mountains. From here the hiking trail climbs up through the greenery past the old mill and shortly afterwards reaches a gravel road. This road begins from the closed hotel "Medjuriječje" and leads some two kilometers along the river to the homestead of Milivoj Bulatović where it ends. Passing these lonely houses, after a few minutes walk one reaches the new, wooden bridge from which remarkable views along the river can be enjoyed. Further on and deeper into the canyon, where there is very little sunshine and where it's always chilly, is the **Bijeli Narini cascade** famous for its beauty as the water bubbles and breaks on the rocks (note that this phenomenon is far from impressive in high summer). Continuing the hike one reaches the most attractive part of the canyon with the narrow path cut into the primeval rock rising vertically above the green river. The tour ends in the village of **Velje Duboko** ("Great Deep") that has nested itself in a picturesque valley in front of the canyon. The village, with small houses surrounded with walnut, plum and apple trees, is a much needed break from the inhospitable conditions of the canyon. It is one of the chief villages of the Rovci clan that got its name from the looks of their settlements (*rovati* – to dig into).

Velje Duboko is a good starting point to reach **Kapetanovo Lake** high in the Mt Žurim (6km, 3 hours walk). The picturesque glacial lake lies 1,678m above sea level in a desolate place stripped of most vegetation and surrounded by a *katun* settlement. It is quite large (480 by 360m) and has a distinctive, dark green, almost black water as a result of its depth (max. 37m) that also keeps it cold

Minute beauty of the mountain flowers

throughout the year. From here it's a half hour climb to the smaller **Manito Lake** underneath the top of Mt Stožac and a 2 hour climb to the peak of **Kapa Morača** (2,226m) overlooking the source of river Morača. The other way to reach Kapetanovo Lake is a 5 hour walk from the Krnovo pass on the Nikšić-Žabljak road.

❷ Morača Monastery

> 47 km from Podgorica
> 23 km from Kolašin
> 28th of August

Morača Monastery is set in a spectacular position right at the beginning of the dreaded canyon of River Morača, in the very midst of the highest mountains of Montenegro. The position is further emphasized by the scenic Svetigora waterfall some 25 meters high, plunging noisily just behind the complex, making it one of the famous motifs on many pictures. The monastery was founded in 1251-52 by Prince Stefan, son of Vukan and grandson of Stefan Nemanja, the founder of the Nemanjić dynasty. Its main church, dedicated to the Assumption is a fine example of mature Raška style of Serbian medieval ecclesiastical architecture – single nave with a narthex, cupola above the square base, semicircular apse and a chapel on each side. The details, such as the main portal and the double windows, are clearly Romanesque and reveal that the builders came from the town of Kotor. The monastery was looted (including its copper roof) and burnt down by the Turks in 1504 and remained in ruins until the renovation of 1574 when the best Serb artists of the time were summoned to help. In the 16th

and the 17th c. it became an important artistic and cultural centre and played an important role in political life. Most notable of such events was when in 1608 Serb patriarch Jovan came to the monastery to convene with the local clan leaders and request help from the Savoy dynasty against the Turks, but the scheme met with no response. In the 1877 war the monastery was a site where the advancing Turkish army was stopped with a heroic defense led by its abbot Mitrofan Ban, the future metropolitan of Cetinje.

The **western portal** of the Church of Assumption is made of dark stone and with somewhat naïve representations of the Virgin Mary, Crucifixion and beasts of hell. Above the door is the original inscription by the patron and a fresco of the Virgin surrounded with angels. This painting is one of the rare surviving medieval originals as almost all other frescoes here date from the time of the renovation but copy the themes represented by the destroyed medieval ones. The western front of the church is additionally decorated with now bleached wall-paintings including the large representations of St Demetrios and St George on horseback. These frescoes as well as those in the narthex date from 1616 and are the work of Georgije Mitrofanović who was invited to come from

Morača Monastery lying below the highest peaks of the Dinaric Alps

Rich colours of Morača's bountiful frescoes

remarkable large icons and the gilded crucifix that alone took 11 years to carve, dates from the very beginning of the 17th c. One should also note the portrait of Vukić Vučetić who led the group of local donors who paid for the renovation. In the church are displayed some of the monastery's many valuable **icons** such as those by the painter Jovan: one portrays

which one can also see the construction of the monastery. The small **chapel** to the left of the narthex is dedicated to St Steven, protector saint of the Nemanjićs and of Prince Stefan. Its excellent frescoes are also the work of painter Jovan from 1642. Among them the most important is the one depicting St Steven leading the patron (carrying the model of his church) to the Virgin.

The small **Church of St Nicholas**, lying closer to the entrance of the monastery compound was built in 1639 on the foundations of the medieval tower which once guarded the gates. The monastic tradition holds the church to be even

he famed Monastery of Hilandar on Holy Mt Athos. Before you enter notice the fine door from the same period, influenced strongly by the contemporary oriental art. The most impressive compositions in the **narthex** are the huge Tree of Jesse on the north wall, Last Judgment as well as the Christ sitting on the throne in the composition known as the "Emperor of the Emperors". The walls of the **nave** were painted by priest Strahinja of Budimlje: the Dormition of the Virgin, seen above the door, and scenes from the life of St Elijah on the north wall. One of the rare surviving original frescoes from the 13th c. is the "Ravens feeding Saint Elijah" hidden in the diaconicon (to the left of the altar), regarded by many as one of the masterpieces of its time. The frescoes of the Annunciation and the Deisis are from the same period. The splendid **iconostasis**, with

St Nicholas healing the King Stefan Dečanski

St Sava and his father St Simeon (Nemanja's monastic name), with the life of St Sava depicted in the smaller pictures around it; similar to it is the one representing St Luke painting the icon of the Mother of God, in

older than the main one, but this was probably invented at the time of construction as building of new churches was prohibited in the Ottoman Empire. Its frescoes dating from

---

WHERE TO EAT IN THE MORAČA AREA

Crkvine
Podgorica highway (9 km from Kolašin) , 069/308-335; open 06-23h
Set on a high mountain pass from which open amazing panoramic views of the Morača canyon, this restaurant has a menu offering a standard set of international and national dishes.

The crooked Monks' Bridge

1639, work of painter Jovan, rank amongst the best of their time. The main subject on its walls is the life and miracles of St Nicholas, displayed with some interesting iconographic solutions such as the scene "St Nicholas saving the boy from the Saracens" in which the Saracens are portrayed as Turks dressed in contemporary fashion and seated *alla turca* on an oriental rug. In other frescoes the saint helps the seafarers, gives sight back to the Serbian king Stefan Dečanski and introduces Prince Stefan to the Mother of God. Also notable are the frescoes of St Sava and St Simeon as well as the large composition of the Assumption above the entrance.

Not a long way up the river is the **Monks' Bridge** (*Kaludjerski most*). This half ruined piece of amateur engineering was built by the monastery fraternity in 1842 at the point where the river gets very narrow. One of its arches collapsed and was replaced by a wooden construction, which still stands giving it a hazardous look, but is nevertheless still in use.

❸ Kolašin

📖 3,000

ℹ️ Mirka Vešovića bb, 020/864 254

🚉 Dulovine, 020/865-212

🚌 Mojkovačka bb, 020/864-033

Travelling from the seaside and Podgorica, Kolašin is the first town in the mountains you will come across. Just an hour's drive from Podgorica makes a world of difference: at the altitude of 965m, the climate here is much colder while all forests around the town generate a pleasant cool breeze. The hottest summer days are easy to bear, while in the winter there is plenty of snow on the mountains. The position of the town is fascinating as well: it lies on a plateau between the mountain giants – Bjelasica on the east and Sinjajevina to the northwest. The same plateau is the watershed between Tara that continues northwards and Morača that descends to the south. All of this creates potential for Kolašin to become a perfect weekend break

for people from the capital and a town with the most promising future in tourism.

The town was founded in the mid 17th c. as a Turkish military outpost in the middle of the rebellious clans of Brda and Herzegovina. Therefore its history in the next few centuries was comprised of almost innumerable Christian raids on the town and Muslim efforts to submit the highlanders. Since most of the residents of Kolašin were converts to Islam from the very same clans they fought against, the fighting was fierce and ruthless providing epic singers on both sides with lots of heroes and their deeds. The town was annexed by Montenegro in 1878, the Muslims moved out and Kolašin started all over again. The central square and a couple of streets around it were all that was created in its slow development.

Disregarding its potential, Kolašin is still just a small mountain town whose sleepy atmosphere is broken only by lively café life in which skiers and mountaineers mingle with the locals. The central square, **Trg Boraca**, is the focus of town life. Its edges are formed by one-storied houses whose stoic appearance warns of the long harsh winters. In its centre is the social-realist **monument to the**

allen in WWII
nd behind it a
modernist edifice
of the local town
ouncil that with
ts sharp angles
mitates the
ooftops of the
neighboring houses.
Next to the small
notel "Brile" is the
eat of the National
Park "Biogradska
ora" (*Trg Boraca*
, 020/865-625)
hat covers the most
magnificent part of
Mount Bjelasica. In the
nfo-center (*open 7.30-*
4.30) one can obtain
naps and souvenirs.
Close by is also the tiny
Town Museum (*Muzej*
rada Kolašina; Trg Boraca
; 020/864-344; open on
vorkdays 8-15) with an
thnograpic collection
of the region, collection
on history prior to 1941
nd the section on the
partisans in WWII. On
he farther side of Trg
Boraca stands the tall
notel "Bianca", pride
of the local tourist offer
nd the classiest meeting
pot in town. On the
other side of the square

Central square of Kolašin

is the Četvrte proleterske Street in which most of the towns cafés are concentrated. At the end of the street is another small square and then to its right a mound on which the town church built shortly after 1878 stands.

The most unusual attraction in Kolašin is its **Botanical Garden "Dulovine"** (*Botanička bašta "Dulovine", prearrangement needed on tel. 020/865-477*) on the southern outskirt of the town. The garden is privately owned and quite small so it doesn't stick out from the other houses. To find it go past the rear of the train station, then past the pine woods and then watch for the sign - the Garden is one of the houses to your left. The owner and your guide through the garden is the amazing Daniel Vincek, enthusiast and Montenegrin mountain buff since he came here 40 years ago. His botanical garden presents the flora of continental Montenegro with many rare and endemic species whose life and peculiarities are brought to life by Mr. Vincek's stories.

WHERE TO EAT IN KOLAŠIN

Savardak
Road to ski-center Jezerine (3km from the town centre), 020/864-204; open 09-22h
The old shepherd's hut of wood and straw, savardak, has been recreated on the outskirts of Kolašin as a superb restaurant serving national cuisine. You can choose to sit in its dim interior or outside by the stream and enjoy a number of Montenegrin specialties such as the incredibly tasty polentas *cicvara* and *kačamak* served by friendly staff.

Vodenica
Junaka Breze bb, 020/865-338; open 10-23h
"The Watermill" is a charming national restaurant very near to Kolašin's main street. It has been put to its current use with as little intervention to its original looks as possible which make it a sight

worth seeing. This long-standing favourite both for the tourists and the locals alike serves excellent dishes, prepared in the traditional way. To enjoy them freshly prepared you should preorder a few hours in advance.

Planinar
Trg Borca; 020/865-212; open 9-24h
This cozy place in the centre of Kolašin serves both as a café popular with the middle aged locals and as a restaurant that serves very good food at low prices. Efficient and friendly service.

❹ Bjelasica

ℹ️ Buda Tomovića, Kolašin
020/665-625

Holding a central position in East Montenegro, this giant of a mountain can be seen from all around. Its main ridge spans 29km from Mojkovac to Andrijevica with its highest peak being Crna glava at 2,139m. The mountain got its name after the snowcaps on its tops which remain gleamingly white (*bijela*) during most of the year.

Eastern part of the mountain is protected as the **"Bio- gradska gora" National Park** with Biogradsko jezero Lake as its central and most easily accessible feature. Bear in mind that the Park is open for visits only from the 1st of May to the 15th of October; outside this period all facilities are closed as well as the road at its entrance. To reach it look for a green sign announcing the park some 14km from Kolašin in the direction of Mojkovac; take a right turn immediately after the sign across a narrow bridge. The road climbs 3km through a deep virgin forest where trees as tall as 60m and up to 500 years old block almost all sunlight. The road ends on the shore of Biogradsko jezero (1,094m), with its tranquil green water surrounded by unspoiled forest of maple, birch, fir and 84 other tree species. Here one can find souvenir and a map shop, a restaurant (*open 9 to 21 h, 069/032-601*) and several small cabins that can be rented. On

Biogradsko Lake and the dense virgin forest around it

the shore of the lake is also a pier with boats for rent. The lake is surrounded with a 3,5km long trail suitable for easy, relaxing walk passing over several bridges and pontoons snaking across many streams feeding the lake. Fishing is allowed but only on Tuesdays and Sundays with a proper license which can be obtained for €10 in the souvenir shop. The catch is limited to three pieces. Fishing on the other lakes on Mt Bjelasica is not allowed.

Ski center Jezerine is located some 8km to the east of Kolašin. A rather bumpy road leads to a spacious parking lot. The center has five ski-lifts - one double-chaired, three gondolas and a baby lift with one gondola working also in the evenings. There are also two restaurants here offering a range of cooked dishes at slightly higher prices than in Kolašin. The ski slopes of Jezerine are well-kept and can be quite demanding with some descends reaching the gradients of up to 60 degrees; for the less

Jezerine ski centre

Flocks grazing the pastures of Bjelasica

experienced there is a mid-way station. Very rarely will you encounter crowds on the slopes here as accommodation capacities in Kolašin are still low.

Approximately one hour climb uphill from Jezerine lies **Eko katun Vranjak**, a group of 21 small cottages built to resemble the nearby traditional shepherds' lodgings. The cottages are directly below the peak Trojeglava (2,072 m) from which open magnificent views southwards and eastwards. Vranjak is also an ideal starting point for hiking to the other major peaks of Bjelasica. The stay in this marvelous ambiance can be booked from 15th June to 20th September with the owner (*see p. 257*).

Mt Bjelasica offers excellent conditions for **hiking** with its various changing terrains such as deep forests, clear grassy pastures and rocky peaks. Many clear springs provide plenty of water and its woods offer shelter from the

sun in hot summer days. All together there are ten marked hiking trails with most of the tours starting from Kolašin or Mojkovac and some from the side of Berane and Andrijevica. The shortest way to Crna glava peak is from Jezerine by the way of Zekova glava and Pešića jezero (3h), while the route from Lake Biogradsko across Dolovi Lalevića and Svatovsko groblje takes 4 hours. Apart from the peaks the usual destinations for hikers are five glacial lakes of Bjelasica, the most scenic being **Pešića jezero** (1820m) and somewhat smaller **Ursulovačko jezero** (1895m). On the mountain there are five mountain huts all run by societies from the surrounding towns. Some are pretty old while others, such as those owned by "Džambas" and "Bjelasica", are brand new and up to the highest standards in their class (*see pp. 257-258*).

 Bijelo Polje

📖	16,000
▣	Nedakusi, 050/ 21-488
▣	Nedakusi, 050/478-560
▦	Tamburitza Festival (first weekend in August)

If visiting Montenegro by car, it is almost impossible to miss this town that owes much of its prominence to the Podgorica-Belgrade road which passes through it. This "White Field" in the valley of the Lim River which was named after its abundant daisies (*bijela rada*) was well populated already in the Middle Ages. However, the town itself appeared first in the late 16th c. as a trading post next to the monastery of Nikoljac (*see below*) and was initially called Nikolj-pazar, but this name gave way to the name of the field in which it spread. The face of the oriental small-town changed drastically during the days of socialist Yugoslavia when it was industrialized and rebuilt to a great extent.

The unusual shapes of Saints Peter & Paul Church in Bijelo Polje

Today, it is best known for the sparkling mineral water "Rada" which is drunk all over the country.

The best known historic monument of Bijelo Polje is the **Church of Saints Peter & Paul** (*Crkva svetih Petra i Pavla*) that lies immediately to the left of the main road from Podgorica towards Belgrade. This unusually looking small church was built in 1195-99 by prince Miroslav, brother of Serbian ruler Stefan Nemanja, who governed a region of the state reaching from here to Dubrovnik, known at the time as Hum and later as Herzegovina. When in the mid 13th c. the seat of the bishop of Hum was transferred here, the church got its two high towers (25m) – an obligatory element of all cathedrals. After the Turkish conquest the church was turned into a mosque, one tower was pulled down while the other was kept as a minaret. It remained a Muslim shrine until 1922 when it was returned to the orthodox community.

This tiny church of odd shapes has a rectangular apse and a blind dome and is the earliest example of western pre-Romanesque tradition in Orthodox architecture, a clear sign that it was constructed by builders from the Adriatic coastline invited here by prince Miroslav. The main stone portal still bears the original Cyrillic inscription with prince Miroslav's dedication. Only a few fragments of the original fresco-painting remain to this day. The one just to the left of the entrance is by far the most important:

here we see the remains of the portrait of prince Miroslav, with the model of the church in his hand. By using this image the modifications inflicted during many centuries of its existence were reversed so the original look of the church could be restored during the 1962 restoration works. One ca easily distinguish most of these modifications on the interior walls: even a *mihrab*, a niche designating the direction of Mecca, still endures on the right hand wall. The few remaining frescoes were painted around 132 and are fine examples of

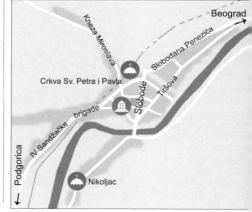

The reconstructed House of Risto Ratković

the monumental style prevalent in Serbia at the time. Church of St Peter & Paul is also known for its connection to Miroslav Gospel (*Miroslavljevo jevandjelje*), a 12th c. illuminated manuscript written on the orders of prince Miroslav for this church. The Gospel is one of the oldest examples of the Serbian redaction of the Old Church Slavonic language and contains 300 splendid miniatures from Byzantine and Romanesque tradition. During the centuries it was kept in the Serb Hilandar monastery on Mt Athos, it was then carried by the Serbian army in WWI to Greece and is today kept in the Belgrade's National Museum as one of its most valuable works of art.

The town's centre is a square with a pleasant park highlighted by a social realist monument to the fallen in WWII. The main town street, the pedestrian Ulica

Slobode, branches from the square. Of the lower side of the square begins a small street in which one can see the recently reconstructed **House of writer Risto Ratković**, the nicest

050/431-579; open Monday to Friday 8-16; entry fee €1) located in the white-washed house (1905) of the old high-school. In the museum one can see Neolithic artifacts found in the surrounding area, an interesting example of a plough from the Roman era, medieval weapons, various folk costumes, numismatic collection (mostly Roman, Medieval Serbian and Montenegrin coins) and finally documents, photos and weapons from WWII.

The other ecclesiastical monument of Bijelo Polje, the **Nikoljac Church**, lies on the opposite

Nikoljac Church, a 16th century ecclesiastical monument

example of oriental architecture in the town. Regrettably, the house is closed for visits. One block above the square lies Radnička street with its **Local Museum** (*Zavičajni muzej; tel.*

side of the town from St Peter & Paul's (*refer to map*). The church which once belonged to the monastery of the same name was built around 1560 and was one of the largest Serb churches

WHERE TO EAT IN BIJELO POLJE

Durmitor
Rakonje bb (on the Kolašin road, 2km from the centre); 050/488-111; open 07-24h
With very little competition in the town, this restaurant with rooms to let is the best place to dine in Bijelo Polje. Its specialties are the almost always spinning spit-roasts, a sure favorite with the locals.

Redjina
Omladinska bb; 050/315-99; open 07-22h
A small and friendly place in the town centre offering snacks and the usual choice of main meals such as pizzas and grills.

Detail from the iconostasis

6　Berane

👥 12,000

ℹ️ 051/236-664, toberane@cg.yu

🚌 Dušana Vujoševića bb, 051/234-892

🏛️ Djurdjevdan Festivities (early May)

constructed under the Ottoman rule. Its form is one of a basilica with three distinctive parts and a large octagonal cupola. Apart from the faded frescoes on its western façade the rest of the exterior is plainly painted in white while the roof is covered with gray shingles. The interior, on the other hand, is one of the most impressive in the whole of Montenegro since it is completely covered in frescoes from the late 16th c. The frescoes depict the cycles of the life of Christ, the life of St John the Baptist and the miracles of St Nicholas but also some unusual scenes such as the eternal suffering of sinners (to the right of the entrance), amongst them a dishonest innkeeper and a miller with the tools of their trade hanging from their necks. The highlight of the church is without a doubt its splendid iconostasis: opulently carved and ornamented in gold, with an inspired work of crucifixion surrounded with seemingly free-standing stars and angels as well as a number of exceptional icons dating from the 16th to the 19th c. The most interesting of these icons is the one of St Nicholas with scenes from his life (1677, *to the right*), painted by Radul, one of the most talented icon-painters of his day. Note also the unusually tall 16th c. candlesticks of white marble standing in front of the iconostasis.

The town of Berane is the centre of Upper Lim valley. It lies in the region known since medieval times as Budimlje, a prosperous county that lay in the middle of the medieval Serbian state. The town itself is actually the youngest in the whole of Montenegro. Its beginning lies in the year 1862 when the Turks built their barracks in the field near the village of Beran to watch over the region of Andrijevica, won by Montenegro in 1860. The town grew around officers' houses but the orthodox population did not settle in larger numbers until its liberation in 1912 when Berane became the seat of a district and got a high school, the only such institution in this part of the country. From 1949 to 1992 the town was renamed to Ivangrad after Ivan Milutinović, one of the leading communists and leaders of the uprising in WWII. The sign with the old name can still be seen on some old notice boards so don't get confused.

Though quite large, Berane is uninteresting apart from the weird blend of oriental neglect witnessed in crumbling old houses, socialist blocks, street sellers as well as utterly chaotic driving. The main street, Igumana Mojsija

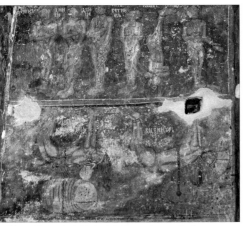

The suffering in hell depicted on a frescoe in the Nikoljac Church

House of Gavro Vuković

Zečevića, is a wide pedestrian promenade filled with cafés. At its upper end is a square with the seat of the local community. Facing it is the House of Gavro Vuković, local chief and the first minister of foreign affairs of Montenegro, which was built in 1913 in a modest variation of current European fashion. To your right is the building housing the **Polimski muzej** (*Miloša Mališića bb, open in summer months 10-13 and 17-20 h, entrance fee €1.50, exhibition texts in English*) with an interesting collection of archeological, historical and ethnographic items. The most interesting are the 14th c. chain mail, old firearms and costumes from the Lim region.

By far the most interesting monument in Berane is the **Monastery of Djurdjevi stupovi** ("George's Towers"), the seat of the orthodox bishopric. It is located on the western outskirt of the town: follow the sign to get off the main road to Andrijevica and then take the third street to your right. The church dedicated to St George was built at the end of the 12th c. by *Župan* Prvoslav, cousin of Stefan Nemanja. Unusually long but nevertheless harmonious church is a result of three building stages. The part with a cupola is the oldest and was done by maritime builders, which were preferred by the Nemanjićs. The

higher part with a belfry was added around 1219 when St Sava established here one of the seven bishoprics of the newly founded autonomous Serbian church. Originally the edifice boasted not one but two towers, the feature that earned it its name. On the west side the church ends with the outer narthex from the 18th c. The interior is plain and comprises only a few frescoes that over the centuries survived five annihilations of the monastery. Djurdjevi stupovi was an important centre for local Christians, especially of the Vasojevići clan. It was

An emroidered womens costume, Polimski muzej

Djurdjevi Stupovi monastery at dusk

here that in 1829 abbot Mojsije Zečević led the assembly that revised and adopted collectively the traditional clan laws. This set of commandments known as *Vasojevićki zakon*, presents a short, easily comprehensible and merciless rules of survival in those cruel and lawless times.

ENVIRONS:

Some 15km to the east of Berane is Mt Cmiljevica (1963m) under which is located the **ski-centre Lokve** with a freshly reconstructed hotel of the same name and three ski-lifts leading to five ski pistes.

❼ Andrijevica

 1,050

This miniature shanty town lies on a small plateau overlooking the river Lim. Even at its height of 800m above sea level it is still overshadowed with high mountains covered in deep green forests. In the Middle Ages a church was built here by Andrija, a prince of the offshoot branch from the Nemanjić dynasty. His church called Andrijevna survived until 1765 when it was leveled to the ground during a Turkish punitive expedition against the Vasojevići clan, which inhabits this

area. When Montenegro acquired control over the Vasojevići in the mid 19 c, the ground of the valley of Lim, where previously stood Andrijevna Church, became once again an interesting site for a centr of a rural region which had no other town at all and with time Andrijevic grew one house at a time. Between the two World Wars it grew even faster a the seat of a large county was located here. This continued until in 1960 al of the administration was transferred to Berane or Plav and the town started slowly to die out.

All the town's amenitie are located in its main street which also serves as the road from Berane to Plav. Side by side stand half-ruined houses of traditional design with white-painted walls and shingled roofs, socialist apartment blocks and hal finished family houses of newer origin. In front of its few shops one can ofte

GUSLE – THE CALL OF THE PAST

Gusle is a Serb national instrument of ancient origin similar to a fiddle but with only one string (or exceptionally in some areas, two strings) where the sound is produced by pulling the bow over the string while holding the instrument in one's lap. The created sound is sharp, dramatic, almost unpleasant and – contrary to the looks - it takes a lot of skill to make it. But the sole sound of gusle is not important on its own as it is always accompanied by singing of the guslar. His chant is a kind of lament repeated over and over, highly intonated and hypnotic, more a recitation than a real song. This comes from the fact that with gusle one always sings epic songs, telling the deeds of heroes and heroic acts and it has been so for centuries. The oldest songs accompanied by gusle come from the Middle Ages and sing about Kosovo Battle and the legendary hero Kraljević Marko. Their glory days were during the times when they replaced both books and newspapers for the poor and illiterate peasants, singing about the lost freedom of the Serbs and encouraging men to new heroic acts. The instrument and its songs are still alive today, telling stories of current events from its own, archaic point of view. *Guslarske vječeri*, the "Evenings of guslars" are still a usual kind of pastime in many towns and guslars are still highly revered and appreciated. In Montenegro it is almost impossible to imagine a home without a family owned gusle hung on the wall, usually richly carved with interesting national symbols, mythological or historical representations.

The forbidding peaks of Komovi emerging from the green fields

see small mountain horses patiently waiting for their master to finish his shopping. However, even such small backwater town is undoubtedly the most important settlement around and is therefore a convenient place to stop for supplies before beginning a trip to the mountains surrounding it, the most notable amongst them being Komovi. The only historical monument in Andrijevica is **Knjaževac,** a nice park whose main feature is a stone church built by prince Nikola in 1887. Facing it are two monuments: the smaller one with an eagle atop erected in memory to the fallen in 1912-1918 wars while the other, more abstract, commemorates the inhabitants of the area who died in WWII.

❽ Komovi

> 20 km from Andrijevica

Together with Durmitor and Prokletije massifs, Komovi is one of the most impressive ranges in Montenegro and indeed in the whole of the Dinaric Alps. The mountain is bordered with Tara to the west and Lim to the east from where it ascends to 1900 meters, where a series of smaller plateaus above the forest level make it perfect for *katuni*, the shepherds' summer houses of, which are remarkably almost all still in function. From the tableland rise the bare rocky peaks – Kom Kučki (2487m) to the west and to the east Kom Vasojevićki (2461m), both named after clans

whose mutual border they form.

Komovi are easily accessed by Andrijevica-Kolašin road that winds upwards to **Trešnjevik** pass, recognizable by the small inn of Savo Lekić. Here you can sip a drink, taste a game delicacy, get information about

Savo Lekić, the proud owner of the Trešnjevik inn

the area or just enjoy the merry company of the locals. From this point a 6km long gravel road branches out leading to the idyllic grassland plateau of **Štavna** with shepherd huts and freely grazing flocks of sheep, cows and horses. This is also the location of

WHERE TO EAT IN ANDRIJEVICA

Most
Most Bandovića (road to Berane); 069/563-791; open 07-01h
The name of this restaurant ("The Bridge") explains its setting, with a large terrace overlooking the fast waters of the river. The menu offers a good choice of grills and national dishes, occasionally also some trout.

A traditional stone house from the vicinity of Andrijevica

the "Eko katun", a new complex of ten huts, each with five beds with all the luxuries of civilization (*see p. 259*). With its wide vistas to the south and its relative flatness, Štavna is a perfect place to pitch your tents.

The rugged, inhospitable looking and in some places almost vertical sides of this mountain are a real challenge for climbers. The climb to Vasojevićki Kom (2½ h) is somewhat easier, while the one to Kučki Kom (3½ h) should only be attempted by experienced climbers and is best achieved from its south face. There is also a nice circular walk around both peaks: from Štavna to Ljuban ridge, then to the source of Crnja river, then below Kučki Kom to the Carine *katun* at the southern face of the mountain and back along the eastern side. Following a slow pace, the walk will take you a whole day.

❾ Plav

📖 3,600
ℹ️ 051/252-888
🚌 Road to Andrijevica, 051/251-371

The small town of Plav has a most spectacular setting: it lies 900m above sea level near a large lake at the east edge of a broad and fertile valley which is bound on all sides by high mountains. Before reaching the town one first observes the **Plavsko Lake**, the largest and the most beautiful of several glacier lakes of the Prokletije Mountains which are mirrored on its surface. The lake is almost 5km long and 2km wide with its

deepest at 9 meters. Its always cold waters have a dark blue (*plavo*) colour, which offers one of the explanations for the town's name. The lake is fed by the water from the River Ljuča coming from the west while from its northern end Lim, the longest river in Montenegro, flows out. Plavsko Lake is very rich in fish, especially in trout, huchen and grayling. The shores are covered in reed and there aren't many places suitable for swimming apart from the wooden pier on its east side.

The town of Plav was first mentioned in the 13th c. as a village of fishermen in possession of Serbian kings that kept the monopoly on the fishing here. Additionally, it functioned as a commercial centre on the busy road from Podgorica to the Lim valley. Plav developed further after the Ottoman conquest in the mid 15th c. and especially at the beginning of the 17th c. when it got a small fort and a permanent garrison; it was during this era that most of the population converted to Islam, the religion still practiced by most of the locals. The place

Plavsko Lake with Prokletije mountains visible in the distance

lived its life of seclusion until 1878 when, by the word of the Peace treaty of Berlin, this area was supposed to become a part of the Princedom of Montenegro. The local Muslims rose to arms against this decision and after fierce resistance managed to reverse the decision and stay in the Ottoman

An old mosque in Plav

The stout Redžepagić Tower

Empire. Nevertheless, the old Empire's rule came to an end in 1912 when the Montenegrin army seized the area. Unfortunately for the region, the newly formed Albanian state got a small portion of the old road to Podgorica and thus Plav was denied its most important route, left with only a single road leading towards the north. This was the beginning of the end for this area which became

known for its high emigration. Today most of the people born in Plav live abroad and the town gets alive only during their summer vacations when they return to see their relatives.

Though it consists mostly of new houses the town's physiognomy is still very oriental. At the entrance to its centre is a small roundabout with a post office. On a small mound to the right is Plav's most important sight, the **Old Mosque** (*Stara džamija*). Made in combination of wood and stone, this typical mosque of the western Balkans was constructed in the mid 18th c. on the site of an older one.

The mosque's porch has some fine carvings. To the left of the roundabout opens a view of the large **Imperial Mosque** (*Carska džamija*) constructed in 1909 with the donation from the Sultan Abdul Hamid II, thus its name. In 1924 the mosque was turned into a warehouse, later into a school and even into a police station and has only recently been returned to its original purpose. From the roundabout starts the narrow *čaršija*, the main trading street where most of the businesses, cafés and institutions are located. At its end take the street to the right and walk past another small mosque with a nicely carved wooden minaret to reach the **Redžepagić Tower**, standing tall in the middle of the courtyard outlined by family homes that surround it. The tower is probably the

Wooden windows on an old house

Beautiful wilderness of Hridsko Lake

oldest building in the town, dating from the late 16th or early 17th c. The first two floors are made of stone and are about one meter thick, while the wooden top floor with a typical steep roof was added somewhat later. The towers such as this one were built by local landowners to serve as their homes which could easily be transformed into impregnable forts. If you look closely, you will notice that several other houses around here are in fact adapted towers.

Plav is a convenient starting place for excursions to the mountains Kofiljača and Bogićevica spreading to the south of it. There is a

Spring flowering in the fields of Mt Bogićevica

marked route leading to Kofiljača's highest peak **Horolac** (2199m) starting

from Bogajiće village, immediately to the south of the town. The walking tour lasts approximately 3 hours. In a spectacular setting in the heart of the wilderness of Mt Bogićevica, at the height of 1960m, the **Hridsko Lake** (*Hridsko jezero*) is located and surrounded with Macedonian pine wood. One can drive to the village of Babino Polje (12km to the east of the town) but to continue beyond one needs a four-wheel

WHERE TO EAT IN PLAV

Belle Ami
Racina bb; 051/252-727; open 07-24h
This restaurant is as exclusive as it gets in Plav: with a cozy separate dining room and a choice of wines, it offers some international-style dishes in addition to the grills and several specialties of the national cuisine.

Djerdan
Glavice bb (behind bus station); tel. 051/25-25-03; open 07-24h
This inexpensive place has a warm atmosphere created by the locals who come here for a coffee or ćevapčići and other grills to accompany their long conversations. The place also serves soup and a cooked dish of the day.

Lovac
Highway to Gusinje; 051/251-392; open 07-23h
The restaurant lies on the northern side of the Plav Lake.
Although away from the town it is frequented for its good food, which apart from grills and local specialties also includes game. The restaurant also offers several rooms for rent.

drive vehicle as the last part of the road is in very bad condition. Alternatively, a walk to the Lake will take you some two hours from Babino Polje.

⑩ Gusinje

 1,700

Located in a fertile valley underneath the craggy Prokletije Mountains with Albania being behind the first peaks to the west and the south, Gusinje finds itself at the end of all roads. This tiny town once had much more importance as it lay on the road to Podgorica. In the 18th c. it was the seat of a county and had 600 houses with 200 shops, but since in 1912

century by Mehmed-pasha Bushati, the Turkish vizier of Shkoder (today Albania). Curiously, the graves of the town's fallen communists are located in the mosque's yard. If you take a short walk thorough Gusinje you will notice many fine examples of Balkan-oriental houses and some of the towers also, but all in a state of utter neglect. It is interesting to notice that this small place has a catholic and an orthodox church as well.

A restaurant on the Ali-pasha's Springs

has an impression that water is coming from all sides carried by a number of streams and spilling all over the field. The streams remain cold throughout the year as they are provided with water from the melting snowcaps. The springs got their name after the famous local hero Ali-pasha of Gusinje, who led the resistance against the Montenegrin annexation of the area in 1878-81. On every August the 2nd, on the day of St Elijah (*Ilindan*), all people originating from Gusinje gather here in celebration, a spontaneous outburst of folklore, sorrow for the homeland left behind and a display of riches gained abroad (mostly in the USA and Germany). There is a very nice restaurant "Vodenica" (Watermill) on the site.

Unusual old houses abound in Gusinje

the road was severed by the borderline the town lost its importance completely and in the last forty years it dwindled to half its size.

The best known monument in Gusinje is the **Vizier's Mosque** (*Vezirova džamija*) structured in a typical local style and built at the end of the 17th

The most famed spot for picnics in the vicinity of Gusinje are the illustrious **Ali-pasha's Springs** (*Ali-pašini izvori*) 2km to the south of town. In this remarkable place one

WHERE TO EAT IN GUSINJE

Primorka
Čaršijska bb, 051/256-333; open 07-23h
A nice eatery in the central town street offering snacks, soups and grills at bargain prices.

⑪ Prokletije

7km from Gusinje

Prokletije (literally "Cursed Mountains", in Albanian *Bjeshkët e Nemuna*) is the southernmost ridge of the Dinaric Alps. In a wider sense these mountains stretch from Shkoder in the west to Peć in the east, spreading through three states - Albania, Montenegro and Serbia - and representing the natural borderline between them. However, their name suggests a somewhat different view: they were considered "cursed" by the shepherds for their inaccessibility, lack of water and pastures, in fact they were unsuitable for any kind of life - these extremely rough conditions can only be found in the area south of Gusinje, which is considered to be the core of the Prokletije ridge. This part of Prokletije is the most impressive, its wilderness and the sheer size of its jagged stone cliffs make it a terrifying proposition. This is also where the Prokletije's highest peak, Maja Jezerces / Jezerski vrh (2694m), looms. The massif is ideal for hiking and alpinism

meadows, peaks rising towards the skies and marvelous panoramic views, Prokletije are an astonishing sight even for those who are not attempting to climb one of its peaks.

The look of Prokletije is due to the intensive

Prokletije Mountains are a prize for avid climbers

and although it lacks facilities and many marked paths it offers a feeling of discovery and walking off the beaten track. Moreover, with their alpine

glaciation process when glaciers pushed down from the mountains carving deep valleys between the peaks. Two of these valleys lead closer to the heart of the

Inaccessible alpine terrain of Prokletije

Old ladies in Grbaja valley

massif – Grbaja in the west and Ropojana to the east.

From Gusinje one reaches **Grbaja** by the way of Dolja village (7km). As you approach this valley in front of you opens one of the most picturesque views in Montenegro – an idyllic vale of green grass with a stream in its middle and birch woods on its sides, bordered with steep mountains finishing with bare stone peaks. To your left rise the Karanfili peaks topped by Veliki vrh (2490m) while on your right are Popadija (2056m) and Volušnica (1876m). Grbaja valley is some 3km long and it slowly rises towards the south with three lovely fields opening one after another. Apart from its enchanting beauty, Grbaja is also the usual starting point for hikers because of its **two mountain huts**. The one run by "Radnički" mountaineering association from Belgrade is open to all hikers without any charge but is very

basically equipped; the key to the hut is kept in the local police office in Gusinje and you should feel free to ask for it. The other hut is run by the local "Karanfili" association and is fully furnished but also charges €5 for the night (*contact person Mr Rifat Mulić*). Starting from Grbaja all hiking tours are fully marked. Before starting you should get a proper map (you can obtain a very basic one from Mr. Mulić for €1) and take a lot of water with you as the upper areas are waterless.

Continuing southwards from Ali-pasha's Springs (*see previous chapter*) the road follows the Skakavac stream, past the village of Vusanje and

slowly enters the valley of **Ropojana**, squeezed from all sides by high peaks. If you're interested in staying longer in this area or are willing to climb some of the peaks it is advisable to report to the border police in their base south of the Vusanje village.

At the other side of Vusanje one comes to the **Grlja Waterfall**. At this spot the Grlja River makes a sudden turn and falls from a 15m high

Splashing energy of Grlja waterfall

Ropojana valley

cliff into a stone abyss from which a chilling spray rises. Not far away up the river is another waterfall, but this one is sheltered in the woods and impossible to see from the road. However, if you're walking you will certainly hear its roar. Just after the waterfall the stream slows down in a place known as **Savino oko** ("St Sava's Eye"), where the striking blue water reveals unusually great depth; this is due to a strong underwater spring that adds much to the stream's strength. Four kilometers further to the south, deeper in the narrowing field of Ropojana, lays the **Čemerikino Lake**. This wild and inaccessible lake disappears in high summer. Note that the Montenegrin-Albanian border lies directly on the other side of the lake.

From Ropojana one can climb the Rosni vrh / Maja Rosit (2522m, right on the border). From Zastan to the left of Ropojana one can advance to the central part of Prokletije with Maja Jezerce lying in Albania some 7km south of here. The climb from the end of the asphalt road takes some 10 hours in one direction and is therefore recommended to do it in two days with an overnight camp. There are no border controls from the Albanian side but if you want to be on the safe side you can announce your group to the Albanian police.

Turning left from Vusanje one comes to Zarunica hamlet; to the north of it is the green Bor ridge (2102m) and to the south the desolate massif of Belič with the highest peak of Maja Kolata / Kolac (2530m) a few hundred meters into Albania.

⑫ Rožaje

 9,300

 Maršala Tita bb, 051/270-158

051/271-115

Rožaje is the centre of a mountainous region in the far east of Montenegro. It lies in the valley traversed by the fast and cold river Ibar which springs nearby, along which passes the road leading to Novi Pazar in Serbia. In the town a road branches off and leads across the snowy Kulina pass descending towards Peć in the region of Kosovo.

The town was first mentioned in the 17th c. under the name Trgovište ("Market") as the peasants from the surrounding mountains came here to sell their meat, skins and dairy products and this tradition continued until not long ago. The name Rožaje, coming from the two crags rising above the town which reminded of horns (*rogovi*), was used simultaneously with

Blue waters of Savino oko underwater spring

Trgovište but became official only after the town was incorporated into Montenegro in 1912. At the end of the 17th century the orthodox population had to flee because they sided with the Austrians and against their Turkish masters; the area was gradually resettled but this time all the newcomers had to accept Islam and the whole area remains almost entirely Muslim to this day.

There is little left to witness the town's history. Until a few decades ago its most lovely feature was the multitude of surviving old houses with high shingled roofs but today you will find only a few of these, most in ruined state, while the rest of the town has been taken by tall new houses of strange post-modern shapes and colours. The most important monument in

the town is the **Ganića kula**, a tall tower built in 1802 by local landowners to serve as an easily defendable home. When the reconstruction works end, it will house the eagerly expected local museum. There are **two**

A wonderfully preserved homestead

old mosques in Rožaje: the older one, Kurtagića džamija, dates from 1697 but following its incompetent reconstruction bears little signs of antiquity; on the other hand, Kučanska džamija, though much younger (1830) retains the features of traditional architecture.

Of much more interest than the town itself are its environs

– Rožaje is surrounded with magnificent range of mountains such as Cmiljevica (1,963m), Hajla (2,403m) and Žljeb (2,155m) to the south and Turjak (1,573m) to the north. The lower regions are hidden in thick forests while above them rise stony peaks attractive for hiking or even free climbing. The area is well known for its abundance in mushrooms, blueberries, blackberries and many rare and endemic flowers. Following a trail along river Ibar in the southwest direction for 10km will lead you to its beautiful springs (*vrelo Ibra*), where six pretty streams join to form the river that will continue for another 272km until its confluence in West Morava. Located just 4km from Rožaje on the highway towards Berane is the **ski-centre Turjak** with a hotel of the same name and two ski lifts.

WHERE TO EAT IN ROŽAJE

Duga
Rasadnik (on Berane road); 051/278-266; open 07-22h
Located just off the main road to Berane this restaurant tucked in greenery enjoys a more peaceful setting, seemingly far from the town. Very nicely furnished, this restaurant serves excellent national cuisine specialties at prices slightly higher than the average.

Košuta
Turjak ski centre; tel. 069/217-066; open 08-22h
This large restaurant caters for the visitors of the Turjak ski centre. Covered in warm wood and embellished with ethno details it serves mostly national cuisine dishes.

M Petrol
Zeleni bb (on Novi Pazar road); 051/274-202; open 07-00h
Disregarding its setting next to a petrol station of the same name in the shabby industrial zone at the exit of the town, this restaurant has very few faults; on the contrary, it ranks amongst the most exclusive in the town, popular with both locals and the regular guests of Rožaje. The range of dishes is standard fare with grills and national dishes predominating, the portions are large and the food tasty.

Hotel

Motel

Villa/Private Pension

Agrotourism accommodation

Hostel

PRICE RANGE - for one person in a two-bed room (including breakfast, service and tax). Small icons present facilities in each Hotel.

number of rooms number of beds

308/373

> 100 Euro
50 - 100 Euro
35 - 50 Euro
25 - 35 Euro
12 - 25 Euro
< 12 Euro

Kolašin: Bianca Resort & Spa ★ ★ ★ ★

115/138

Mirka Vešovica bb

+ 382 (0)20 863 077

www.biancaresort.com

One of the finest and most luxurious hotels of inland Montenegro, situated in the forest near the centre of Kolašin. It has elegant and warm interiors created exclusively with wood and stone. The hotel offers its conference hall, excellent spa center, indoor swimming pool, gym and other modern facilities to its guests.

Kolašin: Brile ★ ★ ★

9/25

Ul.Buda Tomovića 2

+ 382 (0)20 865 021

www.brile.info

This small, family run hotel has become one of the best known tourist locations in the town. The rooms are modernly furnished and comfortable. It also has a small sauna with hydro massage and a restaurant offering national dishes and Italian specialties.

Kolašin: Djevojački most

10/20

Bakovići bb

+ 382 (0)20 867 100

www.montenegro.com

This brand new hotel is on the main exit from Kolašin towards Mojkovac. Elegantly designed and modernly equipped it has medium sized, well-appointed rooms.

Kolašin: Čile ★ ★ ★

12/33

Ul. Ranka i Strahinje Miloševića

+ 382 (0)20 865 039

www.zlatnido.com

This basic hotel has comfortable though rather plainly furnished rooms. Its restaurant ranks among the best in Kolašin and is good value for money.

Kolašin: Hotel Garni ★ ★

7/16

IV Proleterske

+ 382 (0)20 865 484

www.brile.info

This unassuming hotel lies on Kolašin's main promenade. The rooms are small but nevertheless comfortable and clean. The hotel's restaurant offers very good Italian cuisine.

Kolašin: Lipka

72/84

Mojkovačka 20

+ 382 (0)20 863 200

www.lipka-hotel.com

This luxury hotel in the centre of Kolašin is owned by Russians and oriented towards the Russian guests. It has a small spa center with two saunas, massage tables, jacuzzi and a fitness gym. The interior and the rooms are a combination of rustic wood and modern furniture, stylish and comfortable.

Kolašin: Vila Jelka ★ ★

10/25

Partizanska bb

+ 382 (0)20 860 150

www.vilajelka.cg.yu

This private pension is one of the leaders of local tourism in Kolašin organizing many activities and adventures. The rooms are small and basically equipped but cozy. Their restaurant offers domestic food grown on their own farm.

KOLAŠIN: Bakić ★ ★

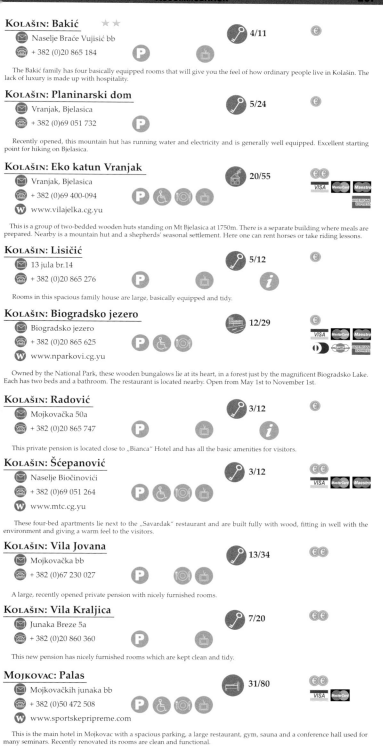

✉ Naselje Braće Vujisić bb

☎ + 382 (0)20 865 184

🔑 4/11

The Bakić family has four basically equipped rooms that will give you the feel of how ordinary people live in Kolašin. The lack of luxury is made up with hospitality.

KOLAŠIN: Planinarski dom

✉ Vranjak, Bjelasica

☎ + 382 (0)69 051 732

🔑 5/24

Recently opened, this mountain hut has running water and electricity and is generally well equipped. Excellent starting point for hiking on Bjelasica.

KOLAŠIN: Eko katun Vranjak

✉ Vranjak, Bjelasica

☎ + 382 (0)69 400-094

🌐 www.vilajelka.cg.yu

20/55

This is a group of two-bedded wooden huts standing on Mt Bjelasica at 1750m. There is a separate building where meals are prepared. Nearby is a mountain hut and a shepherds' seasonal settlement. Here one can rent horses or take riding lessons.

KOLAŠIN: Lisičić

✉ 13 jula br.14

☎ + 382 (0)20 865 276

🔑 5/12

Rooms in this spacious family house are large, basically equipped and tidy.

KOLAŠIN: Biogradsko jezero

✉ Biogradsko jezero

☎ + 382 (0)20 865 625

🌐 www.nparkovi.cg.yu

12/29

Owned by the National Park, these wooden bungalows lie at its heart, in a forest just by the magnificent Biogradsko Lake. Each has two beds and a bathroom. The restaurant is located nearby. Open from May 1st to November 1st.

KOLAŠIN: Radović

✉ Mojkovačka 50a

☎ + 382 (0)20 865 747

🔑 3/12

This private pension is located close to „Bianca" Hotel and has all the basic amenities for visitors.

KOLAŠIN: Šćepanović

✉ Naselje Biočinovići

☎ + 382 (0)69 051 264

🌐 www.mtc.cg.yu

3/12

These four-bed apartments lie next to the „Savardak" restaurant and are built fully with wood, fitting in well with the environment and giving a warm feel to the visitors.

KOLAŠIN: Vila Jovana

✉ Mojkovačka bb

☎ + 382 (0)67 230 027

🔑 13/34

A large, recently opened private pension with nicely furnished rooms.

KOLAŠIN: Vila Kraljica

✉ Junaka Breze 5a

☎ + 382 (0)20 860 360

🔑 7/20

This new pension has nicely furnished rooms which are kept clean and tidy.

MOJKOVAC: Palas

✉ Mojkovačkih junaka bb

☎ + 382 (0)50 472 508

🌐 www.sportskepripreme.com

31/80

This is the main hotel in Mojkovac with a spacious parking, a large restaurant, gym, sauna and a conference hall used for many seminars. Recently renovated its rooms are clean and functional.

MOJKOVAC: Dulović ★ ★ ★

✉ Trg Ljubomira Bakoča bb

☎ + 382 (0)50 472 615

8/19

As this small hotel lies close to the sports' hall of Mojkovac it is visited by sportsmen but also by others interested in outdoor activities such as rafting, hiking etc., which are organized by the hotel.

MOJKOVAC: Ravnjak ★ ★

✉ Naselje Bistrica, Mojkovac

☎ + 382 (0)50 472 144

8/19

Lying at the very entrance to the Durmitor-Tara National Park, this small hotel is best known for its renowned restaurant.

MOJKOVAC: Krstac ★ ★

✉ Stevanovac

☎ + 382 (0)50 795 003

12/23

This motel is situated about a kilometer from the centre of Mojkovac, on the road towards Bijelo Polje. Five more bungalows are due to be opened during the summer of 2008.

MOJKOVAC: Planinarski dom Džambas

✉ Katun Kutijevci

☎ + 382 (0)67 878 938

4/40

Far from a usual mountain hut in Montenegro, it is well furnished and comfortable, and provides the cozy feel of a wooden hut in the wilderness of Bjelasica, 1432m above sea level.

MOJKOVAC: Eko katun Dobrilovina

✉ Dobrilovina

☎ + 382 (0)67 511 755

4/16

This group of four houses built with wood to resemble the old houses of the region lies at the entrance of the Durmitor-Tara National Park, some 25km drive from Mojkovac.

MOJKOVAC: Eko katun Filipović

✉ Uloševina, Bojna Njiva

☎ + 382 (0)67 517 957

19/47

1.5km from the Mojkovac-Bijelo Polje road, in a field amidst a birch forest, on 1100m above sea level lies this group of 14 huts and two houses. The food served here is locally produced and organic.

BIJELO POLJE: Durmitor

✉ Rakonje bb, Bijelo Polje

☎ + 382 (0)50 488 111

18/38

A small and basic motel on the Mojkovac road with a national cuisine restaurant in the basement.

BIJELO POLJE: Novoprevoz

✉ Slobodana Pejovica bb (old bus station)

☎ + 382 (0)50 432 219

7/17

Recently opened, this decent but very basic pension is the only accommodation where you can spend a night in central Bijelo Polje.

BERANE: Hotel S ★ ★ ★

✉ Mitropolita Pajsije

☎ + 382 (0)51 232 031

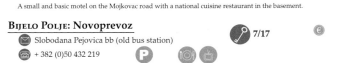

7/13

A new hotel in the center of town, just by the main market. Small and somewhat constricted, but cosy and comfortable with all basic tourist amenities.

BERANE: Buče ★ ★ ★

✉ Berane

☎ + 382 (0)69 458 566

5/10

This small motel some 2km from the center of Berane offers very basic accommodation but is clean and tidy. It has a large terrace overlooking the River Lim, an ideal place to taste their excellent food, above all trout and other river fish.

BERANE: Vidikovac

✉ Dušana Vujoševica 1

☎ + 382 (0)51 233 071

🔑 8/17   €€

This private pension is located just across the local bus station but is surprisingly quiet once inside. The rooms are new, clean and well furnished. In the basement the hotel has a restaurant of the same name serving good food.

ANDRIJEVICA: Komovi

✉ Branka Deletića bb

☎ + 382 (0)51 243 016

🌐 www.hotelkomovi.com

🛏 43/99   €€€

Recently given a new flair, this is the only hotel in Andrijevica and the outlaying area. It has a conference hall, sports grounds and a spacious dining hall. The simple rooms are clean and spacious.

ANDRIJEVICA: Most   ★ ★ ★

✉ Most Bandovića, Andrijevica

☎ + 382 (0)69 563 791

🏨 3/6   €€

A small basic motel whose main asset is a restaurant preparing very good specialties of national cuisine.

ANDRIJEVICA: Eko dom Trešnjevik

✉ Trešnjevik

☎ + 382 (0)51 236 097

🏠 1/6   €

The inn at the Trešnjevik pass offers a decent 6-bed hut ideal as a starting place for hiking in Komovi or as an overnight resting place in this far flung region.

ANDRIJEVICA: Eko katun Štavna

✉ Štavna

☎ + 382 (0)51 243 150

🏘 20/50   €

A group of newly built huts that fit well with the environment of Štavna katun. At 1800m above sea level and far from any civilization it is perfect for a holiday in the wilderness and ideal for those willing to climb Mt Komovi, which is within hand's reach.

PLAV: Aqua Eco Village

✉ Gusinjski put

☎ + 382 (0)51 252 432

🌐 www.turistickonaseljeaqua.net

🏘 10/26   €€

This unique place on the shore of the Plav Lake offers bungalows and apartments but it also has a small convention hall, a large terrace, a mini Zoo-garden and a children's park, not to mention that you can even take their boats to row around the lake for free!

ROŽAJE: Rožaje   ★ ★ ★ ★

✉ Maršala Tita bb

☎ + 382 (0)51 240 100

🌐 www.hotelrozaje.cg.yu

🛏 33/59   €€€€€ VISA MasterCard Maestro

The hotel is situated in the very heart of the town. Recently renovated in a very luxurious fashion it has all the amenities one can ask for although the interior with its fancy period furnishing is on the brink of distasteful. A small casino, sauna, sun-bed lounge and even Turkish baths are at the guests' disposal.

ROŽAJE: Grand

✉ Novo naselje

☎ + 382 (0)69 465 539

🏨 20/40   €

This motel lying on the exit for Berane has very comfortable, clean rooms with showers at bargain basement prices.

ROŽAJE: Duga

✉ 13. jula bb

☎ + 382 (0)51 287 266

🔑 7/18   €€

This private pension is located in the tranquil surroundings at the exit towards Berane, and has a convenient location for those visiting the ski centers of Turjak and Hajla.

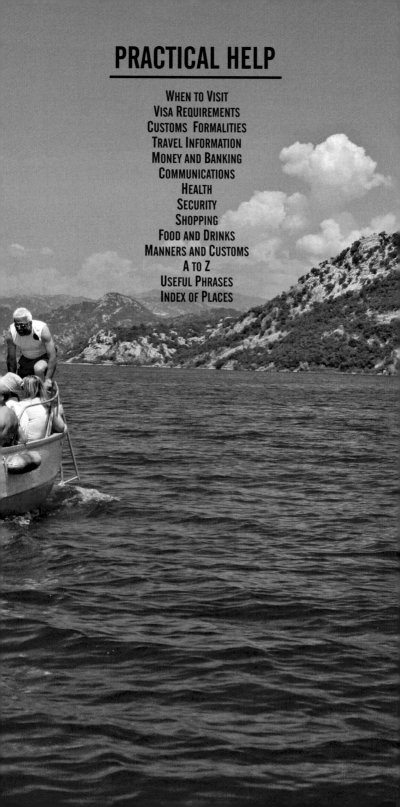

PRACTICAL HELP

WHEN TO VISIT
VISA REQUIREMENTS
CUSTOMS FORMALITIES
TRAVEL INFORMATION
MONEY AND BANKING
COMMUNICATIONS
HEALTH
SECURITY
SHOPPING
FOOD AND DRINKS
MANNERS AND CUSTOMS
A TO Z
USEFUL PHRASES
INDEX OF PLACES

WHEN TO VISIT

Montenegro is appealing for visits in all seasons since its varied climate and geography offer a change of scenery and activities within only a couple of hours drive.

Spring. April in the coastal area usually sees people lightly dressed but with umbrellas as this is the rainiest month of the year. Weather allowing, the bathing season starts around May 1st when the sun shines brightly enough to convince even the most wary. During this month the usual sight in coastal resorts are older European tourists strolling around or drinking coffee, enjoying off-season prices; most of the beach bars and services are just opening and are not fully operational. The mountain rivers are swollen with melting snow and if you enjoy white-water rafting May and June are the months for your visit. Mountain peaks are still covered with snow and sudden weather changes may easily bring another snow storm; the locals who had ran away from the fierce winter and the isolation are now returning. This is the most idyllic season in the lower inland areas and a good opportunity to see Lake Skadarsko at its largest when it is teaming with birdlife, the green leaves in the usually sun-scorched Podgorica and the nearby waterfalls of the River Cijevna in all their magnificence.

Summer. By the beginning of June the tourist season starts to gain force, but the prices of accommodation during this month are still significantly lower than those from the 1st of July. The real tourist invasion comes in July and August when the seaside becomes crammed with visitors of all ages and profiles bringing the rundown infrastructure to the verge of breakdown. Cafés and nightclubs are all open, local music festivals and cultural events follow one another but if you're not looking for loud fun, girls on swarming beaches and being seen, this is the time of year to avoid. The season is also in full swing in the

Autumn arrives early in the high mountains

mountains but the crowds are not so evident here and a few more people in the uninhabited highlands is always appreciated. Many Montenegrins head off to the freshness of the mountains to visit their relatives and in these months even the isolated villages seem alive once more. It is still summer in September, only the days are shorter, but by the middle of the month the beaches have emptied and are left over to the enjoyment of the few remaining tourists.

Autumn. October is mild in the littoral but is the last month to finish what needs to be done in the high mountains as by its end it will almost surely start to snow. In November one day might be sunny and the next stormy but by now all of the tourist businesses have closed and the littoral has fallen into its winter slumber.

Winter. The skiing season starts in December and peaks between New Year's Eve and mid February, though

Enjoy empty beaches in the pre-season

good ski conditions last all the way through April; prices reflect the number of visitors. This is definitely not a season to travel around the interior as severe weather conditions may close many roads for days. Podgorica is coldish and gray while the coastal areas see some sunshine breaking through the rainy clouds. There are very few tourists around and you will be able to observe the locals in their relaxed everyday routine. You will also experience towns such as Kotor or Budva the way they were before the age of mass-tourism.

Visa Requirements

Citizens of European Union member states can enter and stay in the Republic of Montenegro with their identity cards. The citizens of Switzerland, Norway, Israel, Croatia, United States of America, Canada, Singapore, Republic of Korea, Australia and New Zealand may enter and stay up to 90 days with any type of travel document valid for at least six months with regard to the last day of their stay in the country. Providing you list a valid reason your visa can be extended locally for additional 90 days at the fee of approximately €100. Still, what most of the residing foreigners do is just make a daytrip to Dubrovnik or some other location near the border and re-enter for another 90 days. Though this is tolerated try not to abuse the goodwill of the authorities and push your luck too far.

The citizens of the Russian Federation, Ukraine and Albania may enter and stay on the territory of the Republic of Montenegro with all types of travel documents, but only for tourist visits up to 30 days.

The citizens of Bosnia and Herzegovina, Slovenia, Croatia and Macedonia may enter and stay up to 30 days on the territory of the Republic of Montenegro with a personal ID card plus a tourist pass issued at border crossings.

The citizens of other countries need visas; however, it is possible to issue a visa or a tourist pass at the Republic of Montenegro border

EMBASSIES OF MONTENEGRO

GREAT BRITAIN
11 Waterloo Place, London SW1Y4AU
Tel: 00 44 20 78 63 88 06

ITALY
Via Antonio Gramsci 9
00197 Roma
Tel: 0039-06-45471660
e-mail: montenegro-roma@libero.it

FRANCE
Boulevard St Germain
Paris 7ème
tel: +33 1 53 63 80 30
e-mail: ambasadacg@orange.fr

UNITED STATES
1610 New Hampshire Avenue
N.W. Washington DC 20009
tel: + 1 202 234 6108

GERMANY
tel: + 49 30 25 29 19 96
Rudolf-von Gneist-Gasse 1
10785 Berlin

crossings, but only in cases of direct entry to the territory of Montenegro.

For all further information related to consular matters (e. g. visas, citizenship, estates etc.) please contact by telephone or e-mail one of the diplomatic/consular missions from the list.

Customs Formalities

Generally speaking, Montenegrin customs officials are not too eager, one could almost say that they are lax. The frontier between Serbia and Montenegro has only recently became a borderline and official crossings and passport-controls are still a novelty. If arriving from Belgrade on the train you might not even see the border guards. Nevertheless, obeying the following rules is recommended if you wish to have a trouble-free stay.

All travelers require a **passport** valid

Border crossing with Bosnia-Herzegovina at Šćepan polje

for the duration of their stay, and should ensure that it is stamped on entry.

One can bring an unlimited amount of **currency** into the country but is obliged to declare currency in excess of €2,000 upon entry and must obtain a declaration form from customs officials that must be presented on departure. The amount you can take out is limited to €500 unless more has been declared on entry.

The latest regulations limit the amount of **food and beverages** which can be brought into the country to 5l of water, a 1l alcoholic drink, 2l non-alcoholic, a kilogram of dried fruits and vegetables, and 1kg of purchased foodstuffs.

Persons traveling with expensive **electronic equipment** such as cameras or computers should list these items on a declaration issued by the authorities, (ask if needed) this ensures that they can be taken out upon departure.

By the letter of the law visitors staying in private accommodation should register with the police station responsible for the area in which they are staying within 24 hours of arrival but barely anyone complies with this and this permit is almost never checked.

TRAVEL INFORMATION

Arriving by Air

Montenegro is served by two international airports. One is in the capital, Podgorica, the other on the seaside, in Tivat. Dubrovnik airport in Croatia is also very close to the

Inside Podgorica airport

Montenegrin border and many tourists use this route as well.

Podgorica airport, better known as "Golubovci" after a nearby village, is located 12km from the centre of the city to the southwest. It is rather small but very smart since it has been recently renovated. Here one can find all the tourist amenities such as car-hire desks, a bank, duty-free shop,

DIPLOMATIC MISSIONS TO PODGORICA

ALBANIA
Stari Aerodrom, Zmaj Jovina 30
Tel: 020/652-796

AUSTRIA
Kralja Nikole 104
Tel: 020/601-580
Fax: 020/624-344
e-mail: podgorica-ob@bmaa.gv.at

BULGARIA
Vukice Mitrović 10
Tel: 020/655-009
Fax: 020/655-008
email: bg.embassy.me@abv.bg

CHINA
Radosava Burića 4a
Tel/fax: 020/609-275

CROATIA
Adresa: Vladimira Ćetkovića 2
Tel: 020/269-760
Fax: 020/269-810

CZECH REPUBLIC
Kralja Nikole b.b.
Tel: 020/648-347
e-mail: kjpodgorica@seznam.cz

FRANCE
Atinska 35
Tel/fax: 020/655-348
e-mail. france@cg.yu

GERMANY
Hercegovačka 10
Tel/fax: 020/667-285
website: www.beograd.diplo.de
e-mail: l@podg.diplo.de

GREECE
Atinska 4
Tel. 020/655-544
Fax. 020/655-543

HUNGARY
Kralja Nikole 104
Tel. : 020/602-880
Fax: 020/625-243
e-mail: hunoffice.pg@cg.yu

ITALY
Džordža Vašingtona 83
Tel. 020/234-661
Fax: 020/234-663
website: www.conspodgorica.esteri.it/Consolato_Podgorica
e-mail: segreteria.podgorica@esteri.it

MACEDONIA
Hercegovačka 49/III
Tel: 020/667-415
Fax: 020/667-205
e-mail: mkgkpodgorica@cg.yu

RUSSIA
Veliše Mugoše 1
Tel/fax: 020/272-460
e-mail: gencons.ru@cg.yu
konzpitanja@cg.yu

SLOVENIA
13 Jul bb, PC «Čelebić»
Tel: 020/208-020
Fax: 020/237-095
e-mail: kpg@gov.si

UNITED KINGDOM
Bulevar Svetog Petra Cetinjskog 149
Tel: 020/205-460
Fax: 020/205-441

UNITED STATES
Kruševac bb
Tel: 020/225-417
Fax: 020/241-358

Airport Podgorica (TGD)
Tel: +382 (0)20 243 007
+382 (0)20 244-916

Airport Tivat (TIV)
Tel: + 382 (0)32 671 337
+382 (0)32 670 930

souvenir shops, two restaurants and the offices of five airlines (Montenegro Airlines, Jat Airways, Adria, Austrian and Malev). From this airport there are regular direct flights to Belgrade, London, Rome, Ljubljana, Budapest, Zurich, Vienna, Frankfurt and Paris as well as many charter flights. The airport's working hours are from 6 to 23h. There should be minibuses ready to take you to the city after every flight. Another option is taking a taxi, which should cost you €8-10 to the centre of Podgorica. Be sure to agree the price at least approximately before getting into a taxi since overpricing can occur. It is common to haggle for a better price but no taxi driver will be willing to go under €5. See bellow for more on taxis.

Tivat airport lies in the Gulf of Kotor, 3km from the town of the same name and 4km from Kotor. The airport is tiny and rather basic but has all the facilities as the one in Podgorica including car-hire desks, a bank and a restaurant. There are regular flights to Belgrade while other international flights are concentrated in the summer season only. There are many shuttle buses running to Budva (c. €3.50) and in the direction of Herceg Novi (c. €8). Taking a taxi should cost you somewhat more, around €15 to Budva.

Dubrovnik airport "Ćilipi" is just 24km away from Herceg Novi, the closest Montenegrin town. There are many regular bus departures to Montenegro from the bus station in Dubrovnik, mostly to Herceg Novi, but also to other coastal towns and to Podgorica.

Montenegro's national carrier "Montenegro Airlines" has offices in Budapest, Frankfurt, Ljubljana, Milan, Paris, Rome, Vienna and Zurich.

There are direct flights **from London** by Jat to Podgorica (every day) and to Tivat during the summer season as well as to Dubrovnik by British Airways (every day) and Croatia Airlines (at least once a day). **From Dublin** Air Lingus flies to Dubrovnik every second day. There are flights **from Paris** to Dubrovnik operated by Croatian Airlines several times per day, by Montenegro Airlines a couple of times weekly, to Tivat twice weekly (except in the winter) and to Podgorica by Adria Airways daily. **From Zurich** there are flights two times a week by Montenegro Airlines and every day by Adria Airways. The latter company flies each day **from Brussels and Amsterdam** to Podgorica. **From Budapest** Malev flies to Podgorica and Dubrovnik several times a week and Montenegro airlines to Podgorica twice a week.

Arriving by Bus

Montenegro is well connected by bus services to all the neighbouring countries except Albania. There are regular daily lines from Zagreb, Dubrovnik, Sarajevo, Belgrade and Istanbul. Furthermore there are also

AIRLINE OFFICES

Montenegro Airlines
www.montenegroairlines.cg.yu
Podgorica
Slobode 23, tel: 020/664-411
Budva
Slovenska obala bb, tel: 033 451 735
Kotor
Stari grad 320 (building of the Tourist Faculty), tel. 032/304-860

JAT Airways
www.jat.com
Podgorica
Trg Republike 20, tel. 020/665-350, 020/664-750
Budva
Mediteranska 2, tel: 033/451-210
Tivat
032/671-186

Austrian Airlines
www.aua.com
Podgorica Airport
Tel: 020/606-170

Malev
www.malev.com
Podgorica
020/625-242

Adria Airways
www.adria-airways.com
Podgorica
Ivana Vujoševića 46, tel: 020/241-154

Montenegro Airlines

direct lines to several central European cities such as Vienna, Munich, Stuttgart and Frankfurt.

Travelling by Bus

Being the only link to most of the towns and villages, the bus network of Montenegro is comprehesive. Podgorica's bus station has departures for every town several times a day. Some are operated by coaches and others by minibuses, the later having slightly cheaper fares. The quality of coaches and minibuses is variable, from the very confortable new ones

Bus in front of Kotor's Old Town

to those that have rattled around for ages, seen mostly inland. Large items of baggage carry an extra charge and are stored in the trunk (keep the receipt you get from the driver). If you're not getting off at important stops (that is, larger towns) be sure to notify the driver of your destination since it is possible to get off at any desired location (some other point in town, a mountain pass etc.) and not just at the bus stations.

Examples of some prices from Podgorica (aproximately, as prices may vary slightly depending on the bus company):
- to Cetinje €2
- to Budva (via Cetinje) €5
- to Kotor (via Cetinje and Budva) €6
- to Herceg Novi (via Risan) €8
- to Nikšić €3
- to Plužine €7
- to Zabljak (via Nikšić) €9
- to Plav €8

To get to the furthest point reachable by public transport and to villages off the main roads use the local transportation. Each town has local bus lines operating to the villages that have

BUS STATIONS' NUMBERS

Podgorica 020/620-430,
Berane 051/34-892,
Pljevlja 051/81-040,
Herceg Novi 031/21-225,
Budva 033/41-600,
Cetinje 041/21-052,
Ulcinj 030/81-225
Kotor 032/325-809

any kind of road leading to them. Needless to say, these buses are not too precise and, with rare exception, are in poor condition.

Except for a few larger towns, bus stations are just waiting rooms with a café and a dubious toilet, while some are just points in town where the buses stop with no infrastructure at all (for example in Cetinje). If you can't see the timetable it could be that there isn't one but the locals at the station should know it well. If the ticket counter is closed (or there isn't one) it is usual to buy the ticket on board and this way it is even cheaper as you are not charged the station service tax. However, if the counter is open buy the ticket there since the bus could be overcrowded. Aditional care is needed because on some buses they will sell you a ticket even if they don't have any seating space left.

Useful phrases
Does this bus go to … - *Ide li ovaj autobus do …*
Could you stop at … - *Da li bi mogli da stanete kod …*

Arriving by Train

Though it exists on the map, the line to Shkoder in Albania has been abandoned for decades and there is only one country you can come from by train – Serbia. There are daily departures from Belgrade, Novi Sad,

Railway station in Podgorica

Niš and Subotica. The ride from Belgrade should last around 8 hours but due to delays it can easily prolong to 10 or even 12 hours. Therefore it is highly advisable to travel during the night and book a sleeping car (3 or 6 beds). A place in a 6-bed compartment costs roughly €30 (or 2500 Serbian dinars). From mid-June to mid-September booking

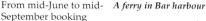

A ferry in Bar harbour

could be tricky as all the trains are packed full and you should try to do so well in advance. Note that the usual procedure is for the conductor to take your ticket in order to know when to wake you up in the morning when he will give it back to you. In order to be sure that you will have a seat during your whole trip in an ordinary 2nd class compartment in the high tourist season you should buy a reservation (*rezervacija*) which costs roughly €5. The same goes for the trip in the other direction from Podgorica towards Belgrade. During the summer season the evening train from Belgrade also carries cars.

Traveling by Train

The only operational train line in Montenegro is the famed Belgrade-Bar railway. In Montenegro it links Podgorica to Sutomore and Bar in the littoral and to Kolašin, Mojkovac and Bijelo Polje in the northeast. The line to Nikšić is operational but used only for cargo trains. This is the cheapest way to cover these distances but on the other hand the trains could be overcrowded and are almost always late. If you're short on time, you can purchase your ticket on the train with an additional fee.

Examples of prices from Podgorica are: to Bar €1.40, to Kolašin €2.20 and to Bijelo Polje €2.90.

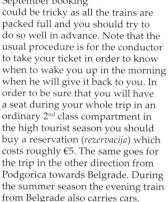

RAILWAY STATIONS' NUMBERS

Podgorica 020/63-36-63
Bar 030/301-615
Bijelo Polje 050/478-560
Kolašin 020/865-212

Arriving by Boat

There are regular car-ferry lines to the port of Bar from Bari and, less often, from Ancona (mostly only in July and August). Their frequency depends on the season but there is at least one a day during the summer and from mid September three a week. Except in the high season when there are some daytime crossings, the usual time of sailing out for both the ferry from Bari and the one from Bar is in the evenings; with a journey that takes 7 to 10 hours they reach the other shore in the early morning. The cheapest seats are about €50, a bed in a cabin c. €60 while the cheapest fare for a car is around €68. Embarkation taxes are charged extra. If you plan to return the same way the return tickets will save you a good deal of money.

On arriving with your own boat see page 43.

Traveling by Car

By far the swiftest way to move around the country and to reach all but the remotest of its corners is by car. However, driving in Montenegro can be very demanding. Due to the mountainous landscape most of the roads wind endlessly above the deep abysses of the canyons and at the same time most of them are also of bad quality. Furthermore, the local drivers are renowned for their perilous driving and care little for signs, restrictions and rules. All of this means that one should not engage in the adventure of driving in Montenegro if not an experienced driver, and secondly that one should be extremely careful and always expect the unexpected from fellow drivers.

The motorized tourist should have a valid international drivers' license. UK citizens need no more than their valid driving license. If not in possession of a Green Card and if your insurance is not valid in Montenegro you will have to buy short-term insurance at the border-crossing.

Additionally, you will be charged an "ecological tax" of €10-30 for your car valid for one year.

Seat belts are obligatory in the two front seats. If not signposted differently, the speed limit is 80km/h on country roads and 60km/h when passing through populated areas. The blood-alcohol level tolerated is up to 0.03% which is equal to a bottle of bear, a glass of wine or a shot of brandy. Use of mobile phones while driving is forbidden although you will rarely see anyone sticking to this rule. You should keep your headlights turned on at all times. On unmarked crossings you should give way to the vehicles joining from the right. The flashing of the lights by on-coming drivers is almost always a warning of a police speed trap in front but could also be a warning of some other approaching danger.

Po kiši i snijegu – Speed limit or warning during wet conditions
Jedan smjer – One way street

Petrol stations are mostly situated at the exits of towns while in rural areas they are few and far between. Check your gasoline meter when going deeper into the countryside. You will find the 24h petrol stations on our inner cover road map. The other stations open at 7 a.m. and close at 8 p.m. In the summer many extend their working hours to 10 o'clock in the evening. All of the stations sell premium super,

unleaded (*bezolovni*), diesel and eco diesel while autogas is still a rarity. All of them cost roughly €1 per liter, except diesel which is €0.90.

There are no motorways in Montenegro. In recent years some of the roads have been fixed up but most of them are still in an appalling condition with uneven road surfaces and many potholes. The major roads (marked by an orange line on our inner cover map) are the only real roads by western standards and all have only one lane in each direction. None are lit and have only a center line. All the other roads are much narrower, almost without any markings and abound with blind corners.

The circular **road through Boka Kotorska** is of good quality but curvy and passes through many towns and villages in some of which (such as Muo or Prčanj) the road narrows to just one lane. During the summer half of the year it is congested, with lots of cars parked on its edges and pedestrians crossing it

Kamenari-Lepetane ferry shortens the travel time around Boka Kotorska considerably

frequently. If in hurry, you can shorten the route from Kotor to Herceg Novi by taking a **Kamenari-Lepetane ferry** that connects the shores of the Gulf at its narrowest point. The ferries leave every 15 minutes and cost €2 one way. Mind you, in the summer the multitude of cars cueing in long lines to get on the ferry makes it doubtful if you will really save any time.

The **Adriatic Highway** (*Jadranska magistrala*) from Tivat to Ulcinj is in decent condition but the traffic on it is always heavy and taking a left hand turn from the road or getting back onto it can be very problematic. The part passing through Budva is jam packed in the summer season and don't be surprised if you stop for some minutes or move at a snail's pace. From Bar southwards

One of many Eko petrol stations

the road allows faster driving and the jams are less frequent except when in the late afternoon the bathers from the Velika plaža beach all jostle on the road back to Ulcinj.

Sheep blocking a minor road on Durmitor

The **Budva-Cetinje road** is used as the main route towards Podgorica and further on to Serbia and is therefore packed with busses and sometimes even with heavy goods lorries. The ascent is often slow but things are better in its last stretch where the road gets the alternately used third lane. However, be extremely careful as this road takes the greatest toll in lives each year.

The **road from Nikšić to Risan** is undergoing major reconstruction in its middle part. The Nikšić-Velusi road is a usual two-lane road with light traffic. The problematic part is the one around Grahovo where the road becomes slightly better than an asphalted caravan track from days long gone. Its last third is a brand new three-lane road. The last part, the descent to Risan, is another ordeal with especially demanding serpentines and many very tight curves: you will be forced to bypass other vehicles only at the broadenings above the edge of a cliff.

The modern Sozina tunnel (charged two ways €2.50 for a car) connecting Petrovac with Virpazar has drastically shortened the route **from the seaside to Podgorica**. From Virpazar onwards to the capital the road is mainly straight and clear but still bears a lot of traffic, especially near Podgorica where the city's suburbs have grown along it.

The road connecting **Podgorica to Cetinje** is used by many come rain or shine but is in good condition.

Nevertheless, this makes it dangerous because of extremely fast driving and overtaking in all places. In the part closer to Cetinje it is freshly restored and gets a third lane but one should keep to the right line as speeding and overtaking are at their worst here.

There are no good roads from **Cetinje to Nikšić**, all of them being village roads often turning into little better than dirt tracks. As a result, one needs to go via Podgorica.

The route from **Podgorica to Nikšić** passes through the valley of the Zeta River and is mostly wide and undemanding. Keep to the speed limit as there are frequent speed traps along the way.

The road from **Nikšić to the border of Bosnia-Herzegovina** has three distinctive parts. The opening part ascends up and its surface has many bumps and holes. The part across the plateau of Piva is straight and with almost no traffic at all. The third part starts from Plužine and takes you through the canyon of the River Piva with its many tunnels. This last part is almost impregnable in the winter when snow and ice descend upon it. Note that the road from the Šćepan Polje border pass is in very bad condition all the way to Brod.

The road leading from **Podgorica to Bijelo Polje** (and further on to Belgrade, Serbia) carries a huge volume of traffic with lots of trucks and busses. The part from Podgorica to Kolašin passes the spectacular canyon of the Morača River with many tunnels and curves.

A bridge across the Piva Lake

Though secured with safety barriers along its entire length it leaves no margin for mistakes.

From the **two approaches to Žabljak** the one from Mojkovac is in much better condition although drivers won't be able to enjoy the scenery of the Tara River canyon for the many curves and blind corners. The road from Nikšić is mostly of tolerable quality but nearly without any markings.

The road from **Bijelo Polje to Berane** and further on to Plav follows the flow of the River Ibar and is mostly clear and only with milder curves. The Berane-Rožaje road is somewhat more demanding.

Traffic signs follow the usual European pattern. Though many signs need renovation, the main

Hitchhikers, recently a more common sight

which is often the only solution to find one's way.

Da li je ovo selo… - Is this the village of…
Vodi li ovaj put za… - Does this road go to…

If in need of **roadside assistance** call AMSCG (Auto Association of Montenegro) on telephone number **9807**. The number for the traffic police is the same as for the ordinary police, 93.

There are a number of **car rental** agencies in Montenegro with their posts in major towns and at the airports. The price for a budget vehicle including insurance is roughly €40-50 for 100km limited mileage per day and €50-60 for unlimited mileage. Check the insurance policy cover as they differ considerably. Most of the agencies have a minimum age requirement ranging from 20 to 22 years.

Tourist signalization in Kotor

roads are marked decently enough to keep you informed on the driving conditions and your position but are light years away from the quantity of information that one finds in Western Europe. On minor roads signs are a rarity and should not be expected, not even those announcing entrance into a populated place. Note that some signs still display "Titograd" for Podgorica and "Ivangrad" for Berane, their communist era names. Many of the signs are misused for advertising including that of the many car towing services (*šlep služba*), which might be of use. In recent years much has been done to improve the **tourist signalization** and their brown and white signs can be seen regularly. However, most of them will show you only the first turn that you need to take, leaving you stranded afterwards. To carry on to your destination, you will need to study your map or consult the locals,

CAR RENTALS

Podgorica Airport
- Europcar +382(0)20 606 310
- Delta Car +382(0)67 259 800
- Meridian +382(0)69 316 666
- Budget +382(0)20 643 490

Tivat Airport
- Europcar +382(0)32 671 894
- Meridian +382(0)69 060 525

Podgorica
- Meridian +382(0)20 234 944

Budva
- Europcar, 13. jula bb, +382(0)33 401 730
- Meridian, Mediteranski sportski centar, +382(0)33 454 105

Kotor
- Ineska +382(0)32 330 063
- Sun +382 (0)69 448 600

Bar
- Meridian, Jovana Tomaševića 30, +382 (0)30 314 000

Traveling by Bicycle

Cycling is not a usual activity in Montenegro and there are no such things as cycle lanes on the roads. It is not recommended to cycle along major roads as they are narrow, bumpy and the drivers pay little attention to cyclists and pedestrians. Minor roads provide safer conditions but they are mostly full of potholes and bumps so additional care is needed. Bicycles can

Clear road for cyclists

be carried onto the train provided that it is not packed full and that you can find a place in which they won't be a nuisance (usually by the entrance, facing the toilet). Conductors are usually tolerant of this but on some occasions they might consider it a problem; we advise you to pretend you don't understand or, as a last resort, to give a Euro or two to solve the "problem". Taking some spare parts with you might be a good idea since there are almost no specialist repair shops beyond rental agencies.

Hitchhiking

In the Montenegrin car-loving culture thumbing a lift is a far from usual method of travel but it is also not unheard of. It might take you some time and patience but in the end it will get you to the desired location. The number of people willing to stop is proportionally opposite to the number of cars passing by so that fetching a ride in the middle of nowhere is usually more effective. Don't be surprised if in a place like this you are offered a lift without asking.

Taxis

There are plenty of taxis around Podgorica, the coastal resorts as well as in some towns in the interior. Except in the capital, taxis are used much more in order to reach surrounding villages or other towns than to roam around the town itself. There are a lot of unregistered taxi drivers with suspicious taxi meters; those at the airports and stations who annoyingly advertise their services are the worst kind and will almost surely overcharge you. If possible, it is always best to ask someone to call you a taxi by phone. If not, pick out a vehicle which has a taxi sign and looks decent, they are not hard to find. If any doubt remains, ask the driver *Po taksimetru?* – "By the meter?" Some taxis charge you for the start of the ride, others don't but all are quite inexpensive – under €0.60 per kilometer – which should get you from one end of the capital city to the other for no more than €3. Note that the minimal price in most taxis is one Euro, which means that this is what you pay even if the meter shows less. In coastal towns taxis are somewhat more expensive but a ride in Budva should not exceed the price of €5. Intercity drives are more expensive still but are not unreasonable: from Podgorica to Kolašin you will pay approximately €55, to Cetinje €20 and to Budva €45.

A taxi crossing the Podgorica's Millenium Bridge

TAXIS IN PODGORICA

Podgorički taksi – 9704

Bel taxi – 9800
/these two are the best for longer rides, while for the shorter ones there's not much difference/

City taxi – 9711

Alo taxi – 9700

Orange taxi – 9707

MONEY AND BANKING

The official **currency** of Montenegro is the Euro even though the country is not a part of the Eurozone. Montenegro used the Deutschmark from 1999 to protect against the instability of the Yugoslav Dinar and the influence of Yugoslav president Milošević, switching to the Euro in 2002. Serbian Dinars are not accepted and it could be difficult to exchange them. There are several problems involved in using the Euro in Montenegro, the most inconvenient for the tourist being that fares under 10 Eurocents are never returned since there isn't enough small change in circulation.

Except in the capital, **exchange offices** (*menjačnica*) are infrequent but banks and even larger post offices will exchange the money, though always with a commission charge. The larger hotels also have exchange bureaus. You will find several exchange booths in Podgorica and Tivat airports, on major bus and train stations and even on a few border crossings. Currency changers usually deal with US Dollars and Swiss Franks which are exchanged without or with low commission; check the commission fares (*provizija*) for other currencies. The rates are not fixed but can vary insignificantly. Always ask for a receipt and count the given money at the counter. Purchasing the British Pound and other currencies might be more difficult as exchange offices rarely have sufficient amounts available.

Montenegro is still generally a cash economy. **Credit cards** are accepted in a growing number of upmarket hotels, travel agents, restaurants and larger stores, but corner shops, bars and other smaller stores will only accept cash. It is a good idea to carry enough cash for your daily needs. Amongst international credit cards the most accepted are Visa, Maestro and Master card. **Cash dispensers** (ATMs) are few and far between but are most often to be found next to the bank. They operate in several languages – English, German, Italian etc. You will be charged a fee for each withdrawal by your card issuer. Atlas Mont Bank and Euromarkets will exchange Euro **travelers' cheques**, but obtaining cash with travelers' cheques in any other currency could be problematic.

Bank accounts are easily opened with a valid passport but you should carefully inquire which bank to choose as some charge for withdrawals.

Cash transfers to and from abroad are somewhat difficult: all international transfers to and from Montenegro are required to pass through clearing banks in order to keep control of the number of Euros in the country, which means that transfers can take anything from 5 to 10 working days. Commissions for this kind of transfer are hefty and differ significantly from bank to bank (typically 15 Euros for a transfer up to €1000). For fast money transfers there are several branches of Western Union around but sending money out of the country is not possible.

Banking hours are 8-19 on workdays and 8-13 on Saturdays.

See also "Customs Formalities" (*p. 263*).

COMMUNICATIONS

Making a local call is fairly simple as only the subscriber's number needs to be dialed. For long-distance calls within the country you will need to dial the area code first (for instance Podgorica 020, Kotor 032, Budva 033). To call abroad first dial 00, than the area code for the country you are calling, then the city code and then the number (for example 00-30-210-4444444, 30 for Greece, 210 for Athens).

The country code for Montenegro is **382**.

The place to make cheap long-distance phone calls is the **post office** (*pošta*) where you will be directed to the phone booth and charged at the end of the call. Post offices are open 8-19 on workdays, 8-13 on Saturdays and are

Cash machine in Budva

The yellow colours of the post office

closed on Sundays. In town centres one can find phone booths which except pre-paid cards.

Many of the hotels have direct dial telephone facilities and the better ones also additionally offer fax, internet or secretarial services. Check the unit charge as telephone charges can vary substantially.

Postage stamps (*marka*) can be purchased at the post offices. For sending a postcard or a letter abroad you will be charged €0.50. Postboxes are rarely found anywhere other than in or in front of post offices. Letters to most European countries take 7 to 10 days to arrive. If you would like to speed up the process you should ask

for airmail (*avionska pošiljka*) which will add 10 to 20 Euro cents (depending on the distance) to the cost of postage. Postal service can be erratic and should not be fully relied upon. If you need something to arrive safely, it is advisable to use a western courier service. The poste restante system functions reasonably well especially in the post offices in larger towns. Make sure that the delivery is clearly marked "poste restante".

Foreign newspapers are to be found only in the better stocked newsstands in coastal resorts. English language broadcasting can be heard from the BBC World Service on short wave on 9410 kHz from 6-8 a.m. and 4-6 p.m., 12095 kHz 7-10 a.m., 6195 kHz from 6 to 10 in the evening. The Voice of America is broadcast on 9760 and 6040 kHz. Satellite and cable TV is fast becoming a regular feature in larger towns and thus also in the local apartments to rent.

Internet cafés are not widely found outside the capital and tourist areas. The usual charge is around €1 per hour. Wireless internet connection is usually found only in up-market hotels and larger cafés.

There are three **mobile phone operators** in Montenegro: Promonte (numbers beginning with 069; call center number 9898), T-Mobile (067, call center - 9899) and Mtel (068, call center 9868). SIM cards with some pre-paid credit on them can be purchased easily at the branches of these companies at a cost of roughly €7. All operators claim to have 98% of the country covered but one should not rely on mobile phones in remote mountain areas.

HEALTH

No **inoculations** are needed for Montenegro but you are advised to be up to date on tetanus and polio. Hepatitis A may occur. Rabies is present and for those at risk vaccination prior to arrival may be considered.

It is wise to take out comprehensive **travel insurance** so that your expenses are covered in case of treated illness or accident both in state-run and in private clinics. Medical staff in Montenegro are generally well trained and some will even speak English. However, the health system is far below western standards and occasionally suffers from shortages. In case you don't have medical insurance

INTERNET CAFÉS

Kotor
- Forza Club, Trg od oružja, Old Town
- IDK, Stari Grad 317
- Internet eg, Bokeška 20

Herceg Novi
- PC World, Mihajla Mustura 7
- Microbeat, Mića Valića 3

Danilovgrad
- Insomnia, Novice Škerovića bb

Podgorica
- Juventas, Trg Božane Vučinić bb (behind "Metalka" building)
- www.Club, Bokeška 4
- Net centar, Vučedolska 13 (across the National Theatre)

Žabljak
- Hit, Vučedolska bb

Budva
- PC centar, Mediteranska 4
- Quasar, Slovenska obala bb
- Santa Maria, Toplički put bb (business centre)

Nikšić
- Hardnet, VI crnogorske brigade bb

all but emergency treatment will require payment, most usually in cash. In case of emergency call **94** for the ambulance service (*hitna pomoć*). There are a number of private clinics around and the cost of treatment in these is a bit less expensive then elsewhere in Europe.

A well stocked pharmacy

Pharmacies (*apoteka*) are well stocked and easy to find. They follow the usual working hours (8-20) but are closed on Sundays when in larger towns there should be one which is on duty (*dežurna apoteka*). In Podgorica it's the one in Novaka Miloševa St. (off the Slobode St.). Many of the branded medicines you might be acquainted with will have different names in local pharmacies so be sure to known the generic name of the drug or take your prescription with you. If you are reluctant to use other medicine or to buy them as imported goods at higher prices be sure to take a good supply with you. Condoms (*kondomi*) can be purchased in pharmacies or, more easily, in corner kiosks.

Tap **water** is safe to drink in all places except in some summer resorts during July and August when there are regular water shortages. Bottled water is widely available in all well supplied shops. Water from most fountains and some of the roadside drinking wells is not safe to drink – these are marked with a warning sign *Voda nije za piće*.

Local meat, cheese, poultry and fish are all considered safe to eat. Hygiene standards are quite high in most hotels and restaurants except in the bottom end ones. Most incidents of light food poisoning come from fast food kiosks where the meat wasn't kept soundly refrigerated, so you should think twice before eating at an unknown place of dubious appearance.

Jellyfish are rare in Montenegrin waters but can be stumbled upon. Burnings and welts from these will subside of their own accord in a few hours. If you happen to step onto an urchin living on underwater rocks near the coast you should remove the spines from your foot or they will fester. Mosquitoes carry no diseases in Montenegro but can be a real nuisance; insecticide vaporizers and repellents are available in better stores and in pharmacies. On adders see page 39.

SECURITY

Street crime on foreigners is generally low in Montenegro. One should beware of pick pocketing in busy tourist areas as well as on trains, busses and in airports. Armed robberies are almost unheard of. Extra precaution should be taken if leaving a luxury car in an unattained parking place – put all your bags, no matter what's in them, in the trunk or some other place where they can't be seen. The greatest danger for the visitor, though rare, might come from mafia shootings or fights of hot-tempered youths. To reduce the possibility of witnessing the former one should avoid places frequented by suspiciously looking local or Russian "businessmen". General attitude towards foreign tourists is generous and friendly but this might not be the case with some local youths. To avoid conflict with them, ignore any provocations, remain calm and collected if spoken to in a mocking way and, most importantly, do not try to outsmart or out do them in any way. Contrary to many European cities the streets of Montenegrin towns are quite safe after dark though it is wise to stay out of secluded places.

The Montenegrin police badge

Political and ethnic tensions still run high in Montenegro. One should avoid discussions on these themes and just keep listening to the stories you're told. Generally speaking, Montenegrins don't like being contradicted on any matter and keeping uncompromisingly to your points might easily result in quarrels or losing friends.

Women traveling solo should feel safe and comfortable but will also experience an unusual level of unwanted attention in bars and discotheques, less in the streets, be it staring or rude remarks. A girl sitting on her own in a café is bound to be approached for a conversation – try not to be impolite but keep to yourself if you are not interested. Montenegrin men are great gentlemen to those of their heart's desire but do not like being rejected.

Topless bathing is usual on most beaches but should be avoided in areas with a Muslim majority such as Ulcinj and its riviera. Full nudity is tolerated only on nudist beaches (*nudistička plaža*).

Although homosexuality is not illegal, display of same-sex affection in public places will arouse discontent and mocking behaviour.

Montenegro lies on the main corridor for drug trafficking from Middle East to Western Europe and consequently there are a number of illegal substances on the streets. Possession and trafficking of drugs is punishable by law and may result in jail sentences.

You are obliged to carry your passport at all times as a means of identification, but this is not strictly observed by the police. We advise you to make a copy of your passport (and other important documents) and keep it in a safe place so that you can easily get a replacement travel document in case your passport gets lost or stolen.

There are many stray dogs around so avoid strolling in secluded places on your own. If you stumble on a pack of dogs act normally as attacks on people are rare.

There are no landmines scattered around Montenegro and all regions, including the border areas, are safe for hiking.

In a case of emergency, call the police on 92, or 112 (free of charge) from a mobile phone.

SHOPPING

Montenegro is definitely not a place for shoppers; those who consider their vacation a perfect time for spending money will be a bit disappointed with the notion that most of the goods in shops have been imported and are only slightly cheaper than back home. Visitors in search of a **souvenir** won't have an easy time either: though souvenir shops are improving, most items on offer are still either unimaginative (mugs, plates, T-shirts

Traditional patterns on a rug

with Montenegrin national symbols) or of problematic quality. If you can't find a specialized souvenir shop, try the local tourist information offices most of which have a few items on sale.

Apart from the classic touristy souvenirs your best buy might be traditional **handicrafts** such as wooden spoons and other kitchen utensils, clay vessels, copper coffee pots, wooden shepherd flutes, heavy woolen sweaters or the traditional leather shoes *opanci*. The whole, splendidly intricate

Dolls depicting a Montenegrin and his wife

national costume (or even some sophisticated part of it), as well as the national instrument *gusle* may be found in some souvenir shops but are beyond the budget of ordinary tourists.

Almost all of the orthodox monasteries have small shops in which you can buy small wooden crosses, candles, incense etc. **Icons** (also sold in souvenir shops) are mostly reproductions, those carved in wood are somewhat pricier, while the hand-painted (*ručno slikana*) or even gold icons can be recognized by their higher prices.

One of the most usual things to carry back home from Montenegro is a bottle of fine wine, *lozova* brandy or

The green market of Kotor

locally made olive oil. One other choice might be a jar of *slatko*, a traditional fruit preserve.

Most Montenegrin towns have a regular market day once a week, while in larger cities **green markets** function every day. Here you will find a choice of fresh fruits, vegetables, fish, honey, home-made cheese, rakijas or herbs at prices generally lower than in supermarkets. Apart from their groceries section, many also feature clothes, electronic equipment and smuggled food goods. They open early and clear up at about 2 p.m. Most of the items will have prices displayed but a little bit of haggling is acceptable.

The first to open in the morning are bakeries – at 6 or 7 a.m. but most of the smaller ones also tend to close in the

early afternoon. Usual **working hours** of local shops are 7-20 or 8-21, Monday to Saturday. Other shops open at 8 or 9 a.m. and close at 8-9 p.m. On Sundays many businesses are closed, while some stores and corner shops stay open to 3 p.m. During the season, shops in tourist centers stay open until midnight.

FOOD & DRINK

It is hard to imagine a Montenegrin from the olden days caring too much for what he eats. Firstly because - with a few exceptions - he didn't have much to eat, and second since, until well into the 20th c, food was foremost a means to survive and not a pleasure. On the other hand, in search of food people found and tried almost all the edible things around them, preparing them in many imaginative ways. Bearing this in mind you will appreciate more the traditional Montenegrin cuisine which is all about simply prepared, straightforward tasty food that keeps you well fed.

The climate and geographic conditions split the land into two utterly different zones of traditional cookery: the Adriatic one, restricted to the narrow strip by the sea, and the mountainous continental zone.

The staple foods of the continental part of Montenegro are potato, corn and cereals but above all the **dairy products** from sheep and cows, the most precious possession of every highlander. Since milk was difficult to preserve it was by and large converted into cheese (*sir*). Domestically prepared cheese from full fat milk is still the most common type enjoyed all over the country. Its forms are not yet standardized and hence it covers a range from softer (but not creamy), young cheese (*mladi*) to semi-aged (*stari*), which is never aged to such an extent that it can't be cut with a fork. Recently, more people have been

Njeguški sir, a well-known delicacy

Kačamak *and* **cicvara**, *best when served with sour milk*

As the sheep and goats were too valuable for their milk, wool and skin, they were rarely slaughtered for meat, which was eaten only on holidays and by the well-off. Perhaps as a reaction to this forced semi-vegetarian diet practiced for many centuries modern Montenegrins are great lovers of meat, which is often eaten on its own and in large quantities. The **meat** (*meso*) most commonly eaten in the interior is mutton (*ovčetina*) or the highly-praised lamb (*jagnjetina*) prepared in many tasty ways such as dried (*sušena*), cooked (*kuvana*), steamed (*na pari*), cooked in milk (*u mlijeku*) or roasted in a pot placed under the smouldering coals (*ispod sača*). Veal (*teletina*) is a more recent newcomer while chicken (*piletina*) and pork (*svinjetina*) play a minor role in

encouraged to once more produce *prljo*, a traditional soft cheese that is low in fat. *Kisjelo mlijeko* (literary "sour milk") is a kind of yoghurt so thick that it is eaten with a spoon; it is served with most simple meals or consumed on its own as a refreshing and tasty snack or as a starter. The most cherished dairy specialty is *kajmak* or *skorup*, a very fat cream of strong flavour, which is eaten on its own, mixed in many traditional meals but also added to many new dishes as a quintessential ingredient that adds that local feel. One of the old dishes eaten with kajmak is *kačamak* - a tasty mush usually prepared from cornmeal, similar to Italian polenta; when it is referred to as *smočani* this means that it is cooked with melted cheese and kajmak. Similar to this is *cicvara*, where flour is cooked in melted

Njeguški pršut ham

kajmak. When well-prepared both dishes are impossible to resist but do bear in mind that they are also very heavy and that you'll need to be really hungry to eat a whole portion. *Popara* or *masanica* is prepared of stale bread, cheese and kajmak cooked slightly in boiling water; it never caught on as a dish in restaurants but it is frequently eaten at home. These three classic Montenegrin dishes were once considered meals appropriate for lunch but are nowadays eaten also for breakfast or dinner. To drink with these try *varenika* – cooked milk or *grušava*, its saltier and fattier version.

traditional cookery but are found in a number of classic specialties from modern times (*see below*). One thing you should not miss is *pršut* – ham, salted and then smoked for a long time and served thinly sliced to enhance its delicious taste.

A delicacy which never fails to delight the locals are **spit roasts** (*pečenje*). Today they are in demand at almost all celebrations while some restaurants, mostly highway-inns, have built their fame around them, and despite the fact that they offer various meals most of their guests arrive only for this indulgence. The most usual

Lamb on spit roast, a must-try delicacy

collard greens. Nettles are also consumed as delicacy, enjoyed mostly in the form of soup (*čorba od kopriva*). Beans (*grah* or *pasulj*) are consumed in several varieties – as a thick soup with dried meats (*čorbast pasulj*) or roasted with lots of onions (*prebranac*).

Fish (*riba*) plays a minor role in Montenegrin continental cuisine since most of the areas were far from sizable rivers. However, the vegetarian fare carried through the long and strictly observed fasts proscribed by the Orthodox Church was enhanced by river and lake fish. From the native river species trout (*pastrmka* or *pastrva*) and sprout (*mladica*) are the only ones to make

type of spit roast in Montenegro is lamb (*jagnjetina*) or piglet (*prasetina*) both ordered by the kilo, which is a bit of a gamble since the meat comes with bones and other hardly edible parts.

Bread (*hljeb*) in the old times used to be baked out of barley or, later, corn. Today you can consider yourself lucky if you find these, but wheat bread baked in the restaurants, mostly *ispod sača*, is a delicacy of its own. *Proja* is a tasty corn bread, rich in fat and sometimes with cheese added to it. Another bread-like snack is *priganice*, a kind of doughnut served with cheese, kajmak, honey or jam. It is almost impossible to imagine a complete meal without the ever popular **pies** (*pite*) such as *gužvara* and *sirnica* with cheese and eggs, *zeljanica* with spinach, onions and cheese, *krompiruša* with potatoes or *heljdija* from buckwheat - another crop adapted perfectly to the harsh mountain climate. A special kind of pie is *izljevuša* whose mixed dough is spilled (*izljevati*) into a bowl and then baked.

The most typical **vegetable** (*povrće*) in Montenegro is the potato (*krtola* or *krompir*) which was introduced in the early 19th c. and from that time on enhanced the diet preventing famine in difficult years. Another well-known vegetable in Montenegro is collard greens (*raštan*), a plant of the cabbage family but of somewhat wilder appearance and taste. Cooked with potatoes and dried mutton it makes a meal of distinctive taste. A dish of similar taste to this one is *japraci* where veal and rice are rolled in leaves of

A variety of vegetables and fish from Lake Skadarsko

it to restaurant menus. The situation in continental Montenegro differs only in the region around Skadarsko Lake which is incredibly rich in fish, primarily bleak (*ukljeva*), carp (*krap* or *šaran*) and sneep (*skobalj*, rarely consumed these days). The traditional way of preparing bleak is to dry it above the fireplace (*dimljena*) before grilling it, while carp is often fried together with prunes or consumed smoked.

In contrast to the continental part, the popular diet in the maritime region was always based on fish from the sea. The range of fresh **sea fish** in any decent restaurant is wide - hake (*oslić*), mackerel (*skuša*), red mullet (*barbun*), bass (*brancin*), gilt-poll (*orada*), dentex (*zubatac*), groper (*škarpina*), eel (*jegulja*), sole (*list*) etc. Sometimes they are priced by the kilo and you can choose a fish proportional to your appetite. The larger fish such as swordfish (*sabljarka*) or ray (*raža*) are served by the slice without bones. The simplest way of preparing, but also the best to retain the taste of the fish, is to grill it smeared with spiced olive oil (*na žaru* or more unusually *sa gradela*). As a side dish with these you can try risotto (*rižoto*), sometimes also coloured by squid-ink (*crni rižoto*), chard (*blitva*) with potatoes or a simple potato salad. The other ways to enjoy your fish are *pržena* - fried in

Freshly caught sea fish

olive oil with lemon juice, laurel and parsley, *lešo* – cooked in water, oil, vinegar and spices, then *pohovana* - fried in breadcrumbs, or - typically for Montenegro - from a pot kept under the coals (*ispod sača*). Fish stew (*brodet*) is made of several types of fish cooked for a longer period and served with polenta/kačamak. Fish soup (*riblja čorba*) is prepared from various kinds of fish cooked the longer the better, with every chef keeping his ingredients and

Mussles and **Krstač** *wine*

their proportion a secret. Other fruits of the sea are also frequent on menus - squid (*lignje*), scampi (*škampi*), rose shrimps (*kozice* or *gambori*) and lobster (*jastog*) being the usual selection. Octopus (*hobotnica*) can be prepared in several tasty ways but is most popular as salad (*salata od hobotnice*) served as a starter. Mussels (*mušlje* or *dagnje*) are as a rule eaten *na buzaru* - stewed in a tasty sauce of wine, oil, garlic and

parsley. The second most important ingredient of maritime cuisine are **olives** (*masline*), still grown in many areas along the coast (mostly around Bar and Ulcinj as well as on the Luštica peninsula) and their oil, the only oil as far as the chefs of the Adriatic are concerned. One of the specialties here is the old, ripe cheese kept in olive oil (*sir iz ulja*). As with all the other delicacies from the seaboard, this mixture is also seasoned with aromatic herbs which grow in abundance on the hill-sides, such as rosemary, sage, parsley etc. These are also an important ingredient in creating *pašticada*, a beef stew served with *makaruli* – macaroni of black wheaten flour. Two specialties specific to the town of Ulcinj are *bamje* (okra) served with veal, and *imam bajedi* – eggplant braised with onions, garlic, tomato and spices.

In the last century Montenegrin cuisine outshone its previous simplicity. Dishes from neighbouring lands were adopted and others were created from local ingredients in a more modern fashion. The traditional dishes which are found all over the Balkans became familiar in Montenegro to such an extent that nobody considers them foreign any more. One of the most popular is *sarme*, sauerkraut rolls stuffed with minced meat and rice; they are prepared mostly at home in large quantities and people live on them for days as it is considered that they get better with time. *Punjene paprike* are bell peppers stuffed with minced meat, rice and tomatoes. *Djuveč* is a rich casserole in which you will find meat accompanied by potatoes, green beans, tomatoes, onions, eggplant etc. *Pilav* is a dish of oriental origin with sliced chicken baked together with rice and onion. Sauerkraut (*kisjeli kupus*) is also featured as a popular winter salad,

Grilled fish served with vegetables

sprinkled with hot paprika. *Turšija* is a name for various kinds of vegetables (cucumbers, carrots, cauliflower, tomatoes) which are pickled in brine and eaten during the winter. In the summer, fresh garden salads of tomato, cucumbers, onions and peppers are often consumed. The most popular amongst them is a relative newcomer from Serbia - *šopska salata*, combined out of all these vegetables and then covered with soft cheese. A popular addition to many dishes is *ajvar* – a pasty mix of baked peppers, eggplant and garlic similar to salsa. The most popular soup in restaurants these days is *teleća čorba*, a creamy concoction of vegetables and veal that melts in the mouth. Similar to it is the mushroom soup (*čorba od pečuraka*) while *pileća supa* is a clear chicken broth.

The most-loved new arrival is **grilled meat** (*roštilj*) called commonly *leskovački*, named after the south Serbian town from which it gets its distinctive form and excellent taste. Almost all of the places in which you can eat will have some specialty from the grill, and though these can considerably vary in quality they are all very tasty. Grilled meat Leskovac-style is also the base for many fast food eateries and kiosks on which the young population can live for days. In smaller towns the kebab grills (*ćevapdzinica*) are more or less the only kind of places to sit down and enjoy a meal. The most popular of the grilled dishes are *ćevapi* – small minced meat rolls (usually ten of them), *pljeskavica* – a minced pork and veal roll sprinkled with spices, *ražnjići* –slices of veal and pork grilled on skewers. All of these are eaten with large amounts of chopped onions (*crni luk*) but in simple places that is all you will get with them so you should opt for a salad on the side.

There is an enormous number of **Italian** restaurants in Montenegro and on top of this the usual non-national type of restaurant also bases its menu on various pizzas, pastas or lasagna. Note that many of the original Italian recipes have been remodeled slightly to suit local taste better, which in most cases means more meat and fat. Others are made fully out of local specialties such as kajmak, *kulen* (spicy sausage), pršut etc. and offer an interesting crash course in the flavours of Montenegro.

The new dishes prepared with traditional ingredients are a regular feature of all menus. *Njeguški stek* is veal filled with *njeguški pršut* ham and feta or some other cheese. Similar to it are *popeci* (sometimes additionally labeled *podgorički*) – veal stuffed with cheese and ham, fried in breadcrumbs.

The list of **deserts** in most restaurants is not particularly inventive – ice-creams (*sladoled*), fruit salads (*voćni kup*), pancakes (*palačinke*) and similar. The situation is better in pastry-shops (*poslastičarnica*) where you will find a mix of sweets influenced by Vienna and those of oriental origin (baklava, *kadaif*…). In older establishments you will also find *boza*, a refreshing drink made out of corn flour.

Bakeries (*pekara*) in Montenegro have grown out into a distinctive brand

Ćevapčići with kajmak cream

Fresh figs sold on stands on the sides of the road

visited in the morning, at midday or late at night primarily for the reason of obtaining a cheap and tasty snack. Bakeries serve almost exclusively a wide array of salty pastries, though some might have sweet ones too. The major test of any bakery is its *burek*, a greasy round pie with meat, cheese, mushrooms or with no filling, consumed traditionally with yoghurt sold on the spot. Other snacks found here are *pogačice* (small leafy breads), *pite* (classic pies in many variations) as well as croissants, sandwiches or even slices of pizza.

Considering all the eating habits of Montenegro, **vegetarians** will not have an easy time. Only the better restaurants will have a vegetarian menu, in some you will be able to compile a meal of salads and side dishes, and in others, especially in smaller establishments and in far flung places, trying to order a non-meat dish is going to raise eyebrows or will even be considered as next to impossible.

Imate li neko jelo bez mesa? – Do you have some dish without meat?
Ima li u ovom jelu mesa? – Does this dish contain meat?
Ja sam vegetarijanac. – I'm a vegetarian.

The best known drink of the Balkans is **rakija**, a generic name for a potent spirit distilled from various kinds of fruit. Making one's own at home is still a matter of pride for any respectful rural household, resulting in a great variety of tastes depending on the quality and skills of the maker. In the region where vine is cultivated one makes **lozova** *rakija* (called simply *loza* by those who feel more familiar with it), prepared from grapes and similar to Italian grappa. The distinctive taste of Montenegrin lozova comes from the indigenous grapevine variety *vranac* but those made of other grapes can be equally tasty. The one brand synonymic with Montenegro is "Crnogorska lozova rakija" produced in large quantities by "Plantaže" from Podgorica and found all over the country. You can't really miss it and, in any case, to spend your holiday in Montenegro without savoring this drink would be a great pity. Two more prestigious brands from the same producer are "Prvijenac" and "Kruna". Two other well known kinds which are bottled and found in shops are "Sjekloća" from Crmnica, and "Institutova" produced by the Biotechnical Institute, but both are out of reach for those with a lighter purse. Other rakijas made in Montenegro are *šljivovica* from plums, *kruškovača* from pears and *kajsijevača* from apricots.

Distilling **rakija brendy**

None of these are branded but they can still be found on the menus of many restaurants.

Climate favourable for growing vineyards is found only in coastland and around Lake Skadarsko. Sadly, the vineyards in Boka and the Littoral have disappeared due to demand for construction land and to easier occupations (such as renting out rooms) so that nowadays **wine** production in the coastland doesn't surpass household needs. One region that kept its production is Crmnica, around the townlet of Virpazar on Skadarsko Lake, though its output is also only a fraction of what it used to be. The two domestic sorts native to the area dominate – *vranac* and *kratošija*. Vranac ("the black one") in particular has grown to be associated with Montenegro. It is a wine of dark ruby colour, with a robust and full-bodied aroma. The only market-orientated producer here is the Sjekloća homestead with its vranac wine but in many villages you will find home-made wine for sale. This is also the wine offered in many restaurants in this region under the name *domaće* ("domestic"). The main producer of wine in Montenegro is the once state-owned "Plantaže" company with its huge vineyards in Čemovsko polje south of Podgorica. Here they produce an array of red wines such as the "Crnogorski vranac", "Crnogorski cabernet", "Crnogorski merlot" as well as blended "Sasso Negro" and "Perla Negra". White wines are represented by the native sort of this warm, lowland area "Crnogorski krstač" - which is grown nowhere else in the world - as well as by "Crnogorski Chardonnay", "Crnogorski Sauvignon" and "Podgoričko bijelo". The 0.7 bottles are filled with premium wine while those of one liter are quality wines. The large production of these fine wines fully covers the needs of Montenegro and you will find them in all shops and restaurants.

"Trebjesa" in the town of Nikšić is the only brewery in Montenegro but its "Nikšićko pivo" **beer** is of such quality that one tends to look no further. Apart from this palatable lager it also produces an excellent *tamno* (dark) variety as well as premium "Nik Gold" and light "Nik Cool". The beer is sold in 0.33 and 0.5 liter glass bottles as well as in considerably cheaper 2 liter plastic

Krstač and Vranac are the most famous sorts of wine in the country

ones. Other beer varieties widely available in Montenegro are Bavaria, Heineken, Laško from Slovenia et cetera. Note that, like in other south European countries, beer in Montenegro is drunk extremely cold in all seasons.

The origins of **medovina** (mead) go back to the early middle ages when this alcoholic beverage of fermented honey was made and consumed by the Old Slavs, who were celebrated as the most skilful beekeepers of Europe. The high pastures with their many aromatic flowers are still ideal for bees and the recipe for mead has not been forgotten. This sweet but refreshing drink is found in many national restaurants but you can also savor it from many individual producers. If you purchase a bottle or two of medovina pay attention because unless kept refrigerated the fermenting process will continue and it will become fizzy and eventually undrinkable.

A drink inseparable from a friendly chat in a street café or at home is **coffee** (*kafa*) which is as a result drunk in large quantities all over Montenegro. Coffee is also the drink you will be offered upon entering someone's house and with which each meal is usually rounded off. Until not long ago, when ordering

Nikšić dark beer

Black coffee in local style

"a coffee" you would without any doubt be served a strong, **black coffee**, called *turska* (Turkish) or just *crna* (black), made out of grounded coffee beans added to boiling water in small copper pots called *džezva*. Upon ordering, it is customary to specify the quantity of sugar you want in it – *sladja* for sweet, *srednja* for medium and *gorča* without any sugar - otherwise you will get sugar to sweeten it yourself. In cafés caring for old time customs the coffee will be accompanied by a glass of cold water and in some places even with a piece of Turkish delight. Nowadays it has become more fashionable to drink espresso and you will find that many trendy cafés and restaurants won't go to the trouble of preparing Turkish coffee. *Nes (kafa)* is a generic name for all types of instant coffees, regardless of the brand; you can order it hot (*topli*) or cold (*hladni*).

Montenegrins are very fond of mineral water (*kisjela voda*) and there are several domestic brands around (like "Rada" from Bijelo Polje). The mineral water will often be served together with a glass of rakija or a coffee. Asking for water (*voda*) will usually get you tap water and to order bottled water ask for *flaširana voda*.

AVERAGE PRICES IN RESTAURANTS

Plate of fish or veal soup – €1.50
Njegoški pršut ham (150g) – €6.00
Fresh salad – €1.50
Squid (250g) – €8.00
Scoop of ice-cream – €0.50
Njeguški stek - €7.50

Bottle of Nikšićko beer (0.33l) – €1.50
Bottle of Vranac wine (0.7l) – €10.00
Shot of loza brandy (0.03l) – €1.00
Cup of black Turkish coffee - €0.70
Cup of espresso – €0.80
Coca-Cola (0.25l) – €1.50

MANNERS & CUSTOMS

Until recently one of the most popular jokes about Montenegrins was that the problems in their customer service stem from the fact that proud warriors cannot be changed overnight into humble waiters and chefs. Surely, Montenegrins are a nation in transition who are changing *en route* from shepherds clinging to their traditions to businessmen and tourism industry workers. These changes are also causing a transformation of the national temperament: once stiff and sober in order to remain heroic and just, modern day Montenegrins are more relaxed, reckless and hedonistic. Their feisty humor is unbeatable and ever-present, delivered in such a way that one wonders whether to laugh or to take it seriously. In so far as these

Neighbourly chat in Perast

generalizations hold true Montenegrins are very intelligent, witty and quick to learn. If their talents are put to a good use they become top artists, managers, professors and doctors who compete with the best in their field elsewhere in the world. If misused, their sharpness is easily twisted into a talent for scams, organizing unscrupulous gangs and mafia networks that have given Montenegrins a bad name in many places.

As a nation, Montenegrins are very warmhearted and welcoming. Hospitality is the dearest obligation of every host, be it the person you are staying with, a good friend or just an acquaintance; don't be surprised if you are treated to coffee or rakija by a total stranger as many people consider it an honour to have a visitor in their far-flung corner of the earth. Hospitality is practiced particularly in rural areas where it is treated with an air of seriousness and where it often tends to overwhelm, especially in terms of eating and drinking.

When meeting people for the first time shake hands sturdily, say your first name or if presented by someone else add the phrase "Drago mi je" (Pleased to meet you). Formal greetings are "Dobro jutro!" (Good morning, but note that this is used only in the early morning, not at 11 a.m. like in English), "Dobar dan!" ("Good day!") and "Dobro vječe!" (Good evening, again only at dusk and during the evenings). On formal occasions surnames and names are preceded with titles "gospodin" for Mister, "gospodjica" for Miss and "gospodja" for Mrs. Stand up when you're meeting older people and women but try not to be too formal. On meeting the people you already know shake hands and say either "Zdravo!" (Hello) or, even more casually, "Dje si?" (What's up?). Younger women will kiss friends on the cheek instead of shaking hands, but will do this only with those they know well. When meeting old friends after a longer period or at any kind of celebration it is usual to kiss on alternate cheeks two or three times and even hug affectionately. A fair amount of physical contact (tapping on the shoulder, taking by the hand and similar) is usual and should be viewed as an act of closeness. The same hugging and kissing procedure precedes cordial departures. The usual goodbyes are the formal "Dovidjenja!" (Goodbye) or more familiar "Zdravo!" or "Ćao!" (Ciao).

Although at their first meeting with you Montenegrins may seem a bit reserved this is likely to disappear after only a few minutes. Anyone whom they met several times is counted as a friend and treated to intimate stories;

proportionally they will show interest in your life, political views, likes and dislikes or other topics you might find unusual but this should not offend since it is considered a normal basis for conversation.

On entering someone's house you will be treated to a coffee (almost always a strong black one), rakija or a juice, possibly home made. If offered, don't miss the delicious preserves called *slatko*, served in small pots, of which you should take one or two teaspoons. On first entering a household it is customary to bring with you a small symbolic gift – a bottle of wine, some coffee, chocolate, flowers or something similar. When toasting say "Živjeli!" or when drinking with only one person "Zdravo bio!" (May you be healthy);

Regular toasting brings people together

it is very important to touch glasses and look into the eyes of the people you're toasting with. Beware that your glass will be refilled as soon as you have finished it; the best defense against this is to leave a sip or two until you're prepared to leave. It happens frequently that people are invited to lunch or dinner and you should not hesitate as it is not purely a gesture of politeness.

During meals there aren't too many rules to obey. Helping yourself to some more food without hesitation is not unusual and will spare you the even larger amounts of food your hosts are likely to serve you. Try to taste everything you're offered so as not to offend the hosts. The courses (appetizer, soup, main dish and a dessert) are accompanied by saying "Prijatno!" (Bon appetite) and answering "Hvala, takodje!" (Thanks, the same to you).

The greatest honor for every guest is

Traditional bread baked for **slava**

to be invited to a *slava*, the celebration of a family's saint day. The most common amongst them are Nikoljdan (St Nichola's – 19th December), Arandjelovdan (St Michael – 21st November), Jovanjdan (St John's – 20th January) and Djurdjevdan (St George's – 6th May) when most people roam around visiting their friends and relatives. You could bring a small, symbolic gift, but you will be accepted equally even if you don't. The most conventional greeting is "Srećna slava!" followed by kissing on the cheeks. Upon entering the house you will be offered *žito* - a wheat, nuts and honey cake of which you should take a spoon or two after making the sign of the cross (if you're Christian, of course). After this all you should do is enjoy yourself and drink eagerly at all the toasts.

HOLIDAYS

January 1st and 2nd – New Year's Day
January 7th and 8th - Orthodox Christmas
April 17th-20th (4 days) – Orthodox Easter
(only for 2009)
May 1st and 2nd – May Day
May 21st – Independence Day
July 13th – Statehood Day

The local's skills in foreign languages depend on their age and education. Most of the younger people will at least understand English and will know a couple of phrases. The second language spoken is Italian, then Russian and more rarely German. Knowledge of any Slavic language is fairly useful as many words and phrases are common or similar.

Govorite li engleski / ruski / italijanski / njemački? – Do You speak English / Russian / Italian / German?

If invited for a drink in a café it is highly probable that your host will strongly insist on paying the whole bill.

Taking it easy while fishing

As there is no point in arguing it is best to buy a round yourself when he/she is not around to pay, but be careful not to equal the amount as this might be considered offensive. Sharing payment around the table is not considered convivial. Ask to add some money but try not to be too precise as bargaining over cents is considered avaricious.

Montenegrins are not formal in the least when it comes to clothing. Most of them tend to overdress but there are few occasions in private life apart from weddings or funerals when there is a dress code to obey.

Though Montenegrin girls dress provocatively and act quite free one should not expect too much from the first few "dates". Patriarchal morality still looms over and in a society as small as that in Montenegro no girl wants to be labeled as "easy going".

When asking for something politely use the phrase "molim Vas" (please). Using this at the end of each and every sentence will be considered much too formal so try to apply it only when you're really in need of something.

A TO Z

Bartering is not customary and will be tolerated only in certain places for instance greenmarkets, provided you are willing to spend a somewhat larger amount of money.

Shopwindow in Budva's Old Town

Business Hours: Government and business offices usually work from 8 a.m. to 4 p.m. Monday to Friday. Department stores and supermarkets are generally open from 8 a.m. to 8 or 9 p.m. (*see p. 276*). 24-hour shops or kiosks are common. Most restaurants are open until midnight. This is also when the cafés and clubs should turn their loud music off. On most of the public holidays (*see p. 285*) the majority of shops will be open. The only exceptions are 1st-2nd January, Christmas Day and the first day of Easter.

Churches: Most of the large town churches are open throughout the day whilst those in villages are open only at service times, usually at 7.30 a.m. (8.30 on Saturdays, 9 a.m. on Sundays) and 5 p.m. Upon entering the church one is required to act politely, not to laugh or raise your voice. Enter decently dressed – no swimsuits, shorts, miniskirts or even uncovered shoulders. Take your hat off. Women are expected to cover their heads although this rule is not too strictly obeyed. In orthodox churches women are not allowed in the sanctuary behind the iconostasis. Moving around during service is not encouraged and men should keep to the right while women to the left of the church. There are no entry fees but one could bestow a small donation or buy some items, if there are any for sale (usually to the left of the entrance). Ask for permission if you want to take pictures, especially in the church.

Cinemas are rare and mostly in bad condition. Though they offer latest releases, the repertoire is limited to the most popular movies. All foreign films are subtitled, never dubbed. Evening shows are more expensive that those before 8 p.m.

Electric current: 220 Volts, with plugs of two round pins.

Local Time is GMT + 1 hour. From end-March to end-October the time is GMT + 2 hrs. So, when it is noon in Podgorica, it is 11 a.m. in London and 6 a.m. in New York.

Museums rarely open every day. Most are closed on Monday but some close on Sunday. Specific opening hours are provided in the texts on particular museums. Last entrance is usually

A service in an orthodox church

30 to 40 minutes before closing time. Occasionally the captions are written in English and it is sometimes possible to find a booklet describing the display in some major language. "Is there anything about the museum in English/German/French?" – *Imate li nešto o muzeju na engleskom/njemačkom / francuskom?*

With little to no restrictions, photography can be freely enjoyed

Regarding **photography** there are a few restrictions. In many of the churches and most museums it is forbidden to take pictures. Photography is also forbidden near military and police objects. Care should be taken before taking photos of policemen and one should always ask for permission. "May I take a picture of you?" – *Smijem li da Vas slikam?*

Public Toilettes: There are only a few around - the best places to look for them are bus and railway stations, though these are mostly unbearably filthy. Be prepared with a small soap and some toilette paper. A far better solution is to try a restaurant or a café. "Pardon me; may I use your toilette?" – *Oprostite, smijem li se poslužiti vašim Ve-ceom?* The signs say *muški* (or just "M") for men's and *ženski* ("Ž") for women's.

Smoking is allowed in almost all places and, as people do smoke a lot, can be quite annoying for the non-smokers. Some restaurants have a non-smoking area (*dio za nepušače*) but most bars and clubs will be unbearably smoky.

Tipping is not obligatory but it is usual in taxis and restaurants to round up the sum to the nearest whole followed with the phrase *U redu je* ("OK"), provided you are satisfied with the service, of course. This applies even to the smallest bills.

Weights and Measures. The metric system is used in Montenegro, the same as in the rest of continental Europe. The unit of length is *metar*, for weight it's *gram* and for capacity *litar*.

Wheelchair Access is very poor and is to be found only in a few upmarket places and some governmental institutions.

Crowded street cafe in Herceg Novi

USEFUL PHRASES

In the table below you will find the 30 letters of the Montenegrin alphabet. Latin letters are in black and their Cyrilic equivalents in gray, as both alphabets are officially in equal use. The pronunciation of each letter is described through words in English. The order given here is alphabetical but many of the listings will follow the order of the Cyrillic alphabet (called *azbuka*) which goes like this: a-b-v-g-d-dj-e-ž-z-i-j-k-l-lj-m-n-nj-o-p-r-s-t-ć-u-f-h-c-č-dž-š.

A a А а - father	L l Л л - look
B b Б б - bed	Lj lj Љ љ – million
C c Ц ц - lots	M m М м - me
Č č Ч ч - chalk	N n Н н - no
Ć ć Ћ ћ - ciao	Nj nj Њ њ - canyon
D d Д д - day	O o О о - door
Dj dj (Ђ đ) Ђ ђ - schedule	P p П п - pig
Dž dž Џ џ - jack	R r Р р - room
E e Е е - men	S s С с - son
F f Ф ф - fish	Š š Ш ш - she
G g Г г - good	T t Т т - top
H h Х х - his	U u У у - rule
I i И и - he	V v В в - very
J j Ј ј - you	Z z З з - zoo
K k К к - kind	Ž ž Ж ж - leisure

TIME

One minute	Minut минут	meenoot
One hour	Sat сат	ssaht
Half an hour	Po sata по сата	poh sahta
Monday	Ponedeljak понедељак	ponedelyak
Tuesday	Utorak уторак	ootorak
Wednesday	Srijeda сриједа	sreeyedah
Thursday	Četvrtak четвртак	chetvrhtak
Friday	Petak петак	petak
Saturday	Subota субота	soobota
Sunday	Nedjelja неђеља	nedyelya

NUMBERING

0	Nula нула	noola
1	Jedan један	yedan
2	Dva два	dvah
3	Tri три	tree
4	Četiri четири	chehteeree
5	Pet пет	pet
6	Šest шест	shehsst
7	Sedam седам	sedahm
8	Osam осам	osahm
9	Devet девет	dehvet
10	Deset десет	desset
11	Jedanaest једанаест	yedanahest
12	Dvanaest дванаест	dvahnahest
13	Trinaest тринаест	treenahest
14	Četrnaest четрнаест	chetrnaest
15	Petnaest петнаест	petnahest
16	Šesnaest шеснаест	shehssnaest
17	Sedamnaest седамнаест	sehdamnahest
18	Osamnaest осамнаест	osahmnahest
19	Devetnaest деветнаест	dehvetnahest
20	Dvadeset двадесет	dvahdeset
21	Dvadeset i jedan двадесет и један	dvahdeseteeyedan
30	Trideset тридесет	treedehset
40	Četrdeset четрдесет	chetrdehset
100	Sto сто	stoh
200	Dvesto двесто	dvestoh
1000	Hiljadu хиљаду	heelyadoo

DURING SHOPPING

How much does it cost?	Pošto je ovo? Пошто је ово?	poshtoh ye ovo
I would like…	Volio bih… Волио бих…	voleeoh beeh
Do you have…	Imate li… Имате ли…	eemate lee
I'm just looking.	Samo gledam. Само гледам.	samoh gledam
Do you take credit cards?	Primate li kreditne kartice? Примате ли кредитне картице?	preemateh lee kreditne kartitse
What time do you close?	Kada zatvarate? Када затварате?	kadah zat-varahtey
Expensive	Skupo Скупо	skoopoh
Cheap	Jeftino Јефтино	jefteenoh
Size (clothes)	Veličina Величина	vehleechinah
Size (shoes)	Broj Број	broy
White	Bijelo Бијело	beeyeloh
Black	Crno Црно	tsrnoh
Red	Crveno Црвено	tsrvenoh
Yellow	Žuto Жуто	zhootoh
Green	Zeleno Зелено	zelenoh
Blue	Plavo Плаво	plavoh

IN COMMUNICATION

Yes	Da / Да	dah
No	Ne / Не	neh
Please	Molim Vas / Молим Вас	moleem vas
Thank you	Hvala Vam / Хвала Вам	hvahlah
Excuse me	Izvinite / Извините	izveeneeteh
Hallo	Zdravo / Здраво	zdravoh
Goodbye	Dovidjenja / Довиђења	dohveedyenya
Good night	Laku noć / Лаку ноћ	lakoo noch
Morning	Jutro / Јутро	yootroh
Afternoon	Popodne / Поподне	popodney
Evening	Vječe / Вјече	vyeche
Yesterday	Juče / Јуче	yooche
Today	Danas / Данас	danas
Tomorrow	Sjutra / Сјутра	syootrah
Here	Ovdje / Овдје	ovdyeh
There	Onamo / Онамо	onamoh
What?	Što? / Што?	shtoh
When?	Kada? / Када?	kada
Why?	Zašto? / Зашто?	zashtoh
Where?	Gdje? / Гдје?	gdye
How are You?	Kako ste? / Како сте?	kakoh steh
Very well, thank you.	Dobro, hvala. / Добро, хвала.	dobroh, hvahlah
Pleased to meet you.	Drago mi je. / Драго ми је.	dragoh mee yey
See you soon.	Vidimo se. / Видимо се.	veedeemoh se
That's fine.	U redu je. / У реду је.	oo redoo yey
Do you speak English?	Govorite li engleski? / Говорите ли енглески?	govoreetey lee engleskee

VERY USEFUL

Big	Veliko / Велико	veleekoh
Small	Malo / Мало	maloh
Hot	Vruće / Вруће	vroochey
Cold	Hladno / Хладно	hlahdno
Good	Dobro / Добро	dobro
Bad	Loše / Лоше	loshe
Open	Otvoreno / Отворено	otvohrenoh
Close	Zatvoreno / Затворено	zatvohrenoh
Left	Lijevo / Лијево	leeyevoh
Right	Desno / Десно	dessnoh
Straight on	Pravo / Право	pravoh
Near	Blizu / Близу	bleezoo
Far	Daleko / Далеко	dalekoh
Up	· Gore / Горе	gorey
Down	Dole / Доле	doley
Entrance	Ulaz / Улаз	oolahz
Exit	Izlaz / Излаз	eezlahz
Toilet	Ve-ce (WC) / Ве-це	vey-tsey

IN THE RESTAURANT

Menu	Jelovnik/meni / јеловник/мени	yelovneek/menee
Wine list	Vinska karta / винска карта	veenskah kartah
Glass	Čaša / чаша	chashah
Bottle	Boca / боца	botsah
Knife	Nož / нож	nozh
Fork	Viljuška / виљушка	vilyooshkah
Spoon	Kašika / кашика	kasheekah
Breakfast	Doručak / доручак	doroochak
Lunch	Ručak / ручак	roochak
Dinner	VJečera / вјечера	vyehcherah
Main course	Glavno jelo / главно јело	glavnoh yeloh
Starters	Predjelo / предјело	predyeloh
Soup	Supa / Čorba / супа / чорба	ssoopah / chorbah
Fish	Riba / риба	reebah
Meat	Meso / месо	messo
Vegetarian	Vegetarijanski / вегетаријански	vegetareeyanskee
Vinegar	Sirće / сирће	seerche
Oil	Ulje / уље	oolye
Barbecued	Na žaru / на жару	na zharoo
baked	Pečeno / печено	pechenoh
fried	Prženo / прžено	przhenoh
cheese	Sir / сир	seer
rice	Riža / рижа	reezha
pork	Svinjetina / свињетина	sweenyeteenah
chicken	Piletina / пилетина	peeleteenah
bread	Hljeb / хлеб	hlyeb
pie	Pita / пита	peetah
ice-cream	Sladoled / сладолед	slahdoled
cake	Kolač / колач	kolach
water	Voda / вода	vodah
coffee	Kafa / кафа	kafah
tea	Čaj / чај	chay
wine	Vino / вино	weenoh
bear	Pivo / пиво	peevoh
brandy	Rakija / ракија	rakeeyah

INDEX OF PLACES

Note: Letters "ć" and "č" follow "c", "dj" follows "d", "lj" follows "l". "š" goes after "s" and "ž" after "z". Names printed in CAPITAL LETTERS reffer to destinations that are divided into chapters.

Ada Bojana 142
Ali-pašini izvori, springs 251
Andrijevica 246
Arza, fort 101

Bar 135, 267
Bečići 126
Berane 244
Besac, castle 168
Beška, monastery of 170
Bijela 67
Bijelo Polje 241
Biogradska gora, National Park 240
Biogradsko Lake 240
Bjelasica, Mt 240
Bobotov kuk, peak 215
Brštanovica, camp 209
BUDVA 14, 120
Buljarica, beach 118

CETINJE 14, 174
Cijevna, river 162
Crkvice 70
Crmnica 168
Crna Gora, village 213
Crno jezero, lake 211
Crvena glavica, beach 117
Crvena plaža, beach 118

Čanj, beach 118

Dobrilovina, monastery 207
Dobrota 91
Doclea see Duklja
Dodoši 167
Donja Lastva 97
Draga, river 209
Dražin Vrt 77
Drobni pijesak 117
Duklja, ruins of 162
Durmitor, Mt 14, 210

Djurdjevića Tara, bridge of 208
Djurdjevi stupovi, monastery 245

Godimlje 169
Gornja Lastva 97
Gospa od Škrpjela, islet 72
Grab, camp 209
Gradište, monastery 132
Grbaja, valley 253
Grmožur, castle 169
Gusinje 251

Haj Nehaj, castle 134
HERCEG NOVI 56

Hridsko jezero, Lake 250

Igalo 62
Ivanova korita 189

Jaz, beach 116
Jezerine, ski center 240

Kamenari 268
Kapa moračka, peak 235
Kapetanovi jezero, lake 235
Karuč 167
Kolašin 238
Komarnica, river 215
Komovi, Mt 247
Kosmač, fort 126
Kostanjica 171
KOTOR 14, 79
Krajina, region 169
Kraljičina plaža, beach 117, 129
Krivošije, region of 70
Kruče, beach 119

Lepetane 98, 268
Lesendro, isle 167
Lokve, ski centre 246
Lovćen, Mt 189
Lučice, beach 118
Luštica, peninsula 100

Ljuta, river 77
Ljutica, river 208

Maljevik, beach 118
Mamula, fort 102
Medun 163
Meljine 64
Miločer, beach 129
Mirište, beach 101
Mogren, beach 116
Morača monastery 14, 236
Moračnik, monastery of 170
Mratinje 218
Mrkovi 102
Mrtvica, river 234
Muo 93
Murići 170

Nedajno 219
Nevidio, gorge 216
Nikšić 222

Njeguši 192

Orahovac 77
Orjen, Mt 65

Ostrog, monastery 194
Ostros 171
Ostrvo cvijeća see Prevlaka
Otok, islet 99

Paštrovići, clan 133
Perast 14, 71
Perazića do, beach 117
Petnjica 217
Petrovac 117, 131
Pešića jezero, lake 241
Pišće 219
Piva, canyon 217
Piva monastery 14, 219
Piva, region of 217
Plav 248
Plava spilja, cave 101
Plavsko jezero, lake 248
Pljevlja 204
PODGORICA 156, 264
Podi 65
Podmaine, monastery 125
Pošćenje 217
Praskvica, monastery 129
Prčanj 94
Prečista Krajinska, ruins of 172
Prevlaka, islet 98
Prokletije, mountain range 14, 252
Pržno, beach 117

Radovanići 102
Radovan luka 209
Radovići 100
Ratac, ruins of monastery 134
Reževići, monastery 130
Rijeka Crnojevića 172
Risan 68
Rose 103
Rožaje 254

Savina, monastery 63
Savin kuk, peak 212
Scutari Lake see Skadarsko Lake
Seoca 169
Skadarsko Lake 14, 165
Slovenska plaža, beach 116
Soliosko polje, bird sanctuary 99
Sopot, well 70

Starčeva gorica, monastery of 170
Stari Bar 136
Stoliv 96
Sušica, river 209
Sušičko Lake 215
Sutomore 118, 134
Svač, ruins of 143
Sveta Trojica, monastery 205
Sveti Djordje, islet 72
Sveti Marko, islet 99
Sveti Nikola, isle 126
Sveti Stefan 128

Šas 143
Šasko Lake 143
Šćepan polje 209, 218
Škrka, lakes of 214
Štavna, katun of 247

Tara, river 14, 207
Tepca 209
Tivat 97, 265
Topla 61
Topolica, beach 118
Trsa 219
Trsteno, beach 116
Turjak, ski centre 255

Ulcinj 138
Utjeha, beach 119

Valdanos, beach 119
Velika plaža, beach 141
Veliki pijesak, beach 119
Velje Duboko 235
Verige, straits 68
Vir, estavelle of 225
Virpazar 168
Vranjina 167

Zelenika 64

Žabljak 211
Žabljak Crnojevića 164
Žanjica, beach 101
Ženska voda, beach 119
Žukotrlica, beach 118

CIP – Каталогизација у публикацији
Народна библиотека Србије, Београд

338.48 (497 . 16) (036)

DULOVIĆ, Vladimir
    Montenegro in your hands : travel guide / [Vladimir Dulović ; photos Dragan Bosnić
... et. al.] – 1st ed. – Beograd : Komshe , 2008 (Beograd : Publikum) . 292 str. : fotogr. ,
geogr. karte ; 23 cm

Podaci o autoru preuzeti iz kolofona . – Na oba spojna lista geogr. karte. – Tiraž 1.500.

ISBN 978-86-86245-08-3

a) Туризам – Црна Гора – Водичи
COBISS . SR – ID 148040204

Montenegro Adventures

www.montenegro-adventures.com

Your getaway to Montenegro

* Hotels * Villas * Apartments * Rural Accommodation *
* Business Travel * Conferences & Meetings * Incentive Trips *
* Excursions * Tours * Activity Holidays * Adventure Travel *
* Transfer * Transportation *

Tel: +382-20-202-380 +382-20-244-228
Mob: +382-69-315-601